CCST
Cisco® Certified Support Technician
Study Guide
Cybersecurity Exam

Todd Lammle
Jon Buhagiar
Donald Robb
Todd Montgomery

SYBEX®
A Wiley Brand

Copyright © 2025 by John Wiley & Sons Inc. All rights reserved, including rights for text and data mining and training of artificial intelligence technologies or similar technologies.

Published by John Wiley & Sons, Inc., Hoboken, New Jersey.
Published simultaneously in Canada.

No part of this publication may be reproduced, stored in a retrieval system, or transmitted in any form or by any means, electronic, mechanical, photocopying, recording, scanning, or otherwise, except as permitted under Section 107 or 108 of the 1976 United States Copyright Act, without either the prior written permission of the Publisher, or authorization through payment of the appropriate per-copy fee to the Copyright Clearance Center, Inc., 222 Rosewood Drive, Danvers, MA 01923, (978) 750-8400, fax (978) 750-4470, or on the web at www.copyright.com. Requests to the Publisher for permission should be addressed to the Permissions Department, John Wiley & Sons, Inc., 111 River Street, Hoboken, NJ 07030, (201) 748-6011, fax (201) 748-6008, or online at http://www.wiley.com/go/permission.

The manufacturer's authorized representative according to the EU General Product Safety Regulation is Wiley-VCH GmbH, Boschstr. 12, 69469 Weinheim, Germany, e-mail: Product_Safety@wiley.com.

Trademarks: Wiley and the Wiley logo, and the Sybex logo are trademarks or registered trademarks of John Wiley & Sons, Inc. and/or its affiliates in the United States and other countries and may not be used without written permission. All other trademarks are the property of their respective owners. John Wiley & Sons, Inc. is not associated with any product or vendor mentioned in this book.

Limit of Liability/Disclaimer of Warranty: While the publisher and author have used their best efforts in preparing this book, they make no representations or warranties with respect to the accuracy or completeness of the contents of this book and specifically disclaim any implied warranties of merchantability or fitness for a particular purpose. No warranty may be created or extended by sales representatives or written sales materials. The advice and strategies contained herein may not be suitable for your situation. You should consult with a professional where appropriate. Further, readers should be aware that websites listed in this work may have changed or disappeared between when this work was written and when it is read. Neither the publisher nor authors shall be liable for any loss of profit or any other commercial damages, including but not limited to special, incidental, consequential, or other damages.

For general information on our other products and services or for technical support, please contact our Customer Care Department within the United States at (800) 762-2974, outside the United States at (317) 572-3993 or fax (317) 572-4002. For product technical support, you can find answers to frequently asked questions or reach us via live chat at https://sybexsupport.wiley.com.

Wiley also publishes its books in a variety of electronic formats. Some content that appears in print may not be available in electronic formats. For more information about Wiley products, visit our web site at www.wiley.com.

Library of Congress Control Number applied for:

Paperback ISBN: 9781394207350
ePDF ISBN: 9781394207374
ePub ISBN: 9781394207367

Cover Image: © Jeremy Woodhouse/Getty Images
Cover Design: Wiley
Printed and bound by CPI Group (UK) Ltd, Croydon, CR0 4YY
C9781394207350_240325

Contents at a Glance

Contents

Acknowledgments

There were many people who helped us build the new Cisco certification books in 2023 and 2024. First, Kenyon Brown helped us put together the direction for the books and managed the internal editing at Wiley, so thank you, Ken. Kim Wimpsett was the development editor and worked diligently for many months keeping these books moving along.

We also thank content refinement specialist Sowmini Durairaj, the copyeditor Lori Martinsek, the proofreader Tiffany Taylor, and the indexer Tom Dinse.

About the Authors

Todd Lammle is the authority on Cisco certification and internetworking and is Cisco certified in most Cisco certification categories. He is a world-renowned author, speaker, trainer, and consultant. Todd has three decades of experience working with LANs, WANs, and large enterprise licensed and unlicensed wireless networks, and lately he's been implementing large Cisco Security networks using Firepower/FTD and ISE.

His years of real-world experience are evident in his writing; he is not just an author but an experienced networking engineer with very practical experience from working on the largest networks in the world, at such companies as Xerox, Hughes Aircraft, Texaco, AAA, Cisco, and Toshiba, among many others.

Todd has published over 130 books, including the very popular *CCNA: Cisco Certified Network Associate Study Guide, CCNA Wireless Study Guide, CCNA Data Center Study Guide, and CCNP Security*—among over a hundred more—all from Sybex. He runs an international consulting and training company based in northern Idaho where he spends his free time in the mountains playing with his golden retrievers.

You can reach Todd through his website at `www.lammle.com`.

Jon Buhagiar, BS/ITM, MCSE, CCNA, is an information technology professional with two decades of experience in higher education and the private sector.

Jon currently serves as supervisor of network operations and is currently the director of information technology at RareMed Solutions, Pittsburgh Technical College. In this his role, he manages projects related to the IT infrastructure and cloud services that serve multiple pharmacies operated by RareMed Solutions. In addition, he is responsible for the technology that support hundreds of care specialists that raise the quality of life for many patients all over the world.

He was previously the supervisor of network operations at Pittsburgh Technical College, where he managed the data center, network infrastructure operations, and IT operations and was involved in the management of projects supporting the quality of education at the College. He also served as an adjunct instructor in the College's School of Information Technology department, where he has taught courses for Microsoft and Cisco certification. Jon has been an instructor for 20+ years at several colleges in the Pittsburgh area, since the introduction of the Windows NT MCSE in 1998.

Jon earned a bachelor of science degree in information technology management from Western Governors University. He also achieved an associate degree in business management from Pittsburgh Technical College. His most recent certifications include Windows Server 2016 Microsoft Certified Solutions Expert (MCSE) and Cisco Certified Network Associate (CCNA). Other certifications include CompTIA Network+, CompTIA A+, and CompTIA Project+.

In addition to his professional and teaching roles, Jon has authored many books with Wiley Sybex over the past 10 years, including the Second Edition CCNA Certification Practice Tests 200-301 (Sybex 2023) Comp-TIA Network+ Study Guide: Exam N10-009 (Sybex Study Guide), along with Todd Lammle (Sybex 2024). Jon has spoken at several conferences about spam and email systems. He is an active radio electronics hobbyist and has held a ham radio license for the past 20 years, KB3KGS. He experiments with electronics and has a strong focus on the Internet of Things (IoT).

Donald Robb, widely recognized online as "The Packet Thrower," brings over two decades of experience in the IT industry. His career has spanned a diverse array of roles, beginning with help desk support and evolving into a position as one of the most respected consultants in the field. Donald has honed expert-level skills across various IT domains, including networking, security, collaboration, data center management, wireless technologies, and service providers. His depth of knowledge and technical expertise have made him a sought-after professional in the industry.

Currently, Donald is a principal network architect for Walt Disney Studios. In this role, he serves as a subject matter expert on various technologies, playing a critical role in shaping the company's network architecture and ensuring its reliability and performance. His work involves leading the design and implementation of complex networks and guiding teams and stakeholders through the technical intricacies of modern IT infrastructures.

Over the years, Donald has collaborated with major industry vendors and smaller, specialized companies, earning many advanced certifications along the way. His achievements include becoming a double JNCIE and obtaining most of Cisco's professional-level certifications, demonstrating his deep technical proficiency and commitment to continuous learning. His expertise has also been recognized through his selection as a Cisco Champion for four consecutive years, an honor awarded to top influencers in the networking community.

In addition to his hands-on work in the field, Donald has made significant contributions to IT education. He has had the privilege of working alongside Todd Lammle, a legendary figure in the IT world, coauthoring several books and developing courses that have helped countless professionals advance their careers. Through his extensive experience, certifications, and educational efforts, Donald Robb has solidified his reputation as a leading authority in the IT industry.

Todd Montgomery has been in the networking industry for more than 40 years. Todd holds many Cisco, AWS, CompTIA, and Juniper certifications. Todd has spent most of his career in the field working on-site in data centers throughout North America and around the world.

He has worked on the most advanced networks of equipment manufacturers, systems integrators, and end users in the data center and cloud computing environments of the private sector, service providers, and the government sector. Todd most recently worked as a data center network automation engineer in Austin, Texas, involved in network implementation and support of emerging data center technologies and AWS public cloud services.

Introduction

Welcome to the exciting world of security and your path toward Cisco certification. If you've picked up this book because you want to improve yourself and your life with a better, more satisfying, and secure job, you've chosen well!

Whether you're striving to enter the thriving, dynamic security sector or seeking to enhance your skill set and advance your position within it, being Cisco certified can seriously stack the odds in your favor to help you attain your goals. This book is a great start.

Cisco certifications are powerful instruments of success that also markedly improve your grasp of all things internetworking. As you progress through this book, you'll gain a strong, foundational understanding of security that reaches far beyond Cisco devices. And when you finish this book, you'll be ready to tackle the next step toward Cisco certification.

Essentially, by beginning your journey toward becoming Cisco certified, you're proudly announcing that you want to become an unrivaled security expert, a goal that this book will help get you underway to achieving.

Congratulations in advance for taking the first step toward your brilliant future!

 To find your included bonus material, as well as additional Todd Lammle videos, and extra practice questions, please see www.lammle.com/ccst.

Cisco's CCST Certifications

It used to be that to secure the holy grail of Cisco certifications—the CCIE—you passed only one written test before being faced with a grueling, formidable hands-on lab. This intensely daunting, all-or-nothing approach made it nearly impossible to succeed and predictably didn't work out too well for most people.

Cisco responded to this issue by creating a series of new certifications, which not only created a sensible, stepping-stone-path to the highly coveted CCIE prize, but it also gave employers a way to accurately rate and measure the skill levels of prospective and current employees.

The CCNA and CCNP exams were then created as a stepping stone, and they are still the most popular certifications in the world. This exciting paradigm shift in Cisco's certification path truly opened doors that few were allowed through before!

Now Cisco has reached down and created a new introduction level certification program, below the CCNA, called the Cisco Certified Support Technician (CCST). There are two exams, two certs, called Network and Cybersecurity.

CCST Networking certification validates an individual's skills and knowledge of entry-level networking concepts and topics. The certification demonstrates foundational knowledge and skills needed to show how networks operate, including the devices, media, and protocols that enable network communications.

The Cisco Certified Support Technician (CCST) Networking certification is also a first step toward working on achieving your CCNA Certification.

The Cisco Certified Support Technician (CCST) Cybersecurity certification validates a candidate's skills and knowledge of entry-level cybersecurity concepts and topics, including security principles, network security and endpoint security concepts, vulnerability assessment and risk management, and incident handling.

The Cisco Certified Support Technician (CCST) Cybersecurity certification is also a first step toward CyberOps Associate certification.

This book is a powerful tool to get you started in your Cisco certification studies, and it's vital to understand that material in it before you go on to conquer any other certifications!

 Exam policies can change from time to time. We highly recommend that you check both the Cisco and Pearson VUE sites for the most up-to-date informa-tion when you begin your preparation, when you register, and again a few days before your scheduled exam date.

Tips for Taking the CCST Cybersecurity Exam

Here are some general tips for taking your exam successfully (assuming you are going in person as online testing is available as well):

- This is not like the CCNA or other Cisco certification tests that are available on www.vue.com. You need to instead go to https://www.certiport.com/locator to both register and pay for your exam. You can take the exams in person at a center, or in your home or office, under direct video and audio supervision. For exams at home informa-tion and to sign up, call (800) 589-6871.

- Bring two forms of ID with you. One must be a photo ID, such as a driver's license. The other can be a major credit card or a passport. Both forms must include a signature.

- Arrive early at the exam center so you can relax and review your study materials, particularly tables and lists of exam-related information. After you are ready to enter the testing room, you will need to leave everything outside; you won't be able to bring any materials into the testing area.

- Read the questions carefully. Don't be tempted to jump to an early conclusion. Make sure you know exactly what each question is asking.

- Don't leave any unanswered questions. Unanswered questions are scored against you. There will be questions with multiple correct responses. When there is more than one correct answer, a message at the bottom of the screen will prompt you to either "choose two" or "choose all that apply." Be sure to read the messages displayed to know how many correct answers you must choose.

■ When answering multiple-choice questions you're not sure about, use a process of elimination to get rid of the obviously incorrect answers first. Doing so will improve your odds if you need to make an educated guess.

Who Should Read This Book?

You—if want to pass the CCST Cybersecurity exam and pass it confidently! This book is chock-full of the exact information you need and directly maps to CCST Cybersecurity exam objectives, so if you use it to study for the exam, your odds of passing shoot way up.

And in addition to including every bit of knowledge you need to learn to pass the exam, We have included some really great tips and solid wisdom throughout the chapters, to equip you even further to successfully work in the real IT security world.

What's Included in the Book

We have included several study tools throughout the book:

Assessment Test   At the end of this introduction is an assessment test that you can use to check your readiness for the exam. Take this test before you start reading the book; it will help you determine the areas you might need to brush up on. The answers to the assessment test questions appear on a separate page after the last question of the test. Each answer includes an explanation and a note telling you the chapter in which the material appears.

Objective Map and Opening List of Objectives   In this introduction you'll find a detailed exam objective map showing you where each of the exam objectives is covered in this book. In addition, each chapter opens with a list of the exam objectives it covers. Use these to see exactly where each of the exam topics is covered.

Exam Essentials   Each chapter, just after the summary, includes a number of exam essentials. These are the key topics you should take from the chapter in terms of areas to focus on when preparing for the exam.

Chapter Review Questions   To test your knowledge as you progress through the book, there are review questions at the end of each chapter. As you finish each chapter, answer the review questions, and then check your answers—the correct answers and explanations are in the Appendix. You can go back to reread the section that deals with each question you got wrong to ensure that you correctly answer the next time you're tested on the material.

Interactive Online Learning Environment and Test Bank

The interactive online learning environment that accompanies CCST Cybersecurity provides a test bank with study tools to help you prepare for the certification exam—and increase your chances of passing it the first time! The test bank includes the following tools:

Sample Tests   All of the questions in this book are provided, including the assessment test, which you'll find at the end of this introduction, and the chapter tests that include the review questions at the end of each chapter. In addition, there is a practice exam. Use these questions to test your knowledge of the study guide material. The online test bank runs on multiple devices.

Flashcards   Approximately 100 questions are provided in digital flashcard format (a question followed by a single correct answer). You can use the flashcards to reinforce your learning and provide last-minute test prep before the exam.

Other Study Tools   A glossary of key terms from this book and their definitions are available as a fully searchable PDF.

Go to http://www.wiley.com/go/sybextestprep to register and gain access to this interactive online learning environment and test bank with study tools.

How to Use This Book

If you want a solid foundation for the serious effort of preparing for the Cisco CCST Cybersecurity exam, then look no further because we have spent countless hours putting together this book with the sole intention of helping you pass it!

This book is loaded with valuable information, and you will get the most out of your study time if you understand how I put the book together. Here's a list that describes how to approach studying:

1. Take the assessment test immediately following this introduction. (The answers are at the end of the test, but no peeking!) It's okay if you don't know any of the answers—that's what this book is for. Carefully read over the explanations for any question you get wrong and make note of the chapters where that material is covered.

2. Study each chapter carefully, making sure you fully understand the information and the exam objectives listed at the beginning of each one. Again, pay extra-close attention to any chapter that includes material covered in questions you missed on the assessment test.

3. Answer all the review questions related to each chapter. Specifically note any questions that confuse you and study the corresponding sections of the book again. And don't just skim these questions—make sure you understand each answer completely.

4. Before you take your test, be sure to visit my website for questions, videos, audios, and other useful information.

5. Test yourself using all the electronic flashcards. This is a brand-new and updated flashcard program to help you prepare for the latest Cisco CCST Cybersecurity exam, and it is a great study tool.

I tell you no lies—learning every bit of the material in this book is going to require applying yourself with a good measure of discipline. So try to set aside the same time period every day to study, and select a comfortable and quiet place to do so. If you work hard, you will be surprised at how quickly you learn this material.

What Does This Book Cover?

This book covers everything you need to know to solidly prepare you for getting into your CCST studies. Be advised that just because much of the material in this book won't be official Cisco CCST objectives in the future doesn't mean you won't be tested on it. Understanding the foundational, real-world cybersecurity information and skills offered in this book is critical to your certifications and your career!

So, as you move through this book, here's a snapshot of what you'll learn chapter by chapter:

Chapter 1: Security Concepts   In this chapter you will begin learning basic security concepts. The security concepts include vulnerabilities, threats, exploits, as well as the difference between these concepts. You will then learn about common threats and vulnerabilities, such as malware, ransomware, and other common tactics.

Chapter 2: Network Security Devices   This chapter will describe network infrastructure and technologies that support network security, such as virtualization, honeypots, intrusion detection systems (IDS), and many other devices.

Chapter 3: Network Security Concepts   Chapter 3 will cover a lot of common network concepts that you would find in the CCST Networking certification. However, the concepts will be explained and highlighted as they pertain to network security.

Chapter 4: Network Device Access   This chapter will explain the difference between authentication, authorization, and accounting (AAA) that is used with Remote Authentication Dial-In User Service (RADIUS), as well as multifactor authentication (MFA), and password policies.

Chapter 5: Secure Access Technology   This chapter will cover the various technologies that allow you to secure communications over an insecure network, such as access control lists (ACLs), firewalls, Virtual Private Network (VPN) connections, and Network Access Control (NAC). Encryption types and the protocols that use them will also be covered.

Chapter 6: OS Basics and Security   This chapter will focus on the various operating systems and their various security features, such as Windows Defender, host-based firewalls, and file and directory permissions. In addition this chapter will cover the importance of software and hardware updates. To round this topic of operating system security, system logs will be covered in entirety.

Chapter 7: **Endpoint Security**   This Chapter will take a deep dive into endpoint security, such as the various built-in tools that can help us collect data. This chapter will also cover the basics of hardware and software inventory, program deployments, data backups, regulatory compliance, and bring your own device (BYOD) strategies.

Chapter 8: **Vulnerability Management**   Chapter 8 will focus on risk management strategies, such as risk ranking, approaching risk management, risk mitigations strategies, risk associated with data types, and the levels of risk. In addition, this chapter will give you a fundamental understanding of how to identify risk and mitigate risk.

Chapter 9: **Vulnerability Management**   This chapter explains the various ways that you can manage vulnerabilities in your organization, such as identification, management, and mitigation. Threat intelligence techniques are also covered that explain how the industry catalogs vulnerabilities, identifies trends, and mitigates vulnerabilities.

Chapter 10: **Disaster Recovery**   This chapter explains disaster recovery for business continuity and recovery. The chapter will cover how disasters might happen, what to do when it happens and the planning around disasters to get your organization operating again.

Chapter 11: **Incident Handling**   This chapter explains how security events are found with the help of Security Information and Event Management (SIEM) systems. The chapter will also explain the importance of security orchestration, automation, and response (SOAR) systems to help automate and orchestrate a remediation to an event. Common compliance frameworks for incident handling are also explained along with their reporting and notification requirements.

Chapter 12: **Digital Forensics**   This chapter will explain digital forensics and the attack attribution processes. Some of the concepts covered will be Cyber Kill Chain, MITRE ATT&CK Matrix, and tactics, techniques, procedures (TTPS), as well as evidence and the proper handling of evidence.

Chapter 13: **Incident Response**   The last chapter will describe the elements of a cybersecurity incidence response. This chapter will include the National Institute of Standards and Technology (NIST) standard for incident response, and how to implement a policy, plan, and the various procedural elements.

Exam Objectives

Speaking of objectives, you're probably pretty curious about those, right? Cisco asked groups of IT professionals to fill out a survey rating the skills they felt were important in their jobs, and the results were grouped into objectives for the exam.

This is a list of objectives and which chapter the objectives are covered in. Remember that a single objective can be covered in multiple chapters.

OBJECTIVE MAP

Objective	Chapter(s)
1.0 Essential Security Principles	**1, 4, 5**
1.1. Define essential security principles	1
• Vulnerabilities, threats, exploits, and risks; attack vectors; hardening; defense-in-depth; confidentiality, integrity, and availability (CIA); types of attackers; reasons for attacks; code of ethics	1
1.2. Explain common threats and vulnerabilities	1
• Malware, ransomware, denial of service, botnets, social engineering attacks (tailgating, spear phishing, phishing, vishing, smishing, etc.), physical attacks, man in the middle, IoT vulnerabilities, insider threats, Advanced Persistent Threat (APT)	1
1.3. Explain access management principles	4
• Authentication, authorization, and accounting (AAA); RADIUS; multifactor authentication (MFA); password policies	4
1.4. Explain encryption methods and applications	5
• Types of encryption, hashing, certificates, public key infrastructure (PKI); strong vs. weak encryption algorithms; states of data and appropriate encryption (data in transit, data at rest, data in use); protocols that use encryption	5
2.0 Basic Network Security Concepts	**2, 3, 5**
2.1. Describe TCP/IP protocol vulnerabilities	3
• TCP, UDP, HTTP, ARP, ICMP, DHCP, DNS	3
2.2. Explain how network addresses impact network security	3
• IPv4 and IPv6 addresses, MAC addresses, network segmentation, CIDR notation, NAT, public vs. private networks	3

(Continued)

(Continued)

Objective	Chapter(s)
2.3. Describe network infrastructure and technologies	**2**
• Network security architecture, DMZ, virtualization, cloud, honeypot, proxy server, IDS, IPS	2
2.4. Set up a secure wireless SoHo network	**2**
• MAC address filtering, encryption standards and protocols, SSID	2
2.5. Implement secure access technologies	**5**
• ACL, firewall, VPN, NAC	5
3.0 Endpoint Security Concepts	**6, 7**
3.1. Describe operating system security concepts	**6**
• Windows, macOS, and Linux; security features, including Windows Defender and host-based firewalls; CLI and PowerShell; file and directory permissions; privilege escalation	6
3.2. Demonstrate familiarity with appropriate endpoint tools that gather security assessment information	**7**
• netstat, nslookup, tcpdump	7
3.3. Verify that endpoint systems meet security policies and standards	**7**
• Hardware inventory (asset management), software inventory, program deployment, data backups, regulatory compliance (PCI DSS, HIPAA, GDPR), BYOD (device management, data encryption, app distribution, configuration management)	7
3.4. Implement software and hardware updates	**6**
• Windows Update, application updates, device drivers, firmware, patching	6
3.5. Interpret system logs	**6**
• Event Viewer, audit logs, system and application logs, syslog, identification of anomalies	6

(*Continued*)

(Continued)

Objective	Chapter(s)
5.2. Explain digital forensics and attack attribution processes	**12**
• Cyber Kill Chain, MITRE ATT&CK Matrix, and Diamond Model; Tactics, Techniques, and Procedures (TTP); sources of evidence (artifacts); evidence handling (preserving digital evidence, chain of custody)	12
5.3. Explain the impact of compliance frameworks on incident handling	**11**
• Compliance frameworks (GDPR, HIPAA, PCI-DSS, FERPA, FISMA), reporting and notification requirements	11
5.4. Describe the elements of cybersecurity incident response	**13**
• Policy, plan, and procedure elements; incident response life cycle stages (NIST Special Publication 800-61 sections 2.3, 3.1–3.4)	13

Like all exams, the CCST Cybersecurity certification from Cisco is updated periodically and may eventually be retired or replaced. At some point after Cisco is no longer offering this exam, the old editions of our books and online tools will be retired. If you have purchased this book after the exam was retired, or are attempting to register in the Sybex online learning environment after the exam was retired, please know that we make no guarantees that this exam's online Sybex tools will be available once the exam is no longer available.

Assessment Test

1. Which form of social engineering is nothing more than looking over someone's shoulder while they enter or view sensitive information?

   A. Shoulder surfing

   B. Phishing

   C. Tailgating

   D. Whaling

2. What is a method for stopping tailgating?

   A. User authentication

   B. Access control vestibules

   C. Strong passwords

   D. Change SSIDs

3. Susan is interested in securing her SOHO wireless network. What should she do to be assured that only her devices can join her wireless network?

   A. Enable WPA2

   B. Enable MAC filtering

   C. Enable port security

   D. Disable SSID broadcasts

4. Which statement is correct about WPA?

   A. WPA was released at the same time as WEP.

   B. WPA was released as a fix for poor coverage.

   C. WPA was released as a fix for poor encryption.

   D. The Wi-Fi Alliance wanted to rebrand WEP with WPA.

5. How does TCP guarantee delivery of segments to the receiver?

   A. Via the destination port

   B. TCP checksums

   C. Window size

   D. Sequence and acknowledgment numbers

6. What is required before TCP can begin sending segments?

   A. Three-way handshake

   B. Port agreement

   C. Sequencing of segments

   D. Acknowledgment of segments

7. Which method is used to direct communications to a group of computers that subscribe to the transmission?

   A. Unicast

   B. Broadcast

   C. Multicast

   D. Anycast

8. Which factor of authentication requires you to present something that is unique to you and can't be copied?

   A. Password

   B. Signature

   C. Fingerprint

   D. Location

9. What is the end device that sends credentials for 802.1X called?

   A. Authenticator

   B. Supplicant

   C. AAA server

   D. RADIUS server

10. What can you use to protect against spoofing of internal IP addresses on the perimeter of your network?

   A. ACLs

   B. Intrusion detection systems

   C. SSL

   D. Host intrusion detection systems

11. Which benefit of using a secure VPN allows verification that a packet was not tampered with in transit?

   A. Authentication

   B. Data integrity

   C. Anti-replay

   D. Confidentiality

12. What is an advantage of using a standard ACL?

   A. More secure

   B. Less processing overhead

   C. More specific rules

   D. Blocking of applications

13. Which extension is used with the Windows batch scripting language?

   A. .vbs

   B. .js

   C. .bat

   D. .py

14. Chelsea is worried about the threat of malware on the network. She wants every workstation to have installed software that will detect worms and Trojan horses. What type of software should she install?

   A. Malware

   B. Antivirus

   C. Software firewalls

   D. Spyware

15. Which of the following is *not* an NTFS permission? (Choose the best answer.)

   A. Full Control

   B. Write

   C. Read & Execute

   D. Change

16. You manage the IT department for an organization and want to enforce restrictions so that company-owned devices do not record via the camera and microphone. What can you implement?

   A. Antivirus software

   B. MDM software

   C. Firewall software

   D. BYOD policy

17. You are an employee of an organization that works with information identifying citizens in the United States and Europe. Which regulations should you adhere to?

   A. PCI DSS

   B. HIPPA

   C. GDPR

   D. PHI

18. Which information is not commonly found in the initial form for a change request?

   A. Reason

   B. Priority

   C. Risk analysis

   D. Change rollback plan

19. You just found out that your internal core router has a remote-control vulnerability. What is the risk level that you would associate with this?

   A. Low

   B. Medium

   C. High

   D. No risk

20. Which threat intelligence plans are long-term and high level?

   A. Strategic

   B. Tactical

   C. Operational

   D. Technical

21. Which of the following is an active reconnaissance tactic?

   A. Vulnerability scanning

   B. DNS enumeration

   C. Network traffic analysis

   D. OSINT

22. Which backup media is the slowest from which to recover?

   A. Disk-to-tape

   B. Disk-to-disk

   C. Disk-to-flash

   D. Disk-to-cloud

23. What is the definition of the recovery point objective?

   A. How long it will take to back up a data set

   B. How current the data is on backup media

   C. How long it will take to restore a data set

   D. How large the current data set is

24. Which regulations are enforced on education providers?

   A. GLBA

   B. FERPA

   C. SOX

   D. HIPAA

25. Which model was developed by Lockheed Martin, to provide a framework used to identify and prevent cyber intrusions?

   A. Cyber Kill Chain

   B. Diamond Model

C. MITRE ATT&CK Matrix

D. TTPs

26. A disgruntled employee is found to have leaked the parts used for a new product for your organization. What type of threat is this an example of?

A. Supply chain

B. Insider threat

C. DDoS attack

D. Phishing

Answers to Assessment Test

1. A. Shoulder surfing involves looking over someone's shoulder as they enter information. Phishing is the act of attempting to steal credentials by sending an email that takes you to a fraudulent login. Tailgating is the act of following a person through an access control point and using their credentials. Whaling is a form of phishing that targets high-profile individuals.

2. B. Using access control vestibules, also known as mantraps (small rooms that limit access to one or a few individuals) is a great way to stop tailgating. User authentication will not prevent or stop tailgating. Strong passwords will not prevent tailgating because tailgating is a physical security problem. Changing SSIDs will not stop tailgating because tailgating does not pertain to wireless.

3. B. Enabling MAC filtering on the access point will allow the devices that she specifies. Enabling WPA2 encryption will not prevent unauthorized access to the SOHO network. Port Security is enabled on wired network switches to prevent unauthorized access. Disabling the SSID from broadcasting will not prevent unauthorized access.

4. C. After the weaknesses in WEP encryption were discovered, the Wi-Fi Alliance rushed the release of the WPA security protocol. The WPA security protocol incorporated the 802.11i standard of TKIP, which allowed for better integrity of 802.11 transmissions. The WPA security protocol was released after the WEP security protocol. The WPA security protocol did not address any problems related to coverage. It was not a rebranding of the WEP security protocol; it was intended to be a replacement.

5. D. TCP guarantees delivery of segments with sequence and acknowledgment numbers. At the transport layer, each segment is given a sequence number that is acknowledged by the receiver. The source and destination ports are used for the delivery of segments, but they do not guarantee delivery. TCP checksums are used to detect errors in segments but do not guarantee delivery. Window size is used to adjust buffer size on the sending and receiving hosts.

6. A. A three-way handshake is required between sender and receiver before TCP can begin sending traffic. During this three-way handshake, the sender's window buffer size is synchronized with the receiver's window buffer size. Ports are not agreed upon; they are used for the addressing of traffic at the transport layer. The sequencing and acknowledgment of segments is a function of the TCP protocol.

7. C. Multicast is used to allow computers to opt into a transmission. Examples of uses for multicast are video, routing protocols, and imaging of computers, to name a few. A unicast address is a single valid IP address for direct communications purposes between two hosts. A broadcast will forward a message to all computers in the same subnet. A multicast address is a single address that is selectively sent to a multicast group of hosts. Anycast is a way of allowing the same IP address on multiple machines in different geographical areas. The routing protocol is used to advertise in routing tables the closest IP by the use of metrics.

8. C. Your fingerprint is an example of something that you are, because it is unique to you. A password is something that you know. A signature is something that you do, as it is unique to how you sign and can be forged. A location is somewhere you are, according to you GPS location.

9. B. The end device that sends credentials is called the supplicant. The supplicant is a piece of software in the operating system that supplies the credentials for AAA authentication. The authenticator is the wireless access point (WAP) or switch configured for 802.1X. The AAA server is normally a RADIUS server or TACACS+ server that is configured for 802.1X.

10. A. Access control lists (ACLs) are an effective way to mitigate spoofing of internal IPs from outside the trusted network. ACLs are used to control traffic by either allowing, denying, or logging traffic depending on specific conditions. An intrusion detection system (IDS) can be used to notify you if it detects an attack, but it will not prevent an attack. Secure Sockets Layer (SSL) communications offer both encryption and authentication of the data via certificate signing. This would prevent tampering of the data end to end, but it will not prevent spoofing. A host intrusion detection system (HIDS) is an application that runs on a host to detect intrusions. A HIDS is similar to an IDS, but it is all software based and resides on the host it is to protect.

11. B. Data integrity is one of the benefits of using a secure VPN protocol. To ensure its integrity, a packet is sealed with a hash that must be calculated to the same hash on the other side when it is received and decrypted. Authentication is a benefit to using a VPN in that both parties are authenticated before network transmission begins. Anti-replay is a byproduct of authentication and data integrity; packets cannot be replayed without authentication between both parties and a rehashing of the packets. Confidentiality is created with any VPN because of the end-to-end encryption.

12. B. An advantage of a standard access control list (ACL) is that they require less processing overhead from the ASIC or CPU (depending on the platform). Since they only inspect layer 3 headers, no further decapsulation is required for layer 4. The level of security is not increased or decreased when using standard access control lists. If a higher level of specificity for the condition is required, then extended access lists should be used. Blocking of specific applications can only be achieved with extended access lists because the source and destination ports can be specified.

13. C. The `.bat` extension is used with the Windows batch scripting language. The `.vbs` extension is used with VBScript language. The `.js` extension is used with the JavaScript scripting language. The `.py` extension is used with the Python scripting language.

14. B. Antivirus software is an application that is installed on a system to protect it and to scan for viruses as well as worms and Trojan horses. Malware is malicious software that once installed on a system causes malicious activity. Software firewalls will not detect Trojan horses and worms. Spyware is malicious software that monitors user activity and offers unsolicited pop-up advertisements.

15. D. Change is a share permission; the similar permission in NTFS is Modify. Full Control, Write, and Read & Execute are NTFS permissions.

16. B. Implementing mobile device management (MDM) software can help you enforce restrictions of mobile device recordings. Antivirus software and firewall software do not restrict camera and microphone usage. A BYOD policy will not enforce restrictions of camera and microphone usage.

17. C. You should adhere to regulation based on General Data Protection Regulation (GDPR) for EU citizens. Health Insurance Portability and Accountability Act (HIPPA) is a law that applies to health care. Payment Card Industry Data Security Standard (PCI DSS) is a standard of processes and procedures used to handle data related to transactions using payment cards. Protected health information (PHI) refers to any information used in the health care industry to describe a patient or aliment.

18. C. The risk analysis is typically not included in the initial request form for change submitted to the change advisory board. Any risk included in this initial form will be a narrow view from the requestor. The function of the change advisory board is to perform the risk analysis organization-wide. Reason, priority, and change rollback plan are all commonly found in the initial form for a change request.

19. C. Since this is your core router the impact is high and the remote-control vulnerability is also high risk. Therefore, this should be taken care of immediately. All other answers are incorrect.

20. A. Strategic threat intelligence is aimed at less technical people, and more toward decision makers and C-suite level people in the organization. Tactical threat intelligence is technically focused for security analysts. Operational threat intelligence is aimed at managers that have a working knowledge of the various TTPs a threat actor might use. Technical threat intelligence is very low-level and aimed at the technical aspect of tools used by both threat actors and security professionals.

21. A. Vulnerability scanning is an active reconnaissance tactic because it interacts with the network. DNS enumeration is a passive reconnaissance tactic because it can be done without anyone knowing. Network traffic analysis is just that, analysis, and therefore it is a passive tactic. Open source intelligence (OSINT) uses publicly available information and therefore it is considered a passive tactic.

22. D. Disk-to-cloud is the slowest recovery method because you must recover from the cloud over a network connection. Disk-to-tape is the not the fastest because you must re-tension the tape and then locate the data on the tape to recover it. Disk-to-disk is the fastest recovery method and backup method as well, because you are backing up from a disk to another disk attached via the network. Disk-to-flash is not a backup method, because of the price of flash.

23. B. The recovery point objective (RPO) is how current the data is on the backup media and to what point you can recover to. How long it takes to back up the data set is the backup window. How long it will take to restore the data set is the recovery time objective (RTO). The size of the current data set is an incorrect answer.

24. B. Family Educational Rights and Privacy Act (FERPA) affects education providers and organizations that process student records. The Gramm–Leach–Bliley Act (GLBA) affects providers of financial services and safeguards customer information. The Sarbanes–Oxley Act (SOX) is enforced by the Securities and Exchange Commission (SEC) and regulates sensitive financial information and financial records. The Health Insurance Portability and Accountability Act (HIPAA) affects health care providers and providers that process health records.

25. A. The Cyber Kill Chain model was developed by Lockheed Martin. It is a common framework used to identify and prevent cyber intrusion. The Diamond Model is used for incident analysis and maps out components of an intrusion. The MITRE ATT&CK Matrix was develop by the MITRE corporation to map out the stages of an attack. The MITRE ATT&CK Matrix uses tactic, threats, and procedures (TTPs) to carry out each stage of an attack.

26. B. This is a classic example of an insider threat, typically these threat stem from disgruntled employees or corporate espionage. A supply chain threat is when someone injects malware or malicious intent into the supply chain for a product. A distributed denial of service (DDoS) is an attack where several hosts attack a single host, knocking it offline. Phishing attacks are attempt to manipulate recipients into sharing sensitive information.

Chapter

1

Security Concepts

THE FOLLOWING CCST EXAM TOPICS ARE COVERED IN THIS CHAPTER:

✔ **1.0 Essential Security Principals**

- 1.1. Define essential security principles

  Vulnerabilities, threats, exploits, and risks; attack vectors; hardening; defense-in-depth; confidentiality, integrity, and availability (CIA); types of attackers; reasons for attacks; code of ethics

- 1.2. Explain common threats and vulnerabilities

  Malware, ransomware, denial of service, botnets, social engineering attacks (tailgating, spear phishing, phishing, vishing, smishing, etc.), physical attacks, man in the middle, IoT vulnerabilities, insider threats, Advanced Persistent Threat (APT)

It's true. . .you're not paranoid if they really are out to get you. Although "they" probably aren't after you personally, your network—no matter the size—is seriously vulnerable, so it's wise to be very concerned about keeping it secure. Unfortunately, it's also true that no matter how secure you think your network is, it's a good bet that there are still some very real threats out there that could breach its security and totally cripple your infrastructure!

I'm not trying to scare you; it's just that networks, by their very nature, are not secure environments. Think about it—the whole point of having a network is to make resources available to people who aren't at the same physical location as the network's resources.

Because of this, it follows that you've got to open access to those resources to users you may not be able to identify. One network administrator I know referred to a server running a much-maligned network operating system as "a perfectly secure server until you install the network interface card (NIC)." You can see the dilemma here, right?

Okay, with all this doom and gloom, what's a network administrator to do? Well, the first line of defense is to know about the types of threats out there, because you can't do anything to protect yourself from something you don't know about. But once you understand the threats, you can begin to design defenses to combat bad guys lurking in the depths of cyberspace just waiting for an opportunity to strike.

I'm going to introduce you to some of the more common security threats and teach you about the ways to mitigate them. I'll be honest—the information I'll be giving you in this chapter is definitely not exhaustive. Securing computers and networks is a huge task, and there are literally hundreds of books on this subject alone. To operate securely in a network environment, you must understand how to speak the language of security. As in any field, there is terminology.

In this chapter, you will learn the common types of attacks that all network professionals should understand to secure an enterprise network.

To find your included bonus material, as well as Todd Lammle videos, practice questions, and hands-on labs, please see www.lammle.com/ccst.

Technology-Based Attacks

Technology-based attacks are those that take advantage of weaknesses in software and the protocols that systems use to communicate with one another. This contrasts with attacks that target environmental or human weaknesses (covered later in this chapter). In this section, you'll learn about attacks that target technologies.

Denial of Service (DoS)/Distributed Denial of Service (DDoS)

A denial of service (DoS) attack does exactly what it sounds like it would do—it prevents users from accessing the network and/or its resources. Today, DoS attacks are commonly launched against a major company's intranet and especially its websites. "Joe the Hacker" (formerly a plumber) thinks that if he can make a mess of, say, Microsoft's or Amazon's website, he's done that company some serious damage. And you know what?

He's right!

Even though DoS attacks are nasty, strangely, hackers don't respect other hackers who execute them because they're really easy to deploy. It's true—even a pesky little 10-year-old can execute one and bring you to your knees. (That's just wrong!) This means that "real" bad guys have no respect for someone who uses DoS attacks, and they usually employ much more sophisticated methods of wreaking havoc on you instead. I guess it comes down to that "honor among thieves" thing. Still, know that even though a DoS-type attack won't gain the guilty party any esteemed status among "real" hackers, it's still not exactly a day at the beach to deal with.

Worse, DoS attacks come in a variety of flavors. Let's talk about some of them now.

The Ping of Death

Ping is primarily used to see whether a computer is responding to IP requests. Usually, when you ping a remote host, what you're really doing is sending four normal-sized Internet Control Message Protocol (ICMP) packets to the remote host to see whether it's available. But during a ping-of-death attack, a humongous ICMP packet is sent to the remote host victim, totally flooding the victim's buffer and causing the system to reboot or helplessly hang there, drowning. It's good to know that patches are available for most operating systems to prevent a ping-of-death attack from working.

Distributed DoS (DDoS)

Denial of service attacks can be made more effective if they can be amplified by recruiting helpers in the attack process. In the following sections, some terms and concepts that apply to a distributed denial of service attack are explained.

Botnet/Command and Control

A botnet is a group of programs connected on the Internet for the purpose of performing a task in a coordinated manner. Some botnets, such as those created to maintain control of Internet Relay Chat (IRC) channels, are legal, whereas others are illegally created to foist a DDoS. An attacker can recruit and build a botnet to help amplify a DoS attack, as illustrated in Figure 1.1.

The steps in the process of building a botnet are as follows:

1. A botnet operator sends out viruses or worms whose payloads are malicious applications, the bots, infecting ordinary users' computers.

2. The bots on the infected PCs log into a server called a command-and-control (C&C) server under the control of the attacker.

3. At the appropriate time, the attacker, through the C&C server, sends a command to all bots to attack the victim at the same time, thereby significantly amplifying the effect of the attack.

Traffic Spike

One of the hallmarks of a DDoS attack is a major spike in traffic in the network as bots that have been recruited mount the attack. For this reason, any major spike in traffic should be regarded with suspicion. A network intrusion detection system (IDS) can recognize these traffic spikes and may be able to prevent them from growing larger or in some cases prevent the traffic in the first place.

Some smaller organizations that cannot afford the pricier intrusion prevention systems (IPSs) or IDSs make use of features present on their load balancers. Many of these products include DDoS mitigation features such as the TCP SYN cookie option. It allows the load balancer to react when the number of SYN requests reaches a certain point. At that point, the device will start dropping requests when the SYN queue is full.

Coordinated Attack

Another unmistakable feature of a DDoS attack is the presence of a coordinated attack. As shown in Figure 1.1 and as just described in the section "Botnet/Command and Control," to properly amplify the attack the bots must attack the victim at the same time. The coordination of the bots is orchestrated by the command-and-control server, depicted in Figure 1.1. If all the bots can be instructed to attack at precisely the same second, the attack becomes much more overwhelming to the victim.

Friendly/Unintentional DoS

An unintentional DoS attack (also referred to as an attack from "friendly fire") is not caused by malicious individuals; instead, it's a spike in activity to a website or resource that overpowers its ability to respond. In many cases, it is the result of a relatively

FIGURE 1.1   Botnet.

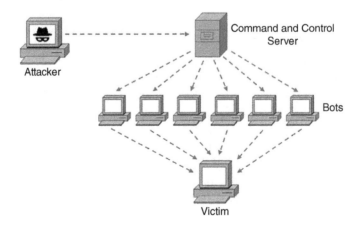

unknown URL suddenly being shared in a larger medium such as a popular TV or news show. For example, when Michael Jackson died, the amount of Twitter and Google traffic spiked so much that at first it was thought that an automated attack was under way.

Physical Attack

Physical attacks are those that cause hardware damage to a device. These attacks can be mitigated, but not eliminated, by preventing physical access to the device. Routers, switches, firewalls, servers, and other infrastructure devices should be locked away and protected by strong physical access controls. Otherwise, you may be confronted with a permanent DoS, covered in the next section.

Permanent DoS

A permanent DoS (PDoS) attack is one in which the device is damaged and must be replaced. It requires physical access to the device, or does it? Actually, it doesn't! An attack called phlashing attacks the firmware located in many systems. Using tools that fuzz (introduce errors into) the firmware, attackers cause the device to be unusable.

Another approach is to introduce a firmware image containing a Trojan or other type of malware.

Smurf

Smurfs are happy little blue creatures that like to sing and dance, but a Smurf attack is far more nefarious. It's a version of a DoS attack that floods its victim with spoofed broadcast ping messages. I'll talk about spoofing in more detail later; for now, understand that it basically involves stealing someone else's IP address.

Here's how it works: the bad guy spoofs the intended victim's IP address and then sends many pings (IP echo requests) to IP broadcast addresses. The receiving router responds by delivering the broadcast to all hosts in the subnet, and all the hosts respond with an IP echo reply—all of them at the same time. On a network with hundreds of hosts, this results in major network gridlock because all the machines are kept busy responding to each echo request. The situation is even worse if the routers have not been configured to keep these types of broadcasts confined to the local subnet (which thankfully they are by default!). Figure 1.2 shows a Smurf attack in progress.

Fortunately, Smurf attacks aren't very common anymore because most routers are configured in a way that prevents them from forwarding broadcast packets to other networks. Plus, it's really easy to configure routers and hosts so they won't respond to ping requests directed toward broadcast addresses.

SYN Flood

A SYN flood is also a DoS attack that inundates the receiving machine with lots of packets that cause the victim to waste resources by holding connections open. In normal communications, a workstation that wants to open a Transmission Control Protocol/Internet Protocol (TCP/IP) communication with a server sends a TCP/IP packet with the SYN flag set to 1, as

FIGURE 1.2 Smurf attack.

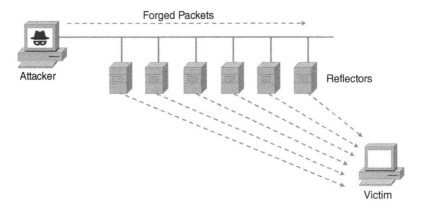

FIGURE 1.3 SYN flood.

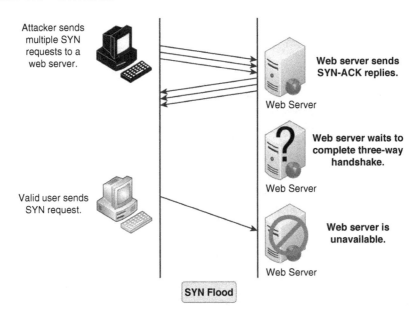

part of the three-way handshake process. The server automatically responds to the request, indicating that it's ready to start communicating with a SYN-ACK. In the SYN flood, the attacker sends a SYN, the victim sends back a SYN-ACK, and the attacker leaves the victim waiting for the final ACK. While the server is waiting for the response, a small part of memory is reserved for it. As the SYNs continue to arrive, memory is gradually consumed. Figure 1.3 shows an example of a simple DoS/SYN flood attack.

You can see that the preyed-upon machine can't respond to any other requests because its buffers are already overloaded, and it therefore rejects all packets requesting connections, even valid ones, which is the idea behind the attack. Crafting a firewall rule to prevent flooding of SYN packets might help. However, if the threat actor can coordinate a large number of SYN packets from distributed hosts, reverse proxies can mitigate the attack.

Reflective/Amplified Attacks

Reflected or amplified attacks increase the effectiveness of a DoS attack. Two of the more effective of these types of attacks involve leveraging two functions that almost all networks use, DNS and NTP. In the next two sections, these attacks are described.

DNS

A DNS amplification attack is a form of reflection attack in that the attacker delivers traffic to the victim by reflecting it off a third party. Reflection conceals the source of the attack. It relies on the exploitation of publicly accessible open DNS servers to deluge victims with DNS response traffic.

The attacker sends a small DNS message to an open resolver using the victim's IP address as the source. The type of request used returns all known information about the DNS zone, which allows for the maximum level of response amplification directed to the victim's server. The attack is magnified by recruiting a botnet to send the small messages to a large list of open resolvers (DNS servers). The response from the DNS server overwhelms the victim, as shown in Figure 1.4.

NTP

Although NTP reflection attacks use the same process of recruiting bots to aid the attack, the attacks are not reflected off DNS servers; they are instead reflected off Network Time Protocol (NTP) servers. These servers are used to maintain time synchronization between devices in a network.

The attacker (and accompanying bots) sends a small spoofed 8-byte UDP packet to vulnerable NTP servers that requests a large amount of data (megabytes worth of traffic) be

FIGURE 1.4 DNS amplification attack.

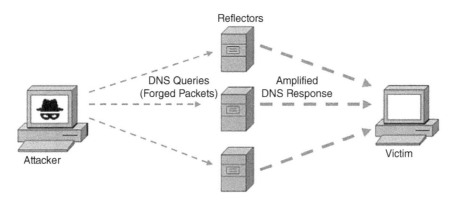

sent to the DDoS's target IP address. The attackers use the `monlist` command, a remote command in older versions of NTP, which sends the requester a list of the last 600 hosts that have connected to that server. This attack can be prevented by using at least NTP version 4.2.7 (which was released in 2010).

On-Path Attack (Previously Known as Man-in-the-Middle Attack)

Interception! But it's not a football, it's a bunch of your network's packets—your precious data. An on-path attack (previously known as a man-in-the-middle attack) happens when someone intercepts packets intended for one computer and reads the data. A common guilty party could be someone working for your very own ISP using a packet sniffer and augmenting it with routing and transport protocols. Rogue ATM machines and even credit-card swipers are tools that are also increasingly used for this type of attack. Figure 1.5 shows an on-path/man-in-the-middle attack.

DNS Poisoning

DNS clients send requests for name to IP address resolution (called queries) to a DNS server. The search for the IP address that goes with a computer or domain name usually starts with a local DNS server that is not authoritative for the DNS domain in which the requested computer or website resides. When this occurs, the local DNS server makes a request of the DNS server that does hold the record in question. After the local DNS server receives the answer, it returns it to the local DNS client. After this, the local DNS server maintains that record in its DNS cache for a period called the Time to Live (TTL), which is usually an hour but can vary.

FIGURE 1.5   On-path/man-in-the-middle attack.

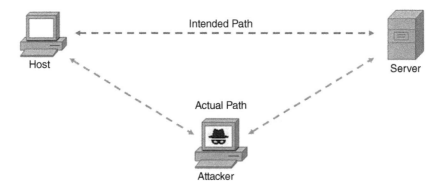

In a DNS cache poisoning attack, the attacker attempts to refresh or update that record when it expires with a different address than the correct address. If the attacker can convince the DNS server to accept this refresh, the local DNS server will then be responding to client requests for that computer with the address inserted by the attacker. Typically, the address they now receive is for a fake website that appears to look in every way like the site the client is requesting. The hacker can then harvest all the name and password combinations entered on their fake site. This type of attack is really a combination of a DNS cache poisoning attack and a phishing attempt.

To prevent this type of attack, the DNS servers should be limited in the updates they accept. In most DNS software, you can restrict the DNS servers from which a server will accept updates. This can help prevent the server from accepting these false updates.

VLAN Hopping

VLANs, or virtual LANs, are Layer 2 segmentation in a switched network. A VLAN may also span multiple switches. When devices are segregated into VLANs, access control lists (ACLs) can be used in a router to control access between VLANs in the same way it is done between real LANs. When VLANs span switches, the connection between the switches is called a trunk link, and it carries the traffic of multiple VLANs. Trunk links are also used for the connection from the switch to the router.

A VLAN hopping attack results in traffic from one VLAN being sent to the wrong VLAN. Normally, this is prevented by the trunking protocol placing a VLAN tag in the packet to identify the VLAN to which the traffic belongs.

This process is shown in Figure 1.6.

The attacker can circumvent this by a process called double tagging, which is placing a fake VLAN tag into the packet along with the real tag. When the frame goes through multiple switches, the real tag is taken off by the first switch, leaving the fake tag.

When the frame reaches the second switch, the fake tag is read, and the frame is sent to the VLAN to which the hacker intended the frame to go.

FIGURE 1.6   VLAN hopping.

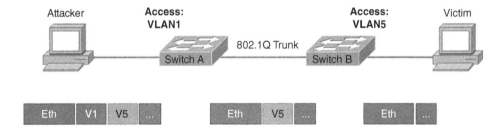

ARP Spoofing

ARP spoofing is the process of adopting another system's MAC address for the purpose of receiving data meant for that system. It usually also entails ARP cache poisoning. ARP cache poisoning is usually a part of an on-path/man-in-the middle attack. The ARP cache contains IP address to MAC address mappings that a device has learned through the ARP process. One of the ways this cache can be poisoned is by pinging a device with a spoofed IP address. In this way, an attacker can force the victim to insert an incorrect IP address to MAC address mapping into its ARP cache. If the attacker can accomplish this with two computers having a conversation, they can effectively be placed in the middle of the transmission. After the ARP cache is poisoned on both machines, they will be sending data packets to the attacker, all the while thinking they are sending them to the other member of the conversation.

Rogue DHCP

Dynamic Host Configuration Protocol (DHCP) is used to automate the process of assigning IP configurations to hosts. When configured properly, it reduces administrative overload, reduces the human error inherent in manual assignment, and enhances device mobility. But it introduces a vulnerability that when leveraged by a malicious individual can result in an inability of hosts to communicate (constituting a DoS attack) and peer-to-peer attacks.

When an illegitimate DHCP server (called a rogue DHCP server) is introduced to the network, unsuspecting hosts may accept DHCP Offer packets from the illegitimate DHCP server rather than the legitimate DHCP server. When this occurs, the rogue DHCP server will not only issue the host an incorrect IP address, subnet mask, and default gateway address (which makes a peer-to-peer attack possible); it can also issue an incorrect DNS server address, which will lead to the host relying on the attacker's DNS server for the IP addresses of websites (such as major banks) that lead to phishing attacks. An example of how this can occur is shown in Figure 1.7.

FIGURE 1.7   Rogue DHCP.

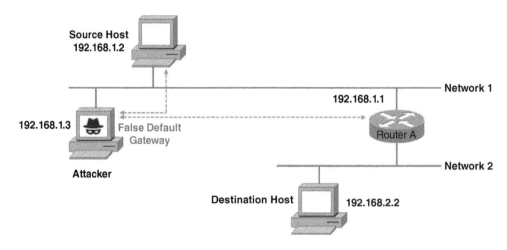

In Figure 1.7, after receiving an incorrect IP address, subnet mask, default gateway, and DNS server address from the rogue DHCP server, the DHCP client uses the attacker's DNS server to obtain the IP address of their bank. This leads the client to unwittingly connect to the attacker's copy of the bank's website. When the client enters their credentials to log in, the attacker now has the client's bank credentials and can proceed to empty out their account.

IoT Vulnerabilities

Thanks to the Internet of Things (IoT), we can finally have our fridge in the kitchen connected to the Internet! But the downside of that magic is that IoT devices tend to be made cheaply, so they don't have a lot of features you can tune, and they usually aren't built with security in mind.

Because of that, IoT devices have become quite the popular attack vector because they are usually directly connected to your network. The best way to protect yourself is to bury your Amazon Echo in your backyard, but if you would prefer to use Alexa, then the next best thing is to make sure your IoT devices are on an isolated wireless network that uses strong wireless security. That way, if someone does hack your fridge, they can't breach your actual network.

There is an enterprise version of IoT called Operational Technology (OT). OT is the other side of the IT coin that is usually staffed by nontechnical engineers who manage the infrastructure used in places such as power companies, oil and gas, and various other plants. Securing OT is the next big gold rush for IT folk because its critical infrastructure typically lacks solid network and security design.

Rogue Access Point (AP)

These are APs that have been connected to your wired infrastructure without your knowledge. The rogue may have been placed there by a determined hacker who snuck into your facility and put it in an out-of-the-way location or, more innocently, by an employee who just wants wireless access and doesn't get just how dangerous doing this is. Either way, it's just like placing an open Ethernet port out in the parking lot with a sign that says "Corporate LAN access here—no password required!"

Clearly, the worst type of rogue AP is the one some hacker has cleverly slipped into your network. It's particularly nasty because the bad guy probably didn't do it to simply gain access to your network. Nope—the hacker likely did it to entice your wireless clients to disastrously associate with their rogue AP instead! This ugly trick is achieved by placing their AP on a different channel from your legitimate APs and then setting its SSID in accordance with your SSID. Wireless clients identify the network by the SSID, not the MAC address of the AP or the IP address of the AP, so jamming the channel that your AP is on will cause your stations to roam to the bad guy's AP instead. With the proper DHCP scope configured on the AP, the hacker can issue the client an address, and once that's been done, the bad guy has basically "kidnapped" your client over to their network and can freely perform a peer-to-peer attack. Believe it or not, this can all be achieved from a laptop while Mr. Hacker simply sits in your parking lot, because there are many types of AP applications that will run on a laptop—yikes!

But you're not helpless—one way to keep rogue APs out of the wireless network is to employ a wireless LAN controller (WLC) to manage your APs. This is a nice mitigation technique because APs and controllers communicate using Lightweight Access Point Protocol (LWAPP) or the newer Control and Provisioning of Wireless Access Points (CAPWAP), and it just so happens that one of the message types they share is called Radio Resource Management (RRM). Basically, your APs monitor all channels by momentarily switching from their configured channel and by collecting packets to check for rogue activity. If an AP is detected that isn't usually managed by the controller, it's classified as a rogue, and if a wireless control system is in use, that rogue can be plotted on a floor plan and located. Another great benefit of this mitigation approach is that it enables your APs to also prevent workstations from associating with the newly exposed rogue.

Evil Twin

An evil twin is an AP that is not under your control but is used to perform a hijacking attack. A hijacking attack is one in which the hacker connects one or more of your users' computers to their network for the purpose of a peer-to-peer attack.

The attack begins with the introduction of an access point (AP) that is under the hacker's control. This access point will be set to use the same network name or SSID your network uses, and it will be set to require no authentication (creating what is called an open network).

Moreover, this access point will be set to use a different channel than the access point under your control.

To understand how the attack works, you must understand how wireless stations (laptops, tablets, and so on) choose an access point with which to connect. It is done by SSID and not by channel. The hacker will "jam" the channel on which your access point is transmitting. When a station gets disconnected from an access point, it scans the area for another access point with the same SSID. The stations will find the hacker's access point and connect to it.

Once the station is connected to the hacker's access point, it will receive an IP address from a DHCP server running on the access point and the user will now be located on the same network as the hacker. At this point, the hacker is free to commence a peer-to-peer attack.

Ransomware

Ransomware is a class of malware that prevents or limits users from accessing their information or systems. In many cases the data is encrypted, and the decryption key is only made available to the user when the ransom has been paid.

Password Attacks

Password attacks are among the most common attacks there are. Cracked or disclosed passwords can lead to severe data breaches. The end game of a phishing attack is often to learn a password. In this section, you'll learn about the two major approaches to cracking a password.

Brute-Force

A brute-force attack is a form of password cracking. The attacker attempts every possible combination of numbers and letters that could be in a password. Theoretically, given enough time and processing power, any password can be cracked. When long, complex passwords are used, however, it can take years.

Setting an account lockout policy is the simplest mitigation technique to defeat brute-force attacks. With such a policy applied, the account becomes locked after a set number of failed attempts.

Dictionary

Similar to a brute-force attack, a dictionary attack uses all the words in a dictionary until a key is discovered that successfully decrypts the ciphertext. Manual brute-force cracking requires considerable time and processing power, and it is very difficult to complete. A dictionary attack uses common passwords or passphrases to try in the password attack, and this reduces the time and resources—that is, if it works! It also requires a comprehensive dictionary of words.

An automated program uses the hash of the dictionary word and compares this hash value to entries in the system password file. Although the program comes with a dictionary, attackers also use extra dictionaries that are found on the Internet.

You should implement a security rule that says that a password must *not* be a word found in the dictionary to protect against these attacks. You can also implement an account lockout policy so that an account is locked out after a certain number of invalid login attempts.

Advanced Persistent Threat

Probably the scariest attack in this chapter is the Advanced Persistent threat (APT), which is when a group such as a government or state actor breaches a system for a long time. These attacks tend to have a goal, so they are well planned and funded, and they are in it for the long haul.

One of the most famous examples is Stuxnet, where US and Israeli intelligence agencies built a worm that lay dormant until it found its way onto computers that ran Iran's secret nuclear program infrastructure. Then it caused havoc.

Hopefully you don't find yourself against such an entity in your day-to-day job, but all you can do is make sure your company's security posture is as strong as possible.

Hardening Techniques

There are many different hardening techniques we can employ to secure our networks from compromise. When evaluating the techniques to be employed in your network, you should keep a few things in mind: evaluate your risk, evaluate the overhead the hardening introduces, and prioritize your list of hardening techniques to be implemented. Many of these hardening techniques are low-hanging fruit and should be employed, such as changing default passwords on network appliances and operating systems. Just make sure you have a system in place so complex passwords are not forgotten and are kept safe. Other techniques might require much more effort, such as patch management and firmware changes. In the following sections, I will introduce you to a few hardening techniques that can be used to secure your organization.

Changing Default Credentials

When installing a network device, the very first thing you must do is log into the device. There is often a standardized default username and password for each vendor or each vendor's product line. Most devices make you change the default password upon login to the device.

Changing the default password to a complex password is a good start to hardening the device. However, changing the username will also ensure that a brute-force attack cannot be performed against the default username. There are many different websites dedicated to listing the default credentials for network devices, so it doesn't take tremendous skill to obtain the default username and password of a device.

Avoiding Common Passwords

Avoiding common passwords is another simple measure to harden a device or operating system. There are several dictionaries that you can find on the Internet that will include common passwords. Some dictionaries are even collections of compromised passwords that have been made public.

When creating a password, it is always best practice to make the password at least 12 to 18 characters, based on the sensitivity of its use. You should always include symbols, numbers, and upper- and lowercase alpha characters. You should also resist substituting characters for symbols that look like the character. This substitution is often called "leet speak," and it is in every downloadable dictionary on the Internet. An example of a "leet speak" password is *p@$$word*. Another common pitfall in creating passwords is the use of words; passwords should be random and complex. An example of a complex password is *GLtNjXu#W6*qkqGkS$*. You can find random password generators on the Internet, such as `https://passwordsgenerator.net/`.

DHCP Snooping

An attack called DHCP spoofing is carried out by an attacker running a rogue DHCP server on your LAN. The rogue DHCP server has particular options set such as DNS or the default gateway in an attempt to redirect valid traffic to an exploited website to further compromise the clients. A rogue DHCP server can also be introduced to create an interruption of service.

DHCP snooping is a feature on Cisco switches as well as other vendor switches. It prevents a rogue DHCP server, also called a spurious DHCP server, from sending DHCP messages to clients. When DHCP snooping is configured on switches, all switchports are considered untrusted ports. Only a trusted port can forward DHCP messages; all untrusted ports are filtered for DHCP messages.

Change Native VLAN

When data is transmitted on a trunk link that is not tagged with a VLAN ID, the data will default to the native VLAN. The native VLAN is also the VLAN used for switch management. The default native VLAN is VLAN 1 on all unconfigured switches from the factory; it is also the default membership for all ports on an unconfigured switch. This creates a potential security issue; if a new switch is plugged into the network and the default VLAN is not changed on the switch ports, a user will have direct access to the management network.

If the native VLAN is not changed from the default, an attacker can use the native VLAN to launch an attack using the Dynamic Trunking Protocol (DTP) or launch a VLAN hopping attack. A DTP attack is performed by plugging a rogue Cisco switch into a port that is set to default trunking negotiation. An attacker can then use the untagged packets to move data on the native VLAN of the trunk. A VLAN hopping attack is when the attacker tags the frame twice. The intended VLAN is tagged, and then the default VLAN of 1 is tagged. When the switch receives the frame on an access link, the first tag is stripped off and then the frame is switched onto the intended VLAN.

You can mitigate the risk of users being exposed to the management VLAN and VLAN hopping by changing the native VLAN to another VLAN number. It is common to change the native VLAN on trunks to VLAN 999 or another unused VLAN. Then do not use VLAN 1 for any device management and create another VLAN for that purpose.

Patching and Updates

When operating systems are installed, they are usually point-in-time snapshots of the current build of the operating system. From the time of the build to the time of install, several vulnerabilities can be published for the operating system. When an operating system is installed, you should patch it before placing it into service. Patches remediate the vulnerabilities found in the operating system and fixed by the vendor. Updates add new features not included with the current build. However, some vendors may include vulnerability patches in updates. Network devices also have patches and updates that should be installed before placing them into service.

After the initial installation of the device or operating system and the initial patches and updates are installed, you are not done! Vendors continually release patches and updates to improve security and functionality, usually every month and sometimes outside of the normal release cycle. When patches are released outside of the normal release cycle, they are called out-of-band patches and are often in response to a critical vulnerability.

Microsoft products are patched and updated through the Windows Update functionality of the operating system. However, when an administrator is required to patch and update an entire network, Windows Server Update Services (WSUS) can be implemented. A WSUS server enables the administrator to centrally manage patches and updates. The administrator can also report on which systems still need to be patched or updated.

Upgrading Firmware

When you purchase a network device, you don't know how long it's been sitting on the shelf of a warehouse. In that time, several exploits could have been created for vulnerabilities discovered. It is always recommended that a device's *firmware* be upgraded before the device is configured and put into service.

Most hardware vendors will allow downloading of current firmware. However, some vendors require the device to be covered under a maintenance contract before firmware can be downloaded. It is also best practice to read through a vendor's changelog to understand the changes that have been made from version to version of firmware.

Defense in Depth

The concept of defense in depth is not the implementation of a single security measure but the combination of several different security measures. This creates a depth to our defense strategy to make is tougher for a bad actor to launch a successful attack and gain access to sensitive data. An example of a defense-in-depth strategy is shown in Figure 1.8 as it applies to a malicious email. The malicious email should be filtered by the spam filter, but if it makes it through the spam filter, then the antivirus and antimalware software should pick up the attempt. If none of the prior detections work at stopping the email, the end-user training should prevent the malicious link in the email from being clicked. However, if it is clicked, then the content filtering software should prevent the exploit from calling back to the server hosting the malware.

FIGURE 1.8   Example of defense in depth.

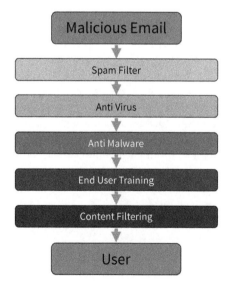

Security in this example is not left to a single mechanism. The collection of these mechanisms makes it tougher for a bad actor to succeed. The following sections cover several different security measures according to the CompTIA Network+ exam objectives, but they in no way cover all of the different security measures out there. It is always best to assess what you are trying to secure first and then identify the weaknesses. Once you understand the weaknesses, security measures can be implemented to address each weakness identified. The result will be a very diverse set of security measures and a defense-in-depth strategy.

Social-Based Attacks

Despite what we see in the movies, most breaches aren't due to a bad guy pressing a few keys on their keyboard and suddenly hacking into the Pentagon. They usually just rely on some of these low-tech attacks.

Social Engineering

The sad reality is that no matter how much money we spend on advanced security solutions to prevent bad actors from messing with the business, the average user can easily be tricked into doing something that can compromise everything.

Social engineering is really just a fancy term for being a conman, where the attacker simply talks their way into getting what they need. This comes in many forms, but essentially the bad actor will pretend to be someone in authority to gain access to information they shouldn't have access to. A common example of this is the hacker phoning a user and claiming to be their tech support so they can try to get the user's account information.

Another popular social engineering attack is the attacker pretending to be a customer and bluffing their way through tech support so they can have the password reset. A good example of this is when a large energy company, Suncor, was crippled because a hacker convinced tech support to reset the Azure Global Administrator's password (they also reset the multi-factor authentication on the account), which gave the hacker complete access to the company's Microsoft infrastructure! Within a couple minutes, the hacker locked out all the IT staff and was able to wreak havoc on all the computers because they were managed by Azure. I certainly wouldn't want to be that tech support person!

The best way to combat this threat is to continuously train staff to be on the lookout for social engineering attempts. For example, there is never a reason for IT to ask a user for their credentials. So, if someone who claims to be in IT asks for that kind of information, users should be taught to hang up and report the incident to the team that handles security.

Insider Threats

Sometimes the bad actor actually works for the company, which makes life harder because they are already on the network. Because of this, a disgruntled worker might take advantage of their existing access to the company systems, or even their position, to do things that can cause all kinds of problems.

A common example of this is when IT staff are laid off: they might leave some going-away presents such as changing passwords or otherwise setting up a time bomb that will take a system offline if not found in time. Hopefully it goes without saying, but never do this! Losing your job is not worth going to prison or getting a large fine.

The best way to reduce the risk of malicious insider threats is to enforce strict least privilege wherever possible; by ensuring that people can't access things they don't need for their day-to-day job, there will be less overall risk. It is also a good idea to have some kind of security monitoring so you can tell if users are misbehaving.

A different version of an insider threat is a user who doesn't mean to be malicious but can compromise your security anyway. Imagine a user brings their personal laptop into the office and decides to directly connect the laptop to the Ethernet jack in their office. Well, if the laptop has malware in it, then it's possible that it can spread across the network and infect all the systems.

My favorite one is when a user wants better wireless in their office area and decides to buy a cheap home router like a D-Link, instead of asking IT to install a proper access point. If they plug the D-Link into the Ethernet jack, then they just created a rogue DHCP server that will accidentally knock all the endpoints in the VLAN offline due to them getting the wrong IP information. This is because the cheap router will almost always be closer to the endpoints than the corporate DHCP server, so it will answer DHCP requests before the proper one can respond.

The best way to handle accidental insider threats so to define strict policies that specify what an employee is and isn't allowed to do; this is typically called an acceptable use policy (AUP). The idea is by explicitly saying that the employee can't use non-IT issued equipment, they can be disciplined if they break the rules. Beyond that, solutions such as Network Access Control (NAC) can help prevent unauthorized devices from being added to the network.

Phishing

Phishing comes in many different forms, but the main idea is that the attacker will send the victim an email that asks the user to click a link that will typically either download some malware or take them to a login page that will steal their credentials if they enter their username and password.

To make things more believable, the attacker will make the email look somewhat official and will pretend to be something urgent like a message from "Netflix" saying your account is delinquent and will be shut down if you don't click the link immediately. You can usually tell a phishing email from the real thing very easily because they tend to be lazy representations that are full of typos and sometimes just flatout use wrong logos or colors.

A more sure-fire way of identifying a phishing email is to look at the email address you received the mail from. The address is usually spoofed by the attacker to make it appear more legitimate. Although it may say something like support@netflix.com..., if you hover your mouse over it, you might see the real address is thisisafakenetflixsupportemail@gmail.com. Likewise, just like social engineering, your bank is never going to ask you for your banking password. So any requests like that can be immediately discarded.

There are also a couple of spin-off versions, such as "smishing," which is the same thing except the attacker texts it to your phone instead. I currently get about 10 texts a day that range from saying my packages can't be delivered, to my online services being shut off for non-pay, to the government deciding to give me money! In fact, I looked at my phone while writing this and found this message:

> *Netflix: We couldn't process your monthly payment, so your account is temporarily on hold. Please update your billing information here: https: Netflix-Canada-update.com*

We also have "vishing" attacks, where you are called on the phone by the attacker instead of them sending you a text or an email. If you have ever received a spam call from "Microsoft" saying they detected a problem with your computer and you need to give them remote access to your computer so they can fix it, they tried to social engineer you into compromising your computer. If you fall for it, they will probably install some lovely malware for you!

The last type of phishing that we will talk about is called spear phishing, and it's basically just a targeted form of phishing. Instead of sending out random emails to see if someone falls for it, the attacker will do more research and send a targeted message to achieve a result.

A frequent example that I see is when the attacker spoofs an email from the company's CEO that is sent to the finance department at 10:50 a.m. The message will say something like "Please pay this $500,000 invoice immediately as the deal needs to close by 11:00 AM. – Mr. CEO"; because of the short deadline, finance might pay the invoice without doing any verification, and the money really goes to the attacker.

Just as with social engineering, the best way to combat the threat is to continuously train users on how to detect phishing attempts and how to deal with them. Security teams frequently will send their own phishing emails to their employees in order to assess them, and those who click the link are treated to some mandatory security training.

Vishing

A vishing attack is similar to a phishing attack, with a small twist. The threat actor will use their voice to attempt to steal credentials, in lieu of a well-crafted email. Typically, the threat actor will call a helpdesk and pretend to be an employee. They will plead with the help desk person to help them change their password, or they could lose their job—something along those lines to pull the heartstrings (so to speak) of the help desk person. These types of attacks are really more social engineering than anything else.

Real Life

In September 2023, a really large cyberattack was carried out on MGM Resorts International. This cyberattack was aided by a successful vishing attempt on MGM's IT helpdesk.

Smishing

The reason these are called smishing attacks is that the Short Message Service (SMS), also known as texting, is the delivery method. A smishing attack involves well-crafted text messages to fool a victim into logging into a phishing site. Other messages might coax them into purchasing and sending gift cards. There are many different variations on this method of attack. If you can motivate a person to carry out an act, it's probably been done via smishing. This is also another good reason to never publish your cellphone number on social media sites such as Facebook or LinkedIn.

Spear Phishing

Another form of phishing is spear phishing. Spear phishing is when the attacker uses information that the target would be less likely to question because it appears to be coming from a trusted source. Suppose, for example, that you receive a message that appears to be from your spouse that says to click to see that video of your children from last Christmas. Because it appears far more likely to be a legitimate message, it cuts through your standard defenses like a spear, and the likelihood that you would click this link is higher. Generating the attack requires much more work on the part of the attacker, and it often involves using information from contact lists, friend lists from social media sites, and so on.

Environmental

Some attacks become possible because we have created an environment that they can develop in and be acted out upon. An example of environmental behavior is the urge for people to pick up a wallet on the street. They might have malicious intent, or they might not. However, they will pick it up and look inside. The environment is a public place, and there is potential for value lost. The following are issues that are created by user behavior that can be carried out by malicious threat actors.

Tailgating

Tailgating is the term used for someone being so close to you when you enter a building that they are able to come in right behind you without needing to use a key, a card, or any other security device. Many social-engineering intruders who need physical access to a site will use this method of gaining entry. Educate users to beware of this and other social-engineering ploys and prevent them from happening.

Access control vestibules (mantraps) are a great way to stop tailgating. An access control vestibule is a series of two doors with a small room between them that helps prevent unauthorized people from entering a building.

Piggybacking

Piggybacking and tailgating are similar but not the same. Piggybacking is done with the authorization of the person with access. Tailgating is done when the attacker sneaks inside without the person with access knowing. This is why access control vestibules (mantraps) and turnstiles deter tailgating, and live guards and security training deters piggybacking.

Shoulder Surfing

Shoulder surfing involves nothing more than watching someone when they enter their sensitive data. They can see you entering a password, typing in a credit card number, or entering any other pertinent information. The best defense against this type of attack is simply to survey your environment before entering personal data. Privacy filters can be used that make the screen difficult to read unless you are directly in front of it.

Malware

Malware is a broad term describing any software with malicious intent. Although we use the terms *malware* and *virus* interchangeably, distinct differences exist between them. The lines have blurred because the delivery mechanism of malware and viruses is sometimes indistinguishable.

A virus is a specific type of malware, the purpose of which is to multiply, infect, and do harm. A virus distinguishes itself from other malware because it is self-replicating code that often injects its payload into documents and executables. This is done in an attempt to infect more users and systems. Viruses are so efficient in replicating that their code is often programmed to deactivate after a period of time, or they are programmed to only be active in a certain region of the world.

Malware can be found in a variety of other forms, such as covert cryptomining, web search redirection, adware, spyware, and even ransomware, and these are just a few. Today the largest threat of malware is ransomware because it's lucrative for criminals.

Ransomware

Ransomware is a type of malware that is becoming popular because of anonymous currency, such as Bitcoin. Ransomware is software that is often delivered through an unsuspecting random download. It takes control of a system and demands that a third party be paid. The "control" can be accomplished by encrypting the hard drive, by changing user password information, or via any of several other creative ways. Users are usually assured that by paying the extortion amount (the ransom), they will be given the code needed to revert their systems back to normal operations. CryptoLocker was a popular ransomware that made headlines across the world, as shown in Figure 1.9.

FIGURE 1.9   CryptoLocker.

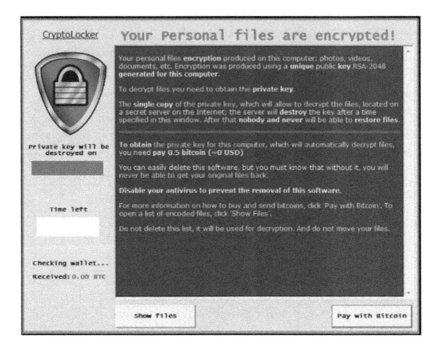

You can protect yourself from ransomware by having antivirus/antimalware software with up-to-date definitions and by keeping current on patches.

Summary

In this chapter, you learned common attack types that you might expect on an enterprise network. These attack types can be categorized into technology-based attacks and those that are the result of human failure or of the network environment that exists.

Technology-based attacks include denial-of-service (DoS)/distributed denial of service (DDoS) attacks, on-path attacks, DNS poisoning, VLAN hopping, ARP spoofing, rogue DHCP, rogue access point (AP), evil twin, ransomware, and password attacks.

Human and environmental attacks include social engineering, phishing, tailgating, piggybacking, and shoulder surfing.

Exam Essentials

Explain common technology-based attacks.   These include (DoS)/distributed denial-of-service (DDoS) attacks, on-path attacks, DNS poisoning, VLAN hopping, ARP spoofing, rogue DHCP, rogue access point (AP), evil twin, ransomware, and password attacks.

Describe (DoS)/distributed denial of service (DDoS) attacks.   This includes the architecture and behavior of a botnet and of the role of the command-and-control-server.

Identify human and environmental attacks.   These include social engineering, phishing, tailgating, piggybacking, and shoulder surfing.

Review Questions

The following questions are designed to test your understanding of this chapter's material. For more information on how to get additional questions, please see www.lammle.com/ccst.

You can find the answers to these questions in Appendix.

1. Which of the following is *not* a technology-based attack?

   A. DoS

   B. Ping of death

   C. Shoulder surfing

   D. Malware

2. A command-and-control server is a part of which of the following attacks?

   A. DDoS

   B. Ping of death

   C. Shoulder surfing

   D. Malware

3. Which of the following is a DoS attack that floods its victim with spoofed broadcast ping messages?

   A. SYN flood

   B. Smurf attack

   C. Land attack

   D. Ping of death

4. Which of the following is an attack that inundates the receiving machine with lots of packets that cause the victim to waste resources by holding connections open?

   A. Ping of death

   B. Zero day

   C. Smurf attack

   D. SYN flood

5. In which of the following does the attacker (and their bots) sends a small spoofed 8-byte UDP packet to vulnerable NTP servers that requests a large amount of data (megabytes worth of traffic) be sent to the DDoS's target IP address?

   A. SYN flood

   B. NTP amplification

   C. Smurf attack

   D. DNS amplification

6. Which of the following was previously known as a man-in-the-middle attack?

   A. VLAN hopping

   B. On-path attack

   C. LAND attack

   D. Smurf attack

7. Double tagging is a part of which of the following attacks?

   A. VLAN hopping

   B. Smurf attack

   C. DDoS

   D. Malware

8. Which of the following is the process of adopting another system's MAC address for the purpose of receiving data meant for that system?

   A. Certificate spoofing

   B. ARP spoofing

   C. IP spoofing

   D. URL spoofing

9. Which of the following is connected to your wired infrastructure without your knowledge?

   A. Rogue AP

   B. Command-and-control server

   C. Zombies

   D. Botnet

10. Which of the following uses the same SSID as your AP?

   A. Rogue AP

   B. Rogue DHCP

   C. Evil twin

   D. Zombie

Chapter

2

Network Security Devices

THE FOLLOWING CCST EXAM TOPICS ARE COVERED IN THIS CHAPTER:

✓ **2.0 Network Security**

- 2.3. Describe network infrastructure and technologies.

  Network security architecture, DMZ, virtualization, cloud, honeypot, proxy server, IDS, IPS

- 2.4. Set up a secure wireless SoHo network.

  MAC address filtering, encryption standards and protocols, SSID

 To find your included bonus material, as well as Todd Lammle videos, practice questions, and hands-on labs, please see www.lammle.com/ccst.

To operate securely in a network environment, one must understand how to speak the language of security. As in any field, there is terminology that must be understood to discuss more involved topics.

In this chapter you will learn the basic concepts, terms, and principles that all network professionals should understand to secure an enterprise network.

If you want to understand the basic wireless LANs (WLANs) most commonly used today, just think 10BaseT Ethernet with hubs. What this means is that our WLANs typically run half-duplex communication—everyone is sharing the same bandwidth, and only one user is communicating at a time.

This isn't necessarily bad; it's just not good enough. Because most people rely on wireless networks today, it's critical that they evolve faster than greased lightning to keep up with our rapidly escalating needs. The good news is that this is actually happening—and it even works securely! We'll discuss these newer, faster technologies in this chapter.

The goal in this chapter is to introduce you to wireless networks and the technologies in use today. I'll also cover the various components used, the IEEE 802.11 standards, wireless installation, and, of course, wireless security.

Confidentiality, Integrity, and Availability (CIA)

The three fundamentals of security are confidentiality, integrity, and availability (CIA), often referred to as the CIA triad. Most security issues result in a violation of at least one facet of the CIA triad. Understanding these three security principles will help ensure that the security controls and mechanisms implemented protect at least one of these principles.

Confidentiality

To ensure confidentiality, you must prevent the disclosure of data or information to unauthorized entities. As part of confidentiality, the sensitivity level of data must be determined before putting any access controls in place. Data with a higher sensitivity level will have more access controls in place than data at a lower sensitivity level. Identification, authentication, authorization, and encryption can be used to maintain data confidentiality.

Integrity

Integrity, the second part of the CIA triad, ensures that data is protected from unauthorized modification or data corruption. The goal of integrity is to preserve the consistency of data, including data stored in files, databases, systems, and networks.

Availability

Availability means ensuring that data is accessible when and where it is needed. Only individuals who need access to data should be allowed access to that data. The two main areas where availability is affected are (1) when attacks are carried out that disable or cripple a system and (2) when service loss occurs during and after disasters. Technologies that provide fault tolerance, such as RAID and redundant sites, are examples of controls that help to improve availability.

Threats

The first line of defense in providing CIA is to know about the types of threats out there, because you can't do anything to protect yourself from something you don't know about. But once you understand the threats, you can begin to design defenses to combat bad guys lurking in the depths of cyberspace just waiting for an opportunity to strike. Threats comes in two forms, internal and external.

Internal

Internal threats are those that are sourced within your own network. These attacks come from inside the firewall. Sadly, we have more to fear from our own users than we do from external hackers (maybe we should treat them better). They have already discovered and penetrated the network, which is two-thirds of the hacking process.

External

External threats come from outside the firewall. These are typically hackers of all abilities. They include script kiddies (amateurs), advanced persistent threats (APT, usually a state-sponsored team), and all types in between. Later you will learn that these two types require a different approach when penetration testing for vulnerabilities.

Network Access Control

Network access control (NAC) is a method of securing network hosts before they're allowed to access the network. Network access control systems that control access to devices based on their security settings include Cisco's Network Admission Control (NAC) and Microsoft's Network Policy and Access Services (NPAS). These systems examine the state of a computer's operating system updates and antimalware updates before allowing access, and in some cases they can even remediate the devices before permitting access. The following sections cover key components of network access control systems.

Posture Assessment

When devices attempt to access the network, the devices are examined closely, which is called a posture assessment. The following items can be checked:

- Antimalware updates
- Operating system updates
- Windows Registry settings

When the assessment is complete and is positive, admission is granted. If problems are found, admission may be denied and the user notified that action must be taken, or the device may be directed to a remediation server that can install missing updates or quarantine the device if necessary.

Guest Network

When a device is attempting to connect to a network using a form of network access control, the device is first placed in a guest network until a posture assessment is performed. Until it is either approved or remediated, it will remain in the guest network. The guest network will not allow access to the balance of the network to prevent the device from introducing issues to the network.

Persistent vs. Nonpersistent Agents

Network access control systems can be deployed using either persistent or nonpersistent agents on the devices. A persistent agent is one that is installed on an NAC client and starts when the operating system loads. This agent provides functionality that may not be present in the nonpersistent agent, such as system-wide notifications and alerts and auto and manual remediation.

A nonpersistent agent is one that is used to assess the device only during the onetime check-in at login, usually through a captive web portal. The nonpersistent, or dissolvable, agent is removed from the device when the authentication web page is closed. It can be used to support the assessment of endpoints not owned by the organization and as such can help to make a bring your own device (BYOD) policy possible.

Honeypot

Another segmentation tactic is to create honeypots and honeynets. *Honeypots* are systems strategically configured to be attractive to hackers and to lure them into spending enough time attacking them while information is gathered about the attack. In some cases, entire networks called *honeynets* are attractively configured for this purpose. You need to make sure that either of these types of systems do not provide direct connections to any important systems. Their ultimate purpose is to divert attention from valuable resources and to gather as much information about an attack as possible. A tarpit is a type of honeypot designed to provide a very slow connection to the hacker so that the attack takes enough time to be properly analyzed.

Wireless Networks

Wireless networks come in many forms, cover various distances, and provide a wide range of bandwidth capacities depending on the type that's been installed. The typical wireless network today is an extension of an Ethernet LAN, with wireless hosts utilizing Media Access Control (MAC) addresses, IP addresses, and so forth, just like they would on a wired LAN.

Figure 2.1 shows a simple, typical WLAN.

Wireless networks are more than just run-of-the-mill LANs—because they're wireless, of course. They cover a range of distances, from short-range personal area networks (PANs) to wide area networks (WANs) that really go the distance.

Figure 2.2 illustrates how different types of wireless networks look and the related distances they'll provide coverage for in today's world.

Now that you've got a mental picture, let's explore each of these networks in more detail.

Wireless Personal Area Networks

A wireless PAN works in a very small area and connects devices such as mice, keyboards, PDAs, headsets, and cell phones to our computers. This conveniently eliminates the cabling clutter of the past. If you're thinking Bluetooth, you've got it, because it's by far the most popular type of PAN around.

PANs are low power, they cover short distances, and they're small. You can stretch one of these to cover about 30 feet max, but most devices on a PAN have a short reach, making

FIGURE 2.1 Wireless LAN distribution system (DS).

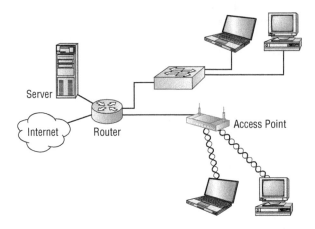

FIGURE 2.2 Today's wireless networks.

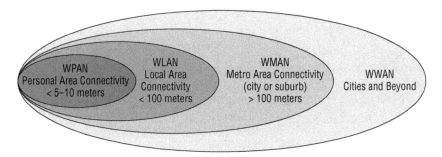

them popular for small and/or home offices. Bigger isn't always better—you don't want your PAN's devices interfering with your other wireless networks, or someone else's. Plus, you've got the usual security concerns to manage. So remember that PANs are the perfect solution for small devices you want to connect to your PC.

The standard use for PANs is unlicensed. This means that beyond initially purchasing PAN-typical devices, the users involved don't have to pay to use the type of devices in this network. This factor definitely encourages the development of devices that can use PAN frequencies.

Wireless Local Area Networks

Wireless LANs (WLANs) were created to cover longer distances and offer higher bandwidth than PANs. They're the most popular type of wireless networks in use today.

The first WLAN had a data rate up to 2 Mbps, could stretch about 200–300 feet, depending on the area, and was called 802.11. The typical rates in use today are higher: 11 Mbps for IEEE 802.11b and 54 Mbps for 802.11g/a.

The ideal for a WLAN is to have many users connect to the network simultaneously, but this can cause interference and collisions because the network's users are all competing for the same bandwidth.

Like PANs, WLANs use an unlicensed frequency band, which means you don't have to pay for the frequency band in order to transmit. And, again, this attribute has resulted in an explosion of new development in the WLAN arena.

Wireless Metro Area Networks

Wireless metro area networks (WMANs) cover a fairly large geographic area such as a city or small suburb. They're becoming increasingly common as more and more products are introduced into the WLAN sector, causing the price tag to drop.

You can think of WMANs as low-budget, bridging networks. They'll save you some real cash compared to shelling out for much more costly leased lines, but there's a catch: in order to get your discount long-distance wireless network to work, you've got to have a line of sight between each hub or building.

Fiber connections are ideal to build an ultra-solid network backbone, so go with them if they're available in your area. If your ISP doesn't offer the fiber option, or you just don't have the cash for it, a WMAN is a perfectly fine and economical alternative for covering something like a campus or another large area, as long as you've got that vital line-of-sight factor in check!

Wireless Wide Area Networks

So far, it's very rare to come across a wireless wide area network (WWAN) that can provide you with WLAN speeds, but there sure is a lot of chatter about them. A good example of a WWAN would be the latest cellular networks, which can transmit data at a pretty good clip. But even though WWANs can certainly cover plenty of area, they're still not speedy enough to replace our ubiquitous WLANs.

Some people—especially those shilling stuff on TV—claim to adore their infallible, turbo-charged cellular networks. These terminally happy people are usually watching high-speed video while uploading images and gaming on their smart phones, but I don't know anyone who lives outside the TV who actually gets that kind of speed. And as for that "coverage anywhere" schtick? Off the set, dead zones and frozen phones are just reality for now.

It's possible that we'll see more efficiency and growth for WWANs soon, but since WWANs are used to provide connectivity over a really large geographic area, it follows that implementing one will separate your cell service provider from a large quantity of cash. So it's going to come to motivation; as more people demand this type of service and are willing to pay for it, cellular companies will gain the resources to expand and improve on these exciting networks.

Another set of positives in favor of WWAN growth and development is that they meet a lot of business requirements, and technology is growing in a direction that the need for this type of long-distance wireless network is getting stronger. So it's a fairly good bet that connectivity between a WLAN and a WWAN will be critical to many things in our future. For instance, when we have more IPv6 networks, the "pass-off" between these two types of networks may be seamless.

Basic Wireless Devices

Although it might not seem this way to you right now, *simple* wireless networks (WLANs) are less complex than their wired cousins because they require fewer components. To make a basic wireless network work properly, all you need are two main devices: a wireless AP and a wireless network interface card (NIC). This also makes it a lot easier to install a wireless network, because basically you just need an understanding of these two components in order to make it happen.

Wireless Access Points

You'll find a central component such as a hub or switch in the vast majority of wired networks, which is there to connect hosts together and allow them to communicate. Wireless technologies also has a component that connects all wireless devices together, only that device is known as a wireless *access point* (AP). Wireless APs have at least one antenna. Usually there are two for better reception (referred to as diversity) and a port to connect them to a wired network.

Figure 2.3 shows an example of a Cisco wireless AP, which just happens to be one of my personal favorites.

FIGURE 2.3 A wireless access point.

APs have the following characteristics:

- APs function as a central junction point for the wireless stations much like a switch or hub does within a wired network. Due to the half-duplex nature of wireless networking, the hub comparison is more accurate, even though hubs are rarely found in the wired world anymore.
- APs have at least one antenna—most likely two.
- APs function as a bridge to the wired network, giving the wireless station access to the wired network and/or the Internet.
- SoHo APs come in two flavors: the stand-alone AP and the wireless router. They can and usually do include functions such as network address translation (NAT) and Dynamic Host Configuration Protocol (DHCP).

Even though it's not a perfect analogy, you can compare an AP to a hub because it doesn't create collision domains for each port like a switch does. But APs are definitely smarter than hubs. An AP is a portal device that can either direct network traffic to the wired backbone or back out into the wireless realm. If you look at Figure 2.1 again, you can see that the connection back to the wired network is called the distribution system (DS), and it also maintains MAC address information within the 802.11 frames. What's more, these frames are capable of holding as many as four MAC addresses, but only when a wireless DS is in use.

An AP also maintains an association table that you can view from the web-based software used to manage the AP. What's an association table? It's basically a list of all workstations currently connected to or associated with the AP, which are listed by their MAC addresses. Another nice AP feature is that wireless routers can function as NAT routers, and they can carry out DHCP addressing for workstations as well.

In the Cisco world, there are two types of APs: autonomous and lightweight. An autonomous AP is one that's configured, managed, and maintained in isolation with regard to all the other APs that exist in the network. A lightweight AP gets its configuration from a central device called a wireless controller. In this scenario, the APs are functioning as antennas, and all information is sent back to the wireless LAN controller (WLC). There are a bunch of advantages to this, such as the capacity for centralized management and more seamless roaming. You'll learn all about using WLCs and lightweight APs throughout this book.

You can think of an AP as a bridge between the wireless clients and the wired network. And, depending on the settings, you can even use an AP as a wireless bridge for bridging two wired network segments together.

In addition to the stand-alone AP, there's another type of AP that includes a built-in router, which you can use to connect both wired and wireless clients to the Internet. These devices are usually employed as NAT routers and are the type shown in Figure 2.3.

Wireless Network Interface Card

Every host you want to connect to a wireless network needs a wireless *network interface card* (NIC) to do so. Basically, a wireless NIC does the same job as a traditional NIC, only instead of having a socket/port to plug a cable into, the wireless NIC has a radio antenna.

Figure 2.4 gives you a picture of a wireless NIC. This wireless card is used in a laptop or desktop computer, and pretty much all laptops have wireless cards plugged into or built into the motherboard.

NOTE   These days it's pretty rare to use an external wireless client card because all laptops come with them built in, and desktops can be ordered with them too. But it's good to know that you can still buy the client card shown in Figure 2.4. Typically, you would use cards like the ones shown in the figure for areas of poor reception or for use with a network analyzer because they can have better range, depending on the antenna you use.

Wireless Antennas

Wireless antennas work with both transmitters and receivers. Two broad classes of antennas are on the market today: *omnidirectional* (or point-to-multipoint) and *directional* (or point-to-point). Refer to Figure 2.3 for an example of omnidirectional antennas attached to the Cisco 800 AP.

FIGURE 2.4   A wireless NIC.

Yagi antennas usually provide greater range than omnidirectional antennas of equivalent gain. Why? Because Yagi antennas focus all their power in a single direction. Omnidirectional antennas must disperse the same amount of power in all directions at the same time, like a large donut.

A downside to using a directional antenna is that you have to be much more precise when aligning communication points. It's also why most APs use omnidirectional antennas—because clients and other APs often can be located in any direction at any given moment.

To get a picture of this, think of the antenna on your car. Yes, it's a non-networking example, but it's still a good one because it clarifies the fact that your car's particular orientation doesn't affect the signal reception of whatever radio station you happen to be listening to. Well, most of the time, anyway. If you're in the boonies, you're out of range and out of luck—something that also applies to the networking version of omnidirectional antennas.

Wireless Principles

Next up, I'm going to cover different types of networks you'll run into and/or design and implement as your wireless networks grow:

- IBSS
- BSS
- SSID
- ESS

Independent Basic Service Set (Ad Hoc)

This is the easiest way to install wireless 802.11 devices. In this mode, the wireless NICs (or other devices) can communicate directly without the need for an AP. A good example of this is two laptops with wireless NICs installed. If both cards were set up to operate in ad hoc mode, they could connect and transfer files as long as the other network settings, such as protocols, were set up to enable this as well. We'll also call this an *independent basic service set (IBSS)*, which is born as soon as two wireless devices communicate.

To create an ad hoc network, all you need is two or more wireless-capable devices. Once you've placed them within a range of 20–40 meters of each other, they'll "see" each other and be able to connect—assuming they share some basic configuration parameters. One computer may be able to share the Internet connection with the rest of them in your group.

Figure 2.5 shows an example of an ad hoc wireless network. Notice that there's no access point!

An ad hoc network, also known as peer-to-peer, doesn't scale well, and I wouldn't recommend it due to collision and organization issues in today's corporate networks. With the low cost of APs, you don't need this kind of network anymore anyway, except for maybe in your home—and probably not even there.

FIGURE 2.5   A wireless network in ad hoc mode.

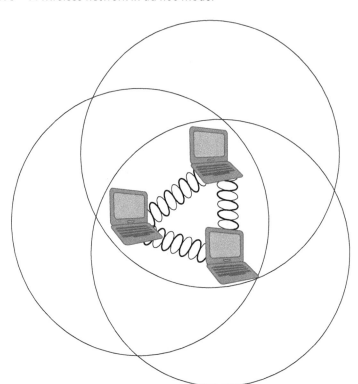

Another con is that ad hoc networks are pretty insecure, so you really want to have the AdHoc setting turned off before connecting to your wired network.

Basic Service Set

A basic service set (BSS) is the area, or cell, defined by the wireless signal served by the AP. It can also be called a basic service area (BSA); the two terms, BSS and BSA, are interchangeable. Even so, BSS is the most common term that's used to define the cell area. Figure 2.6 shows an AP providing a BSS for hosts in the area and the basic service area (cell) that's covered by the AP.

The AP isn't connected to a wired network in this example, but it provides for the management of wireless frames so the hosts can communicate. Unlike an ad hoc network, this network will scale better, and more hosts can communicate because the AP manages all network connections.

FIGURE 2.6   Basic service set/basic service area.

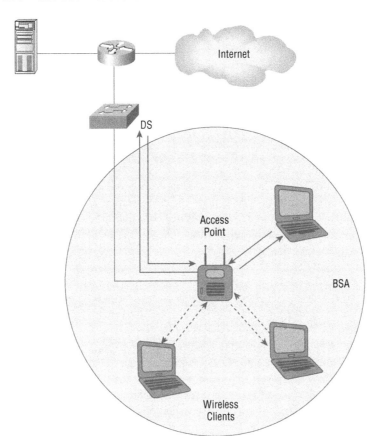

Infrastructure Basic Service Set

In infrastructure mode, wireless NICs communicate only with an access point instead of directly with each other, like they do when they're in ad hoc mode. All communication between hosts, as well as any wired portion of the network, must go through the access point. Remember this important fact: In infrastructure mode, wireless clients appear to the rest of the network as though they are standard, wired hosts.

Figure 2.6 shows a typical infrastructure mode wireless network. Pay special attention to the access point and the fact that it's also connected to the wired network. This connection from the access point to the wired network is called the *distribution system (DS)* and is how the APs communicate to each other about hosts in the BSA. Basic stand-alone APs don't communicate with each other via the wireless network, only through the DS.

Before you configure a client to operate in wireless infrastructure mode, you need to understand SSIDs. The *service set identifier (SSID)* is the unique 32-character identifier that represents a particular wireless network and defines the BSS. And, just so you know, a lot of people use the terms SSID and BSS interchangeably, so don't let that confuse you! All devices involved in a particular wireless network can be configured with the same SSID. Sometimes access points even have multiple SSIDs.

Let's talk about that a little more now.

Service Set ID

Technically, *service set ID* (SSID) is a basic name that defines the basic service area (BSA) transmitted from the AP. A good example of this is "Linksys" or "Netgear." You've probably seen that name pop up on your host when looking for a wireless network. This is the name the AP transmits out to identify which WLAN the client station can associate with.

The SSID can be up to 32 characters long. It normally consists of human-readable ASCII characters, but the standard doesn't require this. The SSID is defined as a sequence of 1–32 octets, each of which may take any value.

The SSID is configured on the AP and can be either broadcasted to the outside world or hidden. If the SSID is broadcasted, when wireless stations use their client software to scan for wireless networks, the network will appear in a list identified by its SSID. But if the SSID is hidden, either it won't appear in the list at all or it will show up as "unknown network," depending on the client's operating system.

Either way, a hidden SSID requires the client station be configured with a wireless profile, including the SSID, in order to connect. And this requirement is above and beyond any other normal authentication steps or security essentials.

The AP associates a MAC address with this SSID. It can be the MAC address for the radio interface itself—called the basic service set identifier (BSSID)—or it can be derived from the MAC address of the radio interface if multiple SSIDs are used. The latter is sometimes called a virtual MAC address, and also referred to as a multiple basic service set identifier (MBSSID), as shown in Figure 2.7.

There are two things you really want to make note of in this figure: first, there's a "Contractor" BSSID and a "Sales" BSSID; second, each of these SSID names is associated with a separate virtual MAC address, which was assigned by the AP.

These SSIDs are virtual, and implementing things this way won't improve your wireless network's or AP's performance. You're not breaking up collision domains or broadcast domains by creating more SSIDs on your AP; you just have more hosts sharing the same half-duplex radio. The reason for creating multiple SSIDs on your AP is so that you can set different levels of security for each client that's connecting to your AP(s).

Extended Service Set

A good to thing to know is that if you set all your access points to the same SSID, mobile wireless clients can roam around freely within the same network. This is the most common wireless network design you'll find in today's corporate settings.

FIGURE 2.7   A network with MBSSIDs configured on an AP.

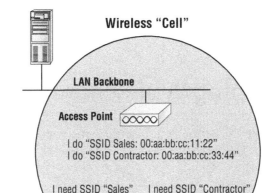

FIGURE 2.8   An extended service set (ESS) network.

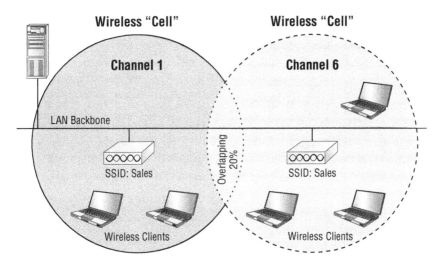

Doing this creates something called an *extended service set (ESS)*, which provides more coverage than a single access point and allows users to roam from one AP to another without having their host disconnected from the network. This design gives us the ability to move fairly seamlessly from one AP to another.

Figure 2.8 shows two APs configured with the same SSIDs in an office, thereby creating an ESS network.

For users to be able to roam throughout the wireless network—from AP to AP without losing their connection to the network—all APs must overlap their neighbor's cells by 20 percent of their signal or more. To make this happen, be sure the channels (frequency) on each AP are set differently.

Nonoverlapping Wi-Fi channels

In both the 2.4 GHz and the 5 GHz frequency bands, channels are defined by the standards: 802.11, 802.11b, and 802.11g use the 2.4 GHz band, also known as the *industrial, scientific, and medical* (ISM) band; and 802.11a uses the 5 GHz band. When two access points are operating in the same area on the same channel or even an adjacent channel, they will interfere with each other. Interference lowers the throughput. Therefore, channel management to avoid interference is critical to ensure reliable operation. This section examines issues that impact channel management.

2.4 GHz Band

Within the 2.4 GHz (ISM) band are 11 channels approved for use in the United States, 13 in Europe, and 14 in Japan. Each channel is defined by its center frequency, but remember, that signal is spread across 22 MHz. There's 11 MHz on one side of the center frequency and 11 MHz on the other side, so each channel encroaches on the channel next to it—even others farther from it to a lesser extent. Take a look at Figure 2.9.

Consequently, within the United States, only channels 1, 6, and 11 are considered nonoverlapping. So, when you have two APs in the same area that are operating on overlapping channels, the effect depends on whether they're on the same channel or on adjacent channels. Let's examine each scenario.

When APs are on the same channel, they will hear each other and defer to one another when transmitting. This is due to information sent in the header of each wireless packet that instructs all stations in the area (including any APs) to refrain from transmitting until the current transmission is received. The APs perform this duty based partially on the

FIGURE 2.9   2.4 GHz band 22 MHz-wide channels.

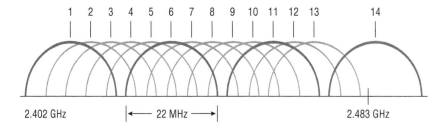

duration field. The end result is that both networks will be slower because they'll be dividing their transmission into windows of opportunity to transmit between them.

When the APs are only one or two channels apart, things get a little tricky, because in this case they may not be able to hear each clearly enough to read the duration field. The ugly result of this is that they'll transmit at the same time, causing collisions that cause retransmissions and can seriously slow down your throughput. Ugh! Therefore, although the two behaviors are different within these two scenarios, the end result is the same: greatly lowered throughput.

5 GHz Band (802.11ac)

802.11a uses the 5 GHz frequency, which is divided into three unlicensed bands called the Unlicensed National Information Infrastructure (UNII) bands. Two bands are adjacent to each other, but there is a frequency gap between the second and third. These bands are known as UNII-1, UNII-2, and UNII-3—the lower, middle, and upper UNII bands, respectively. Each of these bands hosts discrete channels, as in the ISM.

The 802.11a amendment specifies the location of the center point of each frequency, as well as the distance that must exist between the center point frequencies, but it fails to specify the exact width of each frequency. The good news is that the channels only overlap with the next adjacent channel, so it's easier to find nonoverlapping channels in 802.11a.

In the lower UNII band, the center points are 10 MHz apart, and in the other two, the center frequencies are 20 MHz apart. Figure 2.10 illustrates the overlap of the UNII bands (top and bottom), compared to the 2.4 GHz band (middle).

The channel numbers in the lower UNII are 36, 40, 44, and 48. In the middle UNII, the channels are 52, 56, 60, and 64. The channels in UNII-3 are 149, 153, 157, and 161.

2.4 GHz / 5GHz (802.11n)

802.11n builds on previous 802.11 standards by adding *multiple-input multiple-output (MIMO)*, which uses multiple transmitters and receiver antennas to increase data throughput and range. 802.11n can allow up to eight antennas, but most of today's APs use only four to six. This setup permits considerably higher data rates than 802.11a/b/g does.

The following three vital items are combined in 802.11n to enhance performance:

- At the physical layer, the way a signal is sent is changed, enabling reflections and interferences to become an advantage instead of a source of degradation.

- Two 20 MHz-wide channels are combined to increase throughput.

- At the MAC layer, a different way of managing packet transmission is used.

It's important to know that 802.11n isn't truly compatible with 802.11b, 802.11g, or even 802.11a, but it is designed to be backward compatible with them. 802.11n achieves backward compatibility by changing the way frames are sent so they can be understood by 802.11a/b/g.

FIGURE 2.10 5 GHz band 20 MHz-wide channels.

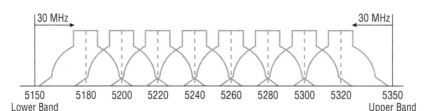

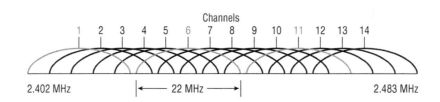

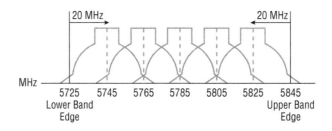

Here's a list of some of the primary components of 802.11n that together sum up why people claim 802.11n is more reliable and predictable:

40 MHz Channels 802.11g and 802.11a use 20 MHz channels and employ tones on the sides of each channel that are not used in order to protect the main carrier. This means that 11 Mbps go unused and are basically wasted. 802.11n aggregates two carriers to double the speed from 54 Mbps to more than 108. Add in those wasted 11 Mbps rescued from the side tones, and you get a grand total of 119 Mbps!

MAC Efficiency 802.11 protocols require acknowledgment of each and every frame. 802.11n can pass many packets before an acknowledgment is required, which saves you a huge amount of overhead. This is called *block acknowledgment*.

Multiple-Input Multiple-Output Several frames are sent by several antennae over several paths and are then recombined by another set of antennae to optimize throughput and multipath resistance. This is called *spatial multiplexing*.

Wi-Fi 6 (802.11ax)

So what is Wi-Fi 6, and is it faster than Wi-Fi 5? Well, I would hope so, since it is one number greater than 5, but that is only because this is the sixth generation of Wi-Fi with enough changes to possibly give us twice the speed, although only time will tell if that is true.

To say that 802.11ax and Wi-Fi 6 are the same thing would definitely be true, and it's great marketing right now for the Wi-Fi manufacturers.

Figure 2.11 shows the difference from 202.11ac (Wi-Fi 5). The first thing you should notice is that 802.1ax uses both 2.4 and 5 GHz, whereas 802.1ac uses only 5 GHz, and 802.1ax has more orthogonal frequency-division multiplexing (OFDM) symbols and a higher modulation, which provides superior data rates.

Some benefits of this newer Wi-Fi 6 technology include the following:

- Denser modulation using 1024 quadrature amplitude modulation (QAM), enabling a more than 35 percent speed burst

- Orthogonal frequency-division multiple access (OFDMA)-based scheduling, to reduce overhead and latency

- Robust high-efficiency signaling for better operation at a significantly lower received signal strength indication (RSSI)

- Better scheduling and longer device battery life with target wake time (TWT)

Interference

One factor that affects wireless performance is outside interference. Because 802.11 wireless protocols operate in the 900 MHz, 2.4 GHz, and 5 GHz ranges, interference can come from

FIGURE 2.11   Comparing Wi-Fi 5 to Wi-Fi 6 Standards.

Parameter	Wi-Fi 5 (802.11ac)	Wi-Fi 6 (802.11ax)
Frequency	5 GHz	2.4 and 5.0 GHz
Bandwidths (channels)	20, 40, 80+80, 160 MHz	20, 40, 80+80, 160 MHz
Access	OFDM	OFDMA
Antennas	MU-MIMO (4 × 4)	MU-MIMO (8 × 8)
Modulation	256QAM	1024QAM
Maximum data rate	3.5 Gb/s	9.6 Gb/s
Maximum users/AP	4	8

TABLE 2.1   Range and speed comparisons.

Standard	802.11b	802.11a	802.11g	802.11n	802.11ac	802.11ax
Speed	11 Mbps	54 Mbps	54 Mbps	300 Mbps	1 Gbps	3.5+ Gbps
Frequency	2.4 GHz	5 GHz	2.4 GHz	2.4/5 GHz	5 GHz	2.4/5/6 GHz
Range (in feet)	100–150	25–75	100–150	>230	>230	Unknown

many sources. These include wireless devices such as Bluetooth, cordless telephones, cell phones, other wireless LANs, and any other device that transmits a radio frequency (RF) near the frequency bands that 802.11 protocols use. Even microwave ovens—a huge adversary of 802.11b and 802.11g—can be serious culprits!

Range and Speed Comparisons

Table 2.1 delimits the range comparisons of each 802.11 standard and shows these different ranges using an indoor open-office environment as a factor. (We'll be using default power settings.)

Wireless Security

Now that we've covered the very basics of wireless devices used in today's networks, let's move on to wireless security.

At the foundational level, authentication uniquely identifies the user and/or machine. The encryption process protects the data or the authentication process by scrambling the information enough that it becomes unreadable by anyone trying to capture the raw frames.

Authentication and Encryption

Two types of authentications were specified by the IEEE 802.11 committee: open and shared-key authentication. Open authentication involves little more than supplying the right SSID, but it's the most common method in use today.

With shared-key authentication, the access point sends the client device a challenge-text packet, which the client must then encrypt with the correct Wired Equivalent Privacy (WEP) key and return to the access point. Without the correct key, authentication will fail, and the client won't be allowed to associate with the access point.

Figure 2.12 shows shared-key authentication.

FIGURE 2.12   Shared-key authentication.

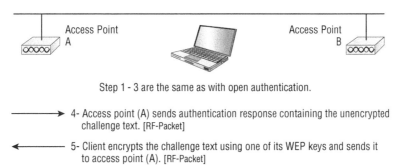

Step 1 - 3 are the same as with open authentication.

4- Access point (A) sends authentication response containing the unencrypted challenge text. [RF-Packet]

5- Client encrypts the challenge text using one of its WEP keys and sends it to access point (A). [RF-Packet]

6- Access point (A) compares the encrypted challenge text with its copy of the encrypted challenge text. If the text is the same, access point (A) will allow the client onto the WLAN. [RF-Packet]

FIGURE 2.13   Open access process.

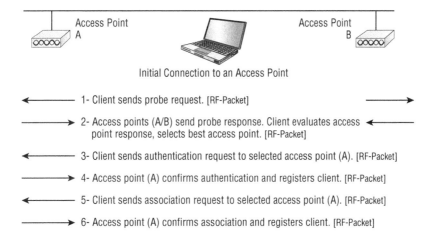

Initial Connection to an Access Point

1- Client sends probe request. [RF-Packet]

2- Access points (A/B) send probe response. Client evaluates access point response, selects best access point. [RF-Packet]

3- Client sends authentication request to selected access point (A). [RF-Packet]

4- Access point (A) confirms authentication and registers client. [RF-Packet]

5- Client sends association request to selected access point (A). [RF-Packet]

6- Access point (A) confirms association and registers client. [RF-Packet]

Shared-key authentication is still not considered secure because all a bad guy has to do to get around it is to detect both the cleartext challenge, the same challenge encrypted with a WEP key, and then decipher the WEP key. It's no surprise that shared-key authentication isn't used in today's WLANs.

All Wi-Fi-certified wireless LAN products are shipped in "open access" mode, with their security features turned off. Although open access or no security sounds scary, it's totally acceptable for places such as public hot spots. But it's definitely not an option for an enterprise organization, and it's not a good idea for your private home network either!

Figure 2.13 shows the open access process.

You can see that an authentication request has been sent and validated by the AP. But when open authentication is used or set to "none" in the wireless controller, the request is pretty much guaranteed not to be denied. For now, understand that this authentication is done at the MAC layer (layer 2), so don't confuse this with the higher-layer authentication we'll cover later, which occurs after the client is associated to the access point.

WEP

With open authentication, even if a client can complete authentication and associate with an access point, the use of WEP prevents the client from sending data to and receiving it from an access point unless the client has the correct WEP key.

A WEP key is composed of either 40 or 128 bits and, in its basic form, is usually statically defined by the network administrator on the access point and on all clients that communicate with that access point. When static WEP keys are used, a network administrator must perform the tedious task of entering the same keys on every device in the WLAN.

Clearly, we now have fixes for this because tackling this manually would be administratively impossible in today's huge corporate wireless networks!

WPA and WPA2: An Overview

Wi-Fi Protected Access (WPA) and WPA2 were created in response to the shortcomings of WEP. WPA was a stopgap measure taken by the Wi-Fi Alliance to provide better security until the IEEE finalized the 802.11i standard. When 802.11i was ratified, WPA2 incorporated its improvements, so there are some significant differences between WPA and WPA2.

These are each essentially another form of basic security that is really just an add-on to the specifications. Even though you can totally lock the vault, WPA/WPA2 pre-shared key (PSK) is a better form of wireless security than any other basic wireless security method I've talked about so far. Still, keep in mind that I did say basic!

WPA is a standard developed by the Wi-Fi Alliance and provides a standard for authentication and encryption of WLANs that's intended to solve known security problems. The standard takes into account the well-publicized AirSnort and man-in-the-middle WLAN attacks. So, of course, we use WPA2 to help us with today's security issues because we can use Advanced Encryption Standard (AES) encryption, which provides for better key caching than WPA does. WPA is only a software update, whereas WPA2 requires a hardware update, but you'd be hard-pressed to find a laptop or any PC today that doesn't have built-in WPA2 support.

The PSK verifies users via a password or identifying code, often called a passphrase, on both the client machine and the access point. A client gains access to the network only if its password matches the access point's password. The PSK also provides keying material that Temporal Key Integrity Protocol (TKIP) or AES uses to generate an encryption key for each packet of transmitted data.

Wi-Fi Protected Access

WPA was designed to offer two methods of authentication in implementation. The first, called WPA Personal or WPA (PSK), was designed to work using a passphrase for authentication, but it improves the level of protection for authentication and data encryption too. WPA PSK uses the exact same encryption as WPA Enterprise—the PSK just replaces the check to a RADIUS server for the authentication portion.

The only known weakness of WPA PSK lies in the complexity of the password or key used on the AP and the stations. If it happens to be one that's easily guessed, it could be susceptible to something known as a dictionary attack. This type of attack uses a dictionary file that tries out a huge number of passwords until the correct match is found. Consequently, this is very time-consuming for the hacker. WPA3's big difference is how it can prevent a dictionary attack.

Because of this, WPA PSK should mainly be used in a small office, home office (SOHO) environment, and in an enterprise environment only when device restrictions, such as voice over IP (VoIP) phones, don't support RADIUS authentication.

WPA2 Enterprise

Regardless of whether WPA or WPA2 is used during the initial connection between the station and the AP, the two agree on common security requirements. Following that agreement, the following series of important key-related activities occur (in this specific order):

1. The authentication server derives a key called the Pairwise Master Key (PMK). This key will remain the same for the entire session. The same key is derived on the station. The server moves the PMK to the AP where it's needed.

2. The next step is called the four-way handshake. Its purpose is to derive another key called the Pairwise-Transient-Key (PTK). This step occurs between the AP and the station and requires the following four steps:

    a. The AP sends a random number known as a nonce to the station.

    b. Using this value along with the PMK, the station creates a key used to encrypt a nonce that's called the snonce, which is then sent to the AP. It includes a reaffirmation of the security parameters that were negotiated earlier. It also protects the integrity of this frame with a MIC. This bidirectional exchange of nonces is a critical part of the key-generation process.

    c. Now that the AP has the client nonce, it will generate a key for unicast transmission with the station. It sends the nonce back to the station along with a group key commonly called a group transient key, as well as a confirmation of security parameters.

    d. The fourth message simply confirms to the AP that the temporal keys (TKs) are in place.

One final function performed by this four-way handshake is to confirm that the two peers are still "alive."

802.11i

Although WPA2 was built with the 802.11i standard in mind, the following features were added when the standard was ratified:

- A list of EAP methods that can be used with the standard
- AES-CCMP for encryption instead of RC4
- Better key management; the master key can be cached, permitting a faster reconnect time for the station

But wait, there's more! There is a new sheriff in town, and its name is WPA3.

WPA3

In 2018, the Wi-Fi Alliance announced the new WPA3, a Wi-Fi security standard to replace WPA2. The WPA2 standard has served us well, but it's been around since 2004! WPA3 will improve on the WPA2 protocol with more security features, just like WPA2 was designed to fix WPA.

What's fun about WPA3 is the naming used to define the handshake as well as the exploits—yes, exploits are already out there! First, remember that WPA2 uses a PSK, but WPA3 has been upgraded to 128-bit encryption and uses a system called Simultaneous Authentication of Equals (SAE). This is referred to as the Dragonfly handshake. It forces network interaction on a login so that hackers can't deploy a dictionary attack by downloading its cryptographic hash and then running cracking software to break it.

Even more fun, the known exploits of WPA3 are called Dragonblood. The reason these Dragonblood exploits are already out is that the protections in WPA2 haven't really changed that much in WPA3—at least, not yet. Worse, WPA3 is backward compatible, meaning that if someone wants to attack you, they can just use WPA2 in an attack to effectively downgrade your WPA3-compatible system back to WPA2!

Like WPA2, the Wi-Fi Protected Access security includes solutions for personal and enterprise networks. But WPA3 offers some very cool new goodies that pave the way for more powerful authentication and enhanced cryptographic clout. It also helps to protect vital networks by preserving resiliency and offers a cleaner approach to security.

Here's a list of characteristics shared by all WPA3 networks:

- They use the latest security methods.
- They don't allow outdated legacy protocols.
- They require the use of Protected Management Frames (PMF).

Like us, our Wi-Fi networks have different levels of risk tolerance according to type and function. For the nonpublic, home, or enterprise variety, WPA3 gives us some cool tools to shut down password-guessing attacks. WPA3 also works with superior security protocols for networks that require or want a higher degree of protection.

As mentioned, WPA3 is backward compatible and provides interoperability with WPA2 devices, but this is really only an option for companies developing certified devices. I'm sure that it will become a required piece over time as market adoption grows.

WPA3-Personal

How does being able to seriously protect your individual users sound? WPA3-Personal provides that capability by offering powerful password-based authentication via SAE. This is a big upgrade from WPA2's PSK and works really well even when users choose simple, easy-to-crack passwords!

Like I said, WPA3 also frustrates a hacker's attempts to crack passwords via dictionary attacks. Some additional perks include the following:

- *Natural password selection:* WPA3 allows users to choose passwords that are easier to remember.

- *Ease of use:* WPA3 delivers enhanced protections with no change to the way users connect to a network.

- *Forward secrecy:* WPA3 protects data traffic even if a password is compromised after the data was transmitted.

WPA3-Enterprise

Basically, wireless networks of all kinds gain a lot of security with WPA3, but those with sensitive data on them, like networks belonging to financial institutions, governments, and even enterprises, really get a boost! WPA3-Enterprise improves everything WPA2 offers, plus it really streamlines how security protocols are applied throughout our networks.

WPA3-Enterprise even gives us the option to use 192-bit, minimum-strength security protocols, plus some very cool cryptographic tools to lock things down tight!

Here's a list of the ways WPA3 beefs up security:

- *Sweet feature alert:* WPA3 uses a system called Wi-Fi Device Provisioning Protocol (DPP) that allows users to utilize NFC tags or QR codes to allow devices on the network. Sweet!

- *Authenticated encryption:* 256-bit Galois/Counter Mode protocol (GCMP-256).

- *Key derivation and confirmation:* 384-bit Hashed Message Authentication Mode (HMAC) with Secure Hash Algorithm (HMAC-SHA384).

- *Key establishment and authentication:* Elliptic Curve Diffie-Hellman (ECDH) exchange and Elliptic Curve Digital Signature Algorithm (ECDSA) using a 384-bit elliptic curve.

- *Robust management frame protection:* 256-bit Broadcast/Multicast Integrity Protocol Galois Message Authentication Code (BIP-GMAC-256).

- The 192-bit security mode offered by WPA3-Enterprise ensures that the right combination of cryptographic tools are used and sets a consistent baseline of security within a WPA3 network.

TABLE 2.2   WPA, WPA2, and WPA3 compared.

Security Type	WPA	WPA2	WPA3
Enterprise Mode: business, education, government	Authentication: IEEE 802.1X/EAP Encryption: TKIP/MIC	Authentication: IEEE 802.1X/EAP Encryption: AES-CCMP	Authentication: IEEE 802.1X/EAP Encryption: GCMP-256
Personal Mode: SOHO, home, and personal	Authentication: PSK Encryption: TKIP/MIC	Authentication: PSK Encryption: AES-CCMP	Authentication: SAE Encryption: AES-CCMP
	128-bit RC4 w/TKIP encryption	128-bit AES encryption	128-bit AES encryption
	Ad hoc not supported	Ad hoc not supported	Ad hoc not supported

WPA3 has also improved upon 802.11's open authentication support by giving us something called Opportunistic Wireless Encryption (OWE). The idea behind the OWE enhancement option is to offer encryption communication for networks without passwords. It works by giving every device on the network its own unique key.

This implements something called Individualized Data Protection (IDP), which happens to come in handy for password-protected networks too because even if an attacker gets hold of the network password, they still can't access any other encrypted data!

All good—we've got WPA, WPA2, and now WPA3 covered. But how do they compare? Table 2.2 breaks them down.

Summary

In this chapter, you learned the basic concepts, terms, and principles that all network professionals should understand to secure an enterprise network. We covered concepts such as the CIA triad and internal and external threats.

The second half of this chapter explores the essentials and fundamentals of how wireless networks function. Springing off that foundation, I then introduced you to the basics of wireless radio frequencies and the IEEE standards. We discussed 802.11 from its inception through its evolution to current and near-future standards and talked about the subcommittees who create these standards.

All of this led into a discussion of wireless security—or rather, nonsecurity for the most part—which we went over in detail.

We finished the chapter by bringing you up to speed on TKIP and WPA/WPA2 security solutions—important tools used to protect the wireless LANs of today.

Exam Essentials

Explain common security concepts.   These include the CIA triad, least privilege, zero-trust model, defense in depth, and separation of duties.

Describe key security terms.   Among these are *vulnerabilities, exploits*, and *threats*.

Understand the IEEE 802.11a specification.   802.11a runs in the 5 GHz spectrum, and if you use the 802.11h extensions, you have 23 nonoverlapping channels. 802.11a can run up to 54 Mbps, but only if you are less than 50 feet from an access point.

Understand the IEEE 802.11b specification.   IEEE 802.11b runs in the 2.4 GHz range and has three nonoverlapping channels. It can handle long distances but with a maximum data rate of up to 11 Mbps.

Understand the IEEE 802.11g specification.   IEEE 802.11g is 802.11b's big brother and runs in the same 2.4 GHz range, but it has a higher data rate of 54 Mbps if you are less than 100 feet from an access point.

Understand the IEEE 802.11n specification.   IEEE 802.11n operates in the 2.4 GHz and 5 GHz range. Support for 5 GHz bands is optional. Its net data rate ranges from 54 Mbps to 600 Mbps. The standard also added support for multiple-input, multiple-output (MIMO) antennas.

Understand the IEEE 802.11ac specification.   IEEE 802.11ac-2013 is an amendment that builds on 802.11n. Changes include wider channels (80 or 160 MHz versus 40 MHz) in the 5 GHz band and more spatial streams (up to eight versus four). Wave 2 products include additional features such as MU-MIMO, 160 MHz channel width support, support for more 5 GHz channels, and four spatial streams with four antennas.

Understand the IEEE 802.11ax specification.   IEEE 802.11ax is the successor to 802.11ac. It's marketed as Wi-Fi 6 (2.4 GHz and 5 GHz) and Wi-Fi 6E (6 GHz). It is also known as High Efficiency Wi-Fi, for the overall improvements to Wi-Fi 6. Data rates against the predecessor (802.11ac) are only 39 percent. For comparison, this improvement was nearly 500 percent for the other predecessors.

Understand the different WiFi standards, frequencies, and ranges.   WiFi standards are 802.11a/b/g/n/ac/ax using 2.4 GHz and 5 GHz.

Remember the various service set identifiers (SSIDs).   SSIDs can use a basic service set, an extended service set, an independent service set (ad hoc), and a roaming service set.

Review Questions

You can find the answers to these questions in Appendix.

1. Which of the following is *not* an external threat?
   A. Accidental file deletion by an employee
   B. DoS attack
   C. Fake contractor on site
   D. Malware infection by email

2. Which concern do you have when you encrypt data before sending it?
   A. Accounting
   B. Availability
   C. Integrity
   D. Confidentiality

3. You have decided that the default permission for all files will be *no* access. What principle are you following?
   A. Defense in depth
   B. Need to know
   C. Separation of duties
   D. Zero trust

4. What are you following if you encrypt a file, apply access permissions to it, and lock the door to the room where the server on which the file resides is located?
   A. Defense in depth
   B. Need to know
   C. Separation of duties
   D. Zero trust

5. Which if the following is a method of checking the security health of network hosts before they're allowed to access the network?
   A. NAC
   B. DAC
   C. CVE
   D. CVSS

6. Which encryption type does enterprise WPA3 use?
   A. AES-CCMP
   B. GCMP-256

C. PSK

D. TKIP/MIC

7. What is the frequency range of the IEEE 802.11b standard?

A. 2.4 Gbps

B. 5 Gbps

C. 2.4 GHz

D. 5 GHz

8. What is the frequency range of the IEEE 802.11a standard?

A. 2.4 Gbps

B. 5 Gbps

C. 2.4 GHz

D. 5 GHz

9. What is the frequency range of the IEEE 802.11g standard?

A. 2.4 Gbps

B. 5 Gbps

C. 2.4 GHz

D. 5 GHz

10. You've finished physically installing an access point on the ceiling of your office. At a minimum, which parameter must be configured on the access point in order to allow a wireless client to operate on it?

A. AES

B. PSK

C. SSID

D. TKIP

E. WEP

F. 802.11i

11. Which encryption type does WPA2 use?

A. AES-CCMP

B. PPK via IV

C. PSK

D. TKIP/MIC

12. How many nonoverlapping channels are available with 802.11b?

A. 3

B. 12

    C. 23

    D. 40

13. Which of the following has built-in resistance to dictionary attacks?

    A. WPA

    B. WPA2

    C. WPA3

    D. AES

    E. TKIP

14. What is the maximum data rate for the 802.11a standard?

    A. 6 Mbps

    B. 11 Mbps

    C. 22 Mbps

    D. 54 Mbps

15. What is the maximum data rate for the 802.11g standard?

    A. 6 Mbps

    B. 11 Mbps

    C. 22 Mbps

    D. 54 Mbps

Chapter

3

IP, IPv6, and NAT

THE FOLLOWING CCST CYBER EXAM TOPICS ARE COVERED IN THIS CHAPTER:

✔ **2.0 Network Security**

- 2.1. Describe TCP/IP protocol vulnerabilities

  TCP, UDP, HTTP, ARP, ICMP, DHCP, DNS

- 2.2. Explain how network addresses impact network security

  IPv4 and IPv6 addresses, MAC addresses, network segmentation, CIDR notation, NAT, public vs. private networks

The *Transmission Control Protocol/Internet Protocol (TCP/IP)* suite was designed and implemented by the Department of Defense (DoD) to ensure and preserve data integrity as well as maintain communications in the event of catastrophic war. So it follows that if designed and implemented correctly, a TCP/IP network can be a secure, dependable, and resilient one. In this chapter, I'll cover the protocols of TCP/IP, and throughout this book, you'll learn how to create a solid TCP/IP network with Cisco routers and switches.

We'll begin by exploring the DoD's version of TCP/IP and then compare that version and its protocols with the OSI reference model that we discussed earlier.

Once you understand the protocols and processes used at the various levels of the DoD model, we'll take the next logical step by delving into the world of IP addressing and the different classes of IP addresses used in networks today.

We're then going to dig into network address translation (NAT), dynamic NAT, and port address translation (PAT), also known as NAT overload, which extends address space.

However, what if NAT isn't good enough to use in your cloud-based applications, or your network is just too big, like enterprise worldwide big? This is where IPv6 sings and can be used to solve these types of business case issues. So I'll end the chapter by discussing IPv6, formats, and concepts.

To find up-to-the-minute updates for this chapter, please see `www.lammle.com/ccst`.

TCP/IP and the DoD Model

The DoD model is basically a condensed version of the OSI model that comprises four instead of seven layers:

- Process/application layer
- Host-to-host layer or transport layer
- Internet layer
- Network access layer or link layer

FIGURE 3.1   The DoD and OSI models.

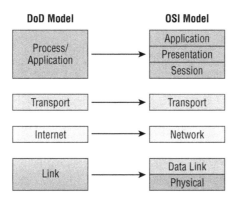

Figure 3.1 offers a comparison of the DoD model and the OSI reference model. As you can see, the two are similar in concept, but each has a different number of layers with different names. Cisco may at times use different names for the same layer, such as both "host-to-host" and "transport" at the layer above the Internet layer, as well as "network access" and "link" used to describe the bottom layer.

> When the different protocols in the IP stack are discussed, the layers of the OSI and DoD models are interchangeable. In other words, be prepared for the exam objectives to call the host-to-host layer the transport layer!

A vast array of protocols join forces at the DoD model's *Process/Application layer*. These processes integrate the various activities and duties spanning the focus of the OSI's corresponding top three layers (application, presentation, and session). We'll focus on a few of the most important applications found in the CCST objectives. In short, the process/application layer defines protocols for node-to-node application communication and controls user-interface specifications.

The *host-to-host layer or transport layer* parallels the functions of the OSI's transport layer, defining protocols for setting up the level of transmission service for applications. It tackles issues such as creating reliable end-to-end communication and ensuring the error-free delivery of data. It handles packet sequencing and maintains data integrity.

The *Internet layer* corresponds to the OSI's network layer, designating the protocols relating to the logical transmission of packets over the entire network. It takes care of the addressing of hosts by giving them an IP (Internet Protocol) address and handles the routing of packets among multiple networks.

At the bottom of the DoD model, the *network access layer or link layer* implements the data exchange between the host and the network. The equivalent of the data link and physical layers of the OSI model, the network access layer oversees hardware addressing and defines protocols for the physical transmission of data. The reason TCP/IP became so

FIGURE 3.2   The TCP/IP protocol suite.

FIGURE 3.2   The TCP/IP protocol suite.

DoD Model

| Application | Telnet | FTP | LPD | SNMP |
| | TFTP | SMTP | NFS | X Window |

| Transport | TCP | | UDP | |

| Internet | ICMP | ARP | | RARP |
| | IP | | | |

| Link | Ethernet | Fast Ethernet | Token Ring | FDDI |

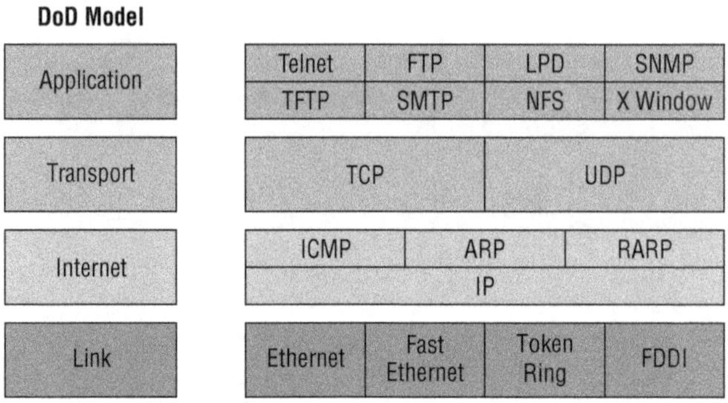

popular is that there were no set physical layer specifications, so it could run on any existing or future physical network!

The DoD and OSI models are alike in design and concept and have similar functions in similar layers. Figure 3.2 shows the TCP/IP protocol suite and how its protocols relate to the DoD model layers.

In the following sections, we will look at the different protocols in more detail, beginning with those found at the process/application layer.

The Process/Application Layer Protocols

Coming up, I'll describe the different applications and services typically used in IP networks, and although there are many more protocols defined here, we'll focus on the protocols most relevant to the CCST objectives. Here's a list of the protocols and applications we'll cover in this section:

- Telnet
- SSH
- FTP
- SFTP
- TFTP
- SNMP
- HTTP
- HTTPS
- NTP
- DNS
- DHCP/BootP
- APIPA

Telnet

Telnet was one of the first Internet standards, developed in 1969, and is the chameleon of protocols—its specialty is terminal emulation. It allows a user on a remote client machine, called the Telnet client, to access the resources of another machine, the Telnet server, in order to access a command-line interface. Telnet achieves this by pulling a fast one on the Telnet server and making the client machine appear as though it were a terminal directly attached to the local network. This projection is actually a software image—a virtual terminal that can interact with the chosen remote host. A drawback is that there are no encryption techniques available within the Telnet protocol, so everything must be sent in clear text, including passwords! Figure 3.3 shows an example of a Telnet client trying to connect to a Telnet server.

These emulated terminals are of the text-mode type and can execute defined procedures such as displaying menus that give users the opportunity to choose options and access the applications on the duped server. Users begin a Telnet session by running the Telnet client software and then logging in to the Telnet server. Telnet uses an 8-bit, byte-oriented data connection over TCP, which makes it very thorough. It's still in use today because it is so simple and easy to use, with very low overhead, but again, with everything sent in clear text, it's not recommended in production.

Secure Shell (SSH)

Secure Shell (SSH) protocol sets up a secure session that's similar to Telnet over a standard TCP/IP connection and is employed for doing things such as logging into systems, running programs on remote systems, and moving files from one system to another. And it does all of this while maintaining an encrypted connection. Figure 3.4 shows an SSH client trying to connect to an SSH server. The client must send the data encrypted!

You can think of it as the new-generation protocol that's now used in place of the antiquated and very unused commands of remote shell (rsh) and remote login (rlogin)—even Telnet.

FIGURE 3.3   Telnet.

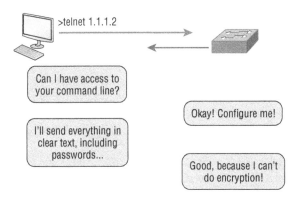

FIGURE 3.4   Secure Shell.

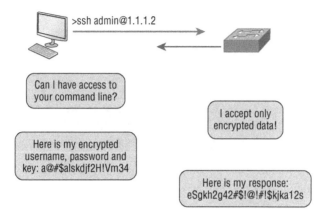

FIGURE 3.5   FTP.

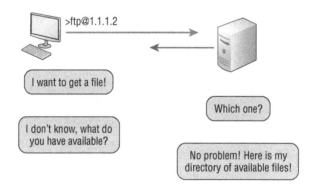

File Transfer Protocol (FTP)

File Transfer Protocol (FTP) actually lets us transfer files, and it can accomplish this between any two machines using it. But FTP isn't just a protocol; it's also a program. Operating as a protocol, FTP is used by applications. As a program, it's employed by users to perform file tasks by hand. FTP also allows for access to both directories and files and can accomplish certain types of directory operations, such as relocating into different ones (Figure 3.5).

But accessing a host through FTP is only the first step. Users must then be subjected to an authentication login that's usually secured with passwords and usernames implemented by system administrators to restrict access. You can get around this somewhat by adopting the username *anonymous*, but you'll be limited in what you'll be able to access.

Even when employed by users manually as a program, FTP's functions are limited to listing and manipulating directories, typing file contents, and copying files between hosts. It can't execute remote files as programs.

FIGURE 3.6   TFTP.

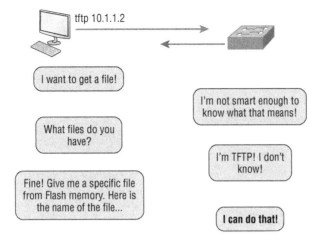

Secure File Transfer Protocol (SFTP)

Secure File Transfer Protocol (SFTP) is used when you need to transfer files over an encrypted connection. It uses an SSH session (more on this later), which encrypts the connection, and SSH uses port 22, hence the port 22 for SFTP.

Apart from the secure part, it's used just as FTP is—for transferring files between computers on an IP network, such as the Internet.

Trivial File Transfer Protocol (TFTP)

Trivial File Transfer Protocol (TFTP) is the stripped-down, stock version of FTP, but it's the protocol of choice if you know exactly what you want and where to find it because it's fast and easy to use!

But TFTP doesn't offer the abundance of functions that FTP does because it has no directory-browsing abilities, meaning that it can only send and receive files (Figure 3.6). Still, it's heavily used for managing file systems on Cisco devices.

This compact little protocol also skimps in the data department, sending much smaller blocks of data than FTP. Also, there's no authentication as with FTP, so it's even more insecure, and few sites support it because of the inherent security risks.

Simple Network Management Protocol (SNMP)

Simple Network Management Protocol (SNMP) collects and manipulates valuable network information, as you can see in Figure 3.7. It gathers data by polling the devices on the network from a network management station (NMS) at fixed or random intervals, requiring them to disclose certain information, or even asking for certain information from the device. In addition, network devices can inform the NMS station about problems as they occur so the network administrator is alerted.

FIGURE 3.7   SNMP.

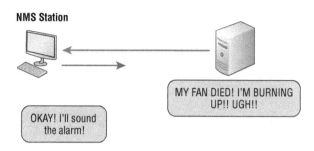

When all is well, SNMP receives something called a *baseline*—a report delimiting the operational traits of a healthy network. This protocol can also stand as a watchdog over the network, quickly notifying managers of any sudden turn of events. These network watchdogs are called *agents*, and when aberrations occur, agents send an alert called a *trap* to the management station.

SNMP Versions 1, 2, and 3

SNMP versions 1 and 2 are pretty much obsolete. This doesn't mean you won't see them in a network now and then, but you'll only come across v1 rarely, if ever. SNMPv2 provided improvements, especially in performance. But one of the best additions was called GETBULK, which allowed a host to retrieve a large amount of data at once. Even so, v2 never really caught on in the networking world, and SNMPv3 is now the standard. Unlike v1, which used only UDP, v3 uses both TCP and UDP and added even more security, message integrity, authentication, and encryption.

Hypertext Transfer Protocol (HTTP)

All those snappy websites comprising a mélange of graphics, text, links, ads, and so on rely on the *Hypertext Transfer Protocol (HTTP)* to make it all possible (Figure 3.8). It's used to manage communications between web browsers and web servers and opens the right resource when you click a link, wherever that resource may actually reside.

In order for a browser to display a web page, it must find the exact server that has the right web page, plus the exact details that identify the information requested. This information must be then be sent back to the browser. Nowadays, it's highly doubtful that a web server would have only one page to display!

Your browser can understand what you need when you enter a Uniform Resource Locator (URL), which we usually refer to as a web address, such as, for example, https://www.lammle.com/order-our-books/ and https://www.lammle.com/blog/.

FIGURE 3.8   HTTP.

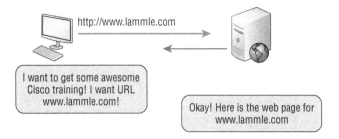

So basically, each URL defines the protocol used to transfer data, the name of the server, and the particular web page on that server.

Hypertext Transfer Protocol Secure (HTTPS)

Hypertext Transfer Protocol Secure (HTTPS) is also known as Secure Hypertext Transfer Protocol. It uses Secure Sockets Layer (SSL). Sometimes you'll see it referred to as SHTTP or S-HTTP, which were slightly different protocols, but because Microsoft supported HTTPS, it became the de facto standard for securing web communication. But no matter—as indicated, it's a secure version of HTTP that arms you with a whole bunch of security tools for keeping transactions between a web browser and a server secure.

It's what your browser needs to fill out forms, sign in, authenticate, and encrypt an HTTP message when you do things online such as make a reservation, access your bank, or buy something.

Network Time Protocol (NTP)

Kudos to Professor David Mills of the University of Delaware for coming up with this handy protocol that's used to synchronize the clocks on our computers to one standard time source (typically, an atomic clock). *Network Time Protocol (NTP)* works by synchronizing devices to ensure that all computers on a given network agree on the time (Figure 3.9).

This may sound pretty simple, but it's very important because so many of the transactions done today are time and date stamped. Think about databases—a server can get messed up pretty badly and even crash if it's out of sync with the machines connected to it by even mere seconds! You can't have a transaction entered by a machine at, say, 1:50 a.m. when the server records that transaction as having occurred at 1:45 a.m. So basically, NTP works to prevent a "back to the future *sans* DeLorean" scenario from bringing down the network—very important indeed!

Domain Name Service (DNS)

Domain Name Service (DNS) resolves hostnames—specifically, Internet names, such as www.lammle.com—to an IP address. But you don't have to actually use DNS. You just type in the IP address of any device you want to communicate with and find the IP address of a URL by using the `nslookup` program. For example, `>nslookup www.cisco.com` will return the IP address resolved by DNS.

FIGURE 3.9 NTP.

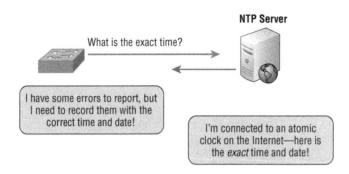

So, if you want to resolve the name *todd*, you must either type in the FQDN of todd. lammle.com or have a device such as a PC or router add the suffix for you. For example, on a Cisco router, you can use the command `ip domain-name lammle.com` to append each request with the lammle.com domain. If you don't do that, you'll have to type in the FQDN to get DNS to resolve the name.

An IP address identifies hosts on a network and the Internet as well, but DNS was designed to make our lives easier. Think about this: what would happen if you wanted to move your web page to a different service provider? The IP address would change, and no one would know what the new one was. DNS allows you to use a domain name to specify an IP address. You can change the IP address as often as you want, and no one will know the difference.

To resolve a DNS address from a host, you'd typically type in the URL from your favorite browser, which would hand the data to the application layer interface to be transmitted on the network. The application would look up the DNS address and send a UDP request to your DNS server to resolve the name (Figure 3.10).

If your first DNS server doesn't know the answer to the query, then the DNS server forwards a TCP request to its root DNS server. Once the query is resolved, the answer is transmitted back to the originating host, which means the host can now request the information from the correct web server.

An important thing to remember about DNS is that if you can ping a device with an IP address but cannot use its FQDN, you might have some type of DNS configuration failure.

Dynamic Host Configuration Protocol (DHCP)/Bootstrap Protocol (BootP)

Dynamic Host Configuration Protocol (DHCP) assigns IP addresses to hosts. It allows for easier administration and works well in small to very large network environments. Many types of hardware can be used as a DHCP server, including a Cisco router.

FIGURE 3.10 DNS.

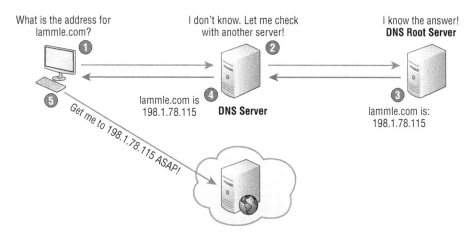

DHCP differs from BootP in that BootP assigns an IP address to a host but the host's hardware address must be entered manually in a BootP table. You can think of DHCP as a dynamic BootP. But remember that BootP is also used to send an operating system that a host can boot from. DHCP can't do that.

But there's still a lot of information a DHCP server can provide to a host when the host is requesting an IP address from the DHCP server. Here's a list of the most common types of information a DHCP server can provide:

- IP address
- Subnet mask
- Domain name
- Default gateway (routers)
- DNS server address
- WINS server address

A client that sends out a DHCP Discover message in order to receive an IP address sends out a broadcast at both layer 2 and layer 3:

- The layer 2 broadcast is all *F*s in hex, which looks like this: ff:ff:ff:ff:ff:ff as the destination MAC address.
- The layer 3 broadcast is 255.255.255.255, which means all networks and all hosts.

DHCP is connectionless, which means it uses User Datagram Protocol (UDP) at the transport layer, also known as the host-to-host layer, which we'll talk about later.

Seeing is believing, so here's an example of output from my analyzer showing the layer 2 and layer 3 broadcasts:

```
Ethernet II, Src: 0.0.0.0 (00:0b:db:99:d3:5e),Dst: Broadcast(ff:ff:ff:ff:ff:ff)
Internet Protocol, Src: 0.0.0.0 (0.0.0.0),Dst: 255.255.255.255(255.255.255.255)
```

The data link and network layers are both sending out "all hands" broadcasts saying, "Help—I don't know my IP address!"

Figure 3.11 shows the process of a client/server relationship using a DHCP connection. This is the four-step process a client takes to receive an IP address from a DHCP server:

1. The DHCP client broadcasts a DHCP Discover message looking for a DHCP server (Port 67).

2. The DHCP server that received the DHCP Discover message sends a layer 2 unicast DHCP Offer message back to the host.

3. The client then broadcasts to the server a DHCP Request message asking for the offered IP address and possibly other information.

4. The server finalizes the exchange with a unicast DHCP Acknowledgment message.

FIGURE 3.11   DHCP client four-step process.

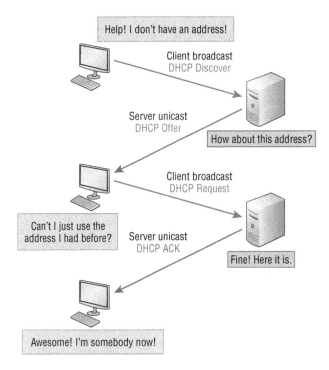

DHCP Conflicts

A DHCP address conflict occurs when two hosts use the same IP address. This sounds bad, and it is! We'll never even have to discuss this problem once we get to the chapter on IPv6!

During IP address assignment, a DHCP server checks for conflicts using the ICMP protocol, similar to the Ping program to test the availability of the address before it's assigned from the pool. If no host replies, then the DHCP server assumes that the IP address is not already allocated. This helps the server know that it's providing a good address, but what about the host? To provide extra protection against that terrible IP conflict issue, the host can broadcast for its own address!

A host uses something called a gratuitous ARP to help avoid a possible duplicate address. The DHCP client sends an ARP broadcast out on the local LAN or VLAN using its newly assigned address to solve conflicts before they occur.

So, if an IP address conflict is detected, the address is removed from the DHCP pool (scope), and it's really important to remember that the address will not be assigned to a host until the administrator resolves the conflict by hand!

Automatic Private IP Addressing (APIPA)

Okay, so what happens if you have a few hosts connected together with a switch or hub and you don't have a DHCP server? You can add IP information by hand, known as *static IP addressing*, but later Windows operating systems provide a feature called *Automatic Private IP Addressing (APIPA)*. With APIPA, clients can automatically self-configure an IP address and subnet mask—basic IP information that hosts use to communicate—when a DHCP server isn't available. The IP address range for APIPA is 169.254.0.1 through 169.254.255.254. The client also configures itself with a default Class B subnet mask of 255.255.0.0.

But when you're in your corporate network working and you have a DHCP server running, and your host shows that it's using this IP address range, it means that either your DHCP client on the host is not working or the server is down or can't be reached due to some network issue. Believe me—I don't know anyone who's seen a host in this address range and has been happy about it!

Now, let's take a look at the transport layer, or what the DoD calls the host-to-host layer.

 If you see an IP address starting with the first two octets of 169.254.x.x, then either you don't have a working DHCP server on the subnet or you have a network connectivity issue.

The Host-to-Host or Transport Layer Protocols

The main purpose of the host-to-host layer is to shield the upper-layer applications from the complexities of the network. This layer says to the upper layer, "Just give me your data stream, with any instructions, and I'll begin the process of getting your information ready to send."

Coming up, I'll introduce you to the two protocols at this layer:

▪ Transmission Control Protocol (TCP)

▪ User Datagram Protocol (UDP)

In addition, we'll look at some of the key host-to-host protocol concepts, as well as the port numbers.

 Remember, this is still considered layer 4, and layer 4 can use acknowledgments, sequencing, and flow control.

Transmission Control Protocol (TCP)

Transmission Control Protocol (TCP) takes large blocks of information from an application and breaks them into segments. It numbers and sequences each segment so that the destination's TCP stack can put the segments back into the order the application intended. After these segments are sent on the transmitting host, TCP waits for an acknowledgment of the receiving end's TCP virtual circuit session, retransmitting any segments that aren't acknowledged.

Before a transmitting host starts to send segments down the model, the sender's TCP stack contacts the destination's TCP stack to establish a connection. This creates a *virtual circuit*, and this type of communication is known as *connection-oriented*. During this initial handshake, the two TCP layers also agree on the amount of information that's going to be sent before the recipient's TCP sends back an acknowledgment. With everything agreed on in advance, the path is paved for reliable communication to take place.

TCP is a full-duplex, connection-oriented, reliable, and accurate protocol, but establishing all these terms and conditions, in addition to error checking, is no small task. TCP is very complicated, so not surprisingly, it's costly in terms of network overhead. And because today's networks are much more reliable than those of yore, this added reliability is often unnecessary. Most programmers use TCP because it removes a lot of programming work, but for real-time video and VoIP, *User Datagram Protocol (UDP)* is often better because using it results in less overhead.

TCP Segment Format

Because the upper layers just send a data stream to the protocols in the transport layers, I'll use Figure 3.12 to demonstrate how TCP segments a data stream and prepares it for the Internet layer. When the Internet layer receives the data stream, it routes the segments as packets through an internetwork. The segments are handed to the receiving host's host-to-host layer protocol, which rebuilds the data stream for the upper-layer applications or protocols.

Figure 3.12 shows the TCP segment format and the different fields within the TCP header. This isn't important to memorize for the Cisco exam objectives, but you need to understand it well because it's really good foundational information.

FIGURE 3.12 TCP segment format.

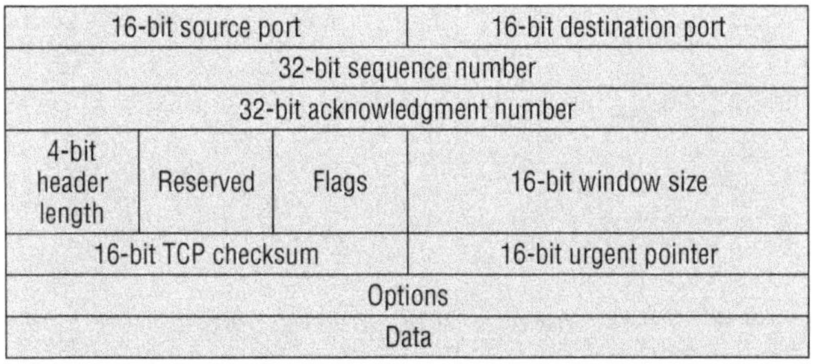

16-bit source port	16-bit destination port
32-bit sequence number	
32-bit acknowledgment number	

4-bit header length	Reserved	Flags	16-bit window size

16-bit TCP checksum	16-bit urgent pointer
Options	
Data	

The TCP header is 20 bytes long, or up to 24 bytes with options. You need to understand what each field in the TCP segment is in order to build a strong educational foundation:

Source Port. This is the port number of the application on the host sending the data, which I'll talk about more thoroughly a little later in this chapter.

Destination Port. This is the port number of the application requested on the destination host.

Sequence Number. A number used by TCP that puts the data back in the correct order or retransmits missing or damaged data during a process called sequencing.

Acknowledgment Number. The value is the TCP octet that is expected next.

Header Length. The number of 32-bit words in the TCP header, which indicates where the data begins. The TCP header (even one including options) is an integral number of 32 bits in length.

Reserved. Always set to zero.

Code Bits/Flags. Controls functions used to set up and terminate a session.

Window. The window size the sender is willing to accept, in octets.

Checksum. The cyclic redundancy check (CRC), used because TCP doesn't trust the lower layers and checks everything. The CRC checks the header and data fields.

Urgent. A valid field only if the Urgent pointer in the code bits is set. If so, this value indicates the offset from the current sequence number, in octets, where the segment of non-urgent data begins.

Options. May be 0, meaning that no options have to be present, or a multiple of 32 bits. However, if any options are used that do not cause the option field to total a multiple of 32 bits, padding of 0s must be used to make sure the data begins on a 32-bit boundary. These boundaries are known as words.

Data. Handed down to the TCP protocol at the transport layer, which includes the upper-layer headers.

Let's take a look at a TCP segment copied from a network analyzer:

```
TCP - Transport Control Protocol
Source Port: 5973
Destination Port: 23
Sequence Number: 1456389907
Ack Number: 1242056456
Offset: 5
Reserved: %000000
Code: %011000
Ack is valid
Push Request
Window: 61320
Checksum: 0x61a6
Urgent Pointer: 0
No TCP Options
TCP Data Area:
vL.5.+.5.+.5.+.5 76 4c 19 35 11 2b 19 35 11 2b 19 35 11
2b 19 35 +. 11 2b 19
Frame Check Sequence: 0x0d00000f
```

Did you notice that everything I talked about earlier is in the segment? As you can see from the number of fields in the header, TCP creates a lot of overhead. Again, this is why application developers may opt for efficiency over reliability to save overhead and go with UDP instead. It's also defined at the transport layer as an alternative to TCP.

User Datagram Protocol (UDP)

User Datagram Protocol (UDP) is basically the scaled-down economy model of TCP, which is why UDP is sometimes referred to as a thin protocol. Like a thin person on a park bench, a thin protocol doesn't take up a lot of room—or in this case, require much bandwidth on a network.

UDP doesn't offer all the bells and whistles of TCP either, but it does do a fabulous job of transporting information that doesn't require reliable delivery, using far less network resources. (UDP is covered thoroughly in Request for Comments [RFC] 768.)

So, clearly, there are times that it's wise for developers to opt for UDP rather than TCP, one of them being when reliability is already taken care of at the process/application layer. Network File System (NFS) handles its own reliability issues, making the use of TCP both impractical and redundant. But ultimately, it's up to the application developer to opt for using UDP or TCP, not the user who wants to transfer data faster!

UDP does *not* sequence the segments and does not care about the order in which the segments arrive at the destination. UDP just sends the segments off and forgets about them. It doesn't follow through, check up on them, or even allow for an acknowledgment of safe arrival—complete abandonment. Because of this, it's referred to as an unreliable protocol. This does not mean that UDP is ineffective, only that it doesn't deal with reliability issues at all.

Furthermore, UDP doesn't create a virtual circuit, nor does it contact the destination before delivering information to it. Because of this, it's also considered a *connectionless* protocol. Because UDP assumes that the application will use its own reliability method, it doesn't use any itself. This presents an application developer with a choice when running the Internet Protocol stack: TCP for reliability or UDP for faster transfers.

It's important to know how this process works because if the segments arrive out of order, which is commonplace in IP networks, they'll simply be passed up to the next layer in whatever order they were received. This can result in some seriously garbled data! On the other hand, TCP sequences the segments so they get put back together in exactly the right order, which is something UDP just can't do.

UDP Segment Format

Figure 3.13 clearly illustrates UDP's markedly lean overhead as compared to TCP's hungry requirements. Look at the figure carefully—can you see that UDP doesn't use windowing or provide acknowledgments in the UDP header?

It's important for you to understand what each field in the UDP segment is:

Source Port.   Port number of the application on the host sending the data.

Destination Port.   Port number of the application requested on the destination host.

Length.   Length of UDP header and UDP data.

Checksum.   Checksum of both the UDP header and UDP data fields.

Data.   Upper-layer data.

UDP, like TCP, doesn't trust the lower layers and runs its own CRC. Remember that the checksum is the field that houses the CRC, which is why you can see the checksum information.

The following shows a UDP segment caught on a network analyzer:

```
UDP - User Datagram Protocol
Source Port: 1085
Destination Port: 5136
Length: 41
Checksum: 0x7a3c
UDP Data Area:
..Z......00 01 5a 96 00 01 00 00 00 00 00 11 0000 00
...C..2._C._C 2e 03 00 43 02 1e 32 0a 00 0a 00 80 43 00 80
Frame Check Sequence: 0x00000000
```

Notice that low overhead! Try to find the sequence number, ack number, and window size in the UDP segment. You can't because they just aren't there!

FIGURE 3.13   UDP segment.

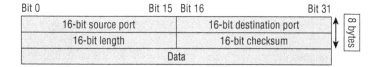

TABLE 3.1 Key features of TCP and UDP.

TCP	UDP
Sequenced	Unsequenced
Reliable	Unreliable
Connection-oriented	Connectionless
Virtual circuit	Low overhead
Acknowledgments	No acknowledgment
Windowing flow control	No windowing or flow control of any type

Key Concepts of Host-to-Host Protocols

Because you've now seen both a connection-oriented (TCP) and connectionless (UDP) protocol in action, it's a good time to summarize the two here. Table 3.1 highlights some of the key concepts about these two protocols for you to memorize.

And if all this isn't quite clear yet, a telephone analogy will really help you understand how TCP works. Most of us know that before you speak to someone on a phone, you must first establish a connection with that other person, no matter where they are. This is akin to establishing a virtual circuit with the TCP protocol. If you were giving someone important information during your conversation, you might say things such as, "You know? or "Did you get that?" Saying things like this is a lot like a TCP acknowledgment—it's designed to get you verification. From time to time, especially on mobile phones, people ask, "Are you still there?" People end their conversations with a "Goodbye" of some kind, putting closure on the phone call, which you can think of as tearing down the virtual circuit that was created for your communication session. TCP performs these types of functions.

Conversely, using UDP is more like sending a postcard. To do that, you don't need to contact the other party first; you simply write your message, address the postcard, and send it off. This is analogous to UDP's connectionless orientation. Because the message on the postcard is probably not a matter of life or death, you don't need an acknowledgment of its receipt. Similarly, UDP does not involve acknowledgments.

Let's take a look at another figure, one that includes TCP, UDP, and the applications associated to each protocol: Figure 3.14 (discussed in the next section).

Port Numbers

TCP and UDP must use *port numbers* to communicate with the upper layers because these are what keep track of different conversations crossing the network simultaneously. Originating-source port numbers are dynamically assigned by the source host and will equal

FIGURE 3.14 Port numbers for TCP and UDP.

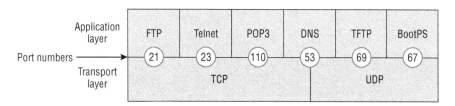

some number starting at 1024. Port numbers 1023 and below are defined in RFC 3232 (or just see www.iana.org), which discusses what we call well-known port numbers.

Virtual circuits that don't use an application with a well-known port number are assigned port numbers randomly from a specific range instead. These port numbers identify the source and destination application or process in the TCP segment.

> The Requests for Comments (RFCs) form a series of notes about the Internet (originally the ARPAnet) started in 1969. These notes discuss many aspects of computer communication, focusing on networking protocols, procedures, programs, and concepts, but they also include meeting notes, opinions, and sometimes even humor. You can find the RFCs by visiting www.iana.org.

Figure 3.14 illustrates how both TCP and UDP use port numbers. I'll cover the different port numbers that can be used next:

- Numbers below 1024 are considered well-known port numbers and are defined in RFC 3232.

- Numbers 1024 and above are used by the upper layers to set up sessions with other hosts and by TCP and UDP to use as source and destination addresses in the segment.

TCP Session: Source Port

Let's take a minute to check out analyzer output showing a TCP session I captured with my analyzer software session:

```
TCP - Transport Control Protocol
Source Port: 5973
Destination Port: 23
Sequence Number: 1456389907
Ack Number: 1242056456
Offset: 5
Reserved: %000000
Code: %011000
Ack is valid
```

```
Push Request
Window: 61320
Checksum: 0x61a6
Urgent Pointer: 0
No TCP Options
TCP Data Area:
vL.5.+.5.+.5.+.5 76 4c 19 35 11 2b 19 35 11 2b 19 35 11
2b 19 35 +. 11 2b 19
Frame Check Sequence: 0x0d00000f
```

Notice that the source host makes up the source port, which in this case is 5973. The destination port is 23, which is used to tell the receiving host the purpose of the intended connection (Telnet).

By looking at this session, you can see that the source host makes up the source port by using numbers from 1024 to 65535. But why does the source make up a port number? To differentiate between sessions with different hosts, because how would a server know where information is coming from if it didn't have a different number from a sending host? TCP and the upper layers don't use hardware and logical addresses to understand the sending host's address as the data link and network layer protocols do. Instead, they use port numbers.

TCP Session: Destination Port

You'll sometimes look at an analyzer and see that only the source port is above 1024 and the destination port is a well-known port, as shown in the following trace:

```
TCP - Transport Control Protocol
Source Port: 1144
Destination Port: 80 World Wide Web HTTP
Sequence Number: 9356570
Ack Number: 0
Offset: 7
Reserved: %000000
Code: %000010
Synch Sequence
Window: 8192
Checksum: 0x57E7
Urgent Pointer: 0
TCP Options:
Option Type: 2 Maximum Segment Size
Length: 4
MSS: 536
Option Type: 1 No Operation
Option Type: 1 No Operation
Option Type: 4
Length: 2
Opt Value:
No More HTTP Data
Frame Check Sequence: 0x43697363
```

And sure enough, the source port is over 1024, but the destination port is 80, indicating an HTTP service. The server, or receiving host, will change the destination port if it needs to.

In the preceding trace, a "SYN" packet is sent to the destination device. This Synch (as shown in the output) sequence is what's used to inform the remote destination device that it wants to create a session.

TCP Session: Syn Packet Acknowledgment

The next trace shows an acknowledgment to the SYN packet:

```
TCP - Transport Control Protocol
Source Port: 80 World Wide Web HTTP
Destination Port: 1144
Sequence Number: 2873580788
Ack Number: 9356571
Offset: 6
Reserved: %000000
Code: %010010
Ack is valid
Synch Sequence
Window: 8576
Checksum: 0x5F85
Urgent Pointer: 0
TCP Options:
Option Type: 2 Maximum Segment Size
Length: 4
MSS: 1460
No More HTTP Data
Frame Check Sequence: 0x6E203132
```

Notice the *Ack is valid*, which means that the source port was accepted and the device agreed to create a virtual circuit with the originating host.

And here again, you can see that the response from the server shows that the source is 80 and the destination is the 1144 sent from the originating host—all's well!

Table 3.2 gives you a list of the typical applications used in the TCP/IP suite by showing their well-known port numbers and the transport layer protocols used by each application or process. It's really key to memorize this table.

Notice that DNS uses both TCP and UDP. Whether it opts for one or the other depends on what it's trying to do. Even though it's not the only application that can use both protocols, it's certainly one that you should make sure to remember in your studies.

 What makes TCP reliable is sequencing, acknowledgments, and flow control (windowing). UDP does not have reliability.

TABLE 3.2 Key protocols that use TCP and UDP.

TCP	UDP
Telnet 23	SNMP 161
SMTP 25	TFTP 69
HTTP 80	DNS 53
FTP 20, 21	BooTP/DHCP 67
DNS 53	NTP 123
HTTPS 443	
SSH 22	
POP3 110	
IMAP4 143	

Okay—I want to discuss one more item before we move down to the Internet layer—session multiplexing. Session multiplexing is used by both TCP and UDP and basically allows a single computer, with a single IP address, to have multiple sessions occurring simultaneously. Say you go to www.lammle.com and are browsing, and then you click a link to another page. Doing this opens another session to your host. Now you go to https://www.lammle.com/self-paced-online/ from another window, and that site opens a window as well. Now you have three sessions open using one IP address because the session layer is sorting the separate requests based on the transport layer port number. This is the job of the session layer: to keep application layer data separate!

The Internet Layer Protocols

In the DoD model, there are two main reasons for the Internet layer's existence: routing and providing a single network interface to the upper layers.

None of the other upper- or lower-layer protocols have any functions relating to routing—that complex and important task belongs entirely to the Internet layer. The Internet layer's second duty is to provide a single network interface to the upper-layer protocols. Without this layer, application programmers would need to write "hooks" into every one of their applications for each different network access protocol. This would not only be a pain in the neck but would also lead to different versions of each application—one for Ethernet, another one for wireless, and so on. To prevent this, IP provides one single network interface for the upper-layer protocols. With that mission accomplished, it's then the job of the Internet Protocol (IP) and the various network access protocols to get along and work together.

All network roads don't lead to Rome—they lead to IP. And all the other protocols at this layer, as well as all those at the upper layers, use it. Never forget that. All paths through the DoD model go through IP. Here's a list of the important protocols at the Internet layer that I'll cover individually in detail coming up:

- Internet Protocol (IP)
- Internet Control Message Protocol (ICMP)
- Address Resolution Protocol (ARP)

Internet Protocol (IP)

Internet Protocol (IP) essentially is the Internet layer. The other protocols found here merely exist to support it. IP holds the big picture and could be said to "see all," because it's aware of all the interconnected networks. It can do this because all the machines on the network have a software, or logical, address called an IP address, which we'll explore more thoroughly later in this chapter.

For now, understand that IP looks at each packet's address. Then, using a routing table, it decides where a packet is to be sent next, choosing the best path to send it upon. The protocols of the network access layer at the bottom of the DoD model don't possess IP's enlightened scope of the entire network; they deal only with physical links (local networks).

Identifying devices on networks requires answering these two questions: Which network is it on? And what is its ID on that network? The first answer is the *software address*, or *logical address*. You can think of this as the part of the address that specifies the correct street. The second answer is the hardware address, which goes a step further to specify the correct mailbox. All hosts on a network have a logical ID called an IP address. This is the software, or logical, address and contains valuable encoded information, greatly simplifying the complex task of routing. (IP is discussed in RFC 791.)

IP receives segments from the host-to-host layer and fragments them into datagrams (packets) if necessary. IP then reassembles datagrams back into segments on the receiving side. Each datagram is assigned the IP address of the sender and that of the recipient. Each router or switch (layer 3 device) that receives a datagram makes routing decisions based on the packet's destination IP address.

Figure 3.15 shows an IP header. This will give you a picture of what the IP protocol has to go through every time user data that is destined for a remote network is sent from the upper layers.

The following fields make up the IP header:

Version.   IP version number.

Header Length.   Header length (HLEN) in 32-bit words.

Priority and Type of Service.   Type of Service tells how the datagram should be handled. The first three bits are the priority bits, now called the differentiated services bits.

FIGURE 3.15 IP header.

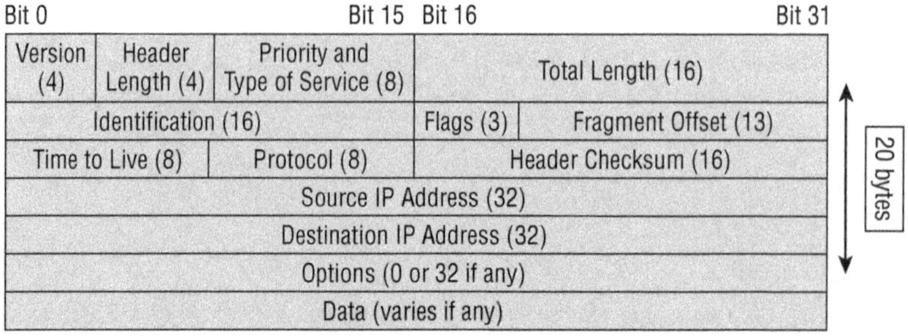

Bit 0			Bit 15 Bit 16		Bit 31
Version (4)	Header Length (4)	Priority and Type of Service (8)	Total Length (16)		
Identification (16)			Flags (3)	Fragment Offset (13)	
Time to Live (8)		Protocol (8)	Header Checksum (16)		
Source IP Address (32)					
Destination IP Address (32)					
Options (0 or 32 if any)					
Data (varies if any)					

20 bytes

Total Length. Length of the packet, including header and data.

Identification. Unique IP-packet value used to differentiate fragmented packets from different datagrams.

Flags. Specifies whether fragmentation should occur.

Fragment Offset. Provides fragmentation and reassembly if the packet is too large to put in a frame. It also allows different maximum transmission units (MTUs) on the Internet.

Time to Live. The time to live (TTL) is set into a packet when it is originally generated. If it doesn't get to where it's supposed to go before the TTL expires, boom—it's gone. This stops IP packets from continuously circling the network looking for a home.

Protocol. Port of an upper-layer protocol; for example, TCP is port 6 and UDP is port 17. Also supports network layer protocols, such as ARP and ICMP, and can be referred to as the Type field in some analyzers. We'll talk about this field more in a minute.

Header Checksum. Cyclic redundancy check (CRC) on the header only.

Source IP Address. 32-bit IP address of the sending station.

Destination IP Address. 32-bit IP address of the station this packet is destined for.

Options. Used for network testing, debugging, security, and more.

Data. After the IP option field will be the upper-layer data.

Here's a snapshot of an IP packet caught on a network analyzer. Notice that all the header information discussed previously appears here:

```
IP Header - Internet Protocol Datagram
Version: 4
Header Length: 5
Precedence: 0
Type of Service: %000
Unused: %00
Total Length: 187
Identifier: 22486
Fragmentation Flags: %010 Do Not Fragment
Fragment Offset: 0
```

```
Time To Live: 60
IP Type: 0x06 TCP
Header Checksum: 0xd031
Source IP Address: 10.7.1.30
Dest. IP Address: 10.7.1.10
No Internet Datagram Options
```

The Type field is typically a Protocol field, but this analyzer sees it as an IP Type field. This is important. If the header didn't carry the protocol information for the next layer, IP wouldn't know what to do with the data carried in the packet. The preceding example clearly tells IP to hand the segment to TCP.

Figure 3.16 demonstrates how the network layer sees the protocols at the transport layer when it needs to hand a packet up to the upper-layer protocols.

In this example, the Protocol field tells IP to send the data to either TCP port 6 or UDP port 17. But it will be UDP or TCP only if the data is part of a data stream headed for an upper-layer service or application. It could just as easily be destined for Internet Control Message Protocol (ICMP), Address Resolution Protocol (ARP), or some other type of network layer protocol.

Table 3.3 is a list of some other popular protocols that can be specified in the Protocol field.

FIGURE 3.16 The Protocol field in an IP header.

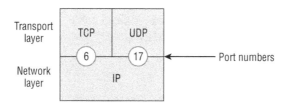

TABLE 3.3 Possible protocols found in the Protocol field of an IP header.

Protocol	Protocol number
ICMP	1
IP in IP (tunneling)	4
TCP	6
UDP	17
EIGRP	88

(*Continued*)

TABLE 3.3 (Continued)

Protocol	Protocol number
OSPF	89
IPv6	41
GRE	47
Layer 2 tunnel (L2TP)	115

You can find a complete list of Protocol field numbers at www.iana.
org/assignments/protocol-numbers.

Internet Control Message Protocol (ICMP)

Internet Control Message Protocol (ICMP) works at the network layer and is used by IP for
many different services. ICMP is basically a management protocol and messaging service
provider for IP. Its messages are carried as IP datagrams. RFC 1256 is an annex to ICMP,
which gives hosts extended capability in discovering routes to gateways.

ICMP packets have the following characteristics:

▪   They can provide hosts with information about network problems.

▪   They are encapsulated within IP datagrams.

The following are some common events and messages that ICMP relates to:

Destination Unreachable.   If a router can't send an IP datagram any further, it uses ICMP to
send a message back to the sender, advising it of the situation. For example, take a look at
Figure 3.17, which shows that interface e0 of the Lab_B router is down.

FIGURE 3.17   ICMP error message is sent to the sending host from the remote router.

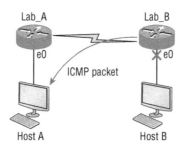

When host A sends a packet destined for host B, the Lab_B router will send an ICMP destination-unreachable message back to the sending device, which is host A in this example.

Buffer Full/Source Quench.   If a router's memory buffer for receiving incoming datagrams is full, it will use ICMP to send out this message alert until the congestion abates.

Hops/Time Exceeded.   Each IP datagram is allotted a certain number of routers, called hops, to pass through. If it reaches its limit of hops before arriving at its destination, the last router to receive that datagram deletes it. The executioner router then uses ICMP to send an obituary message, informing the sending machine of the demise of its datagram.

Ping.   Packet Internet Groper (Ping) uses ICMP echo request and reply messages to check the physical and logical connectivity of machines on an internetwork.

Traceroute.   Using ICMP time-outs, Traceroute is used to discover the path a packet takes as it traverses an internetwork.

Traceroute is usually just called trace. Microsoft Windows uses tracert to allow you to verify address configurations in your internetwork.

The following data is from a network analyzer catching an ICMP echo request:

```
Flags: 0x00
Status: 0x00
Packet Length: 78
Timestamp: 14:04:25.967000 12/20/03
Ethernet Header
Destination: 00:a0:24:6e:0f:a8
Source: 00:80:c7:a8:f0:3d
Ether-Type: 08-00 IP
IP Header - Internet Protocol Datagram
Version: 4
Header Length: 5
Precedence: 0
Type of Service: %000
Unused: %00
Total Length: 60
Identifier: 56325
Fragmentation Flags: %000
Fragment Offset: 0
Time To Live: 32
IP Type: 0x01 ICMP
Header Checksum: 0x2df0
Source IP Address: 100.100.100.2
Dest. IP Address: 100.100.100.1
No Internet Datagram Options
ICMP - Internet Control Messages Protocol
ICMP Type: 8 Echo Request
Code: 0
```

```
Checksum: 0x395c
Identifier: 0x0300
Sequence Number: 4352
ICMP Data Area:
abcdefghijklmnop 61 62 63 64 65 66 67 68 69 6a 6b 6c 6d 6e 6f 70
qrstuvwabcdefghi 71 72 73 74 75 76 77 61 62 63 64 65 66 67 68 69
Frame Check Sequence: 0x00000000
```

Notice anything unusual? Did you catch the fact that even though ICMP works at the Internet (network) layer, it still uses IP to do the Ping request? The Type field in the IP header is 0x01, which specifies that the data we're carrying is owned by the ICMP protocol. Remember, just as all roads lead to Rome, all segments or data *must* go through IP!

> The Ping program uses the alphabet in the data portion of the packet as a payload, typically around 100 bytes by default, unless, of course, you are pinging from a Windows device, which thinks the alphabet stops at the letter *W* (and doesn't include *X*, *Y*, or *Z*) and then starts at *A* again. Go figure!

We'll move on soon, but before we get into the ARP protocol, let's take another look at ICMP in action. Figure 3.18 shows an internetwork—it has a router, so it's an internetwork, right?

FIGURE 3.18   ICMP in action.

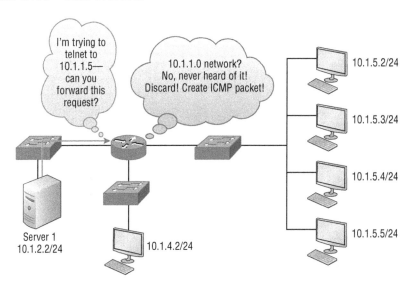

Server 1 (10.1.2.2) telnets to 10.1.1.5 from a DOS prompt. What do you think server 1 will receive as a response? Server 1 will send the Telnet data to the default gateway, which is the router, and the router will drop the packet because there isn't a network 10.1.1.0 in the routing table. Because of this, server 1 will receive an ICMP destination unreachable back from the router.

Address Resolution Protocol (ARP)

Address Resolution Protocol (ARP) finds the hardware address of a host from a known IP address. Here's how it works: when IP has a datagram to send, it must inform a network access protocol, such as Ethernet or wireless, of the destination's hardware address on the local network. Remember that it has already been informed by upper-layer protocols of the destination's IP address. If IP doesn't find the destination host's hardware address in the ARP cache, it uses ARP to find this information.

As IP's detective, ARP interrogates the local network by sending out a broadcast asking the machine with the specified IP address to reply with its hardware address. So basically, ARP translates the software (IP) address into a hardware address—for example, the destination machine's Ethernet adapter address—and from it, deduces its whereabouts on the LAN by broadcasting for this address.

Figure 3.19 shows how an ARP broadcast looks to a local network.

ARP resolves IP addresses to Ethernet (MAC) addresses.

FIGURE 3.19   Local ARP broadcast.

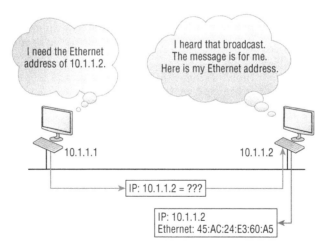

The following trace shows an ARP broadcast—notice that the destination hardware address is unknown and is all *F*s in hex (all 1s in binary)—and is a hardware address broadcast:

```
Flags: 0x00
Status: 0x00
Packet Length: 64
Timestamp: 09:17:29.574000 12/06/03
Ethernet Header
Destination: FF:FF:FF:FF:FF:FF Ethernet Broadcast
Source: 00:A0:24:48:60:A5
Protocol Type: 0x0806 IP ARP
ARP - Address Resolution Protocol
Hardware: 1 Ethernet (10Mb)
Protocol: 0x0800 IP
Hardware Address Length: 6
Protocol Address Length: 4
Operation: 1 ARP Request
Sender Hardware Address: 00:A0:24:48:60:A5
Sender Internet Address: 172.16.10.3
Target Hardware Address: 00:00:00:00:00:00 (ignored)
Target Internet Address: 172.16.10.10
Extra bytes (Padding):
............... 0A 0A 0A 0A 0A 0A 0A 0A 0A 0A 0A 0A 0A
0A 0A 0A 0A 0A
Frame Check Sequence: 0x00000000
```

IP Addressing

One of the most important topics in any discussion of TCP/IP is IP addressing. An *IP address* is a numeric identifier assigned to each machine on an IP network. It designates the specific location of a device on the network.

An IP address is a software address, not a hardware address—the latter is hard-coded on a network interface card (NIC) and used for finding hosts on a local network. IP addressing was designed to allow hosts on one network to communicate with a host on a different network regardless of the type of LANs the hosts are participating in.

Before we get into the more complicated aspects of IP addressing, you need to understand some of the basics. First I'm going to explain some of the fundamentals of IP addressing and its terminology. Then you'll learn about the hierarchical IP addressing scheme and private IP addresses.

IP Terminology

Throughout this chapter, you're being introduced to several important terms that are vital to understanding the Internet Protocol. Here are a few to get you started:

Bit.   A bit is one digit, either a 1 or a 0.

Byte.   A byte is 7 or 8 bits, depending on whether parity is used. For the rest of this chapter, always assume a byte is 8 bits.

Octet.   An octet, made up of 8 bits, is just an ordinary 8-bit binary number. In this chapter, the terms *byte* and *octet* are completely interchangeable.

Network address.   This is the designation used in routing to send packets to a remote network—for example, 10.0.0.0, 172.16.0.0, and 192.168.10.0.

Broadcast address.   The address used by applications and hosts to send information to all nodes on a network is called the broadcast address. Examples of layer-3 broadcasts include 255.255.255.255, which is any network, all nodes; 172.16.255.255, which is all subnets and hosts on network 172.16.0.0; and 10.255.255.255, which broadcasts to all subnets and hosts on network 10.0.0.0.

The Hierarchical IP Addressing Scheme

An IP address consists of 32 bits of information. These bits are divided into four sections, referred to as octets or bytes, with each containing 1 byte (8 bits). You can depict an IP address using one of three methods:

- Dotted-decimal, as in 172.16.30.56
- Binary, as in 10101100.00010000.00011110.00111000
- Hexadecimal, as in AC.10.1E.38

All these examples represent the same IP address. Pertaining to IP addressing, hexadecimal isn't used as often as dotted-decimal or binary, but you still might find an IP address stored in hexadecimal in some programs.

The 32-bit IP address is a structured or hierarchical address, as opposed to a flat or nonhierarchical address. Although either type of addressing scheme could have been used, *hierarchical addressing* was chosen for a good reason. The advantage of this scheme is that it can handle a large number of addresses, namely 4.3 billion (a 32-bit address space with two possible values for each position—either 0 or 1—gives you 2^{32}, or 4,294,967,296). The disadvantage of the flat addressing scheme, and the reason it's not used for IP addressing, relates to routing. If every address were unique, all routers on the Internet would need to store the address of each and every machine on the Internet. This would make efficient routing impossible, even if only a fraction of the possible addresses were used!

The solution to this problem is to use a two- or three-level hierarchical addressing scheme that is structured by network and host or by network, subnet, and host.

This two- or three-level scheme can also be compared to a telephone number. The first section, the area code, designates a very large area. The second section, the prefix, narrows the scope to a local calling area. The final segment, the customer number, zooms in on the specific connection. IP addresses use the same type of layered structure. Rather than all 32 bits being treated as a unique identifier, as in flat addressing, a part of the address is designated as the network address and the other part is designated as either the subnet and host or just the node address.

Next, we'll cover IP network addressing and the different classes of addresses we can use to address our networks.

Network Addressing

The *network address* (which can also be called the network number) uniquely identifies each network. Every machine on the same network shares that network address as part of its IP address. For example, in the IP address 172.16.30.56, 172.16 is the network address.

The *node address* is assigned to, and uniquely identifies, each machine on a network. This part of the address must be unique because it identifies a particular machine—an individual—as opposed to a network, which is a group. This number can also be referred to as a *host address*. In the sample IP address 172.16.30.56, 30.56 specifies the node address.

The designers of the Internet decided to create classes of networks based on network size. For the small number of networks possessing a very large number of nodes, they created the *Class A network*. At the other extreme is the *Class C network*, which is reserved for the numerous networks with a small number of nodes. The class distinction for networks between very large and very small is predictably called the *Class B network*.

Subdividing an IP address into a network and node address is determined by the class designation of our network. Figure 3.20 summarizes the three classes of networks used to address hosts—a subject I'll explain in much greater detail throughout this chapter.

To ensure efficient routing, Internet designers defined a mandate for the leading-bits section of the address for each different network class. For example, because a router knows that a Class A network address always starts with a 0, the router might be able to speed a packet on its way after reading only the first bit of its address. This is where the address schemes define the difference between a Class A, a Class B, and a Class C address. Coming up, I'll discuss the differences between these three classes, followed by a discussion of the Class D and Class E addresses. Classes A, B, and C are the only ranges that are used to address hosts in our networks.

FIGURE 3.20   Summary of the three classes of networks.

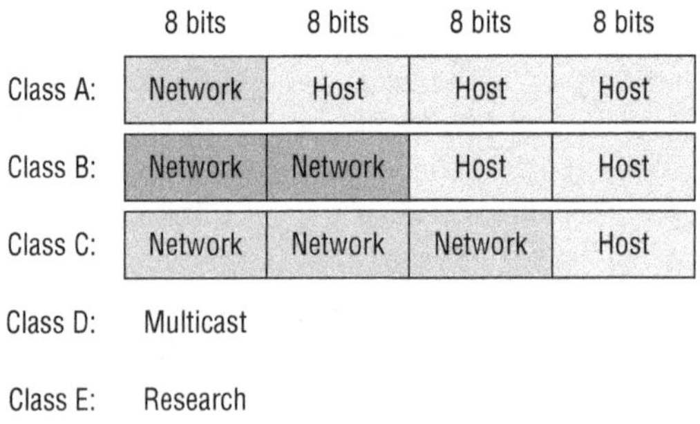

Network Address Range: Class A

The designers of the IP address scheme decided that the first bit of the first byte in a Class A network address must always be off, or 0. This means a Class A address must be between 0 and 127 in the first byte, inclusive.

Consider the following network address:

```
0xxxxxxx
```

If we turn the other 7 bits all off and then turn them all on, we'll find the Class A range of network addresses:

```
00000000 = 0
01111111 = 127
```

So a Class A network is defined in the first octet between 0 and 127, and it can't be less or more. Understand that 0 and 127 are not valid in a Class A network because they're reserved addresses, which I'll explain soon.

Network Address Range: Class B

In a Class B network, the RFCs state that the first bit of the first byte must always be turned on but the second bit must always be turned off. If you turn the other 6 bits all off and then all on, you will find the range for a Class B network:

```
10000000 = 128
10111111 = 191
```

As you can see, a Class B network is defined when the first byte is configured from 128 to 191.

Network Address Range: Class C

For Class C networks, the RFCs define the first two bits of the first octet as always turned on, but the third bit can never be on. Following the same process as the previous classes, convert from binary to decimal to find the range. Here's the range for a Class C network:

```
11000000 = 192
11011111 = 223
```

So if you see an IP address whose first three bits are in the range from 192 to 223, you'll know it is a Class C IP address.

Network Address Ranges: Classes D and E

The addresses between 224 and 255 are reserved for Class D and E networks. Class D (224–239) is used for multicast addresses and Class E (240–255) for scientific purposes, but

TABLE 3.4   Reserved IP addresses.

Address	Function
Network address of all 0s	Interpreted to mean "this network or segment."
Network address of all 1s	Interpreted to mean "all networks."
Network 127.0.0.1	Reserved for loopback tests. Designates the local node and allows that node to send a test packet to itself without generating network traffic.
Node address of all 0s	Interpreted to mean "network address" or any host on a specified network.
Node address of all 1s	Interpreted to mean "all nodes" on the specified network; for example, 128.2.255.255 means "all nodes" on network 128.2 (Class B address).
Entire IP address set to all 0s	Used by Cisco routers to designate the default route. Could also mean "any network."
Entire IP address set to all 1s (same as 255.255.255.255)	Broadcast to all nodes on the current network; sometimes called an *all 1s broadcast* or *local broadcast*.

I'm not going into these types of addresses because they are beyond the scope of knowledge you need to gain from this book.

Network Addresses: Special Purpose

Some IP addresses are reserved for special purposes, so network administrators can't ever assign these addresses to nodes. Table 3.4 lists the members of this exclusive little club and the reasons why they're included in it.

Class A Addresses

In a Class A network address, the first byte is assigned to the network address, and the three remaining bytes are used for the node addresses. The Class A format is as follows:

```
network.node.node.node
```

For example, in the IP address 49.22.102.70, 49 is the network address and 22.102.70 is the node address. Every machine on this particular network would have the distinctive network address of 49.

Class A network addresses are 1 byte long, with the first bit of that byte reserved and the 7 remaining bits available for manipulation (addressing). As a result, the maximum number of Class A networks that can be created is 128. Why? Because each of the 7 bit positions can be either a 0 or a 1, thus 2^7, or 128.

To complicate matters further, the network address of all 0s (0000 0000) is reserved to designate the default route (see Table 3.4 in the previous section). Additionally, the address 127, which is reserved for diagnostics, can't be used either, which means that you can really only use the numbers 1 to 126 to designate Class A network addresses. This means the actual number of usable Class A network addresses is 128 minus 2, or 126.

> The IP address 127.0.0.1 is used to test the IP stack on an individual node and cannot be used as a valid host address. However, the loopback address creates a shortcut method for TCP/IP applications and services that run on the same device to communicate with each other.

Each Class A address has 3 bytes (24 bit positions) for the node address of a machine. This means there are 2^{24}—or 16,777,216—unique combinations and, therefore, precisely that many possible unique node addresses for each Class A network. Because node addresses with the two patterns of all 0s and all 1s are reserved, the actual maximum usable number of nodes for a Class A network is 2^{24} minus 2, which equals 16,777,214. Either way, that's a huge number of hosts on a single network segment!

Class A Valid Host IDs

Here's an example of how to figure out the valid host IDs in a Class A network address:

- All host bits off is the network address: 10.0.0.0.
- All host bits on is the broadcast address: 10.255.255.255.

The valid hosts are the numbers in between the network address and the broadcast address: 10.0.0.1 through 10.255.255.254. Notice that 0s and 255s can be valid host IDs. All you need to remember when trying to find valid host addresses is that the host bits can't all be turned off or on at the same time.

Class B Addresses

In a Class B network address, the first 2 bytes are assigned to the network address and the remaining 2 bytes are used for node addresses. The format is as follows:

```
network.network.node.node
```

For example, in the IP address 172.16.30.56, the network address is 172.16 and the node address is 30.56.

With a network address being 2 bytes (8 bits each), you get 2^{16} unique combinations. But the Internet designers decided that all Class B network addresses should start with the binary digit 1 followed by 0. This leaves 14 bit positions to manipulate, so there are 16,384, or 2^{14} unique Class B network addresses.

A Class B address uses 2 bytes for node addresses. This is 2^{16} minus the two reserved patterns of all 0s and all 1s for a total of 65,534 possible node addresses for each Class B network.

Class B Valid Host IDs

Here's an example of how to find the valid hosts in a Class B network:

- All host bits turned off is the network address: 172.16.0.0.
- All host bits turned on is the broadcast address: 172.16.255.255.

The valid hosts would be the numbers in between the network address and the broadcast address: 172.16.0.1 through 172.16.255.254.

Class C Addresses

The first 3 bytes of a Class C network address are dedicated to the network portion of the address, with only 1 measly byte remaining for the node address. Here's the format:

```
network.network.network.node
```

Using the example IP address 192.168.100.102, the network address is 192.168.100 and the node address is 102.

In a Class C network address, the first three bit positions are always the binary 110. The calculation is as follows: 3 bytes, or 24 bits, minus 3 reserved positions leaves 21 positions. Hence, there are 2^{21}, or 2,097,152, possible Class C networks.

Each unique Class C network has 1 byte to use for node addresses. This leads to 2^{8}, or 256, minus the two reserved patterns of all 0s and all 1s, for a total of 254 node addresses for each Class C network.

Class C Valid Host IDs

Here's an example of how to find a valid host ID in a Class C network:

- All host bits turned off is the network ID: 192.168.100.0.
- All host bits turned on is the broadcast address: 192.168.100.255.

The valid hosts would be the numbers in between the network address and the broadcast address: 192.168.100.1 through 192.168.100.254.

Private IP Addresses (RFC 1918)

The people who created the IP addressing scheme also created private IP addresses. These addresses can be used on a private network, but they're not routable through the Internet. This is designed for the purpose of creating a measure of well-needed security, but it also conveniently saves valuable IP address space.

If every host on every network was required to have real routable IP addresses, we would have run out of IP addresses to hand out years ago. But by using private IP addresses, ISPs, corporations, and home users only need a relatively tiny group of bona fide IP addresses to

TABLE 3.5   Reserved IP address space.

Address class	Reserved address space
Class A	10.0.0.0 through 10.255.255.255
Class B	172.16.0.0 through 172.31.255.255
Class C	192.168.0.0 through 192.168.255.255

connect their networks to the Internet. This is economical because they can use private IP addresses on their inside networks and get along just fine.

To accomplish this task, the ISP and the corporation—the end user, no matter who they are—need to use something called *network address translation (NAT)*, which basically takes a private IP address and converts it for use on the Internet. Many people can use the same real IP address to transmit out onto the Internet. Doing things this way saves megatons of address space—good for us all!

The reserved private addresses are listed in Table 3.5.

IPv4 Address Types

Most people use the term *broadcast* as a generic term, and most of the time, we understand what they mean—but not always! For example, you might say, "The host broadcasted through a router to a DHCP server," but, well, it's pretty unlikely that this would ever really happen. What you probably mean—using the correct technical jargon—is, "The DHCP client broadcasted for an IP address, and a router then forwarded this as a unicast packet to the DHCP server." Oh, and remember that with IPv4, broadcasts are pretty important, but with IPv6, there aren't any broadcasts sent at all.

Okay, I've referred to IP addresses throughout the preceding chapters and now all throughout this chapter, and even showed you some examples. But I really haven't gone into the different terms and uses associated with them yet, and it's about time I did. So here are the address types that I'd like to define for you:

Loopback (Localhost).   Used to test the IP stack on the local computer. Can be any address from 127.0.0.1 through 127.255.255.254.

Layer 2 broadcasts.   These are sent to all nodes on a LAN.

Broadcasts (layer 3).   These are sent to all nodes on the network.

Unicast.   This is an address for a single interface, and these are used to send packets to a single destination host.

Multicast.   These are packets sent from a single source and transmitted to many devices on different networks. Referred to as *one-to-many*.

FIGURE 3.21   Local layer-2 broadcasts.

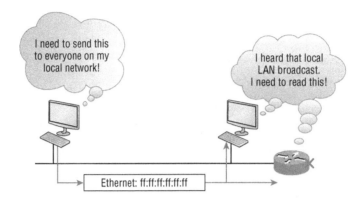

Layer-2 Broadcasts

First, understand that layer-2 broadcasts are also known as hardware broadcasts—they only go out on a LAN, but they don't go past the LAN boundary (router).

The typical hardware address is 6 bytes (48 bits) and looks something like 45:AC:24:E3:60:A5. The broadcast would be all 1s in binary, which would be all *F*s in hexadecimal, as in ff:ff:ff:ff:ff:ff and shown in Figure 3.21.

Every network interface card (NIC) will receive and read the frame, including the router, because this was a layer-2 broadcast, but the router would never, ever forward this!

Layer-3 Broadcasts

Then there are the plain old broadcast addresses at layer 3. Broadcast messages are meant to reach all hosts on a broadcast domain. These are the network broadcasts that have all host bits on.

Here's an example that you're already familiar with: The network address of 172.16.0.0 255.255.0.0 would have a broadcast address of 172.16.255.255—all host bits on. Broadcasts can also be "any network and all hosts," as indicated by 255.255.255.255 and shown in Figure 3.22.

In Figure 3.22, all hosts on the LAN will get this broadcast on their NIC, including the router, but by default the router would never forward this packet.

Unicast Address

A unicast is defined as a single IP address that's assigned to a network interface card and is the destination IP address in a packet—in other words, it's used for directing packets to a specific host.

In Figure 3.23, both the MAC address and the destination IP address are for a single NIC on the network. All hosts on the collision domain would receive this frame and accept it.

FIGURE 3.22   Layer-3 broadcasts.

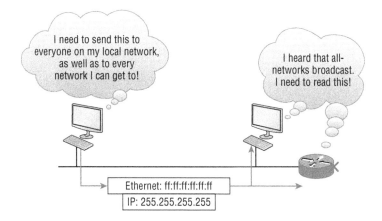

FIGURE 3.23   Unicast address.

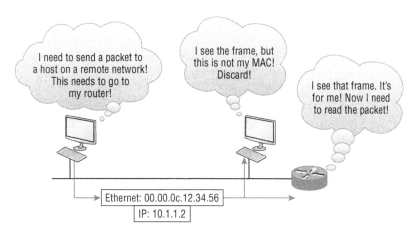

Only the destination NIC of 10.1.1.2 would accept the packet; the other NICs would discard the packet.

Multicast Address

Multicast is a different beast entirely. At first glance, it appears to be a hybrid of unicast and broadcast communication, but that isn't quite the case. Multicast does allow point-to-multipoint communication, which is similar to broadcasts, but it happens in a different manner. The crux of *multicast* is that it enables multiple recipients to receive messages without flooding the messages to all hosts on a broadcast domain. However, this is not the default behavior—it's what we can do with multicasting if it's configured correctly!

FIGURE 3.24   EIGRP multicast example.

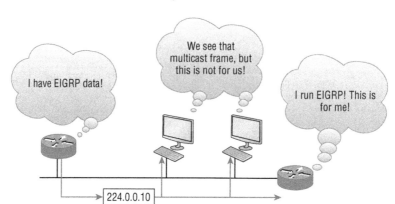

Multicast works by sending messages or data to IP *multicast group* addresses. Unlike with broadcasts, which aren't forwarded, routers then forward copies of the packet out to every interface that has hosts *subscribed* to that group address. This is where multicast differs from broadcast messages—with multicast communication, copies of packets, in theory, are sent only to subscribed hosts. For example, when I say in theory, I mean that the hosts will receive a multicast packet destined for 224.0.0.10. This is an EIGRP packet, and only a router running the EIGRP protocol will read these. All hosts on the broadcast LAN, because Ethernet is what is called a broadcast multi-access LAN technology, will pick up the frame, read the destination address, and then immediately discard the frame unless they're in the multicast group.

This saves PC processing, not LAN bandwidth. Be warned, though—multicasting can cause some serious LAN congestion if it's not implemented carefully! Figure 3.24 shows a Cisco router sending an EIGRP multicast packet on the local LAN, and only the other Cisco router will accept and read this packet.

There are several different groups that users or applications can subscribe to. The range of multicast addresses starts with 224.0.0.0 and goes through 239.255.255.255. As you can see, this range of addresses falls within IP Class D address space based on classful IP assignment.

When Do We Use NAT?

Network address translation (NAT) is similar to Classless Inter-Domain Routing (CIDR) in that the original intention for NAT was to slow the depletion of available IP address space by allowing multiple private IP addresses to be represented by a much smaller number of public IP addresses.

Since then, it's been discovered that NAT is also a useful tool for network migrations and mergers, server load sharing, and creating "virtual servers." So in this chapter, I'm going to describe the basics of NAT functionality and the terminology common to NAT.

Because NAT really decreases the overwhelming number of public IP addresses required in a networking environment, it comes in really handy when two companies that have duplicate internal addressing schemes merge. NAT is also a great tool to use when an organization changes its Internet service provider (ISP) but the networking manager needs to avoid the hassle of changing the internal address scheme.

Here's a list of situations when NAT can be especially helpful:

- When you need to connect to the Internet and your hosts don't have globally unique IP addresses

- When you've changed to a new ISP that requires you to renumber your network

- When you need to merge two intranets with duplicate addresses

You typically use NAT on a border router. For example, in Figure 3.25, NAT is used on the corporate router connected to the Internet.

Now you may be thinking, "NAT's totally cool and I just gotta have it!" But don't get too excited yet because there are some serious snags related to using NAT that you need to understand first. Don't get me wrong—it can truly be a lifesaver sometimes, but NAT has a bit of a dark side you need to know about too. For the pros and cons linked to using NAT, check out Table 3.6.

FIGURE 3.25   Where to configure NAT.

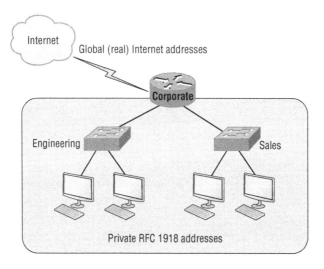

TABLE 3.6   Advantages and disadvantages of implementing NAT.

Advantages	Disadvantages
Conserves legally registered addresses.	Translation results in switching path delays.
Remedies address overlap events.	Causes loss of end-to-end IP traceability.
Increases flexibility when connecting to the Internet.	Certain applications will not function with NAT enabled.
Eliminates address renumbering as a network evolves.	Complicates tunneling protocols such as IPsec because NAT modifies the values in the header.

The most obvious advantage associated with NAT is that it allows you to conserve your legally registered address scheme. But a version of it known as PAT is also why we've only just recently run out of IPv4 addresses. Without NAT/PAT, we'd have run out of IPv4 addresses more than a decade ago!

Types of Network Address Translation

In this section, I'm going to go over the three types of NATs with you:

Static NAT (one-to-one).   This type of NAT is designed to allow one-to-one mapping between local and global addresses. Keep in mind that the static version requires you to have one real Internet IP address for every host on your network.

Dynamic NAT (many-to-many).   This version gives you the ability to map an unregistered IP address to a registered IP address from out of a pool of registered IP addresses. You don't have to statically configure your router to map each inside address to an individual outside address as you would using static NAT, but you do have to have enough real, bona fide IP addresses for everyone who's going to be sending packets to and receiving them from the Internet at the same time.

Overloading (one-to-many).   This is the most popular type of NAT configuration. Understand that overloading really is a form of dynamic NAT that maps multiple unregistered IP addresses to a single registered IP address (many-to-one) by using different source ports. Now, why is this so special? Well, because it's also known as *port address translation (PAT)*, which is also commonly referred to as NAT overload. Using PAT allows you to permit thousands of users to connect to the Internet using only one real global IP address—pretty slick, right? Seriously, NAT overload is the real reason we haven't run out of valid IP addresses on the Internet. Really—I'm not joking!

 I'll show you how to configure all three types of NAT throughout this chapter and at the end of this chapter with the hands-on labs.

NAT Names

The names we use to describe the addresses used with NAT are fairly straightforward. Addresses used after NAT translations are called *global addresses*. These are usually the public addresses used on the Internet, which you don't need if you aren't going on the Internet.

Local addresses are the ones we use before NAT translation. This means that the inside local address is actually the private address of the sending host that's attempting to get to the Internet. The outside local address would typically be the router interface connected to your ISP and is also usually a public address used as the packet begins its journey.

After translation, the inside local address is then called the *inside global address* and the outside global address then becomes the address of the destination host. Check out Table 3.7, which lists all this terminology and offers a clear picture of the various names used with NAT. Keep in mind that these terms and their definitions can vary somewhat based on implementation. The table shows how they're used according to the Cisco exam objectives.

TABLE 3.7   NAT terms.

Names	Meaning
Inside local	Source host inside address before translation—typically an RFC 1918 address.
Outside local	Address of an outside host as it appears to the inside network. This is usually the address of the router interface connected to ISP—the actual Internet address.
Inside global	Source host address used after translation to get onto the Internet. This is also the actual Internet address.
Outside global	Address of outside destination host and, again, the real Internet address.

FIGURE 3.26   Basic NAT translation.

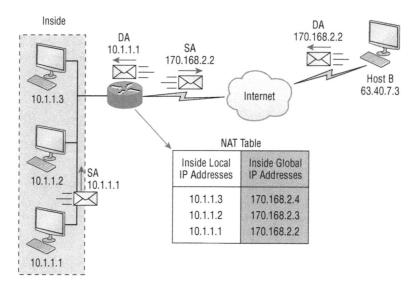

How NAT Works

Okay, it's time to look at how this whole NAT thing works. I'm going to start by using Figure 3.26 to describe basic NAT translation.

In this figure, we can see host 10.1.1.1 sending an Internet-bound packet to the border router configured with NAT. The router identifies the source IP address as an inside local IP address destined for an outside network, translates the source IP address in the packet, and documents the translation in the NAT table.

The packet is sent to the outside interface with the new translated source address. The external host returns the packet to the destination host, and the NAT router translates the inside global IP address back to the inside local IP address using the NAT table. This is as simple as it gets!

Let's take a look at a more complex configuration using overloading, also referred to as PAT. I'll use Figure 3.27 to demonstrate how PAT works by having an inside host HTTP to a server on the Internet.

With PAT, all inside hosts get translated to a single IP address; hence the term *overloading*. Again, the reason we haven't just run out of available global IP addresses on the Internet is because of overloading (PAT).

Take a look at the NAT table in Figure 3.27 again. In addition to the inside local IP address and inside global IP address, we now have port numbers. These port numbers help the router identify which host should receive the return traffic. The router uses the source port number from each host to differentiate the traffic from each of them. Understand that the packet has a destination port number of 80 when it leaves the router, and the HTTP

FIGURE 3.27   NAT overloading example (PAT).

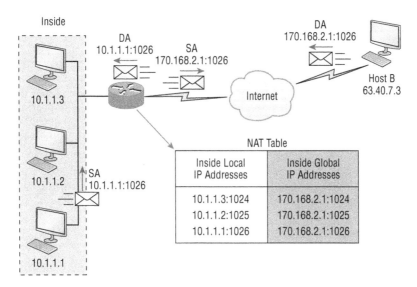

server sends back the data with a destination port number of 1026, in this example. This allows the NAT translation router to differentiate between hosts in the NAT table and then translate the destination IP address back to the inside local address.

Port numbers are used at the transport layer to identify the local host in this example. If we had to use real global IP addresses to identify the source hosts, that's called *static NAT*, and we would run out of addresses. PAT allows us to use the transport layer to identify the hosts, which in turn allows us to theoretically use up to about 65,000 hosts with only one real IP address!

Why Do We Need IPv6?

Well, the short answer is because we need to communicate, and our current system isn't really cutting it anymore. It's kind of like the Pony Express trying to compete with airmail! Consider how much time and effort we've been investing for years while we scratch our heads to resourcefully come up with slick new ways to conserve bandwidth and IP addresses. Sure, variable-length subnet masks (VLSMs) are wonderful and cool, but they're really just another invention to help us cope while we desperately struggle to overcome the worsening address drought.

I'm not exaggerating, at all, about how dire things are getting, because it's simply reality. The number of people and devices that connect to networks increases dramatically each and every day, which is not a bad thing. We're just finding new and exciting ways to communicate to more people, more often, which is a good thing. And it's not likely to go away or even decrease the littlest bit, because communicating and making connections are, in fact, basic human needs—they're in our very nature. But with our numbers increasing along with the rising tide of people joining the communications party increasing as well, the forecast for our current system isn't exactly clear skies and smooth sailing. IPv4, on which our ability to do all this connecting and communicating is presently dependent, is quickly running out of addresses for us to use.

IPv4 has only about 4.3 billion addresses available—in theory—and we know that we don't even get to use most of those! Sure, the use of Classless Inter-Domain Routing (CIDR) and NAT has helped to extend the inevitable dearth of addresses, but we will still run out of them, and it's going to happen within a few years. China is barely online, and we know there's a huge population of people and corporations there that surely want to be. There are myriad reports that give us all kinds of numbers, but all you really need to think about to realize that I'm not just being an alarmist is this: there are about 7 billion people in the world today, and it's estimated that only just over 67 percent of that population is currently connected to the Internet—wow!

That statistic is basically screaming at us the ugly truth that based on IPv4's capacity, every person can't even have a computer, let alone all the other IP devices we use with them! I have more than one computer, and it's pretty likely that you do too, and I'm not even including phones, laptops, game consoles, fax machines, routers, switches, and heaps of other devices we use every day into the mix! So I think I've made it pretty clear that we've got to do something before we run out of addresses and lose the ability to connect with each other as we know it. And that "something" just happens to be implementing IPv6.

IPv6 Addressing and Expressions

Just as understanding how IP addresses are structured and used is critical with IPv4 addressing, it's also vital when it comes to IPv6. You've already read about the fact that at 128 bits, an IPv6 address is much larger than an IPv4 address. Because of this, as well as the new ways the addresses can be used, you've probably guessed that IPv6 will be more complicated to manage. But no worries! As I said, I'll break down the basics and show you what the address looks like and how you can write it as well as many of its common uses. It's going to be a little weird at first, but before you know it, you'll have it nailed!

So let's take a look at Figure 3.28, which has a sample IPv6 address broken down into sections.

FIGURE 3.28   IPv6 address example.

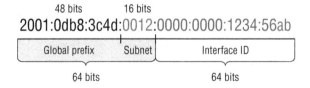

As you can clearly see, the address is definitely much larger. But what else is different? Well, first, notice that it has eight groups of numbers instead of four and also that those groups are separated by colons instead of periods. And hey, wait a second, there are letters in that address! Yep, the address is expressed in hexadecimal just like a MAC address is, so you could say this address has eight 16-bit hexadecimal colon-delimited blocks. That's already quite a mouthful, and you probably haven't even tried to say the address out loud yet!

 There are four hexadecimal characters (16 bits) in each IPv6 field (with eight fields total), separated by colons.

Shortened Expression

The good news is there are a few tricks to help rescue us when writing these monster addresses. For one thing, you can actually leave out parts of the address to abbreviate it, but to get away with doing that you have to follow a couple of rules. First, you can drop any leading zeros in each of the individual blocks. After you do that, the sample address from earlier would then look like this:

```
2001:db8:3c4d:12:0:0:1234:56ab
```

That's a definite improvement—at least we don't have to write all of those extra zeros! But what about whole blocks that don't have anything in them except zeros? Well, we can kind of lose those too—at least some of them. Again referring to our sample address, we can remove the two consecutive blocks of zeros by replacing them with a double colon, like this:

```
2001:db8:3c4d:12::1234:56ab
```

Cool—we replaced the blocks of all zeros with a double colon. The rule you have to follow to get away with this is that you can replace only one contiguous block of such zeros in an address. So if my address has four blocks of zeros and each of them were separated, I just don't get to replace them all because I can replace only one contiguous block with a double colon. Check out this example:

```
2001:0000:0000:0012:0000:0000:1234:56ab
```

And just know that you *can't* do this:

```
2001::12::1234:56ab
```

Instead, the best you can do is this:

```
2001::12:0:0:1234:56ab
```

The reason the preceding example is our best shot is that if we remove two sets of zeros, the device looking at the address will have no way of knowing where the zeros go back in. Basically, the router would look at the incorrect address and say, "Well, do I place two blocks into the first set of double colons and two into the second set, or do I place three blocks into the first set and one block into the second set?" And on and on it would go because the information the router needs just isn't there.

Address Types

We're all familiar with IPv4's unicast, broadcast, and multicast addresses that basically define who or at least how many other devices we're talking to. But as I mentioned, IPv6 modifies that trio and introduces the anycast. Broadcasts, as we know them, have been eliminated in IPv6 because of their cumbersome inefficiency and basic tendency to drive us insane!

So let's find out what each of these types of IPv6 addressing and communication methods do for us:

Unicast.   Packets addressed to a unicast address are delivered to a single interface. For load balancing, multiple interfaces across several devices can use the same address, but we'll call that an anycast address. There are a few different types of unicast addresses, but we don't need to get further into that here.

Global unicast addresses (2000::/3).   These are your typical publicly routable addresses, and they're the same as in IPv4. Global addresses start at 2000::/3. Figure 3.29 shows how a unicast address breaks down. The ISP can provide you with a minimum /48 network ID, which in turn provides you with 16 bits to create a unique 64-bit router interface address. The last 64 bits are the unique host ID.

Link-local addresses (FE80::/10).   These are like the Automatic Private IP Address (APIPA) addresses that Microsoft uses to automatically provide addresses in IPv4 in that they're not meant to be routed. In IPv6, they start with FE80::/10, as shown in Figure 3.30. Think of these addresses as handy tools that give you the ability to throw a temporary LAN together

FIGURE 3.29   IPv6 global unicast addresses.

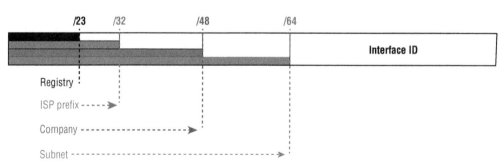

FIGURE 3.30   IPv6 link local FE80::/10: The first 10 bits define the address type.

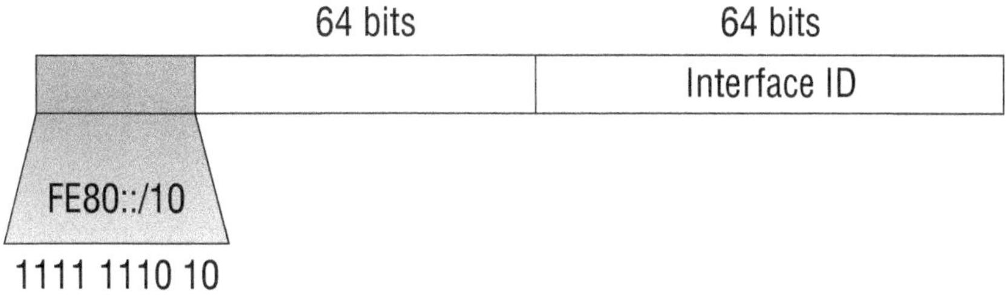

for meetings or create a small LAN that's not going to be routed but still needs to share and access files and services locally.

Unique local addresses (FC00::/7).   These addresses are also intended for nonrouting purposes over the Internet, but they are nearly globally unique, so it's unlikely you'll ever have one of them overlap. Unique local addresses were designed to replace site-local addresses, so they basically do almost exactly what IPv4 private addresses do: allow communication throughout a site while being routable to multiple local networks. Site-local addresses were deprecated as of September 2004.

Multicast (FF00::/8).   Again, as in IPv4, packets addressed to a multicast address are delivered to all interfaces tuned into the multicast address. Sometimes people call them *one-to-many* addresses. It's really easy to spot a multicast address in IPv6 because they always start with *FF*. We'll get deeper into multicast operation coming up, in "How IPv6 Works in an Internetwork."

Anycast.   Like multicast addresses, an anycast address identifies multiple interfaces on multiple devices. But there's a big difference: the anycast packet is delivered to only one device—actually, to the closest one it finds defined in terms of routing distance. And again, this address is special because you can apply a single address to more than one host. These are referred to as *one-to-nearest* addresses. Anycast addresses are typically only configured on routers, never hosts, and a source address could never be an anycast address. Of note is that the IETF did reserve the top 128 addresses for each /64 for use with anycast addresses.

You're probably wondering whether there are any special, reserved addresses in IPv6 because you know they're there in IPv4. Well, there are—plenty of them! Let's go over those now.

Special Addresses

I'm going to list some of the addresses and address ranges (in Table 3.8) that you should definitely make sure to remember because you'll eventually use them. They're all special or reserved for a specific use, but unlike IPv4, IPv6 gives us a galaxy of addresses, so reserving a few here and there doesn't hurt at all!

TABLE 3.8   Special IPv6 addresses.

Address	Meaning
0:0:0:0:0:0:0:0	Equals::. This is the equivalent of IPv4's 0.0.0.0 and is typically the source address of a host before the host receives an IP address when you're using DHCP-driven stateful configuration.
0:0:0:0:0:0:0:1	Equals::1. The equivalent of 127.0.0.1 in IPv4.
0:0:0:0:0:0:192.168.100.1	This is how an IPv4 address would be written in a mixed IPv6/IPv4 network environment.
2000::/3	The global unicast address range.
FC00::/7	The unique local unicast range.
FE80::/10	The link-local unicast range.
FF00::/8	The multicast range.
3FFF:FFFF::/32	Reserved for examples and documentation.
2001:0DB8::/32	Also reserved for examples and documentation.
2002::/16	Used with 6-to-4 tunneling, which is an IPv4-to-IPv6 transition system. The structure allows IPv6 packets to be transmitted over an IPv4 network without the need to configure explicit tunnels.

When you run IPv4 and IPv6 on a router, you have what is called *dual-stack.*

Summary

If you made it this far and understood everything the first time through, you should be extremely proud of yourself! We really covered a lot of ground in this chapter, but understand that the information in it is critical to being able to navigate well through the rest of this book.

If you didn't get a complete understanding the first time around, don't stress. It really wouldn't hurt you to read this chapter more than once. There is still a lot of ground to cover, so make sure you've got this material all nailed down. That way, you'll be ready for more, and just so you know, there's a lot more! What we're doing up to this point is building a solid foundation to build on as you advance.

With that in mind, after you learned about the DoD model, the layers, and associated protocols, you learned about the oh-so-important topic of IP addressing. I discussed in detail the difference between each address class, how to find a network address and broadcast address, and what denotes a valid host address range. I can't stress enough how important it is for you to have this critical information unshakably understood before moving on to Chapter 4!

Because you've already come this far, there's no reason to stop now and waste all those brainwaves and new neural connections. So don't stop—go through the written labs and review questions at the end of this chapter and make sure you understand each answer's explanation. The best is yet to come!

Exam Essentials

Differentiate between the DoD and OSI network models.   The DoD model is a condensed version of the OSI model, composed of four layers instead of seven, but is nonetheless like the OSI model in that it can be used to describe packet creation, and devices and protocols can be mapped to its layers.

Identify process/application layer protocols.   Telnet is a terminal emulation program that allows you to log into a remote host and run programs. File Transfer Protocol (FTP) is a connection-oriented service that allows you to transfer files. Trivial FTP (TFTP) is a connectionless file transfer program. Simple Mail Transfer Protocol (SMTP) is a protocol used to send email.

Identify host-to-host layer protocols.   Transmission Control Protocol (TCP) is a connection-oriented protocol that provides reliable network service by using acknowledgments and flow control. User Datagram Protocol (UDP) is a connectionless protocol that provides low overhead and is considered unreliable.

Identify Internet layer protocols.   Internet Protocol (IP) is a connectionless protocol that provides network address and routing through an internetwork. Address Resolution Protocol (ARP) finds a hardware address from a known IP address. Reverse ARP (RARP) finds an IP address from a known hardware address. Internet Control Message Protocol (ICMP) provides diagnostics and destination unreachable messages.

Describe the functions of DNS and DHCP in the network.   Dynamic Host Configuration Protocol (DHCP) provides network configuration information (including IP addresses) to hosts, eliminating the need to perform the configurations manually. Domain Name Service (DNS) resolves hostnames—both Internet names such as www.lammle.com and device names such as Workstation 2—to IP addresses, eliminating the need to know the IP address of a device for connection purposes.

Identify what is contained in the TCP header of a connection-oriented transmission.   The fields in the TCP header include the source port, destination port, sequence number, acknowledgment number, header length, a field reserved for future use, code bits, window size, checksum, urgent pointer, options field, and finally, the data field.

Identify what is contained in the UDP header of a connectionless transmission.   The fields in the UDP header include only the source port, destination port, length, checksum, and data. The smaller number of fields as compared to the TCP header comes at the expense of providing none of the more advanced functions of the TCP frame.

Identify what is contained in the IP header.   The fields of an IP header include version, header length, priority or type of service, total length, identification, flags, fragment offset, time to live, protocol, header checksum, source IP address, destination IP address, options, and finally, data.

Compare and contrast UDP and TCP characteristics and features.   TCP is connection-oriented, acknowledged, and sequenced and has flow and error control, whereas UDP is connectionless, unacknowledged, and not sequenced and provides no error or flow control.

Understand the role of port numbers.   Port numbers are used to identify the protocol or service that is to be used in the transmission.

Identify the role of ICMP.   Internet Control Message Protocol (ICMP) works at the network layer and is used by IP for many different services. ICMP is a management protocol and messaging service provider for IP.

Define the Class A IP address range.   The IP range for a Class A network is 1–126. This provides 8 bits of network addressing and 24 bits of host addressing by default.

Define the Class B IP address range.   The IP range for a Class B network is 128–191. Class B addressing provides 16 bits of network addressing and 16 bits of host addressing by default.

Define the Class C IP address range.   The IP range for a Class C network is 192 through 223. Class C addressing provides 24 bits of network addressing and 8 bits of host addressing by default.

Identify the private IP ranges.   The Class A private address range is 10.0.0.0 through 10.255.255.255. The Class B private address range is 172.16.0.0 through 172.31.255.255. The Class C private address range is 192.168.0.0 through 192.168.255.255.

Understand the difference between a broadcast, unicast, and multicast address.   A broadcast is to all devices in a subnet, a unicast is to one device, and a multicast is to some but not all devices.

Understand the term *NAT*.   This may come as news to you, because I didn't—okay, failed to—mention it earlier, but NAT has a few nicknames. In the industry, it's referred to as network masquerading, IP masquerading, and (for those who are besieged with OCD and compelled to spell everything out) network address translation. Whatever you want to dub it, basically, they all refer to the process of rewriting the source/destination addresses of IP packets when they go through a router or firewall. Just focus on the process that's occurring and your understanding of it (i.e., the important part), and you're on it for sure!

Remember the three methods of NAT.   The three methods are static, dynamic, and over-loading; the latter is also called PAT.

Understand static NAT.   This type of NAT is designed to allow one-to-one mapping between local and global addresses.

Understand dynamic NAT.   This version gives you the ability to map a range of unregistered IP addresses to a registered IP address from out of a pool of registered IP addresses.

Understand overloading.   Overloading really is a form of dynamic NAT that maps multiple unregistered IP addresses to a single registered IP address (many-to-one) by using different ports. It's also known as *PAT*.

Understand why we need IPv6.   Without IPv6, the world would be depleted of IP addresses.

Understand link-local.   Link-local is like an IPv4 private IP address, but it can't be routed at all, not even in your organization.

Understand unique local.   This, like link-local, is like a private IP address in IPv4 and cannot be routed to the Internet. However, the difference between link-local and unique local is that unique local can be routed within your organization or company.

Remember IPv6 addressing.   IPv6 addressing is not like IPv4 addressing. IPv6 addressing has much more address space, is 128 bits long, and is represented in hexadecimal, unlike IPv4, which is only 32 bits long and represented in decimal.

Review Questions

The following questions are designed to test your understanding of this chapter's material. For more information on how to get additional questions, please see www.lammle.com/ccst.

You can find the answers to these questions in Appendix.

1. Which of the following application layer protocols sets up a secure session that's similar to Telnet?
   - **A.** FTP
   - **B.** SSH
   - **C.** DNS
   - **D.** DHCP

2. What protocol is used to find the hardware address of a local device?
   - **A.** RARP
   - **B.** ARP
   - **C.** IP
   - **D.** ICMP
   - **E.** BootP

3. Which of the following are layers in the TCP/IP model? (Choose three.)
   - **A.** Application
   - **B.** Session
   - **C.** Transport
   - **D.** Internet
   - **E.** Data link
   - **F.** Physical

4. Which class of IP address provides a maximum of only 254 host addresses per network ID?
   - **A.** Class A
   - **B.** Class B
   - **C.** Class C
   - **D.** Class D
   - **E.** Class E

5. Which of the following describe the DHCP Discover message? (Choose two.)

   A. It uses ff:ff:ff:ff:ff:ff as a layer-2 broadcast.

   B. It uses UDP as the transport layer protocol.

   C. It uses TCP as the transport layer protocol.

   D. It does not use a layer-2 destination address.

6. Which layer-4 protocol is used for a Telnet connection?

   A. IP

   B. TCP

   C. TCP/IP

   D. UDP

   E. ICMP

7. Private IP addressing was specified in RFC _____.

8. Which of the following services use TCP? (Choose three.)

   A. DHCP

   B. SMTP

   C. SNMP

   D. FTP

   E. HTTP

   F. TFTP

9. Which of the following is an example of a multicast address?

   A. 10.6.9.1

   B. 192.168.10.6

   C. 224.0.0.10

   D. 172.16.9.5

10. If you use either Telnet or FTP, what layer are you using to generate the data?

    A. Application

    B. Presentation

    C. Session

    D. Transport

11. The DoD model (also called the TCP/IP stack) has four layers. Which layer of the DoD model is equivalent to the network layer of the OSI model?

    A. Application

    B. Host-to-host

    C. Internet

    D. Network access

12. Which two of the following are private IP addresses? (Choose two.)

    A. 12.0.0.1

    B. 168.172.19.39

    C. 172.20.14.36

    D. 172.33.194.30

    E. 192.168.24.43

13. What layer in the TCP/IP stack is equivalent to the transport layer of the OSI model?

    A. Application

    B. Host-to-host

    C. Internet

    D. Network access

14. Which statements are true regarding ICMP packets? (Choose two.)

    A. ICMP guarantees datagram delivery.

    B. ICMP can provide hosts with information about network problems.

    C. ICMP is encapsulated within IP datagrams.

    D. ICMP is encapsulated within UDP datagrams

15. What is the address range of a Class B network address in binary?

    A. 01xxxxxx

    B. 0xxxxxxx

    C. 10xxxxxx

    D. 110xxxxx

16. Which option is a valid IPv6 address?

    A. 2001:0000:130F::099a::12a

    B. 2002:7654:A1AD:61:81AF:CCC1

    C. FEC0:ABCD:WXYZ:0067::2A4

    D. 2004:1:25A4:886F::1

17. Which three statements about IPv6 prefixes are true? (Choose three.)

    A. FF00::/8 is used for IPv6 multicast.

    B. FE80::/10 is used for link-local unicast.

    C. FC00::/7 is used in private networks.

    D. 2001::1/127 is used for loopback addresses.

    E. FE80::/8 is used for link-local unicast.

    F. FEC0::/10 is used for IPv6 broadcast.

18. Which two statements about IPv6 router advertisement messages are true? (Choose two.)

    A. They use ICMPv6 type 134.

    B. The advertised prefix length must be 64 bits.

    C. The advertised prefix length must be 48 bits.

    D. They are sourced from the configured IPv6 interface address.

    E. Their destination is always the link-local address of the neighboring node.

19. Which of the following are advantages of using NAT? (Choose three.)

    A. Translation introduces switching path delays.

    B. NAT conserves legally registered addresses.

    C. NAT causes loss of end-to-end IP traceability.

    D. NAT increases flexibility when connecting to the Internet.

    E. Certain applications will not function with NAT enabled.

    F. NAT remedies address overlap occurrence.

20. Port address translation is also called what?

    A. NAT fast

    B. NAT static

    C. NAT overload

    D. Overloading static

21. Which of the following is considered to be the inside host's address before translation?

    A. Inside local

    B. Outside local

    C. Inside global

    D. Outside global

Chapter

4

Network Device Access

THE FOLLOWING CCST EXAM TOPIC IS COVERED IN THIS CHAPTER:

✔ **1.0 Standards and Concepts**

▪ 1.3. Explain access management principles.

  Authentication, authorization, and accounting (AAA); RADIUS; multifactor authentication (MFA); password policies

▪ 2.5. Implement secure access technologies.

  ACL, firewall, VPN, NAC

In this chapter, we'll learn everything a CCST cyber security professional needs to know about controlling network devices. We will learn how to set up local authentication, and some of this NAC's shortcomings, especially when you have a large network to deal with.

Then we will learn the importance of the AAA model and how it can be applied to various authentication systems. Along the way we will learn about multifactor authentication (MFA) and password policies.

We will follow up this chapter by learning how to apply these concepts to Network Access Control (NAC) systems such as Cisco ISE. This will allow us to control and secure the transient network devices that enter our network every day.

To find your included bonus material, as well as Todd Lammle videos, practice questions, and hands-on labs, please see www.lammle.com/ccst.

Local Authentication

The simplest way to make a login for a Cisco device is to manually create a user account on the device. This means that if we wanted to create a login that Todd can use, we would need to connect to each router in our network and manually add the login commands, as seen in Figure 4.1. Although it isn't a big deal to add an account if your network only has four routers, it can be a daunting task if you need to add Todd to 400 routers.

I remember one time I did some consulting for a large mining company that used local authentication for its network. So before I could start doing any work there…some poor soul had to log into each of 10,000 network devices and make an account for me, and unfortunately, the company didn't have any automation in place. It took a full week!

Creating accounts can be bad enough, but what about if Todd forgets his login and needs to have his password changed? You guessed it, someone will have to manually log into all the devices and change the password for him. Finally, when Todd is done with the project, best practice says that someone should log into to all the devices…again and remove his account.

After reading all that, you would be forgiven for swearing off local accounts for life; however, there is a great use case for keeping at least one local account around, and that is to provide a backup way to log into your devices if some of the other methods we will discuss in

FIGURE 4.1   Local login example.

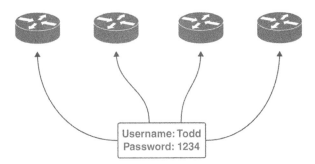

FIGURE 4.2   Local login backup.

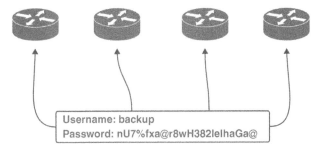

this chapter end up breaking. Because of that, it is a great idea to add a local account with a big scary password on all your network devices, so you don't get locked out if your authentication solution isn't reachable due to an outage. An example can be seen in Figure 4.2.

To configure a local user account, we use the `username` command and specify either a password or a secret. Since this is a security-focused book, we will want to use the `secret` option because it encrypts the password for us.

We shouldn't use the `password` option when making accounts these days because it is stored in the configuration as cleartext. To prove that I created Todd's account using the password option and then ran a `show  run` to display the password:

```
R01(config)#username todd password 1234
 WARNING: Command has been added to the configuration using a type 0 password.
However, recommended to migrate to strong type-6 encryption
R01(config)#
R01(config)#
*Sep 28 04:43:26.824: %AAAA-4-CLI_DEPRECATED: WARNING: Command has been added
to the configuration using a type 0 password. However, recommended to migrate
to strong type-6 encryption
R01(config)#do show running-config | in username
username todd password 0 1234
```

But if I do the same thing with the `secret` option, we can see that it is encrypted:

```
R01(config)# no username todd
This operation will remove all username related configurations with same
name. Do you want to continue? [confirm]
R01(config)#username todd priv 15 secret 1234
R01(config)#do sh run | in username
username todd privilege 15 secret 9
$9$pvuw1rurjUmqAk$ky8n1snhQW7oGW81W6r2jotIXBJ4FRG0PQ7dm8DttCg
```

 You can encrypt cleartext passwords with the `service password-encryption` command, but it is better to just use `secret`.

The last thing we need to do is enable local authentication; by default, a Cisco router will use line authentication instead of what is defined by the username command. We can change that by adding the command `login local` for the vty lines:

```
R01(config)#line vty 0 15
R01(config-line)#login local
```

Now we can login using Todd's account!

```
> ssh todd@10.30.10.230
(todd@10.30.10.230) Password:


R01>
```

AAA Model

The majority of an administrator's day-to-day job is managing users and managing and monitoring access to resources. These day-to-day tasks can be summarized with the AAA model. The AAA model is a security framework that defines the administration of authentication, authorization, and accounting. You will find references to the AAA model when configuring network switches, routers, or RADIUS servers, just to name a few. The AAA model is referred to anywhere you need to authenticate users, authorize access, and account for the authorized or unauthorized access. In the following sections, you will learn the basic concepts of the AAA model.

Authentication

When a user wants to access a resource, they must first prove their identity with the act of *authentication*, which states they are who they say they are. As shown in Figure 4.3, a user provides their authentication credentials to the identity store, where the credentials are

FIGURE 4.3 Authentication components.

Credentials

Identity store

validated. A user can provide authentication credentials using several different factors. The most common authentication factors are something you know (passwords), something you have (smartcard), and something you are (biometrics). Besides the various factors of authentication, there are several protocols that can be used to transmit credentials or aid in the authentication of a user. In the following sections, I will cover in detail all of the various protocols as well as the various factors of authentication that can be used to authenticate a user or computer.

Multifactor Authentication

All authentication is based on something that you know, have, are, or do, or your location. A common factor of authentication is a password, but passwords can be guessed, stolen, or cracked. No one factor is secure by itself, because by themselves they can be compromised easily. A fingerprint can be lifted with tape, a key can be stolen, or a location can be spoofed.

Multifactor authentication (MFA) helps solve the problem of a compromised single-factor authentication method by combining the authentication methods. With multifactor authentication, a single factor will no longer authenticate a user; two or more of the factors discussed in this section are required for authentication. This makes the credentials of the user more complex to compromise.

One of the most common examples where MFA is used in everyday life is at an ATM. To withdraw money, a user must provide a card (one factor) and a PIN (a second factor). If you know the PIN but do not have the card, you cannot get money from the machine. If you have the card but do not have the PIN, you cannot get money from the machine.

In this section, we will cover the most common two-factor (2FA)/MFA methods used by protected applications. The following methods are generally used in conjunction with a traditional username and password combination. It should be assumed that when we talk about 2FA, it provides the same functionality as MFA. MFA just has more than two factors of authentication. For the rest of this section, we will use the term MFA.

Something You Know.   Computing has used the factor of something a person knows since computer security began. This is commonly in the form of a username and password. We can make passwords more complex by requiring uppercase, lowercase, numeric, and symbol combinations. We can also mandate the length of passwords and the frequency with which they are changed. However, the username/password combination is among the most common types of credentials to be stolen because they can be phished or sniffed with a keylogger.

Something You Have.   Authentication based on something a person has relates to physical security. When we use a key fob, RFID tag, or magnetic card to enter a building, we are using something we have. An identification badge is something we have, although technically it is also something we are if it has a picture of us on it. Credit cards have long since been something we have to authenticate a transaction. Within the past two decades, they have also become the most stolen credentials. Recently, credit cards have implemented a new authentication method called Europay, MasterCard, and Visa (EMV). EMV will make it harder to steal and duplicate cards. However, if a card is lost, it can still be used by an unscrupulous person because it is something you physically have.

Something You Are.   A decade or so ago, authenticating a user based on something they are was science fiction. We now have biometric readers built into our phones for our convenience! All we need to do is place our finger on the reader, speak into the phone, or allow the phone to recognize our face, and we are instantly logged in. Computers can be outfitted with fingerprint readers to allow logon of users based on their fingerprint as well. When this technology entered the market, there were various ways to get around it, such as tape-lifting a print, playing back someone's voice, or displaying a picture of a person for the camera. These systems have gotten better since they have entered the market by storing more points of the fingerprint, listening to other aspects of a user's voice, and looking for natural motion in the camera.

Somewhere You Are.   A relatively new factor of authentication is based on somewhere you are. With the proliferation of Global Positioning System (GPS) chips, your current location can authenticate you for a system. This is performed by creating authentication rules on the location. GPS sensors are not the only method of obtaining your current location. Geographic IP information queried from Geo-IP services can also be used for the authentication process. We can restrict login to a specific IP or geographic location based on the IP address provided.

Something You Do.   Another relatively new factor of authentication for network systems is based on something you do. Although it has been used for hundreds of years for documents and contracts, a signature is something you do, and you don't even think about how you do it. It is unique to you and only you because there is a specific way you sign your name. Typing your name into the computer is something you do and don't think about, but there is a slight hesitation that you make without knowing it. Algorithms pick up on this and use the keystrokes as a form of authentication. Arguably, it can be considered biometrics because it is something your brain does without you consciously thinking about it.

Multifactor Authentication Methods

Now that you understand the various factors of authentication, let's examine the various methods to employ MFA. Depending on the application, you may see any number of these methods being used for MFA. In the example shown in Figure 4.4, the MFA method can be replaced with any of the following methods to provide MFA for the application.

FIGURE 4.4 Authentication methods.

Email. Some applications will use email as an MFA method. However, using email as an MFA option is probably the least secure method. This is mainly because people reuse passwords. For example, if your banking website username and password are compromised (something you know) and you reuse the same credentials on email, it provides no protection. The threat actor will quickly log into your email and use it as a factor of authentication. Ideally the email account is protected with MFA in a way that it requires something you have.

Email is useful as a notification method when someone logs into a secure login. However, keep in mind the threat agents know this as well. If your email account is compromised, a threat agent will often create a rule in your email box to dump these notifications directly to the trash. They have also been known to create forwarding rules to redirect communications directly to their own disposable email account.

Short Message Service. Some applications will allow the use of short message service (SMS) text messages as the MFA method. When this method is used, a simple text message is sent to the user's phone number. The message will contain a random five- to eight-digit code that the user will use to satisfy the MFA requirement. When you first set up this MFA method, the protected application will request the code before turning on MFA. This is done to verify that the phone number is correct and that you can receive text messages before the security is applied to your account.

Voice Call. Some applications that are protected by MFA will allow voice calls to be initiated to the end user. This is usually done if the person does not have a phone that accepts text messages. The voice call will recite a five- to eight-digit code that the user will use to satisfy the MFA requirement. This process is similar to SMS, with the difference being it is an automated voice call.

Time-Based Hardware and Software Tokens. *Time-based hardware tokens* are devices that enable the user to generate a one-time password (OTP) to authenticate their identity. SecurID from RSA is one of the best-known examples of a physical hardware token, as shown in Figure 4.5.

Time-based hardware tokens operate by rotating a code every 60 seconds. The token typically uses the time-based one-time password (TOTP) or HMAC-based one-time password (HOTP) algorithm to calculate the rotating code. This rotating code is combined with a user's PIN or password for authentication. A time-based hardware token is considered multifactor authentication because it is something you have (hardware token) along with something you know, such as your PIN or password.

FIGURE 4.5 An RSA security key fob.

A new type of time-based hardware token is becoming the new standard, and it can be considered a time-based software token or soft token. It operates the same as a hardware token, but it is an application on your cell phone that provides the code. Google Authenticator is one example of these types of applications. Microsoft also has an authenticator application similar to Google Authenticator.

When configuring MFA on an application, you have two ways of adding an account to the authenticator application. You can take a picture of a quick response (QR) code, or you can enter a security code into the authenticator application. If you choose to use a QR code, then the application turning on the MFA will present a QR code that can be scanned by the authenticator application. If you choose to use a setup key, the application turning on the MFA will provide a key. There is generally a second step before the application is protected by MFA, where you will be required to enter a code from the authenticator application to the protected application. A lengthy one-time-use backup key is also generated, in case you need to turn MFA off in the event your device is lost or stolen.

Authorization

Authentication is the act of proving you are who you state you are, as we learned in the last section. Authorization dictates what you can do once you are authenticated. And in some cases, authorization can even dictate whether you are even allowed to authenticate. For example, if your IP address is external, you might not even be allowed (authorized) to authenticate.

In the following, we'll learn how authorization is needed when using the following:

- Identity and access management
- Least privilege
- Role-based access control

Identity and Access Management

Identity and Access Management (IAM) is a security framework used for the authentication and authorization of users. The IAM model has been adopted by service providers as a means of managing users with their application. The IAM framework allows a service provider to define the authentication of users by means of a username and password, certificate keypair, or even single sign-on (SSO), just to name a few methods.

The framework also defines the authorization of user access for a resource within the service provider. Many service providers have adopted a model of security in which the object and accompanying permission are defined. This allows granular control of what can be accessed by the user and what can be done with the service or object by the user. For example, if a database is created on a service provider, the specific database can be secured so that a particular user has access only to read objects within the database. However, administrators might have a higher level of permissions to alter information.

Least Privilege

The principle of least privilege is a common security concept that states a user should be restricted to the least amount of privileges that they need to do their job. By leveraging the principle of least privilege, you can limit internal and external threats. For example, if a front-line worker has administrative access on their computer, they have the ability to circumvent security; this is an example of an internal threat. Along the same lines, if a worker has administrative access on their computer and received a malicious email, a bad actor could now have administrative access to the computer; this is an example of an external threat. Therefore, only the required permissions to perform their tasks should be granted to users, thus providing least privilege.

Security is not the only benefit to following the principle of least privilege, although it does reduce your surface area of attack because users have less access to sensitive data that can be leaked. When you limit workers to the least privilege they need on their computer or the network, fewer intentional or accidental misconfigurations will happen that can lead to downtime or help-desk calls. Some regulatory standards require following the principle of least privilege. By following the principle of least privilege, an organization can improve on compliance audits by regulatory bodies.

Role-Based Access Control (RBAC)

As administrators, we are accustomed to file-based access controls and the granularity that accompanies these access control models. However, with today's emerging cloud-based systems, we often do not need the granularity of individual permissions. Role-based access control (RBAC) helps remove the complex granularity by creating roles for users who accumulate specific rights. The user is then given a role or multiple roles in which specific rights have been established for the resource, as shown in Figure 4.6.

FIGURE 4.6   Role-based access.

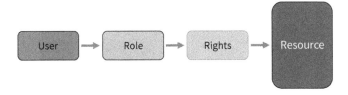

As an example, Microsoft Teams has roles for a Teams meeting. You can be an attendee, presenter, or organizer. The attendee can attend a Teams meeting and share their video and audio feed. The presenter can do that, plus they can share a presentation, mute participants, and perform several other presentation key functions. The organizer can do everything the presenter can do, plus they can create breakout rooms and view attendance. By changing someone's role in the meeting, from attendee to presenter, for example, we can allow them to share a document with the meeting's other attendees. If we had to find the specific permission to allow that person to perform the function, it would take a lot longer and would be prone to error.

Role-based access doesn't stop with just cloud-based applications. We can use role-based access controls in our day-to-day operations by standardizing permissions based on specific roles in our organization. When a marketing person is hired, the standardized role of marketing can be applied. This can be performed with Active Directory groups and the permission groups we include.

Accounting

Accounting is the last A in the AAA model, and after learning about authentication and authorization, this section is where we can see it all together. Ironically, let's use the analogy of a transaction in a physical bank. In Figure 4.7, the customer (user) appears on the far left, and their money (resource) is shown on the far right. As an example, I will use the analogy of a bank transaction in which a customer will withdraw money.

A customer (user) will provide their *authentication* via their account number (something they know) and identification (something they are). The bank teller can then authenticate that they are the person they say they are.

Once the teller has authenticated the customer (user), *authorization* will be checked. With the analogy of a bank, authorization might be how much money is in your bank account. However, a better example is who in the bank is allowed to enter the vault and touch the money! I'm sure even if my bank authenticates me, they won't authorize me to count and withdraw my own money. I'm pretty sure that if I tried, I would go to jail and not collect my

FIGURE 4.7   AAA bank analogy.

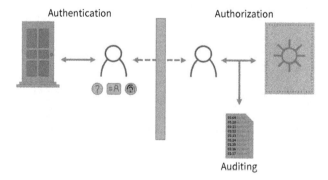

$200. The teller is authorized to touch the money and hand it to you. It is important to note that, in this example, the teller is also authenticated when they come into work, although this authentication process is less rigorous than your authentication process.

Now that you have been authenticated and authorized to receive your money, an audit trail is created. If you had $400 and withdrew $200, your account would be debited $200. The audit trail in this example is the *accounting* process of the AAA system. Accounting allows us to trust, but audit.

In a network system, when a user logs on, they will commonly authenticate with a username and password. When the user tries to access the resource, their authorization to the resource will be checked. If they are authorized to access the resource, the accounting of access will be recorded. It is important to note that accounting can record denied access to a resource as well.

Although the analogy of a bank has to deal with money, and the word *accounting* is synonymous with money, the word *accounting* in the IT world has nothing to do with money. Accounting in the IT world has to do with the audit trail that users and computers leave when they authenticate and access information. The only time the accounting feature has anything to do with money is if your service provider is charging you based on the amount of time you've spent logged in or for the amount of data sent and received.

Common AAA Systems

You should now have a better understanding of the AAA model, as well as how it applies to day-to-day operations. In this section, we will learn about the systems that support the AAA concepts. The following are the two most popular AAA systems that are used by Cisco. In no way are they a complete list of the AAA systems you might work with outside of the exam. However, the knowledge of authentication, authorization, and auditing, along with the following AAA systems, will help you understand other systems better.

Remote Authentication Dial-In User Service

Remote Authentication Dial-In User Service (RADIUS) was originally proposed as an Internet Engineering Task Force (IETF) standard. It has become a widely adopted industry standard for authenticating users and computers for network systems. RADIUS creates a common authentication system, which allows for centralized authentication and accounting.

The origins of RADIUS are from the original Internet service provider (ISP) dial-up days, as its acronym describes. Today, RADIUS is commonly used for authentication of virtual private networks (VPNs), wireless systems, and any network system that requires a common authentication system. RADIUS operates as a client-server protocol. The RADIUS server controls authentication, authorization, and accounting (AAA). The RADIUS client can be wireless access points, a VPN, or wired switches.

The RADIUS client will communicate with the RADIUS server via UDP port 1812 for authentication and UDP port 1813 for accounting. RADIUS is synonymous with the AAA security framework because it provides authentication, authorization, and accounting for users and computers.

Authentication.   The main purpose of the RADIUS server is to provide centralized authentication of users or computers. This can be performed by means of username and password, or authentication can be extended with MFA. We can even authorize computers based on their attributes, such as their MAC address. All of these authentication methods are dependent on the RADIUS installation.

Authorization.   Authorization of a user on a computer to allow a connection to a resource is based on the attributes returned after successful authorization. The returned attributes can be used by the authenticating application to configure the user account or computer with a VLAN, configure a connection type, or even enforce restrictions, just to name a few.

Accounting.   Accounting is performed by recording each transaction to the datastore configured with the RADIUS server. The key takeaway is that the RADIUS server accepts the RADIUS accounting packet and then stores the data.

The RADIUS server can be installed on many different operating systems, such as Linux and Windows. Microsoft Windows Server includes an installable feature, called the Network Policy Server (NPS), which provides RADIUS functionality. The authentication of users and computers is based on Active Directory. The authorization is based on the settings in the NPS. The accounting is directed to a logfile in the file system, but an account can also be configured for a Microsoft SQL database.

Terminal Access Controller Access Control System Plus

The *Terminal Access Controller Access-Control System Plus (TACACS+)* protocol is also an AAA method and an alternative to RADIUS. Like RADIUS, it is capable of performing authentication on behalf of multiple wireless APs, RRAS servers, or even LAN switches that are 802.1X capable. Based on its name, you would think it's an extension of the TACACS protocol (and in some ways it is), but the two definitely are not compatible.

Here are two major differences between TACACS+ and RADIUS:

- RADIUS combines user authentication and authorization into one profile, but TACACS+ separates the two.

- TACACS+ utilizes the connection-based TCP port 49, but RADIUS uses UDP instead.

Even though both are commonly used today, because of these two reasons TACACS+ is considered more stable and secure than RADIUS.

Figure 4.8 shows how TACACS+ works.

When a TACACS+ session is closed, the information in the following list is logged, or accounted for. This isn't a complete list; it's just meant to give you an idea of the type of accounting information TACACS+ gathers:

- Connection start time and stop time

- The number of bytes sent and received by the user

- The number of packets sent and received by the user

- The reason for the disconnection

FIGURE 4.8   TACACS+ login and logout sequence.

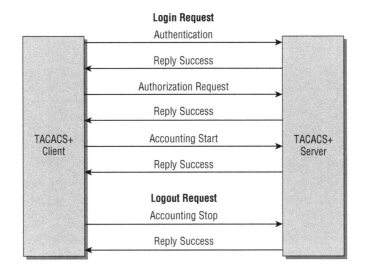

Configuration of AAA

This is where the rubber meets the road, so to speak. Let's configure the AAA model on a
Cisco router. Doing this will centralize the authentication, and it can even allow us to
authorize what an authenticated user can do!

Before we can use AAA on a Cisco router or switch, we need to type `aaa new-model`
to enable it. This is kind of amusing because the `new-model` command has been around
since 2006, so it isn't very new these days:

```
R01(config)#aaa new-model
```

Once AAA is enabled, we need to configure each of the "A's" individually. There are tons
of options here, so we will just focus on what we need to enable a login. The easiest way to
enable AAA authentication is with the `aaa authentication login default local`
command. This tells the router to use the local user database for authentication for everything:

```
R01(config)#aaa authentication login default local
```

Now that we have some basic commands configured, we can create a local user with the
command `username todd password supersecretpassword`:

```
R01(config)#username todd password supersecretpassword
```

We have successfully configured a local AAA server, but we still only have local authentication, which is where the chapter started. If we really want to harness the power of AAA, we need to configure an external RADIUS server. Once the RADIUS server is configured, we can then point our routers and switches to it, and we then have centralized logins.

There are a number of ways we can implement a RADIUS server. For example, we can install and configure a FreeRADIUS server inside a Linux distribution. However, a more popular option is to install the Microsoft feature called Network Policy Server (NPS). Using the Microsoft NPS will allow us to use Active Directory–based users to authenticate on the routers and switches. Don't worry, you can implement Windows groups to control who can authenticate on the routers and switches.

Let's examine the configuration for the router to use the RADIUS server for authentication. On the RADIUS server, we will need to create a client entry for the router. When we create the client entry, we will also be required to configure a shared secret password, as shown in Figure 4.9. This shared secret will also need to be configured on the router (client). The configuration will enable the router to authenticate before passing user authentication traffic.

We will start by configuring a server group called NPS_Servers with the command `aaa group server radius NPS_Servers`. This will place us in the `config-sg-radius` prompt where we will specify the RADIUS server along with the shared secret. with the command `server-private 172.16.1.8 auth-port 1812 acct-port 1813 key ToddPass`. You will notice we are configuring the authentication port of 1812 and the accounting port of 1813. If the RADIUS server is operating on different ports, we can substitute them in this command. We then specify the authentication for login to the group of NPS_Servers with a fallback of local authentication, just in case the RADIUS server is down. This is done with the command `aaa authentication login default group NPS_Servers local`. The last step is to set the exec mode (authorization) for anyone authenticated with the RADIUS server group of NPS_Servers, to include a fallback of local. This is configured with the command `aaa authorization exec default group NPS_Servers local if-authenticated`:

```
R01(config)#aaa group server radius NPS_Servers
R01(config-sg-radius)#server-private 172.16.1.8 auth-port 1812
acct-port 1813 key ToddPass
R01(config)#aaa authentication login default group NPS_Servers local
R01(config)#aaa authorization exec default group NPS_Servers local if-
authenticated
```

There are many other configurations we can perform with RADIUS servers for Cisco routers and switches, but this is the basic configuration you should know for the exam. You should also be able to apply the basic concepts of AAA to routers and switches as we just learned.

FIGURE 4.9   NPS client.

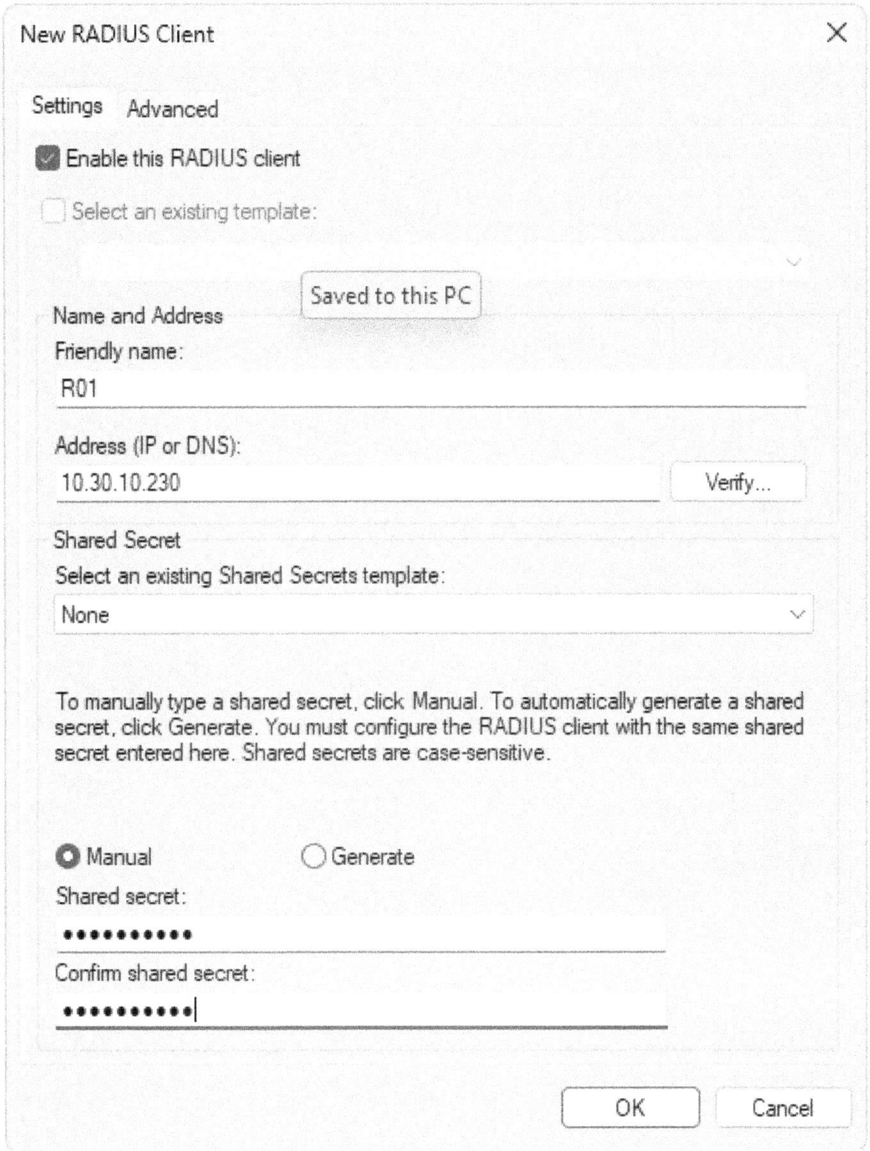

New RADIUS Client   ✕

Settings   Advanced

☑ Enable this RADIUS client

☐ Select an existing template:

Name and Address   ┌─────────────────────┐
                                    │ Saved to this PC   │
Friendly name: └─────────────────────┘

R01

Address (IP or DNS):

10.30.10.230   Verify…

Shared Secret
Select an existing Shared Secrets template:

None   ⌄

To manually type a shared secret, click Manual. To automatically generate a shared
secret, click Generate. You must configure the RADIUS client with the same shared
secret entered here. Shared secrets are case-sensitive.

◉ Manual   ○ Generate

Shared secret:

••••••••••

Confirm shared secret:

••••••••••|

                                            OK   Cancel

RADIUS Login Process

Now that we understand the AAA model and configuration of the AAA model on routers and switches, let's examine the overall login process. The following will explain the flow of logging into a router or switch that uses a RADIUS server, as shown in Figure 4.10.

The router forwards the authentication request to the RADIUS server using UDP port 1812.

The RADIUS server receives the request and makes sure the router is defined as a client in the server configuration by matching the IP that sent the request and seeing whether the router is using the proper shared secret.

Assuming the client matches, the RADIUS server looks at its policy to determine whether the user is allowed to connect. Figure 4.11 shows a typical NPS policy. The gist of the policy is that it will allow connections if the user is in a Windows Active Directory group called "Net Admins."

If the client is authorized to authenticate, then the user's username and password are checked against Active Directory.

The RADIUS server sends back a "pass" or "fail" to the router.

If the router receives a pass, then it allows the connection.

Like many things we cover in this book, RADIUS can be a pretty complex subject with endless options. However, these basic concepts are what will be on the exam.

> Setup and configuration of the RADIUS server is way outside the objectives for the exam. You can learn more about setup and configuration of the NPS at the link `https://learn.microsoft.com/en-us/windows-server/networking/technologies/nps/nps-top`.

FIGURE 4.10 RADIUS flow.

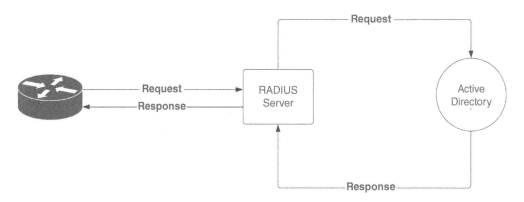

FIGURE 4.11 NPS policy.

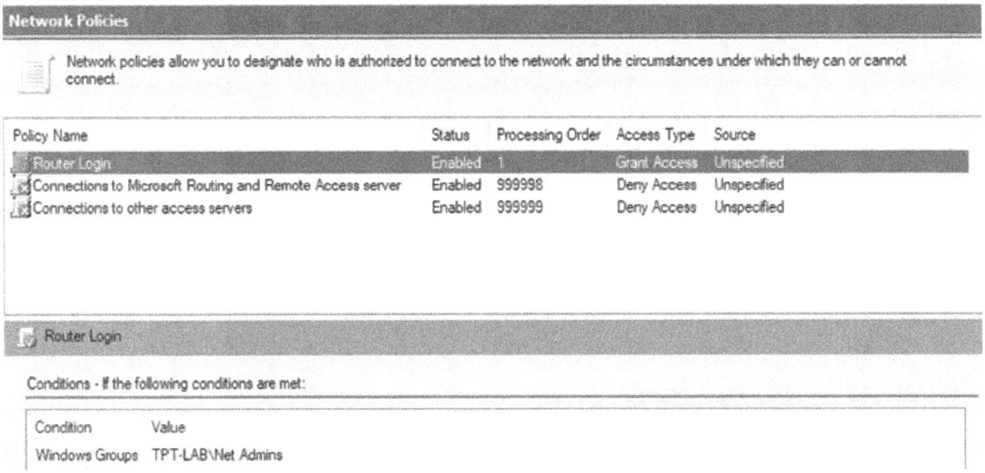

Password Policies

If you recall our local authentication example, we created a user called "todd" with the frankly terrible password "1234." Although it may be easy for Todd to remember, it is about as insecure as possible. One of the ways we can prevent bad passwords is to create a password policy.

A password policy is simply a series of rules that define what is an acceptable password in your network. The exact rules you can define will depend on what solution you are using to make your policy: for example, Microsoft AD will have different options than Cisco Identity Services Engine (ISE). Some common rules can include:

- Minimum password length
- Require uppercase characters
- Require lowercase characters
- Require numbers
- Require symbol characters
- Disallow repeating characters
- Disallow sequential characters
- Disallow common words

Password best practices change from time to time, but generally they always move in the direction of being more complex. Microsoft tends to recommend a minimum password length of eight characters and using a mixed set of characters, but certain solutions will make you set a password that is at least 12 characters.

It may be tempting to say that all users need to have a 50-character password at your company, but you will quickly have an angry mob outside your office if you try to implement such a policy. It can take a lot of time and effort to find a happy balance between secure passwords and not being murdered by the company receptionist.

Aside from controlling what passwords are allowed, password policies also let you set how long before a password expires. After all, even secure passwords need to be changed to reduce the risk of them being compromised. Typically, most organizations set passwords to expire somewhere between every one and two months.

Account Lockout Policy

Configure user account settings to limit the number of login attempts before the account is locked for a period of time. Legitimate users who need to get in before the block expires can contact the administrator and explain why they weren't able to give the right password three times in a row, and non-legitimate users will go away in search of another system to try to enter.

When choosing the number of failed attempts, you need to consider the number of calls you get to the help desk versus the security in having few failed attempts before lockout. You'll find that when you set it to three failed attempts, the help desk will get more calls than necessary, but it allows for better security. Setting the number of failed login attempts to five may be better for users, because many users realize after the third failed attempt that their Caps Lock key was on, but it's less secure than three failed attempts. This setting needs to be evaluated against your security requirement and help desk volume.

You should also consider the length of the lockout. If it's a Monday morning and a person enters their password wrong X number of times and gets locked out, five minutes might be appropriate. The time it takes to get a cup of coffee and unlock might be just enough time on a Monday morning to allow the user to wake up. You can specify these settings for an entire domain, as shown in Figure 4.12. As shown here, the user will be locked out for 30 minutes after three failed attempts. By default, there is no account lockout policy set for a domain.

If a password attack is being executed, having no protection could easily allow millions of password attempts. By setting a failed login attempt counter and a lockout duration, you slow the progress of the attack.

FIGURE 4.12   Account lockout policy settings.

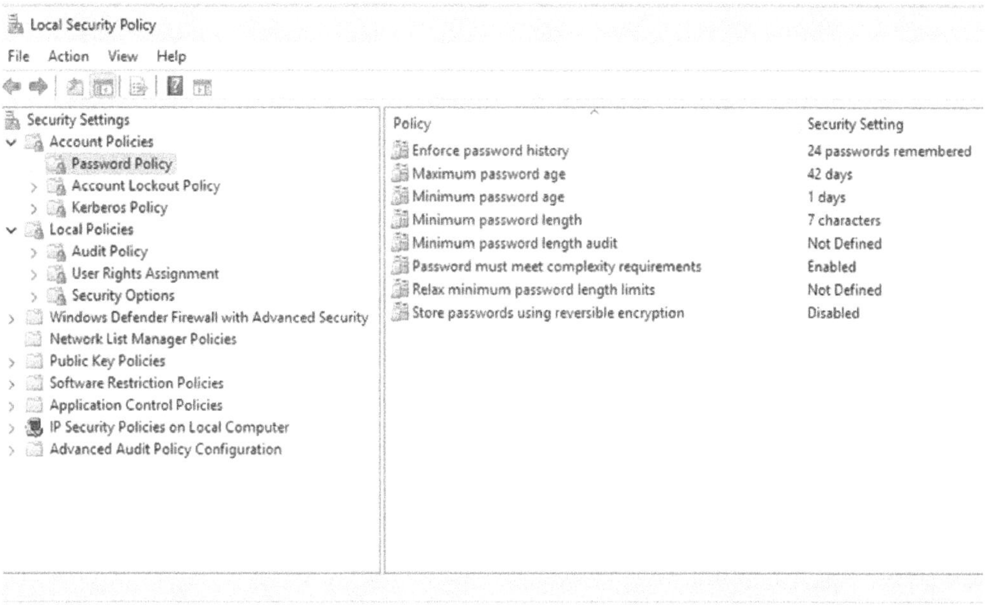

NAC Overview

Network access control (NAC) can be viewed as a simple RADIUS server's big brother. I like to refer to NAC solutions as a Swiss Army Knife for user identity. They provide a ton of features that are geared around identifying users and determining what they are allowed to access on the network. Earlier in the chapter, I mentioned that Cisco ISE is Cisco's RADIUS server, but it is really a powerful NAC solution.

You can think of Cisco ISE having two parts; the first part can be used to provide access for you to administrate your network devices, and the other part focuses on providing access to your users so they can use the network.

Aside from RADIUS, the other device administration option is called Terminal Access Controller Access Control System (TACACS), or just TACACS for short. As an added wrinkle, the Cisco version of TACACS is called TACACS+ because Cisco made some enhancements to the protocol.

We don't need to understand the protocol for the CCST, but the main difference is it has better support for the authorization part of AAA when it comes to device management.

Deploying it in your network is really complicated and can take a lot of effort to implement properly, although Cisco ISE provides several workflows that help you navigate most of the features that you might encounter during implementation.

For example, we could make a policy that only allows certain printers to get online, or we can say you can only access the internal network if your computer's antimalware is up to date. Just to keep things moving along, let's talk through the basic steps for a computer getting online with a wired Ethernet connection.

802.1X

802.1X is an IEEE standard that's used to identify and authorize a user before they are allowed access to the network. 802.1X is used for both wired and wireless network access. When you are using 802.1X with a wired connection, the physical port allows communications of 802.1X credentials. The port will not allow user traffic to be switched until the AAA process is completed and the user or computer is verified.

Think of 802.1X as the mechanism to control the port or wireless association on the switch or wireless access point, respectively. 802.1X still requires a source of authentication, authorization, and accounting too, to complete the AAA model. Therefore, 802.1X can be set up with a RADIUS or TACACS+ server.

If you are following along in this chapter, you probably started putting the boxes together, so to speak. Yes, you can configure 802.1X on a router, switch, or wireless access point with a Microsoft NPS (RADIUS) server. This is actually a very basic configuration and really does nothing more than keep strangers off your network. It does not stop someone from introducing a computer infested with malware into your network. This is where NAC really come in handy. There are many other features, as we will learn.

If we use 802.1X in conjunction with Cisco ISE (NAC) to provide the AAA model, we can then prevent a malicious intent. For example, if a threat actor gets into a company office and manages to plug their laptop into a free Ethernet jack, they won't be able to get anywhere because Cisco ISE will stop the connection until the bad guy can provide the proper credentials to log in to the network. This is often referred to as port-based network access control (PNAC).

802.1X Components

There are three main components of 802.1X that you should be aware of for this exam. A supplicant is some software that lives in a user's device OS, which can be either a native OS feature or a third-party solution such as Cisco Secure Client that is installed on the computer or phone. The authenticator is the network device, and the authentication server is Cisco ISE (NAC), as shown in Figure 4.13.

The job of the supplicant is to collect the device and user credentials on the computer so it can be used for the 802.1X session. Authentication can be done using the computer or user credentials. The consideration when using user authentication is that if you only use the user authentication, the computer will be kicked off the network anytime you aren't logged in. This would mean your computer wouldn't be able to get any patches or necessary updates after hours, and would just be a pain in general. Because of this, we also authenticate the computer so that it always stays online.

FIGURE 4.13 802.1X components.

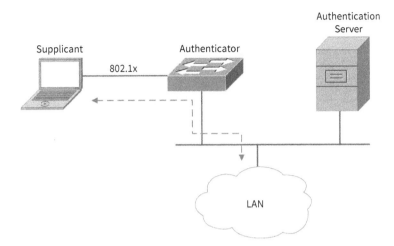

The way this works is that the computer authentication is used when no one is logged in to the computer, and the user authentication is used once someone logs in. You can use both at the same time for extra security if you install the Cisco Secure Client, although a lot of companies stick with the native supplicant to save costs because Secure Client can get expensive if you need to buy it for everyone who uses your network.

If the computer is joined to Active Directory, the supplicant can seamlessly grab the credentials and send them upward to the next component, called the authenticator. It can also prompt the user to enter their username and password, or even use a certificate structure.

The authenticator is just a fancy name for the switchport that the computer is connected to that is configured to do 802.1X. In the case of a wireless connection, the authenticator would be either the access point or the wireless LAN controller, depending on how the wireless network is set up.

The switch will then use RADIUS to contact the Cisco ISE server, which we call the Authentication Server in this context. Finally, ISE will check its policy and decide whether the user is allowed network access or not.

NAC Process

We covered a lot there, so let's quickly recap the steps for a wired Ethernet connection to get online in an 802.1X environment:

1. When a user starts a wired connection, software on their device called a supplicant passes their credentials and/or a certificate over to the switchport it is connected to.

2. The switch is referred to as the authenticator because the switch will send the information over to the authentication server via RADIUS. Authentication server is another name for a NAC, which is Cisco ISE in this example.

3. Cisco ISE will then make sure the request came from a switch it knows about by matching the IP the request came from and checking the shared secret.

4. ISE will then check the authentication policy to see whether the connection is allowed.

5. Finally, ISE will check the authorization policy to determine what the user is allowed to access and send the response back to the authenticator, which then permits the supplicant.

A wireless connection will be similar except it will be using either the access point or the wireless LAN controller for the authenticator instead of a switchport.

Profiling

Profiling is the ability for Cisco ISE to identify endpoints on your network. It does this by matching traffic against several attributes such as MAC address organizationally unique identifiers (OUIs), IP address ranges, Cisco Discovery Protocol (CDP) or Link Layer Discovery Protocol (LLDP) information, and other attributes gleaned from other services. You can create your own profiler rules as needed, but otherwise Cisco ISE ships with 800 built-in ones to get you started. Figure 4.14 shows a policy for an Apple iPhone.

Posturing

Posturing allows you to set criteria for when a device is allowed on the network. It also allows users to automatically remediate their computer if they don't meet the requirements. For example, you can require that their firewall is enabled; if it is not, then you will automatically restrict full network access. This will force the user to turn on the firewall to regain full network access. Figure 4.15 shows a posturing policy that needs an anti-malware solution to be installed on a Windows computer. This is a popular requirement; if someone does not have anti-malware up to date, you can require that they remediate the anti-malware software before they enter into the network.

Bring Your Own Device (BYOD)

The traditional workforce is very quickly becoming a mobile workforce, with employees working from home, on the go, and in the office. Mobile devices such as laptops, tablets, and smartphones are used by employees to connect to the organization's resources.

Bring your own device (BYOD) has been embraced as a strategy by organizations to alleviate the capital expense of equipment by allowing employees to use devices they already own.

The various devices that employees bring into the network are often outside of the organization's control. These devices can pose a severe risk to the network. For this reason, the BYOD network should be segmented from the operational network, and NAC is a great method to achieve this!

FIGURE 4.14   ISE profiling policy.

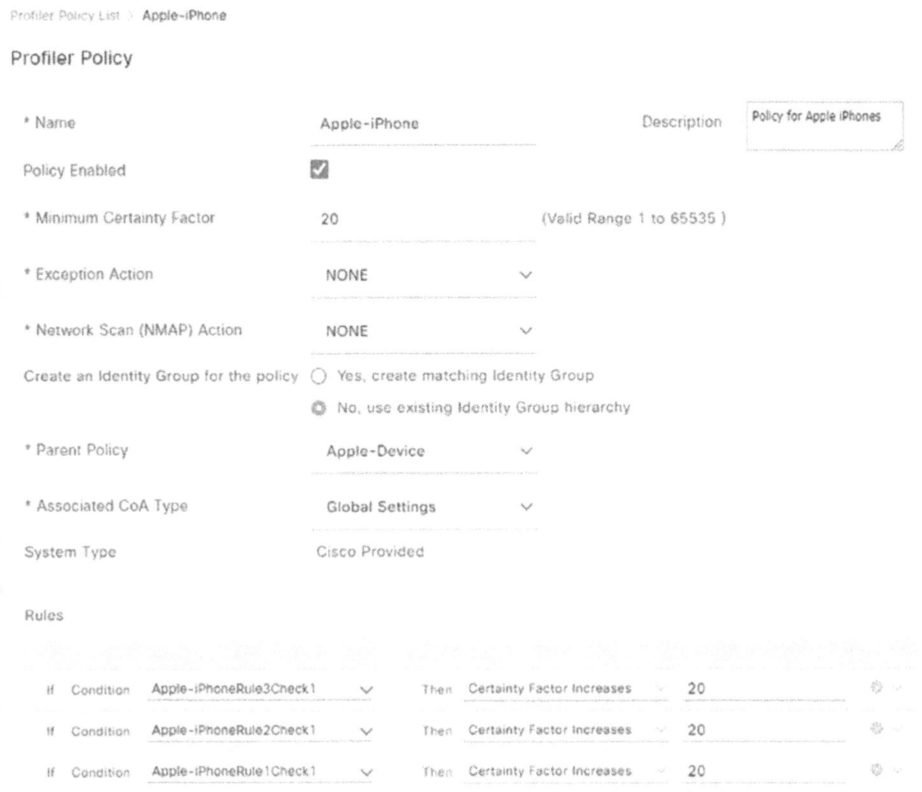

Profiler Policy List > Apple-iPhone

Profiler Policy

* Name	Apple-iPhone	Description	Policy for Apple iPhones
Policy Enabled	☑		
* Minimum Certainty Factor	20	(Valid Range 1 to 65535)	
* Exception Action	NONE ⌄		
* Network Scan (NMAP) Action	NONE ⌄		
Create an Identity Group for the policy	◯ Yes, create matching Identity Group		
	◉ No, use existing Identity Group hierarchy		
* Parent Policy	Apple-Device ⌄		
* Associated CoA Type	Global Settings ⌄		
System Type	Cisco Provided		

Rules

If	Condition	Apple-iPhoneRule3Check1 ⌄	Then	Certainty Factor Increases ⌄	20	⚙ ⌄
If	Condition	Apple-iPhoneRule2Check1 ⌄	Then	Certainty Factor Increases ⌄	20	⚙ ⌄
If	Condition	Apple-iPhoneRule1Check1 ⌄	Then	Certainty Factor Increases ⌄	20	⚙ ⌄

There are pros and cons to this from a security perspective, but it can be cheaper in the long run to give each employee a budget to buy their own computer rather than supplying one and dealing with all the maintenance and support.

Cisco ISE allows users to register their laptops on their own. In a perfect world, users can get themselves online without any IT support help. That never happens, but it is a nice thought.

Guest Network Isolation

Most guests in your network never need to connect to the organization's servers and internal systems. When guests connect to your wireless network, it is usually just to get connectivity to the Internet. Therefore, a guest service set identifier (SSID) should be created that isolates guest traffic from production traffic. These guest network SSIDs are usually created by default on consumer wireless devices. On enterprise wireless LAN controllers, the guest network typically needs to be created.

FIGURE 4.15   Malware posture rule.

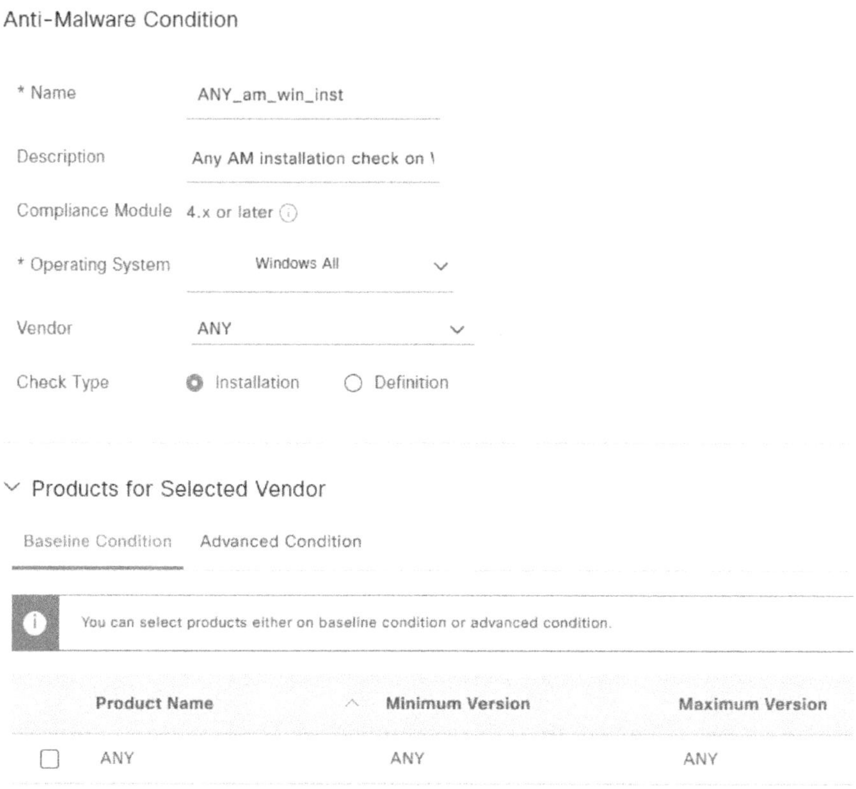

Anti-Malware Condition

* Name	ANY_am_win_inst
Description	Any AM installation check on \
Compliance Module	4.x or later ⓘ
* Operating System	Windows All ⌄
Vendor	ANY ⌄
Check Type	● Installation ○ Definition

⌄ Products for Selected Vendor

Baseline Condition   Advanced Condition

ⓘ   You can select products either on baseline condition or advanced condition.

Product Name ∧	Minimum Version	Maximum Version
☐ ANY	ANY	ANY

Some considerations for the guest network are what is open to guests, how long they have access, how much bandwidth, SSID name—the list goes on, depending on your organization. Guest networks usually don't give totally unrestricted Internet access; certain sensitive ports such as TCP 25 SMTP are normally blocked. The length of time they have access is another concern. Generally, a guest is just that: a guest. So 4 hours, 8 hours, or 24 hours of access seem responsible. This needs to be thought through, as too short a time will create administrative overhead and too long a window of access allows for abuse of service.

Captive Portal

A *captive portal* is a method of redirecting users who connect to wireless or wired systems to a portal for login or agreement to the acceptable use policy (AUP). Using a captive portal is common for guest networks. More than likely, if you have stayed in a hotel that offers wireless, you have been redirected to the captive portal to accept the terms. Some hotels require you to purchase the wireless service; this type of service would also redirect you to the portal for login or payment. Captive portals are not exclusively used for hotels; they are also used for corporate access to an organization's wireless system.

Summary

We started the chapter learning local authentication for Cisco switches and routers. The considerations of scalability became apparent very quickly. We then examined the AAA model of authentication, authorization, and accounting. This provided us a solid foundation for centralized authentication of user accounts.

As we learned each element of the AAA model, we applied real-world applications to each of them. These real-world applications, such as IAM, might not be on the exam, but they provide a clearer picture of how the AAA model is implemented.

We then learned how to configure the AAA model on Cisco routers and switches via command line. We again, applied our knowledge in the prior section to each element of the configuration. We followed up with a complete understanding of the AAA process to cement our knowledge further.

We then learned about the importance of password policies in relation to security. We looked at how the Windows operating system implements certain control for password complexity. In addition, we learned about account lockout policies and how Windows implements controls.

The next major building block we learned in relation to network device access was Network Access Control (NAC). We learned about the importance of controlling access and contrasted the importance of only allowing secure devices. We then examined the systems used with NAC, such as 802.1X, and how the AAA model is applied to 802.1X. We then rounded our knowledge with understanding some of the controls inside the Cisco ISE NAC, such as profiling and posturing of clients and computers.

We then applied our knowledge to transient systems such as BYOD devices. We examined guest network isolation and its importance for security, which further cemented our newly learn knowledge. We also examined the guest user experience with a captive portal.

Exam Essentials

Identify common authentication methods.   These include multifactor methods, Terminal Access Controller Access-Control System Plus (TACACS+), single sign-on (SSO), Remote Authentication Dial-In User Service (RADIUS), multifactor authentication (MFA), including email, hard tokens, soft tokens, short message service (SMS), voice calls, and authenticator applications as factors of authentication.

Understand the various authorization concepts.   Identity and Access Management (IAM) is a security framework. The principle of least privilege defines that an employee is only given the access required to perform their duties. Role-based access is the technique of combining privileges together for common roles in an organization.

Understand how the AAA model is configured.   You should be familiar with the steps to configure the AAA model on Cisco router and switches. You should also understand the various configuration elements and how they apply to the AAA model.

Understand the need for good passwords.   Passwords are the first line of defense for protecting an account. A password should be required for every account, and strong passwords should be enforced. Users need to understand the basics of password security and work to keep their accounts protected by following company policies regarding passwords.

Know the various techniques of implementing network access control.   802.1X, NAC, and Cisco ISE are just a few of the many tactics used for network segmentation covered in this chapter. You should review the various techniques listed in this chapter.

Review Questions

 The following questions are designed to test your understanding of this chapter's material. For more information on how to get additional questions, please see www.lammle.com/ccst.

You can find the answers to these questions in Appendix.

1. The Cisco ISE system is an example of?
   A. NAC
   B. 802.1X
   C. Authenticator
   D. IAM

2. You are implementing a public guest wireless network and require that users accept an acceptable use policy (AUP). What should you implement to accomplish the goal?
   A. ACLs
   B. MAC filtering
   C. Captive portal
   D. 802.1X

3. Which security concept dictates that a user be given only the permission to perform their job?
   A. Zero trust
   B. Role-based access
   C. Least privilege
   D. Defense in depth

4. Which authentication system is an open standard originally proposed by the Internet Engineering Task Force (IETF)?
   A. RADIUS
   B. TACACS+
   C. ISE
   D. IAM

5. Which protocol and port number does RADIUS use for accounting?
   A. TCP/1812
   B. TCP/1813
   C. UDP/1812
   D. UDP/1813

6. Which factor of authentication requires you to present something that is unique to you and can't be copied?

  A. Password

  B. Signature

  C. Fingerprint

  D. Location

7. You are designing a security strategy for a cloud-based application. You want to make it simple for other administrators to grant permissions without complexity. Which security strategy should you implement?

  A. TACACS+

  B. PKI

  C. RBAC

  D. RADIUS

8. Why should you always provide a second method of local authentication when setting up AAA remote authentication with a router or switch?

  A. To allow for a backdoor.

  B. To provide a backup if the RADIUS server is down or unreachable.

  C. The local second method is required.

  D. All of the above.

9. You want all guests to register for wireless Internet access before granting them access. What should you implement?

  A. Captive portal

  B. AAA server

  C. 801.X

  D. RBAC

10. Which port must be open to the RADIUS or AAA server for authentication from the authenticator?

  A. UDP/49

  B. UDP/1821

  C. UDP/1812

  D. UDP/1813

Chapter

5

Secure Access Technology

THE FOLLOWING CCST EXAM TOPIC IS COVERED IN THIS CHAPTER:

✔ **1.0 Standards and Concepts**

  ▪ 1.4. Explain encryption methods and applications.

    Types of encryption, hashing, certificates, public key infrastructure (PKI); strong vs. weak encryption algorithms; states of data and appropriate encryption (data in transit, data at rest, data in use); protocols that use encryption

  ▪ 2.5. Implement secure access technologies: ACL, firewall, VPN, NAC

A large part of cybersecurity is making sure users can safely access company resources that they are allowed to, while also preventing them from accessing areas of the network they aren't. In this chapter, you'll learn some smart solutions that will help you securely access company resources.

We'll start by introducing how to filter traffic with access control lists (ACLs) on routers, and then we'll discuss how newer firewalls handle the job. From there we will get into how encryption and public key infrastructure (PKI) can help keep our data safe.

Finally, we'll dive deep into how these networks utilize IP security to provide secure communications over a public network via the Internet using VPNs with IPSec.

To find your included bonus material, as well as Todd Lammle videos, practice questions, and hands-on labs, please see www.lammle.com/ ccst.

Access Control Lists

Access control lists are one of the most common ways of securing access to resources because they are simple to use once you understand them, and they are decently effective at keeping the bad guys out.

If you have ever been to a nightclub on a Friday night, you can think of an ACL as the bouncer who decides who is and isn't allowed to skip the line. Typically, the bouncer will have a list of names on a clipboard, and if your name is on it then, welcome in! If not, then you had better go to a less picky establishment to party. An ACL on a Cisco device works in a similar way, only instead of matching someone's name, it is usually matching IP addresses or subnets instead.

You might have noticed there is a flaw in my scenario—wouldn't someone who guesses a name on the bouncer's list gain entry? Yes, they would! Basic ACLs are the same way; if a request comes from a network that is permitted, then there is no further inspection, but we'll talk about some more modern ways to handle that as we progress through the chapter.

A common mistake that juniors make is assuming that that ACLs are always used for security purposes, but ACLs are really used in dozens of features inside of Cisco IOS and many other platforms. Anytime you need to match traffic for some reason, ACLs are usually a good candidate. It is really the configuration that calls the ACL that determines whether it is a security feature or not. Saying that, this is a cybersecurity book, so when we talk about ACLs, we are going to mean security ACLs, which are used to block traffic.

An ACL at its core is just a list of statements that are pretty much like if-then statements in programming or scripting languages. If a statement matches, then some kind of action, typically **permit** or **deny,** will happen. If nothing matches, the ACL skips to the next line until it either finds a match or hits the implicit rule at the bottom that will simply apply a deny action to everything.

To reiterate, each statement will either match or not match a condition, and then each condition will typically have a permit or deny action. At the bottom of every ACL is an implicit deny statement that will ensure that anything that isn't matched is blocked.

There are three important rules that you must keep in mind when working with ACLs—not just on Cisco devices, but also on every other vendor device, because they all follow the same rules, whether it's Palo Alto or Cisco Secure Firewall.

The rules are:

- ACLs are always evaluated one line at a time and always in a top-down fashion. This means that when a packet hits an ACL, the router or firewall starts at the first line and works its way down to the last one.

- ACLs only evaluate traffic until the first match; then the action is applied. This means that if a packet matches on the first line of a 100-line ACL, the other 99 lines are never looked at.

- There is an "implicit deny" at the end of the ACL that will silently block all traffic that hits it. This can cause you *a lot* of headaches if you aren't careful when working with ACLs.

Each of these rules has some powerful ramifications when filtering IP packets with access lists, so keep in mind that creating effective ACLs takes some practice!

There are two main types of access lists:

Standard Access Lists.   These ACLs use only the source IP address in an IP packet as the condition test. All decisions are made based on the source IP address. This means that standard access lists basically permit or deny an entire suite of protocols. They don't distinguish between any of the many types of IP traffic such as web, Telnet, or UDP.

Extended Access Lists.   Extended access lists can evaluate many of the other fields in the layer-3 and layer-4 headers of an IP packet. They can evaluate source and destination IP addresses, the protocol field in the network layer header, and the port number at the transport layer header. This gives extended access lists the ability to make much more granular decisions when controlling traffic.

In the old days, when we had to use specific number ranges to create ACLs, we used

- Standard: 1–99 or 1300–1999

- Extended: 100–199 or 2000–2699

If you need a reference, you can always do "**access-list ?**" in a Cisco device's config mode, and the device will happily give you all the ranges you can use for particular kinds of ACLs, although we are just interested in standard and extended:

```
DC1-SW01(config)#access-list ?
  <1-99>             IP standard access list
  <100-199>          IP extended access list
  <1100-1199>        Extended 48-bit MAC address access list
  <1300-1999>        IP standard access list (expanded range)
  <200-299>          Protocol type-code access list
  <2000-2699>        IP extended access list (expanded range)
  <2700-2799>        MPLS access list
  <300-399>          DECnet access list
  <600-699>          Appletalk access list
  <700-799>          48-bit MAC address access list
  dynamic-extended   Extend the dynamic ACL absolute timer
  rate-limit         Simple rate-limit specific access list
```

But fortunately, we have named ACLs these days that let us specify a meaningful name for our ACL instead of trying to remember what access list 2594 does. Fun fact: numbered ACLs are really named ACLs in modern IOS, which means we don't have to worry about some of the pitfalls we used to have to deal with. We aren't going to get into how to use named ACLs in this book, but just be aware they exist.

Before we dive into how to create an ACL, we need to talk about where to apply it; an ACL won't do anything until we add it to an interface and specify a direction. Just like how the order of the ACL matters, the direction we apply it also has an impact on how traffic will be inspected.

Inbound Access Lists.   When an access list is applied to inbound packets on an interface, those packets are processed through the access list before being routed to an outbound interface. Any packets that are denied won't be routed because they're discarded before the routing process is invoked.

Outbound Access Lists.   When an access list is applied to outbound packets on an interface, packets are routed to the outbound interface and then processed through the access list before being queued.

There are some general access-list guidelines that you should keep in mind when creating and implementing access lists on a router:

- You can assign only one access list per interface, per protocol, per direction. This means that when applying IP access lists, you can have only one inbound access list and one outbound access list per interface.

- Organize your access lists so that the more specific tests are at the top.

- Unless your access list ends with a `permit` any command, all packets will be discarded if they do not meet any of the list's tests. This means every list should have at least one `permit` statement or it will deny all traffic.

- Place IP standard access lists as close to the destination as possible. This is the reason we don't really want to use standard access lists in our networks. You can't put a standard access list close to the source host or network because you can only filter based on source address, and all destinations would be affected as a result.

- Place IP extended access lists as close to the source as possible. Because extended access lists can filter on very specific addresses and protocols, you don't want traffic to traverse the entire network just to be denied. By placing this list as close to the source address as possible, you can filter traffic before it uses up precious bandwidth.

Standard Access Lists

Standard IP access lists filter network traffic by examining the source IP address in a packet. You create a *standard IP access list* by using the access-list numbers 1–99 or numbers in the expanded range of 1300–1999 because the type of ACL is generally differentiated numerically. Based on the number used when the access list is created, the router knows which type of syntax to expect as the list is entered. By using numbers 1–99 or 1300–1999, you're telling the router that you want to create a standard IP access list, so the router will expect syntax specifying only the source IP address in the test lines.

The following output displays a good example of the many access-list number ranges that you can use to filter traffic on your network. The IOS version delimits the protocols you can specify access for:

```
Corp(config)#access-list ?
<1-99> IP standard access list
<100-199> IP extended access list
<1000-1099> IPX SAP access list
<1100-1199> Extended 48-bit MAC address access list
<1200-1299> IPX summary address access list
<1300-1999> IP standard access list (expanded range)
<200-299> Protocol type-code access list
<2000-2699> IP extended access list (expanded range)
<2700-2799> MPLS access list
<300-399> DECnet access list
<700-799> 48-bit MAC address access list
<800-899> IPX standard access list
<900-999> IPX extended access list
dynamic-extended Extend the dynamic ACL absolute timer
rate-limit Simple rate-limit specific access list
```

Wow—there sure are a whole lot of old protocols listed in that output! IPX and DECnet would no longer be used in any of today's networks. Let's take a look at the syntax used when creating a standard IP access list:

```
Corp(config)#access-list 10 ?
deny Specify packets to reject
permit Specify packets to forward
remark Access list entry comment
```

As I said, by using the access-list numbers 1–99 or 1300–1999, you're telling the router that you want to create a standard IP access list, which means you can only filter on source IP address.

Once you've chosen the access-list number, you need to decide whether you're creating a `permit` or deny statement. I'm going to create a deny statement now:

```
Corp(config)#access-list 10 deny ?
Hostname or A.B.C.D Address to match
any Any source host
host A single host address
```

The next step is more detailed because there are three options available in it:

1. The first option is the any parameter, used to permit or deny any source host or network.
2. The second choice is to use an IP address to specify either a single host or a range of them.
3. The last option is to use the `host` command to specify a specific host only.

The any command is pretty obvious—any source address matches the statement, so every packet compared against this line will match. The `host` command is relatively simple too, as you can see here:

```
Corp(config)#access-list 10 deny host ?
Hostname or A.B.C.D Host address
Corp(config)#access-list 10 deny host 172.16.30.2
```

This tells the list to deny any packets from host 172.16.30.2. The default parameter is `host`. In other words, if you type **access-list 10 deny 172.16.30.2**, the router assumes you mean host 172.16.30.2, and that's exactly how it will show in your running-config.

But there's another way to specify either a particular host or a range of hosts known as wildcard masking. In fact, to specify any range of hosts, you must use wildcard masking in the access list.

So exactly what is wildcard masking? Coming up, I'm going to show you using a standard access list example. I'll also guide you through how to control access to a virtual terminal.

Wildcard Masking

Wildcards are used with access lists to specify an individual host, a network, or a specific range of a network or networks. The block sizes you learned about earlier used to specify a range of addresses are key to understanding wildcards.

So let's do a quick review of block sizes before we go any further. I'm sure you remember that the different block sizes available are 64, 32, 16, 8, and 4. When you need to specify a range of addresses, you choose the next-largest block size for your needs. So if you need to specify 34 networks, you need a block size of 64. If you want to specify 18 hosts, you need a block size of 32. If you specify only 2 networks, then go with a block size of 4.

Wildcards are used with the host or network address to tell the router a range of available addresses to filter. To specify a host, the address would look like this:

```
172.16.30.5 0.0.0.0
```

The four zeros represent each octet of the address. Whenever a zero is present, it indicates that the octet in the address must match the corresponding reference octet exactly. To specify that an octet can be any value, use the value 255. Here's an example of how a /24 subnet is specified with a wildcard mask:

```
172.16.30.0 0.0.0.255
```

This tells the router to match up the first three octets exactly, but the fourth octet can be any value.

Okay—that was the easy part. But what if you want to specify only a small range of subnets? This is where block sizes come in. You have to specify the range of values in a block size, so you can't choose to specify 20 networks. You can only specify the exact number that the block size value allows. This means that the range would have to be either 16 or 32, but not 20.

Let's say that you want to block access to the part of the network that ranges from 172.16.8.0 through 172.16.15.0. To do that, you would go with a block size of 8, your network number would be 172.16.8.0, and the wildcard would be 0.0.7.255. The 7.255 equals the value the router will use to determine the block size. So together, the network number and the wildcard tell the router to begin at 172.16.8.0 and go up a block size of eight addresses to network 172.16.15.0.

This really is easier than it looks! I could certainly go through the binary math for you, but no one needs that kind of pain because all you have to do is remember that the wildcard is always one number less than the block size. So, in our example, the wildcard would be 7 because our block size is 8. If you used a block size of 16, the wildcard would be 15. Easy, right?

Just to help you understand this, we'll go through some examples to be sure. The following one tells the router to match the first three octets exactly, but that the fourth octet can be anything:

```
Corp(config)#access-list 10 deny 172.16.10.0 0.0.0.255
```

The next example tells the router to match the first two octets and that the last two octets can be any value:

```
Corp(config)#access-list 10 deny 172.16.0.0 0.0.255.255
```

Now, try to figure out this next line:

```
Corp(config)#access-list 10 deny 172.16.16.0 0.0.3.255
```

This configuration tells the router to start at network 172.16.16.0 and use a block size of 4. The range would then be 172.16.16.0 through 172.16.19.255, and by the way, the Cisco objectives seem to really like this one!

Let's keep practicing. What about this next one?

```
Corp(config)#access-list 10 deny 172.16.16.0 0.0.7.255
```

This example reveals an access list starting at 172.16.16.0 going up a block size of 8 to 172.16.23.255.

Let's keep at it. What do you think the range of this one is?

```
Corp(config)#access-list 10 deny 172.16.32.0 0.0.15.255
```

This one begins at network 172.16.32.0 and goes up a block size of 16 to 172.16.47.255. You're almost done—after a couple more, we'll configure some real ACLs:

```
Corp(config)#access-list 10 deny 172.16.64.0 0.0.63.255
```

This example starts at network 172.16.64.0 and goes up a block size of 64 to 172.16.127.255.

What about this last example?

```
Corp(config)#access-list 10 deny 192.168.160.0 0.0.31.255
```

This one shows us that it begins at network 192.168.160.0 and goes up a block size of 32 to 192.168.191.255.

Here are two more things to keep in mind when working with block sizes and wildcards:

- Each block size must start at 0 or a multiple of the block size. For example, you can't say that you want a block size of 8 and then start at 12. You must use 0–7, 8–15, 16–23, etc. For a block size of 32, the ranges are 0–31, 32–63, 64–95, etc.

- The command any is the same thing as writing out the wildcard 0.0.0.0 255.255.255.255.

Wildcard masking is a crucial skill to master when creating IP access lists. It's the same whether you're creating standard or extended IP access lists.

Extended Access Lists

Let's say that you must now allow Sales to gain access to a certain server on the Finance LAN but not to other network services on that LAN for security reasons. Using Figure 5.1, what's the solution?

FIGURE 5.1 Sales to Finance ACL.

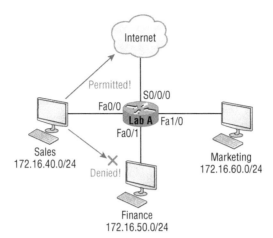

Applying a standard IP access list won't allow users to get to one network service but not another because a standard ACL won't allow you to make decisions based on both source and destination addresses. It makes decisions based only on source address, so we need another way to achieve our new goal—but what is it?

Using an *extended access list* will save the day because extended ACLs allow us to specify source and destination addresses as well as the protocol and port number, which identify the upper-layer protocol or application. An extended ACL is just what we need to effectively allow users access to a physical LAN while denying them access to specific hosts—even specific services on those hosts!

We're going to take a look at the commands we have in our arsenal, but first, you need to know that you must use the extended access-list range from 100 to 199. The 2000–2699 range is also available for extended IP access lists.

After choosing a number in the extended range, you need to decide what type of list entry to make. For this example, I'm going with a deny list entry:

```
Corp(config)#access-list 110 ?
deny Specify packets to reject
dynamic Specify a DYNAMIC list of PERMITs or DENYs
permit Specify packets to forward
remark Access list entry comment
```

And once you've settled on the type of ACL, you need to then select a protocol field entry:

```
Corp(config)#access-list 110 deny ?
<0-255> An IP protocol number
ahp Authentication Header Protocol
eigrp Cisco's EIGRP routing protocol
esp Encapsulation Security Payload
```

```
gre Cisco's GRE tunneling
icmp Internet Control Message Protocol
igmp Internet Gateway Message Protocol
ip Any Internet Protocol
ipinip IP in IP tunneling
nos KA9Q NOS compatible IP over IP tunneling
ospf OSPF routing protocol
pcp Payload Compression Protocol
pim Protocol Independent Multicast
tcp Transmission Control Protocol
udp User Datagram Protocol
```

If you want to filter by application layer protocol, you have to choose the appropriate layer-4 transport protocol after the `permit` or `deny` statement. For example, to filter Telnet or FTP, choose `tcp` because both Telnet and FTP use TCP at the transport layer. Selecting IP wouldn't allow you to specify a particular application protocol later and only filter based on source and destination addresses.

So now, let's filter an application layer protocol that uses TCP by selecting `tcp` as the protocol and indicating the specific destination TCP port at the end of the line. Next, we'll be prompted for the source IP address of the host or network, and we'll choose the any command to allow any source address:

```
Corp(config)#access-list 110 deny tcp ?
A.B.C.D Source address
any Any source host
host A single source host
```

After we've selected the source address, we can then choose the specific destination address:

```
Corp(config)#access-list 110 deny tcp any ?
A.B.C.D Destination address
any Any destination host
eq Match only packets on a given port number
gt Match only packets with a greater port number
host A single destination host
lt Match only packets with a lower port number
neq Match only packets not on a given port number
range Match only packets in the range of port numbers
```

In this output, you can see that any source IP address that has a destination IP address of 172.16.30.2 has been denied:

```
Corp(config)#access-list 110 deny tcp any host 172.16.30.2 ?
ack Match on the ACK bit
dscp Match packets with given dscp value
```

```
eq Match only packets on a given port number
established Match established connections
fin Match on the FIN bit
fragments Check non-initial fragments
gt Match only packets with a greater port number
log Log matches against this entry
log-input Log matches against this entry, including input interface
lt Match only packets with a lower port number
neq Match only packets not on a given port number
precedence Match packets with given precedence value
psh Match on the PSH bit
range Match only packets in the range of port numbers
rst Match on the RST bit
syn Match on the SYN bit
time-range Specify a time-range
tos Match packets with given TOS value
urg Match on the URG bit
<cr>
```

And once we have the destination host addresses in place, we just need to specify the type of service to deny using the "equal to" command, entered as eq. The following help screen reveals the options available now. You can choose a port number or use the application name:

```
Corp(config)#access-list 110 deny tcp any host 172.16.30.2 eq ?
<0-65535> Port number
bgp Border Gateway Protocol (179)
chargen Character generator (19)
cmd Remote commands (rcmd, 514)
daytime Daytime (13)
discard Discard (9)
domain Domain Name Service (53)
drip Dynamic Routing Information Protocol (3949)
echo Echo (7)
exec Exec (rsh, 512)
finger Finger (79)
ftp File Transfer Protocol (21)
ftp-data FTP data connections (20)
gopher Gopher (70)
hostname NIC hostname server (101)
ident Ident Protocol (113)
irc Internet Relay Chat (194)
klogin Kerberos login (543)
kshell Kerberos shell (544)
login Login (rlogin, 513)
lpd Printer service (515)
nntp Network News Transport Protocol (119)
pim-auto-rp PIM Auto-RP (496)
pop2 Post Office Protocol v2 (109)
pop3 Post Office Protocol v3 (110)
smtp Simple Mail Transport Protocol (25)
```

```
sunrpc Sun Remote Procedure Call (111)
syslog Syslog (514)
tacacs TAC Access Control System (49)
talk Talk (517)
telnet Telnet (23)
time Time (37)
uucp Unix-to-Unix Copy Program (540)
whois Nickname (43)
www World Wide Web (HTTP, 80)
```

Now let's block Telnet (port 23) to host 172.16.30.2 only. If the users want to use FTP, fine—that's allowed. The log command is used to log messages every time the access list entry is hit. This can be an extremely cool way to monitor inappropriate access attempts, but be careful because in a large network, this command can overload your console's screen with messages!

Here's our result:

```
Corp(config)#access-list 110 deny tcp any host 172.16.30.2 eq 23 log
```

This line says to deny any source host trying to telnet to destination host 172.16.30.2. Keep in mind that the next line is an implicit deny by default. If you apply this access list to an interface, you might as well just shut the interface down because by default, there's an implicit deny all at the end of every access list. So we've got to follow up the access list with the following command:

```
Corp(config)#access-list 110 permit ip any any
```

The IP in this line is important because it will permit the IP stack. If TCP was used instead of ip in this line, then UDP, etc., would all be denied. Remember, the 0.0.0.0 255.255.255.255 is the same command as any, so the command could also look like this:

```
Corp(config)#access-list 110 permit ip 0.0.0.0 255.255.255.255
0.0.0.0 255.255.255.255
```

But if you did this, when you looked at the running-config, the commands would be replaced with the any any. I like efficiency, so I'll just use the any command because it requires less typing.

As always, once our access list is created, we must apply it to an interface with the same command used for the IP standard list:

```
Corp(config-if)#ip access-group 110 in
```

Or this:

```
Corp(config-if)#ip access-group 110 out
```

Firewalls

ACLs might seem like they would be great for providing simple security, but as you work with them, you will find they can be really limited and inflexible in practice. Because of that, the industry has largely moved on to newer features and solutions to help keep your traffic safe.

One of the problems with the ACLs we have been discussing is that they are stateless. This means that if traffic is permitted in one direction, you will have to also make a rule that permits the inverse traffic. For example, let's say that after reading the previous section you decide to permit all outbound traffic but block all inbound traffic so the hackers can't get you, as shown here:

```
DC1-SW01(config)#ip access-list ext ALLOW-OUTBOUND
DC1-SW01(config-ext-nacl)#permit ip any any
DC1-SW01(config-ext-nacl)#exit
DC1-SW01(config)#ip access-list ext DENY-INBOUND
DC1-SW01(config-ext-nacl)#deny ip any any
DC1-SW01(config-ext-nacl)#exit DC1-SW01(config)#int g0/0
DC1-SW01(config-if)#ip access-group DENY-INBOUND in
DC1-SW01(config-if)#int g0/1
DC1-SW01(config-if)#ip access-group ALLOW-OUTBOUND in
```

If I pinged 8.8.8.8 from the LAN, what would happen is that traffic would leave my router, but the ICMP replies would be blocked by the **DENY-INBOUND** ACL on the WAN interface. To fix that, I would need to explicitly permit the ICMP reply packets above the deny ip any any rule. This makes blocking down the network with ACLs difficult because you need to consider both directions.

Today we tend to solve this by using stateful firewalls instead. A stateful firewall greatly simplifies things by automatically opening the inverse rules for us. If our example was in a modern firewall such as Cisco's Secure Firewall, as seen in Figure 5.2, then all the return traffic permitted by the "Allow Outbound" rule would also be allowed.

Looking closer at Figure 5.2, we can see the "Allow Outbound" rule doesn't refer to interfaces but instead says that the "Inside zone" can talk to the "Outside zone." For right now, zones are just how firewalls group interfaces together so they can manage them more easily. But as you get more advanced in your firewall studies, you'll find that zones are an important piece of how stateful firewalls function. If you were wondering, you can configure

FIGURE 5.2   Secure Firewall.

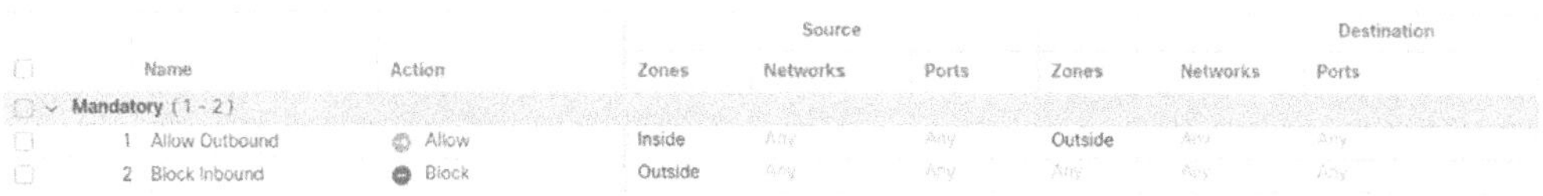

	Name	Action	Source Zones	Source Networks	Source Ports	Destination Zones	Destination Networks	Destination Ports
☐ ˅	Mandatory (1 - 2)							
☐	1 Allow Outbound	⊘ Allow	Inside	Any	Any	Outside	Any	Any
☐	2 Block Inbound	⊖ Block	Outside	Any	Any	Any	Any	Any

FIGURE 5.3   Secure Firewall application policy.

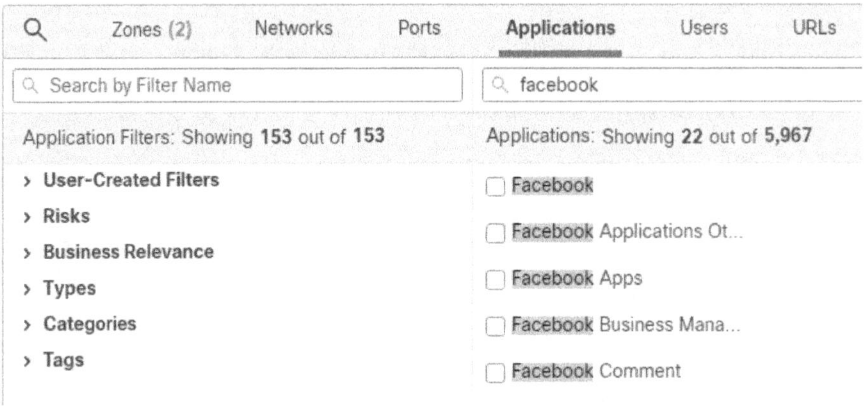

🔍	Zones (2)	Networks	Ports	**Applications**	Users	URLs

🔍 Search by Filter Name	🔍 facebook
Application Filters: Showing **153** out of **153**	Applications: Showing **22** out of **5,967**
› **User-Created Filters**	☐ **Facebook**
› **Risks**	☐ **Facebook** Applications Ot...
› **Business Relevance**	☐ **Facebook** Apps
› **Types**	☐ **Facebook** Business Mana...
› **Categories**	☐ **Facebook** Comment
› **Tags**	

Cisco routers to be a stateful firewall by setting up the Zone Based Firewall feature, but that is way out of scope for this book.

Now that we know how to make more efficient ACLs, we have one more problem that we need to look at: ACLs don't really help with modern traffic because most of our traffic is HTTP based and you'll have a user riot on your hands if you block access to HTTP and HTTPS across the company.

Consider if you wanted to block Facebook on a Cisco router using the skills we have learned so far. You could find out all of Meta's IPs that it uses for Facebook and block them, but that isn't sustainable, and if HR or Marketing needs access to the site for kitty pictures—I mean their job—then you would have a very hard time managing that ACL.

To make the scenario even harder, what if you needed to block only Facebook games but not the rest of the app? That would be impossible without using a next-generation firewall. A *next-generation firewall (NGFW)*, is a firewall that also has a built-in intrusion prevention system (IPS) that can deeply inspect packets before making decisions, as well as other bells and whistles that gives us a lot more functionality.

This allows us to do things such as block traffic based on URLs or even detected applications. Figure 5.3 shows Secure Firewall's ability to block various Facebook apps.

Encryption

Sometimes, like it or not, sending out corporate financial and other types of sensitive data over the Internet just can't be avoided. This is why being able to hide or encode that data with encryption technologies is so vital for shielding it from the prying eyes of a company's competitors, identity thieves—anyone who wants to take a look. Without encryption, our sensitive files and information are essentially being paraded on full display as the data courses over the Internet.

Encryption works by running the data (which when encoded is represented as numbers) through a special encryption formula called a *key* that the designated sending and receiving devices both know. When encrypted data arrives at its specified destination, the receiving device uses that key to decode the data back into its original form.

Back in 1979, the National Security Agency (NSA) classified encryption tools and their associated formulas as munitions, and the NSA has overseen their regulation ever since. The dangerous possibility that hostile nations, terrorists, and criminals may use encrypted communications to plan crimes and go undetected is the compelling reason for doing so. It's also the reason that we're only allowed to export weak encryption methods.

This brings up an important question: exactly how do we measure an encryption algorithm's strength? One way to do that is to measure its bit strength. Until 1998, only software with 40-bit strength or less could be exported, but today, the bar has been raised to 64-bit strength. And by the way, exporting any software with a key length greater than 64 bits is subject to review by the Export Administration Regulations (EAR) required by the U.S. Department of Commerce's Bureau of Industry and Security. This doesn't include exporting to every country because some—like most of those in Western Europe plus Canada, Australia, and Japan—are countries we trust with the technology. But if you happen to be curious or just want to be really careful, check out the current regulations at www.bis. doc.gov/index.php/regulations#ear. Remember, these regulations aren't there to make life a hassle; they're in place to protect us. The greater the number of bits that are encrypted, the tougher it is to crack the code.

 Clearly, the security of monetary transfers is extremely important. The NSA does allow U.S. banks to use more secure encryption methods for this reason and to ensure that they communicate very securely with their overseas branches, customers, and affiliates.

Encrypting passwords being sent from a workstation to a server at login is the most basic need for internal networks, and it's done automatically by most network operating systems today. But legacy utilities such as File Transfer Protocol (FTP) and Telnet don't have the ability to encrypt passwords. Most email systems also give users the option to encrypt individual (or all) email messages, and third-party software packages such as Pretty Good Privacy (PGP) are used by email systems that don't come with encryption abilities of their own. And you already know how critical encryption is for data transmission over VPNs. Finally, encryption capability is clearly very important for e-commerce transactions, online banking, and investing.

I mentioned this earlier, but I didn't tell you exactly what it is: an encryption key is essentially a random string of characters that is used in conjunction with the encryption algorithm. The algorithm is the same for all transactions, but the key is unique to each transaction. Encryption keys come in two flavors: public and private. I'm going to tell you how each one is used next.

Symmetrical Encryption Keys

Using symmetrical key encryption, both the sender and receiver have the same key and use it to encrypt and decrypt all messages. The downside of this technique is that it becomes hard to maintain the security of the key. When the keys at each end are different, it is called asymmetrical or public key. We'll talk about that right after we discuss some encryption standards.

The Data Encryption Standard (DES)

Kudos go to IBM for coming up with one of the most widely used standards: *Data Encryption Standard (DES)*. It was made a standard back in 1977 by the U.S. government. If you want, you can look it up in the Federal Information Processing Standards Publication 46-2 (FIPS 46-2).

Basically, DES uses lookup and table functions, and it actually works much faster than more complex systems. It uses 56-bit keys. RSA Data Systems once issued a challenge to see whether anyone could break the key. A group of Internet users worked together to attempt the task, with each member dealing with a portion of the 72 quadrillion possible combinations. They succeeded and cracked the key in June 1997, after searching only 18 quadrillion keys. Their prize? Knowing they had succeeded when they read a plain-text message that said, "Strong cryptography makes the world a safer place."

Back in the day, DES was a great security standard, but its 56-bit key length has proved to be too short. As I said, the key was first cracked in June 1997. A year later, one was cracked in just 56 hours, and in January 1999, a DES key was broken in a blazing 22 hours and 15 minutes! Not exactly secure, right? We definitely needed something stronger.

Triple Data Encryption Standard (3DES)

That's when *Triple Data Encryption Standard (3DES,* also referred to as *TDES)* came into its glory. Originally developed in the late 1970s, it became the recommended method of implementing DES encryption in 1999. As its name implies, 3DES is essentially three DES encryption methods combined into one.

So 3DES encrypts three times, and it allows us to use one, two, or three separate keys. Clearly, going with only one key is the most unsecure, and opting to use all three keys gives you the highest level of security. Three-key TDES has a key length of 168 bits (56 times 3), but due to a complex type of attack known as *meet-in-the-middle*, it really provides only 112 bits of security. It gets worse farther down the food chain—even though the two-key version has a key size of 112 bits, it actually arms you with only 80 bits of effective security.

Another problem with 3DES is that it's slow. No one likes that, so the National Institute of Standards and Technology (NIST) believes that 3DES will be an effective encryption standard only until sometime around 2030. Even now, it's being phased out in favor of faster methods such as AES.

The Advanced Encryption Standard (AES)

The *Advanced Encryption Standard (AES*, also referred to as *Rijndael)* has been the "official" encryption standard in the United States since 2002. It specifies key lengths of 128, 192, and 256 bits.

The U.S. government has determined that 128-bit security is adequate for things such as secure transactions and all materials deemed Secret, but all Top Secret information must be encoded using 192- or 256-bit keys.

The good news is that the AES standard has proven amazingly difficult to crack. Those who try use a popular method involving something known as a *side channel attack*. This means that instead of going after the cipher directly, they attempt to gather the information they want from the physical implementation of a security system. Hackers attempt to use power consumption, electromagnetic leaks, or timing information (such as the number of processor cycles taken to complete the encryption process) to give them critical clues about how to break the AES system. Although it's true that attacks like these are possible to pull off, they're not really practical to clinch over the Internet.

Hashes

Hashing is a cryptographic process that uses an algorithm to derive a value from a set of clear text to verify that the information came from where it says and that it has not changed. Therefore, we say hashes are used to provide data integrity and origin authentication. Two of the most well-known hashing algorithms are discussed in the following sections.

MD5

The MD5 message-digest algorithm was designed by Ron Rivest, and although it has been shown to have some flaws that cause many to prefer SHA (described in the next section), those flaws are not considered fatal, and it is still widely used to ensure the integrity of transmission. As is the case with most hashing processes, the hash is created from the clear text and then sent along with the clear-text message. At the other end, a second hash of the clear-text data is created using the same algorithm, and if the two hashes match, the data is deemed to be unchanged.

SHA

Secure Hash Algorithm (SHA) is a family of algorithm versions, much like MD5 having multiple versions on its way to becoming MD5. It is published by NIST as a U.S. Federal

Information Processing Standard (FIPS). It operates like any hash does and is considered to be superior to MD5.

Virtual Private Networks

Of course, you've heard the term *VPN* before, and you probably have a pretty good idea of what one is, but just in case: a *virtual private network (VPN)* allows the creation of private networks across the Internet, providing privacy and the tunneling of non-TCP/IP protocols. VPNs are used daily to give remote users and disparate networks connectivity over a public medium such as the Internet instead of using more expensive, permanent means.

VPNs are actually pretty easy to understand. A VPN fits somewhere between a LAN and WAN, with the WAN often simulating a LAN link. Basically, your computer on one LAN connects to a different, remote LAN and uses its resources remotely. The challenge when using VPNs is a big one—security! This may sound a lot like connecting a LAN (or VLAN) to a WAN, but a VPN is much more.

Here's the key difference: a typical WAN connects two or more remote LANs together using a router and someone else's network, such as your Internet service provider's (ISP's). Your local host and router see these networks as remote, not local networks or local resources.

A VPN actually makes your local host part of the remote network by using the WAN link that connects you to the remote LAN. The VPN will make your host appear as though it's actually local on the remote network. This means we gain access to the remote LAN's resources, and that access is also very secure.

And this may also sound a lot like a VLAN definition because the concept is the same: "Take my host and make it appear local to the remote network's resources." Just remember this key distinction: for networks that are physically local, using VLANs is a good solution, but for physically remote networks that span a WAN, you need to use VPNs instead.

Here's a simple VPN example using my home office in Colorado. Here, I have my personal host, but I want it to appear as if it's on a LAN in my corporate office in Texas so I can get to my remote servers. I'm going to go with VPN to achieve my goal.

Figure 5.4 pictures my host using a VPN connection from Colorado to Texas. This allows me to access the remote network services and servers as if my host were right there on the same VLAN.

Why is this so important? If you answered, "Because my servers in Texas are secure, and only the hosts on the same VLAN are allowed to connect to them and use the resources of these servers," you nailed it! A VPN allows me to connect to these resources by locally attaching to the VLAN through a VPN across the WAN. My other option is to open up my network and servers to everyone on the Internet, so clearly, it's vital for me to have a VPN!

FIGURE 5.4   Example of using a VPN.

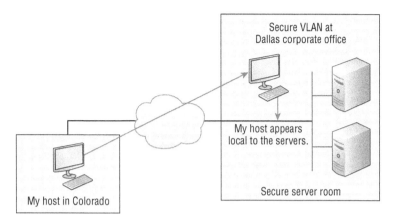

Benefits of VPNs

There are many benefits to using VPNs on your corporate and even home network, including the following:

Security.   VPNs provide security using advanced encryption and authentication protocols, which help protect your network from unauthorized access. IPsec and SSL fall into this category. Secure Sockets Layer (SSL) is an encryption technology used with web browsers and has native SSL encryption known as Web VPN. You can also use the Cisco AnyConnect SSL VPN client installed on your PC to provide an SSL VPN solution, as well as the Clientless Cisco SSL VPN.

Cost Savings.   By connecting the corporate remote offices to their closest Internet provider and creating a VPN tunnel with encryption and authentication, I gain huge savings over opting for traditional leased point-to-point lines. This also permits higher bandwidth links and security, all for far less money than traditional connections.

Scalability.   VPNs scale very well to quickly bring up new offices or have mobile users connect securely.

Compatibility with Broadband Technology.   For remote and traveling users and remote offices, any Internet access can provide a connection to the corporate VPN. This allows users to take advantage of the high-speed Internet access DSL or cable modems offer.

Enterprise- and Provider-Managed VPNs

VPNs are categorized based on the role they play in a business, such as enterprise-managed VPNs and provider-managed VPNs.

FIGURE 5.5   Enterprise-managed VPNs.

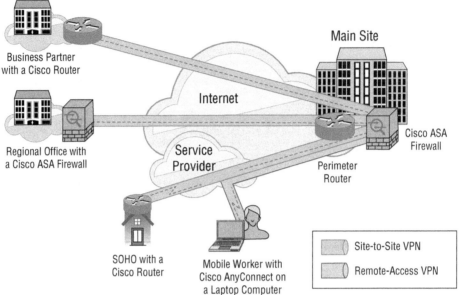

You'll use an enterprise managed VPNs if your company manages its own VPNs. This is a very popular way to provide this service, and it's pictured in Figure 5.5.

There are three different categories of enterprise-managed VPNs:

Remote access VPNs allow remote users such as telecommuters to securely access the corporate network wherever and whenever they need to.

Site-to-site VPNs, or intranet VPNs, allow a company to connect its remote sites to the corporate backbone securely over a public medium such as the Internet instead of requiring more expensive WAN connections.

Extranet VPNs allow an organization's suppliers, partners, and customers to be connected to the corporate network in a limited way for business-to-business (B2B) communications.

Provider-managed VPNs are illustrated in Figure 5.6.

There are two different categories of provider-managed VPNs:

Layer-2 MPLS VPN.   Layer-2 VPNs are a type of VPN that uses MPLS labels to transport data. The communication occurs between routers known as *provider edge* routers (PEs) because they sit on the edge of the provider's network, next to the customer's network.

ISPs that have an existing layer-2 network may choose to use these VPNs instead of the other common layer-3 MPLS VPNs.

FIGURE 5.6   Provider-managed VPNs.

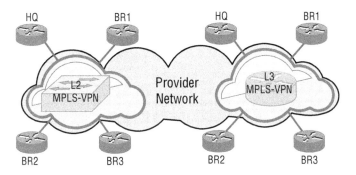

Layer-2 MPLS VPN (VPLS and VPWS):
- Customer routers exchange routes directly.
- Some applications need layer-2 connectivity to work.

Layer-3 MPLS VPN:
- Customer routers exchange routes with SP routers.
- It provides layer-3 service across the backbone.

The two typical technologies of layer-2 MPLS VPN are as follows:

Virtual Private Wire Service (VPWS).   VPWS is the simplest form for enabling Ethernet services over MPLS. It's also known as ETHoMPLS (Ethernet over MPLS) or VLL (Virtual Leased Line). VPWS is characterized by a fixed relationship between an attachment-virtual circuit and an emulated virtual circuit. For example, VPWS-based services are point-to-point Frame-Relay/ATM/Ethernet services over IP/MPLS.

Virtual Private LAN Switching Service (VPLS).   This is an end-to-end service and is virtual because multiple instances of this service share the same Ethernet broadcast domain virtually. Still, each connection is independent and isolated from the others in the network. A learned, dynamic relationship exists between an attachment-virtual circuit and emulated virtual circuits that's determined by the customer MAC address.

In this type of network, the customer manages its own routing protocols. One advantage that a layer-2 VPN has over its layer-3 counterpart is that some applications won't work if nodes aren't in the same layer-2 network.

Layer-3 MPLS VPN.   Layer-3 MPLS VPNs provide a layer-3 service across the backbone, and a different IP subnet connects each site. Because you will typically deploy a routing protocol over this VPN, you need to communicate with the service provider in order to participate in the exchange of routes. Neighbor adjacency is established between your router (called CE) and provider router (called PE). The service provider network has many core routers (called P routers), and the job of the P routers is to provide connectivity between the PE routers.

If you want to totally outsource your layer-3 VPN, then this service is for you. Your service provider will maintain and manage routing for all your sites. From your perspective as a customer who's outsourced your VPNs, it will seem as if your ISP's network is one big virtual switch.

Because they're inexpensive and secure, I'm guessing that you really want to know how to create VPNs now, right? Great! So, there's more than one way to bring a VPN into being. The first approach uses IPsec to build authentication and encryption services between endpoints on an IP network. The second way is via tunneling protocols, which allow you to establish a tunnel between endpoints on a network. Understand that the tunnel itself is a way for data or protocols to be encapsulated inside another protocol—pretty clean!

We'll get to IPsec in a minute, but first, you need to know about four of the most common tunneling protocols in use today:

Layer 2 Forwarding (L2F)

A Cisco-proprietary tunneling protocol that was Cisco's first and created for virtual private dial-up networks (VPDNs). A VPDN allows a device to use a dial-up connection to create a secure connection to a corporate network. L2F was later replaced by L2TP, which is backward compatible with L2F.

Point-to-Point Tunneling Protocol (PPTP)

PPTP was created by Microsoft with others to allow for the secure transfer of data from remote networks to the corporate network.

Layer 2 Tunneling Protocol (L2TP)

L2TP was created by Cisco and Microsoft to replace L2F and PPTP. It merges the capabilities of both L2F and PPTP into one tunneling protocol.

Generic Routing Encapsulation (GRE)

Another Cisco-proprietary tunneling protocol, GRE forms virtual point-to-point links, allowing for a variety of protocols to be encapsulated in IP tunnels. I'll cover GRE in more detail, including how to configure it, at the end of this chapter.

So now that you're clear on both exactly what a VPN is and the various types of VPNs available, it's time to dive into IPsec.

Introduction to Cisco IOS IPsec

Simply put, IPsec is an industry-wide standard framework of protocols and algorithms that allows for secure data transmission over an IP-based network. It functions at layer 3, or network layer of the OSI model.

Did you notice I said "IP-based network"? That's really important because by itself, IPsec can't be used to encrypt non-IP traffic. This means that if you run into a situation where you have to encrypt non-IP traffic, you'll need to create a Generic Routing Encapsulation (GRE) tunnel for it and then use IPsec to encrypt that tunnel!

IPsec Transforms

An *IPsec transform* specifies a single security protocol with its corresponding security algorithm; without these transforms, IPsec wouldn't be able to give us its glory. It's important to be familiar with these technologies, so let me take a second to define the security protocols. I'll also briefly introduce the supporting encryption and hashing algorithms that IPsec relies on.

Security Protocols

The two primary security protocols used by IPsec are *Authentication Header (AH)* and *Encapsulating Security Payload (ESP)*.

Authentication Header (AH)

The AH protocol provides authentication for the data and the IP header of a packet using a one-way hash for packet authentication. It works like this: the sender generates a one-way hash, and then the receiver generates the same one-way hash. If the packet has changed in any way, it won't be authenticated and will be dropped. So basically, IPsec relies on AH to guarantee authenticity.

Let's take a look at this using Figure 5.7.

AH checks the entire packet when in tunnel mode, but it doesn't offer any encryption services. However, using AH in transport mode checks only the payload.

This is unlike ESP, which only provides an integrity check on the data of a packet when in transport mode. However, using AH in tunnel mode and ESP encrypts the whole packet.

FIGURE 5.7 Security protocols.

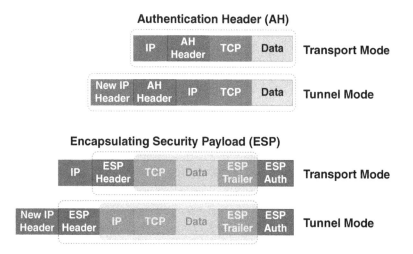

Encapsulating Security Payload (ESP)

So ESP won't tell you when or how the NASDAQ's gonna bounce up and down like a superball, but ESP does a lot for you! It provides confidentiality, data origin authentication, connectionless integrity, antireplay service, and limited traffic-flow confidentiality by defeating traffic-flow analysis—which is almost as good as AH without the possible encryption! Here's a description of ESPs five big features:

Confidentiality (Encryption).   Confidentiality allows the sending device to encrypt the packets before transmitting in order to prevent eavesdropping and is provided through the use of symmetric encryption algorithms such as DES or 3DES. It can be selected separately from all other services, but the type of confidentiality must be the same on both endpoints of your VPN.

Data Integrity.   Data integrity allows the receiver to verify that the data received hasn't been altered in any way along the way. IPsec uses checksums as a simple way to check the data.

Authentication.   Authentication ensures that the connection is made with the correct partner. The receiver can authenticate the source of the packet by guaranteeing and certifying the source of the information.

Anti-replay Service.   Anti-replay election is based on the receiver, meaning the service is effective only if the receiver checks the sequence number. In case you were wondering, a replay attack is when a hacker nicks a copy of an authenticated packet and later transmits it to the intended destination. When the duplicate, authenticated IP packet gets to the destination, it can disrupt services and generally wreak havoc. The *Sequence Number* field is designed to foil this type of attack.

Traffic Flow.   For traffic flow confidentiality to work, you've got to have at least tunnel mode selected. It's most effective if it's implemented at a security gateway where tons of traffic amasses because that's precisely the kind of environment that can mask the true source-destination patterns to bad guys trying to breach your security.

Encryption

VPNs create a private network over a public network infrastructure, but to maintain confidentiality and security, we really need to use IPsec with our VPNs. IPsec uses various types of protocols to perform encryption. The types of encryption algorithms used today are:

Symmetric Encryption.   This type of encryption requires a shared secret to encrypt and decrypt. Each computer encrypts the data before sending info across the network, with this same key being used to both encrypt and decrypt the data. Examples of symmetric key encryption are Data Encryption Standard (DES), Triple DES (3DES), and Advanced Encryption Standard (AES).

Asymmetric Encryption.   Devices that use asymmetric encryption use different keys for encryption than they do for decryption. These keys are called private and public keys.

Private keys encrypt a hash from the message to create a digital signature, which is then verified via decryption using the public key. Public keys encrypt a symmetric key for secure distribution to the receiving host, which then decrypts that symmetric key using its exclusively held private key. It's not possible to encrypt and decrypt using the same key. Asymmetric decryption is a variant of public key encryption that also uses a combination of both a public and private keys. An example of an asymmetric encryption is Rivest, Shamir, and Adleman (RSA).

Looking at Figure 5.8, you can see the complex encryption process.

As you can see from the amount of information I've thrown at you so far, establishing a VPN connection between two sites takes some study, time, and practice. And I'm just scratching the surface here! I know it can be difficult at times, and it definitely takes patience. Cisco does have some GUIs to help with this process, which also come in handy for configuring VPNs with IPsec. Although highly useful and very interesting, they're just beyond the scope of this book, so I'm not going into this topic further here.

FIGURE 5.8   Encryption Process.

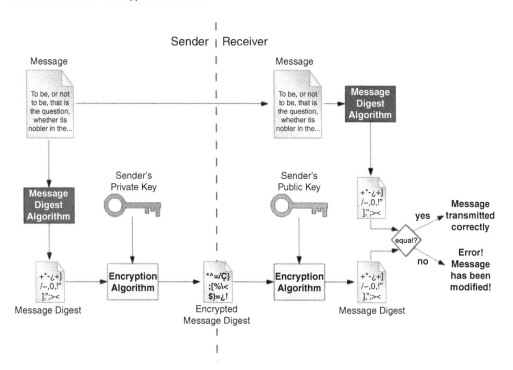

GRE Tunnels

Generic Routing Encapsulation (GRE) is a tunneling protocol that can encapsulate many protocols inside IP tunnels. Some examples would be routing protocols such as EIGRP and OSPF and the routed protocol IPv6. Figure 5.9 shows the different pieces of a GRE header.

A GRE tunnel interface supports a header for each of the following:

- A passenger protocol or encapsulated protocol such as IP or IPv6, which is the protocol being encapsulated by GRE
- GRE encapsulation protocol
- A transport delivery protocol, typically IP

GRE tunnels have the following characteristics:

- GRE uses a protocol-type field in the GRE header, so any layer-3 protocol can be used through the tunnel.
- GRE is stateless and has no flow control.
- GRE offers no security.
- GRE creates additional overhead for tunneled packets—at least 24 bytes.

GRE over IPsec

So as I mentioned, by itself, GRE offers no security—no form of payload confidentiality or encryption whatsoever. If the packets are sniffed over the public network, their contents are in plain text. Although IPsec provides a secure method for tunneling data across an IP network, it definitely has its limitations.

IPsec doesn't support IP broadcast or IP multicast, preventing the use of protocols that need them as routing protocols. IPsec also does not support the use of multiprotocol traffic. But GRE can be used to "carry" other passenger protocols such as IP broadcast or IP

FIGURE 5.9   Generic Routing Encapsulation (GRE) tunnel structure.

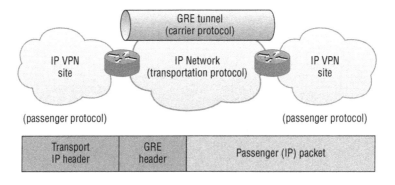

multicast, plus non-IP protocols as well. Using GRE tunnels with IPsec allows you to run a routing protocol, IP multicast, as well as multiprotocol traffic across your network.

With a generic hub-and-spoke topology such as Corp to Branch, you can typically implement static tunnels (usually GRE over IPsec) between the corporate office and branch offices. When you want to add a new spoke to the network, you just need to configure it on the hub router. Also, the traffic between spokes has to traverse the hub, where it must exit one tunnel and enter another. Static tunnels are an appropriate solution for small networks, but not so much as the network grows larger with an increasing number of spokes!

Cisco DMVPN (Cisco Proprietary)

The Cisco Dynamic Multipoint Virtual Private Network (DMVPN) feature enables you to easily scale large and small IPsec VPNs. The Cisco DMVPN is Cisco's answer for allowing a corporate office to connect to branch offices with low cost, easy configuration, and flexibility. DMVPN is composed of one central router like a corporate router, which is referred to as the hub, and the branches as spokes. So the corporate-to-branch connection is referred to as the hub and spoke interconnection. The spoke-to-spoke design is also supported for branch-to-branch interconnections. If you're thinking this design sounds really similar to your old Frame Relay network, you're right! The DMVPN features enable you to configure a single GRE tunnel interface and a single IPsec profile on the hub router to manage all spoke routers. This keeps the size of the configuration on the hub router basically the same even if you add more spoke routers to the network. DMVPN also allows a spoke router to dynamically create VPN tunnels between them as network data travels from one spoke to another.

Cisco IPsec VTI

The IPSec Virtual Tunnel Interface (VTI) mode of an IPsec configuration can seriously simplify a VPN configuration when protection is needed for remote access. And it's a simpler option than GRE or L2TP for the encapsulation and crypto maps used with IPSec. Like GRE, it sends routing protocol and multicast traffic, just without GRE and all the overhead it brings. Simple configuration and routing adjacency directly over the VTI are great benefits! Understand that all traffic is encrypted and that it supports only one protocol—either IPv4 or IPv6, just like standard IPsec.

Public Key Infrastructure

Now that we understand encryption and VPNs a little bit, the question becomes, how can we use it? VPNs authenticate connections in one of two ways: Pre-Share-Key (PSK) and certificates. A PSK is simply a password that is entered between both ends of the VPN tunnel. If you are setting up a VPN between different companies, then sharing the PSK can be a bit of a problem; sometimes it is hidden in emails, sometimes it's painfully spelled out over a phone call, sometimes it's texted to your phone, and sometimes more advanced methods are used, such as a secure password transfer service. When it comes time to change that PSK, you would need to share it with the other side all over again.

Certificates can make your life easier because you don't need to worry about sharing passwords anymore; but like anything in life, they also create own things to worry about instead. The basic idea of certificates is that one is issued to you by your trusted certificate provider to prove who you are. Then the other side also receives one from their trusted certificate provider.

Because your VPN solution would be configured to trust both those certificate providers, it would accept both your certificates as authentication. You can think of it as like the CCST certification you are studying for by reading this book! If I needed to hire for a junior cybersecurity role, I could look for candidates with the CCST: Cyber Security certification on their résumé because I can trust Cisco to only issue that certification to people who were wise enough to buy Todd's and my book.

We call all the components necessary to manage certificates in your organization public key infrastructure (PKI).

Certification Authorities

The previous example mentioned a trusted certificate provider; we call that a Certificate Authority (CA). The main role of a CA is to issue certificates to users and computers. Depending on the solution, you may need to pick between having a certificate that identifies your user or your computer. Sometimes you might need both types of certificates to fully authenticate.

Certificate Authorities can also revoke a certificate to prevent it from being used for authentication anymore. This is useful if an employee leaves the company, if the certificate isn't needed anymore, or if there was a security compromise on the CA so you need to invalidate all certificates. When a certificate is revoked, it is added to something called a Certificate Revocation List, which, as you might have guessed from the name, is a list of revoked certificates. This list is periodically downloaded by devices that rely on the Certificate Authority such as firewalls that are using certificate-based VPNs. There is a more real-time solution called Online Certificate Status Protocol (OSCP), where devices directly query the CA to see whether the certificate is still trusted.

We don't need to get into how to set up a Certificate Authority for this exam, but they come in several flavors. Microsoft includes a full-featured Certificate Authority solution in its Windows Server product, Linux has a variety of open-source packages that can be used depending on the distribution, and you can even use Cisco routers to act as a CA. Figure 5.10 shows a Microsoft CA.

When you first install a Certificate Authority, it will be known as the Root CA because it is the only one around. This is fine for smaller companies, but we generally don't want to work directly with the Root CA because if it becomes compromised, the hacker will get all the keys to the kingdom; we can also get better performance by spreading out the load between different CAs, which we call intermediate certificate authorities.

We can have as many Intermediate CAs as we'll need, and once they are up and running, we don't need to use the Root CA again unless we need to build a new CA. In fact, some companies will shut down the Root CA until it's needed, to ensure the private keys never get stolen. Figure 5.11 shows an example of a certificate hierarchy.

FIGURE 5.10   Certificate authority.

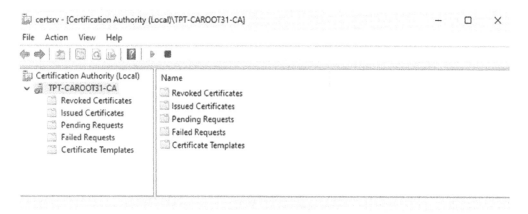

FIGURE 5.11   Certificate hierarchy.

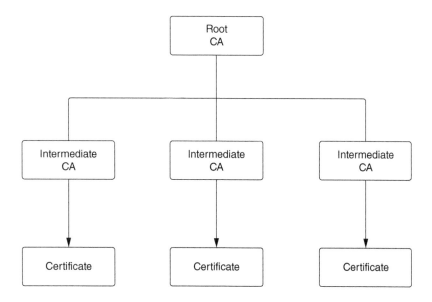

FIGURE 5.12   Real certificate hierarchy.

Figure 5.12 shows a real-world example of this that I got from looking at what CAs www.lammle.com uses. We can see that **Baltimore CyberTrust Root** is the Root CA, **Cloudflare Inc ECC CA-3** is the first intermediate CA, and **sni.cloudflaressl.com** is the actual certificate that was issued.

Certificate Templates

Certificates have plenty of different options including what type of encryption is being used and what the certificate is intended to be used for. CAs make your life easier by using templates to define what characteristics a certificate will have. Figure 5.13 shows an example of some templates defined in my lab's Microsoft CAs.

Certificates

We talked about how to issue certificates, and now it is time to talk about what a certificate really is. A digital certificate provides an entity, usually a user or a computer, with the credentials to prove its identity and associates that identity with a public key.

Certificates are made up of two parts: a public key and a private key. As the names imply, the private key is something you don't want to share with anyone, much like the password to log in to your bank account, because you want to keep your private key a secret. You instead share your public key with anyone who needs it, and they in turn will share their public keys with you.

The last thing we need to decide before we create a certificate is what certificate template we need to use. For this exam, we only really need to know about certificates that are used for a "signature and encryption" purpose, which basically means the certificate can be used to verify an identity and provide encryption. Finally, we can choose whether a certificate will be used to authenticate a server or a client. Server authentication is used for servers and network devices, and client authentication is more used to identify users.

FIGURE 5.13 Certificate templates.

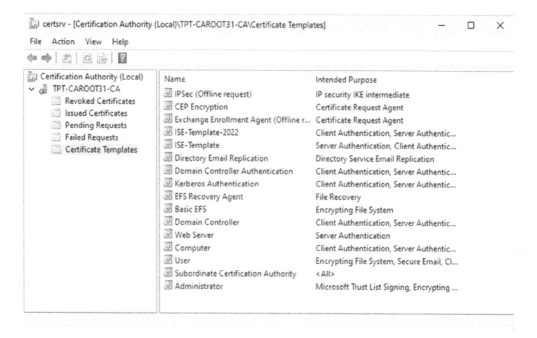

At minimum, a digital certification must provide the serial number, the issuer, the subject (owner), and the public key.

An X.509 certificate complies with the X.509 standard. An X.509 certificate contains the following fields:

- Version
- Serial number
- Algorithm ID
- Issuer
- Validity
- Subject
- Subject public key info
  - Public key algorithm
  - Subject public key
- Issuer unique identifier (optional)
- Subject unique identifier (optional)
- Extensions (optional)

VeriSign first introduced the following digital certificate classes:

- Class 1: For individuals and intended for email. These certificates get saved by web browsers.
- Class 2: For organizations that must provide proof of identity.
- Class 3: For servers and software signing in which independent verification and identity and authority checking is done by the issuing CA.

Summary

In this chapter, you learned some smart solutions that will help you securely access company resources.

We started by introducing how to filter traffic with access control lists on routers, and then we discussed how newer firewalls handle the job. From there we got into how encryption and public key infrastructure can help keep our data safe.

Finally, we dove deep into how these networks utilize IP security to provide secure communications over a public network via the Internet using VPNs with IPSec, and we finished with PKI.

Exam Essentials

Remember the standard and extended IP access-list number ranges.   The number ranges you can use to configure a standard IP access list are 1–99 and 1300–1999. The number ranges for an extended IP access list are 100–199 and 2000–2699.

Understand the term *implicit deny*.   At the end of every access list is an *implicit deny*. This means that if a packet does not match any of the lines in the access list, it will be discarded. Also, if you have nothing but deny statements in your list, the list will not permit any packets.

Understand the standard IP access-list configuration command.   To configure a standard IP access list, use the access-list numbers 1–99 or 1300–1999 in global configuration mode. Choose permit or deny, and then choose the source IP address you want to filter on using one of the three techniques covered in this chapter.

Understand the extended IP access-list configuration command.   To configure an extended IP access list, use the access-list numbers 100–199 or 2000–2699 in global configuration mode. Choose permit or deny, the network layer protocol field, the source IP address you want to filter on, the destination address you want to filter on, and finally, the transport layer port number if TCP or UDP has been specified as the protocol.

Understand the term *virtual private network*.   You must understand why and how to use a VPN between two sites and the purpose that IPsec serves with VPNs.

Understand the function of a firewall.   You must understand why a firewall is more desirable than just using an ACL on a router.

Understand various encryption standards.   You must understand different encryption types and that DES and MD5 are less desirable than more secure options.

Understand the basics of PKI.   You must understand the basics of what PKI is, what a Certificate Authority does, and what a certificate is.

Review Questions

You can find the answers to these questions in Appendix.

1. Which of the following statements is false when a packet is being compared to an access list?

    A. It's always compared with each line of the access list in sequential order.

    B. Once the packet matches the condition on a line of the access list, the packet is acted on and no further comparisons take place.

    C. There is an implicit "deny" at the end of each access list.

    D. Until all lines have been analyzed, the comparison is not over.

2. You need to create an access list that will prevent hosts in the network range of 192.168.160.0 to 192.168.191.0. Which of the following lists will you use?

    A. `access-list 10 deny 192.168.160.0 255.255.224.0`

    B. `access-list 10 deny 192.168.160.0 0.0.191.255`

    C. `access-list 10 deny 192.168.160.0 0.0.31.255`

    D. `access-list 10 deny 192.168.0.0 0.0.31.255`

3. You have created a named access list called BlockSales. Which of the following is a valid command for applying this to packets trying to enter interface Fa0/0 of your router?

    A. `(config)#ip access-group 110 in`

    B. `(config-if)#ip access-group 110 in`

    C. `(config-if)#ip access-group Blocksales in`

    D. `(config-if)#BlockSales ip access-list in`

4. Which access-list statement will permit all HTTP sessions to network 192.168.144.0/24 containing web servers?

    A. `access-list 110 permit tcp 192.168.144.0 0.0.0.255 any eq 80`

    B. `access-list 110 permit tcp any 192.168.144.0 0.0.0.255 eq 80`

    C. `access-list 110 permit tcp 192.168.144.0 0.0.0.255 192.168.144.0 0.0.0.255 any eq 80`

    D. `access-list 110 permit udp any 192.168.144.0 eq 80`

5. Which of the following is an industry-wide standard suite of protocols and algorithms that allows for secure data transmission over an IP-based network that functions at SŁ layer 3, or the network layer of the OSI model?

    A. HDLC

    B. Cable

    C. VPN

    D. IPsec

    E. xDSL

6. Which of the following describes the creation of private networks across the Internet, enabling privacy and tunneling of non-TCP/IP protocols?

   A. HDLC

   B. Cable

   C. VPN

   D. IPsec

   E. xDSL

7. Which of the following older encryption algorithms should never be used?

   A. DES

   B. 3DES

   C. AES

   D. SHA

   E. MD5

8. Which hash algorithm is preferred?

   A. DES

   B. 3DES

   C. AES

   D. SHA

   E. MD5

9. What issues certificates in a PKI model?

   A. Certificate Issuer

   B. Certificate Authority

   C. Certificate Provider

   D. Certificate Master

   E. Certificate Server

10. Which is the name of a secondary Certificate Authority?

    A. Secondary Certificate Authority

    B. Backup Certificate Authority

    C. Intermediate Certificate Authority

    D. Failover Certificate Authority

    E. xCertificate Authority

Chapter

6

OS Basics and Security

THE FOLLOWING CCST EXAM TOPIC IS COVERED IN THIS CHAPTER:

✔ **3.0 Endpoint Security**

- 3.1. Describe operating system security concepts

    Windows, macOS, and Linux; security features, including Windows Defender and host-based firewalls; CLI and PowerShell; file and directory permissions; privilege escalation

- 3.4. Implement software and hardware updates

    Windows Update, application updates, device drivers, firmware, patching

- 3.5. Interpret system logs

    Event Viewer, audit logs, system and application logs, syslog, identification of anomalies

This chapter will focus on the common operating systems and their built-in security features: specifically, the three dominant operating systems of Windows, macOS, and Linux, which you will find on the endpoints in your network environment. We will learn security features of all three operating systems. This will include the hardware and applications that function on these operating systems. We will then finish the chapter by learning all about logging for these operating systems so we can identify security concerns.

To find your included bonus material, as well as Todd Lammle videos, practice questions, and hands-on labs, please see www.lammle.com/ccst.

Operating System Security

The operating system is by far the largest attack vector for threat agents. The software installed on the operating system and the files that the operating system stores are the perfect mixture of targets. Threat actors can target an unpatched application that contains a vulnerability. A threat actor can also sneak a file onto the operating system that is infected with malware. In the following section we will identify security features for the Windows, macOS, and Linux operating systems.

Windows

Windows is mind-bogglingly complex. Other operating systems are complex too, but the mere fact that Windows has nearly 60 million lines of code (and thousands of developers have worked on it!) makes you pause and shake your head. Fortunately, many tens of millions of lines of code are dedicated to features that make the operating system secure. The following are some of the features you need to know for the exam.

Windows Defender Firewall

Windows Defender Firewall is an advanced host-based firewall that was first introduced with Windows XP Service Pack 2. It was integrated and became a security feature with the introduction of Windows Vista. Although host-based firewalls are not as secure as other types of firewalls, Windows Defender Firewall provides much better protection than in previous versions of Windows, and it is turned on by default. Windows Defender Firewall is used to block access from the network, which significantly reduces the surface area of attack for the Windows operating system.

To access Windows Defender Firewall in Windows 10, navigate to Start ➤ Settings Apps ➤ Update & Security ➤ Windows Security ➤ Firewall & Network Protection. To access Windows Defender Firewall in Windows 11, navigate to Start ➤ Settings Apps ➤ Privacy & Security ➤ Windows Security ➤ Firewall & Network Protection. Windows Defender Firewall is divided into separate profile settings: for domain networks (if you're connected to a domain), private networks, and public networks. In Figure 6.1, you can see the default protection for a Windows client not joined to a domain and active on a public network.

Activate and deactivate the firewall   By default, Windows Defender blocks inbound connections, but outbound connections are not blocked by default. You can temporarily deactivate

FIGURE 6.1   Firewall & Network Protection.

FIGURE 6.2 Deactivating Windows Defender Firewall network protection.

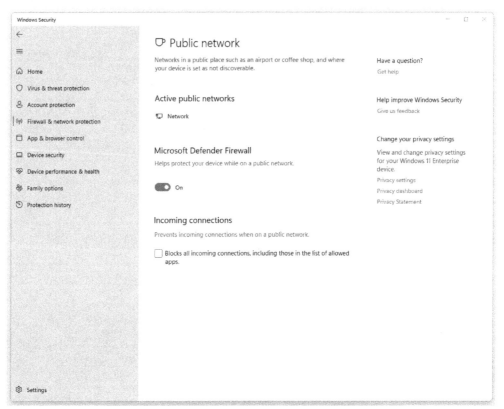

Windows Defender Firewall for a network profile by clicking on the network profile on the Firewall & Network Protection screen and toggling the Windows Defender Firewall setting to Off, as shown in Figure 6.2. Deactivating the firewall protection is extremely useful if you are trying to troubleshoot a network connectivity problem. Dropping the firewall temporarily and testing the incoming connection will confirm whether a firewall adjustment needs to be made or the problem is elsewhere.

Allowing applications   When applications attempt to listen on a port for an incoming connection, the Windows operating system will display a notification asking if you want to allow access. However, if the notification does not display and you determine that an application needs to be allowed through the firewall, you can click Allow An App Through Firewall on the Firewall & Network Protection screen. This will open the Allowed Apps settings page shown in Figure 6.3. Here you can modify the apps that are allowed through the Windows Defender Firewall, as well as add new ones. You will need administrative access to change any network firewall settings.

FIGURE 6.3   Windows Defender Firewall Allowed Apps.

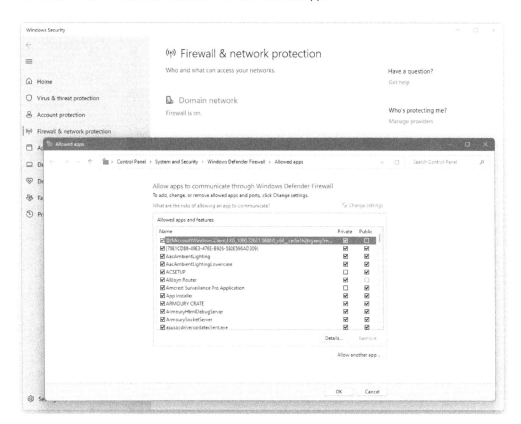

Windows Defender Firewall with Advanced Security   When you allow an application to listen for an incoming connection via the notification dialog box, the operating system creates a rule in the firewall to allow the connection. This is all done for you behind the scenes, and it shows up neatly as an allowed application. However, you can also manually create a rule in Windows Defender Firewall with the Advanced Security MMC, as shown in Figure 6.4. You can open the MMC by clicking Advanced Settings on the Firewall & Network Protection screen.

Here you can configure inbound and outbound rules as well as import and export policies and monitor the security of your system. Monitoring is not confined to the firewall; you can also monitor security associations and connection security rules. In short, Windows Defender Firewall with Advanced Security is an incredibly powerful tool that builds on what Windows Vista originally introduced in 2007. Not only can this MMC snap-in do simple configuration, but it can also configure remote computers and be configured by with Group Policy.

FIGURE 6.4   Windows Firewall with Advanced Security.

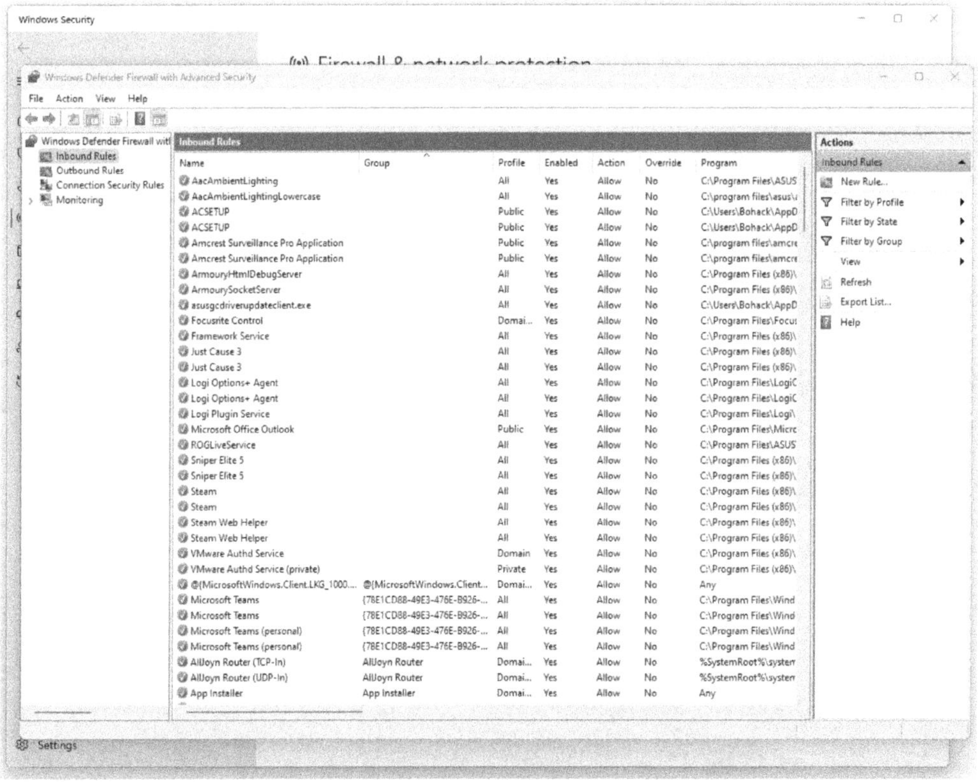

Exceptions   Manual exceptions, also known as firewall rules, are configured on the Inbound Rules tab in the Windows Defender Firewall with Advanced Security MMC. You can click New Rule and configure a firewall rule based on a program, port, predefined rule, or totally custom rule. A rule based on a program allows all incoming connections to the application. A rule based on a port allows you to configure a specific rule based on a TCP or UDP connection to a specific port or range of ports. A predefined rule allows you to modify a predefined rule. A custom rule allows you to configure a program and specific ports; you can even scope it down to the incoming range of IP addresses you will allow. Any of these settings can also be configured after running the New Rule Wizard, as shown in Figure 6.5.

Scripting

Scripting languages do not need to be compiled. They are interpreted by the shell, command line, or external interpreter, as shown in Figure 6.6. The interpreter reads the script and

FIGURE 6.5   Windows Defender Firewall with Advanced Security inbound rules.

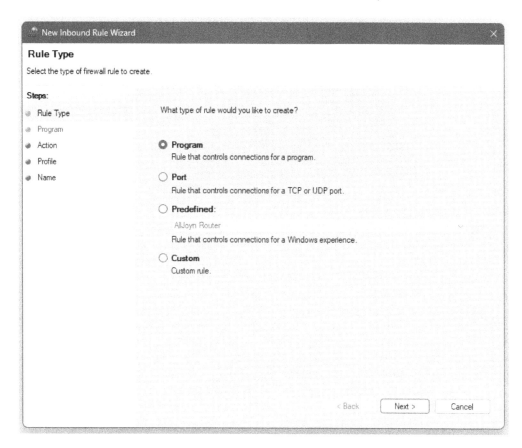

executes the instructions in the operating system. The big difference is that you do not need to compile scripts to executable machine code, such as a C/C++ program. Unfortunately, the higher the level, the less control you have over the process. The benefit is that you can create a script rather quickly, and you don't need to compile it. There are security considerations that this introduces, and they will be covered later in this section.

Another big difference between applications and scripts is that scripts require applications to complete their purpose. If an application doesn't exist for a function in your script, then you should evaluate whether a script is the right course of action. For example, if you need to resize pictures, an application must exist that can be called via the command line that will take the appropriate input and resize the pictures. If an application doesn't exist that can resize the picture, then you might need to write an application that resizes a picture in lieu of a script. A script cannot normally create functions of this nature; it can only call on them.

FIGURE 6.6   Interpreting a scripting language.

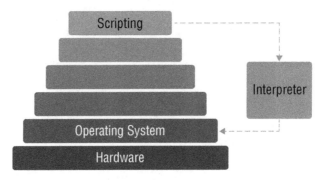

Command Shell/Batch Scripts

The Windows command shell and batch scripts have been around since the release of Microsoft's Disk Operating System (DOS) back in 1981. The original script interpreter was command.com, and since then Windows NT was released, which included an updated command-line interpreter called Command Prompt, or cmd.exe. The original file extension used with batch scripts was .bat, but today both .bat and .cmd can be used to initiate a batch script because they are both associated with the command-line interpreter of cmd.exe.

A Windows batch script is probably the fastest way to get something done when all you need is a list of commands run one after the other. For example, say you need to create new user accounts for a school. You can get the usernames in an Excel sheet, and you can create a script from the entries by using an Excel formula, adding in the column of the username. As an example, the formula ="NET USER" & A1 & "PassW0rd /ADD /DOMAIN" copied into cell B1 will produce the line you need to execute. Then you just need to drag the formula down, and the script will be built. A quick copy and paste, and the script will look similar to the following output. It's a quick and dirty way to create user accounts. Using the combination of an Excel sheet and a copy-and-paste into a batch script is the fastest way to build and execute a laundry list of commands:

```
NET USER UserOne PassW0rd /ADD /DOMAIN
NET USER UserOne PassW0rd /ADD /DOMAIN
NET USER UserOne PassW0rd /ADD /DOMAIN
NET USER UserOne PassW0rd /ADD /DOMAIN
[ Output Cut ]
```

Batch scripts can also contain logic. The following is a simple batch script that tests whether a variable of FLIPFLOP is equal to 0 using an if statement. If FLIPFLOP is equal to 0, the script will proceed to write to the screen the word *Zero*, set FLIPFLOP to a value of 1, and then jump to :LOOP. Because FLIPFLOP is set to 1, it is not equal to 0; so the else clause in the if statement will be processed, the word *One* will be printed to the screen, and FLIPFLOP will then be set to 0, and the script will jump to :LOOP again. This will proceed until Ctrl + C is pressed to stop the processing of the script:

```
@ECHO OFF
REM FlipFlop Script
SET /A FLIPFLOP=0
:LOOP
IF %FLIPFLOP% EQU 0 (ECHO Zero && SET /A FLIPFLOP=1) ELSE (ECHO One && SET /A
FLIPFLOP=0)
GOTO:LOOP
```

PowerShell Scripts

PowerShell allows for the automation and management of the Windows operating systems, as well as cloud-related services such as Microsoft Azure and Microsoft 365. One of the limiting features of any scripting language is its ability to perform a needed task. PowerShell was created to be totally extensible. It was built on the .NET Framework Common Language Runtime (CLR). Any programmable library a .NET application has access to, PowerShell can use, which is what makes it so extensible. It has been used since Windows Server 2008 as a configuration tool for the operating system. In fact, most of the time when you configure a service in the Server Manager tool, you actually run a PowerShell command in the background. Many of the GUI wizards allow you to see the PowerShell script that will be executed so that you can reuse the line in a script of your own.

PowerShell introduced the concept of *cmdlets*. PowerShell has over 100 cmdlets installed, called the core cmdlets. You can always add your own cmdlet by creating a PS1 script and installing it into the PowerShell cmdlet store in the operating system. A cmdlet is simply a verb and noun separated by a dash. Here are a few examples:

Get-Item   Gets an item such as a directory listing, environment variable, or Registry key

Set-Item   Changes the value of an item, such as creating an alias or setting an environment variable

Copy-Item   Copies an item, such as a file or folder

Remove-Item   Deletes an item, such as a file, folder, or Registry key

Move-Item   Moves an item, such as a file, folder, or Registry key

These are just a few of the built-in core cmdlets for PowerShell. Others exist for -Item, such as Rename-Item, New-Item, Invoke-Item, and Clear-Item. Each one performs a corresponding action on the noun following the dash. You can even extend the functionality of a command with your own PS1 cmdlet. There is a Get-Verb command so that you can see all the appropriate verbs that you can use for your own command.

To learn more about creating your own cmdlets, visit: https://learn. microsoft.com/en-us/powershell/scripting/develope r/cmdlet/how-to-write-a-simple-cmdlet?view=powers hell-7.4.

If you use the Get-Item cmdlet and specify a folder, information about that folder will be returned. If you want to see all the other folders contained within that folder, you can use a * wildcard. Or you can use the Get-ChildItem cmdlet and specify the directory, as follows:

```
PS C:\Users\UserOne> Get-item c:\*

    Directory: C:\

Mode                LastWriteTime         Length Name
----                -------------         ------ ----
d-----        11/28/2017   9:52 PM              Dell
d-----         5/16/2018   9:32 PM              NVIDIA
d-----         4/11/2018   7:38 PM              PerfLogs
d-r---         5/28/2018  10:04 PM              Program Files
d-r---         8/12/2018   5:31 PM              Program Files (x86)
d-r---         5/28/2018   6:11 PM              Users
d-----        10/18/2018  10:17 PM               Windows

PS C:\Users\UserOne> Get-ChildItem c:\

    Directory: C:\

Mode                LastWriteTime         Length Name
----                -------------         ------ ----
d-----        11/28/2017   9:52 PM              dell
d-----         5/16/2018   9:32 PM              NVIDIA
d-----         4/11/2018   7:38 PM              PerfLogs
d-r---         5/28/2018  10:04 PM              Program Files
d-r---         8/12/2018   5:31 PM              Program Files (x86)
d-r---         5/28/2018   6:11 PM              Users
d-----        10/18/2018  10:17 PM              Windows
```

When you use the dir command in PowerShell to view a directory listing of files, you are actually using something called an *alias*. The alias then calls the Get-ChildItem cmdlet. To see all the aliases on the operating system, you can use the Get-Alias cmdlet. You can see all the commands mapped over to PowerShell cmdlets, as follows:

```
PS C:\Users\UserOne> get-alias

CommandType     Name
-----------     ----
Alias           % -> ForEach-Object
Alias           ? -> Where-Object
Alias           ac -> Add-Content
Alias           asnp -> Add-PSSnapin
Alias           cat -> Get-Content
Alias           cd -> Set-Location
Alias           CFS -> ConvertFrom-String
Alias           chdir -> Set-Location
Alias           clc -> Clear-Content
```

```
Alias              clear -> Clear-Host
Alias              clhy -> Clear-History
Alias              cli -> Clear-Item
Alias              clp -> Clear-ItemProperty
Alias              cls -> Clear-Host
[ Output Cut ]
```

PowerShell also has a great way to develop scripts in what is called an Integrated Scripting Environment (ISE). The ISE allows you to write a script and test it without having to switch back and forth between a text editor and the execution environment. In addition to writing and the execution environment in the same window, there is a type-ahead feature that allows you to pick a command if you remember only the first few letters, as shown in Figure 6.7. You can also use the Tab key to complete a command, which makes writing scripts easy when you know the first couple of letters. Formatting is also automated and makes for easy-to-read scripts. The formatting highlights variables and commands in different colors so that you can differentiate between the two.

Before any script can be executed on the Windows operating system, you must first allow scripts to run. By default, any PowerShell scripts will be blocked. The following example shows you how to "unrestrict" PowerShell scripts using the `Set-ExecutionPolicy` cmdlet. The `Get-ExecutionPolicy` command will show the current execution policy. The following result shows that the current execution policy is restricted. So, we can use the `Set-ExecutionPolicy -ExecutionPolicy` with the `-ExecutionPolicy`

FIGURE 6.7   PowerShell ISE.

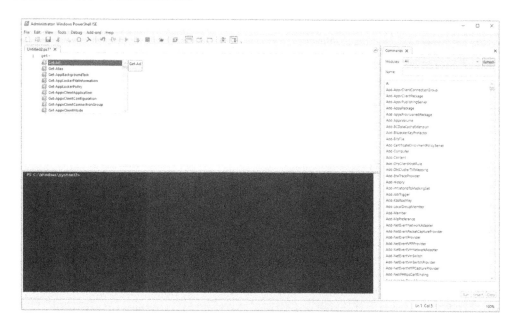

FIGURE 6.8   `Get-ExecutionPolicy` command.

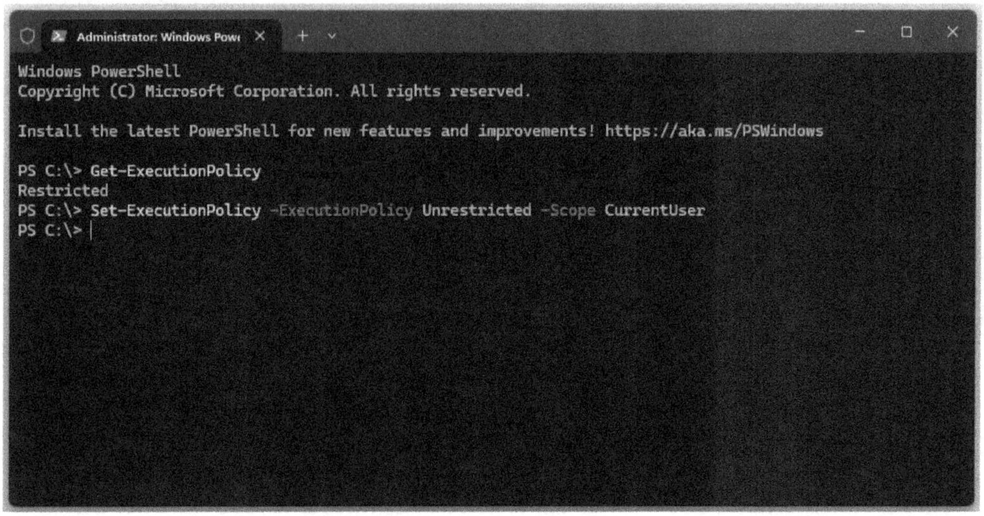

`Unrestricted` switch and parameter to set the execution policy. You will also see that we use the `-scope` switch with the `CurrentUser` parameter (see Figure 6.8). This ensures that we are only going to unrestricted the execution policy for the current user and not the entire operating system:

```
PS C:\> Get-ExecutionPolicy Restricted
PS C:\> Set-ExecutionPolicy -ExecutionPolicy Unrestricted -Scope CurrentUser
PS C:\> Get-ExecutionPolicy Unrestricted
PS C:\>
```

Security Considerations

A common pitfall with scripting is inadvertently introducing a security issue. Security issues come in all different forms when scripting. The most common security issue is the embedding of security credentials in scripts. Regardless of how secure you think the script will be, it's a bad habit and should be avoided at all costs.

That being said, there are instances where embedding a password cannot be avoided. In these situations, you should use mechanisms that are supported in the scripting language to act as a digital locker for your password or methods that encrypt the password. One such mechanism is the `ConvertTo-SecureString` cmdlet. It means more lines of code, more time, and sometimes more aggravation in getting it to work, but the benefit is a secure system.

Another potential problem is the inadvertent introduction of malware with scripting. This usually happens when you need additional functionality, such as email capability or changing a system setting. Windows batch scripting has its limitations, and it is easy to use a third-party tool to get the last bit of functionality out of the script. However, that third-party tool may have malicious intent, and you could introduce that malicious code to the system in which the script is executed. PowerShell has its own potential malware risks; when you add an untrusted module, the same thing could happen.

The best way to avoid these pitfalls is not to shortcut the solution. Do your homework, and avoid embedding passwords or using untrusted modules or third-party utilities in your scripts. It means more work, but this should be factored into your cost-benefit analysis when taking on developing a script.

One last potential issue to consider is that a threat actor will use the command shell or PowerShell scripting language to run malicious commands. Both the batch scripting process and the PowerShell language have the ability to obfuscate the threat actor's payload. The PowerShell language even has the ability to ransom a system itself with simple commands. That doesn't mean there is a command like `set-ransomware` built in, but there are encryption commands built in. A threat actor can easily use these commands to craft a ransomware payload. These attacks are called living of the land (LOTL), and there isn't much you can do to protect yourself. You can just make it harder for the threat actor, such as limiting the scope of unrestricted PowerShell scripts, and be vigilant.

NTFS vs. Share Permissions

The *New Technology File System (NTFS)* was introduced with Windows NT to address security problems. Before Windows NT was released, it had become apparent to Microsoft that a new filesystem was needed to handle growing disk sizes, security concerns, and the need for more stability. NTFS was created to address those issues.

Although the File Allocation Table (FAT) filesystem was relatively stable if the systems that were controlling it kept running, it didn't do well when the power went out or the system crashed unexpectedly. One of the benefits of NTFS was a transaction-tracking system, which made it possible for Windows NT to back out of any disk operations that were in progress when it crashed or lost power.

With NTFS, files, folders, and volumes can each have their own security. NTFS's security is flexible and built in. Not only does NTFS track security in ACLs, which can hold permissions for local users and groups, but each entry in the ACL can specify which type of access is given—such as Read & Execute, List Folder Contents, or Full Control. This allows a great deal of flexibility in setting up a network. In addition, special file-encryption programs were developed to encrypt data while it is stored on the hard disk.

Microsoft strongly recommends that all network shares be established using NTFS. Several current operating systems from Microsoft support both FAT32 and NTFS. It's possible to convert from FAT32 to NTFS without losing data, but you can't do the operation in reverse. (You would need to reformat the drive and install the data again from a backup tape.)

 If you're using FAT32 and want to change to NTFS, the `convert` utility will allow you to do so. For example, to change the E: drive to NTFS, the command is `convert E: /FS:NTFS`.

FIGURE 6.9   Network share permissions and NTFS permissions.

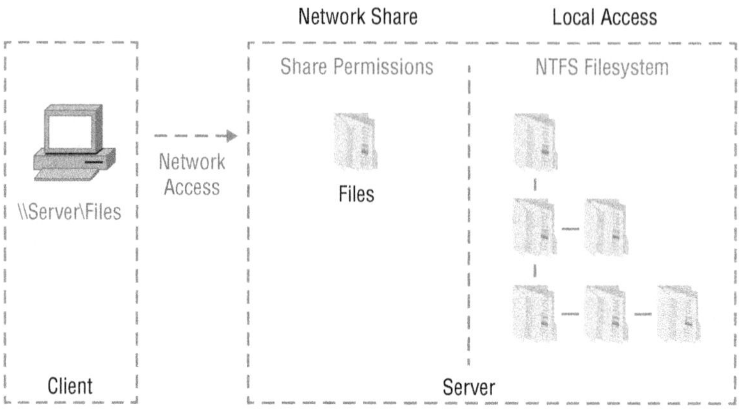

Share permissions apply only when a user is accessing a file or folder through the network, as shown in Figure 6.9. *NTFS permissions* and attributes are used to protect the file when the user is local. With FAT and FAT32, you do not have the ability to assign "extended" or "extensible" permissions, and the user sitting at the console effectively is the owner of all resources on the system. As such, they can add, change, and delete any data or file.

With NTFS as the filesystem, you are allowed to assign more comprehensive security to your computer system, as shown in Table 6.1. NTFS permissions can protect you at the file level. Share permissions can be applied to the folder level only, as shown in Table 6.2. NTFS permissions can affect users accessing files and folders across a network or logged in locally to the system where the NTFS permissions are applied. Share permissions are in effect only when the user connects to the resource through the network.

Allow vs. Deny

Within NTFS, permissions for objects fall into one of three categories: Allow, Deny, or not configured. When viewing the permissions for a file or folder, you can check the box for Allow, which effectively allows the group selected to perform that action. You can also uncheck the box for Allow, which does not allow that group that action, as shown in Figure 6.10. Alternatively, you can check the Deny box, which prevents that group from using that action. There is a difference between not allowing (a cleared check box) and Deny (which specifically prohibits), and you tend not to see Deny used often. Deny, when used, trumps other permissions.

Permissions set on a folder are inherited down through subfolders unless otherwise changed. Permissions are also cumulative; if a user is a member of a group that has Read permission and a member of a group that has Write permission, they effectively have both Read and Write permissions.

TABLE 6.1   NTFS permissions.

NTFS permission	Meaning	Object used on
Full Control	Gives the user all the other choices and the ability to change permissions. The user can also take ownership of the folder or any of its contents.	Folder and file objects
Modify	Combines the Read & Execute permission with the Write permission and further allows the user to delete everything, including the folder.	Folder and file objects
Read & Execute	Combines the Read permission with the List Folder Contents permission and adds the ability to run executables.	Folder and file objects
List Folder Contents	The List Folder Contents permission (known simply as List in previous versions) allows the user to view the contents of a folder and to navigate to its subdirectories. It does not grant the user access to the files in these directories unless that is specified in file permissions.	Folder objects
Read	Allows the user to navigate the entire folder structure, view the contents of the folder, view the contents of any files in the folder, and see ownership and attributes.	Folder and file objects
Write	Allows the user to create new entities within a folder.	Folder and file objects

TABLE 6.2   Share permissions.

Share permission	Meaning
Full Control	Gives the user all the other permissions as well as permission to take ownership and change permissions
Change	Allows the user to overwrite, delete, and read files and folders
Read	Allows the user to view the contents of the file and to see ownership and attributes

Effective Permissions

When a user accesses a file share, both the share permissions and NTFS permissions interact with each other to form the effective permission for the user. Figure 6.11 shows that a user named Fred has logged in and received his access token containing the Sales and R&D

FIGURE 6.10   NTFS folder permissions.

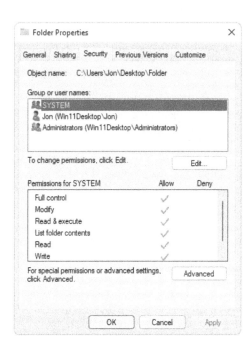

FIGURE 6.11   Effective permissions.

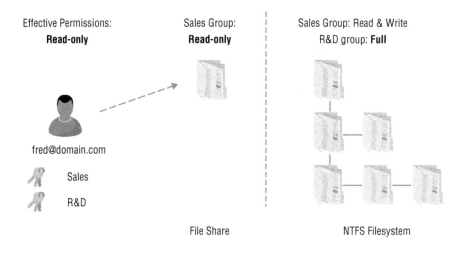

groups, because he is a member of both groups. When Fred accesses the Sales file share, the share permissions define that he has read-only access because he is part of the Sales group. You can see that the NTFS permissions are granting him read and write access because of his Sales group membership, as well as full control because he is also in the R&D group. If Fred were to locally log in to this computer, he would effectively have full control of these files. However, because he is accessing these files from the network, he only has read-only access because of the file-share permissions. The opposite is also true: if he had full permission at the share level and read-only permission at the NTFS level, he would effectively have read-only access.

The rule to figuring out effective permissions is simple: if a user is in more than one group for which there are multiple permissions, take the most permissive permission of NTFS and then the most permissive permission of the share; the effective permission is the more restrictive of the two. There are some circumstances that change this rule slightly when the user (or group) is denied. If a user is in any group that is denied permission at the share or the NTFS level, they are denied for that access level. Therefore, when you derive the more restrictive permission, it will always be a deny for the user. A simple way to remember this is that a deny is a deny.

Moving vs. Copying Folders and Files

When you copy a file, you create a new entity. When you move a file, you simply relocate it and still have only one entity. This distinction is important when it comes to understanding permissions. A copy of a file will have the permissions assigned to it that are already in place at the new location of the file, regardless of which permissions were on the original file.

A moved file, on the other hand, will attempt to keep the same permissions it had in the original location. Differences will occur if the same permissions cannot exist in the new location. For example, if you are moving a file from an NTFS volume to FAT32, the NTFS permissions will be lost. If, on the other hand, you are moving from a FAT32 volume to an NTFS volume, new permissions will be added that match those for newly created entities.

 Folder copy and move operations follow guidelines that are similar to those with files.

Shared Files and Folders

You can share folders, and the files beneath them, by right-clicking the files or folder and choosing Give Access To from the context menu and selecting Specific People. In Windows, the context menu asks you to choose with whom you want to share the folder or file, as shown in Figure 6.12. You can then choose whom to share it with along with their respective permissions. It is important to understand that when you use this method to share files and folders, the share permissions are set to Full Control for the Everyone group.

FIGURE 6.12   Choose people to share with.

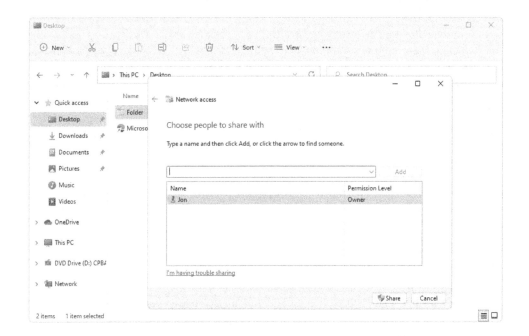

You can access the Advanced Sharing settings by right-clicking the folder you want to share, selecting Properties, then clicking the Sharing tab, and finally selecting Advanced Sharing, as shown in Figure 6.13. This file-sharing method is more traditional with network administrators because every aspect of the share can be controlled. Using this method, only the share permissions are set from this dialog box. The NTFS security permissions are set on the Security tab. In addition, you can add other share names to the same location, limit the number of simultaneous connections, and add comments.

Administrative Shares vs. Local Shares

Administrative shares are automatically created on all Windows operating systems on the network for administrative purposes. These shares can differ slightly based on which operating system is running, but they always end with a dollar sign ($) to make them hidden. There is one share for each volume on a hard drive (C$, D$, and so on) as well as admin$ (the root folder—usually C:\WINDOWS) and print$ (where the print drivers are located). These shares are created for use by administrators and usually require administrator privileges to access.

Local shares, as the name implies, are shares that are created locally by the administrative user on the operating system. The term *local shares* is used to distinguish between automated administrative shares and manually created shares.

FIGURE 6.13   Advanced file and folder sharing.

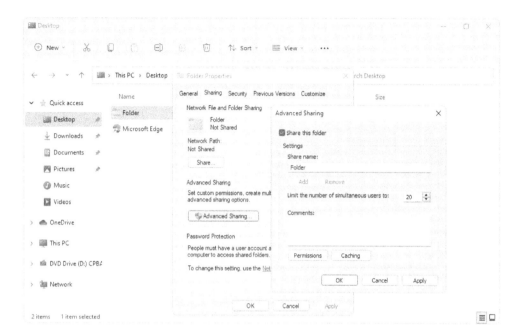

Permission Inheritance and Permissions Propagation

Inheritance is the default throughout the permission structure unless a specific setting is created to override it. A user who has Read and Write permissions in one folder will have them in all the subfolders unless a change has been made specifically to one of the subfolders. If a user has the Write permission, which is inherited from the folder above, the removal of permissions cannot be performed unless inheritance is disabled. Only additional permissions can be added explicitly, because this is actually a new permissions entry and not the removal of an existing permissions entry. You can control NTFS inheritance by right-clicking a folder, selecting Properties, then choosing the Security tab, selecting Advanced, and clicking the Disable Inheritance button, as shown in Figure 6.14.

If the Disable Inheritance button is selected, you will be changing the NTFS security settings on the folder. A second dialog box will pop up, and you must choose to either keep the existing permissions, by selecting Convert Inherited Permissions To Explicit Permissions On This Object, or start fresh with no permissions by selecting Remove All Inherited Permissions From This Object. You should use caution when selecting the latter of the two options, because all folders and files below will inherit and propagate the removal of existing permissions.

If you want to make sure that inheritance and permissions for a folder are propagated to all files and folders below, you can use Replace All Child Object Permission Entries With

FIGURE 6.14   Disabling inheritance.

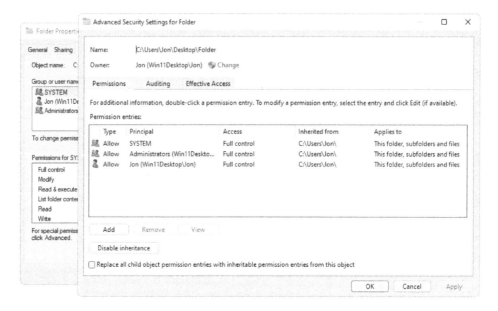

Inheritable Permission Entries From This Object (refer to Figure 6.14). This option will replace every permission in this folder and all the subfolders, regardless of whether explicit permissions were applied further in the folder structure.

In the Advanced Security Settings, you can also configure permissions entries that only apply to the current folder, current folder and files, all folders and files, as well as other variations of these, as shown in Figure 6.15. These settings can change the propagation of file permissions to folders and files.

User Account Control

Looking back at the first Windows operating system, when you installed the operating system the setup process would create a user account for you. This user account was the administrator account. This created a very wide area of attack for a threat actor; they simply had to target an account named administrator, and they had admin credentials!

Today, the installation process of the operating system creates a unique user account for you. The administrator account is still created, but it is disabled by default. This uniqueness of the first account on Windows helped narrow the area of attack. However, it didn't prevent the person on the computer from unknowingly run a malicious application with their administrator privileges. This is where User Account Control (UAC) comes into the picture.

FIGURE 6.15   Permissions entry.

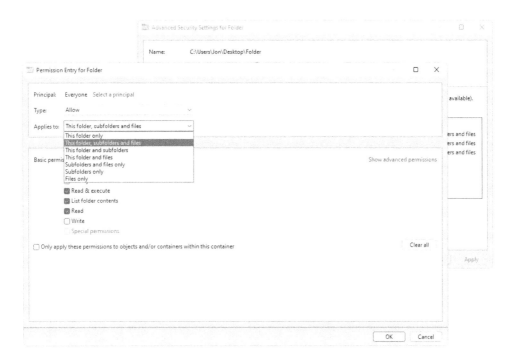

UAC was introduced as a standard security feature with Windows Vista. It was created to reduce the risk of running malware as the administrator account. Nothing stops you from running malware and allowing it via the UAC, but hopefully most people will not allow the malware to continue. Before the UAC, if a program executed, it would execute as the administrator of the computer.

When an administrator logs on to the computer, the full administrator token (privilege) is set aside, and the account will log on as a standard user. The majority of day-to-day activities typically don't require administrator privileges. However, if the administrative privilege is required or requested, the UAC will intervene and prompt the user to either allow or deny the privileges request, as shown in Figure 6.16. If the request is granted, the process requesting the administrator privilege will be allowed to use the privilege for the time it is running.

The UAC will intervene and prompt the user under a few conditions. One condition is running an application or setup that is flagged as requiring administrator privileges. These applications or setup programs will have a yellow and blue shield displayed on their icon. Another condition that will trigger the UAC is certain settings in the operating system that require administrative privileges, as shown in Figure 6.17.

FIGURE 6.16   User Access Control dialog.

FIGURE 6.17   Date and Time settings.

You can manually trigger the UAC dialog by right-clicking an application and selecting Run As Administrator. If a standard user runs an application that requires administrative privileges, or they select Run As Administrator, the operating system will prompt them for the credentials of an administrator.

You can change the behavior of the UAC by clicking the Start Menu ➤ Settings, typing UAC, and selecting Change User Account Control Settings. This will bring up a dialog box with a slider as shown in Figure 6.18.

You can move the slider to select the following options:

Always Notify Me When   This option will notify you when programs try to install software or make changes to your computer. It will also notify you when you make changes to Windows settings. This option will freeze other tasks until you respond.

Notify Me Only When Apps Try To Make Changes To My Computer (Default)   This option is the default when you install the operating system. This option will notify you when programs try to install software or make changes to your computer. It will not notify you

FIGURE 6.18   User Account Control Settings.

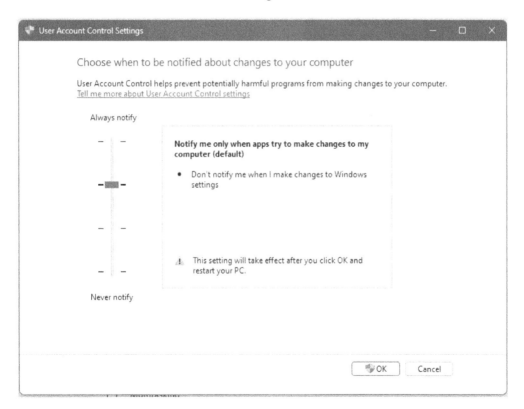

when you make changes to Windows settings. This option will freeze other tasks until you respond.

Notify Me Only When Apps Try To Make Changes To My Computer (Do Not Dim My Desktop)   This option will notify you when programs try to install software or make changes to your computer. It will not notify you when you make changes to Windows settings, and it will not freeze other tasks until you respond.

Never Notify (Disable UAC prompts)   This option will turn off all UAC protection.

Windows Update

When operating systems are installed, they are usually point-in-time snapshots of the current build of the operating system. From the time of the build to the time of installation, several vulnerabilities can be published for the operating system. When an operating system is installed, you should patch it before placing it into service. Patches remediate the vulnerabilities found in the operating system and fixed by the vendor. Updates add new features not included with the current build. However, some vendors may include vulnerability patches in updates. Network devices also have patches and updates that should be installed before placing them into service.

In large-scale networks, the organization may employ a corporate patch-management solution. Microsoft offers a free patch-management solution called Windows Server Update Services (WSUS). Microsoft also sells a licensed solution called Microsoft Endpoint Configuration Manager (MECM), which performs many other functions in addition to patch management. If an update is required and your organization uses one of these products, the patch must be approved, downloaded, and deployed. Third-party patch-management solutions may also be used in your organization. Third-party solutions are usually specific to an application or suite of applications, such as Adobe or Autodesk.

In small office, home office (SOHO) environments and small network environments, the update may be a one-off installation for a specific application. In this case, the update just needs to be downloaded and installed, per the vendor instructions. Always make sure to have a plan to roll back from a bad update. Turning on System Protection is a good idea before the update. If an update fails, you can simply use System Restore to restore the operating system to a prior point in time.

Very rarely, you will find that a Microsoft or third-party update has created a problem on the operating system. When this happens, it's pretty easy to roll back updates by uninstalling them. Simply open the Settings app, select Windows Update, then Update History, and then Uninstall Updates, and finally select the update and choose Uninstall, as shown in Figure 6.19.

On the left of the Installed Updates screen, you can select Uninstall A Program. This will take you to the Programs And Features – Uninstall Or Change A Program screen. From here, you can uninstall third-party updates. After uninstalling an update, it's a good idea to reboot before testing to see whether it fixed the issue.

FIGURE 6.19   Uninstalling an update.

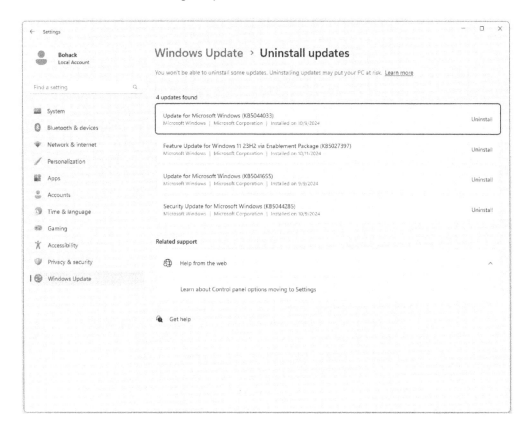

An alternative to uninstalling an update is to use System Restore to revert to an earlier time before the update. However, System Protection must have been turned on before the update was installed. System Protection in Windows 10/11 is turned off by default. You can turn it on by clicking the Start menu, typing **Recovery** and selecting it, and then clicking Configure System Restore, selecting the System drive, clicking Configure, selecting Turn On System Protection, and finally clicking OK.

Application Patching

After the initial installation of the application, you are not done! The installation of a new application just means that you must pay attention to updates for the software. Vendors continually release patches and updates to improve security and functionality, sometimes every month, depending on the application. The Windows operating system has a built-in patch management system. Unfortunately, each application vendor has adopted its own patch management system, and it typically requires the end user to be an administrator to install the new software.

To keep applications patched, administrators have adopted strategies with Microsoft Configuration Manager, formerly System Center Configuration Manager (SCCM), and Intune. These two products allow administrators to deploy applications and applications patches in addition to many other functions. There are many other third-party products that will manage patch management for both the applications and the operating system.

Of course, this is assuming that your clients are the end-compute environment. Many organizations have adopted virtual desktop infrastructure (VDI), or terminal, services. The centralized computer environment allows an administrator to update the application in one location. This of course can be done manually or automatically with one of the tools mentioned earlier.

Device Drivers

Device drivers and firmware can also be installed via Windows Update, Microsoft Configuration Manager, Intune, or third-party tools. Driver and firmware updates are just as important as other Windows Updates. Older versions of drivers and firmware can contain vulnerabilities that threat actors can exploit.

Sometimes the latest drivers can create problems, so it may be necessary to roll back the current driver to a prior version. This action will roll back the driver to the original version detected by Windows, also called the *out-of-box driver*. In some cases, it may roll back to a generic driver, which reduces functionality until a proper driver is installed.

This process can be completed with these steps:

1. Right-click the Start menu.
2. Select Device Manager.
3. Select the device.
4. Right-click, and select Properties from the context menu.
5. Select the Driver tab
6. Click Roll Back Driver.
7. Provide the reason for rolling back the driver.
8. Click Yes, as shown in Figure 6.20.

When the rollback is complete, you should reboot the computer before testing to see whether it fixed the issue.

macOS/Linux

In the beginning there was UNIX. UNIX System 5 (version 5) is an operating system originally created and licensed by AT&T Labs. The UNIX operating system is considered to be the root of all UNIX-based operating systems. In the mid-1970s, the University of

FIGURE 6.20   Rolling back a driver.

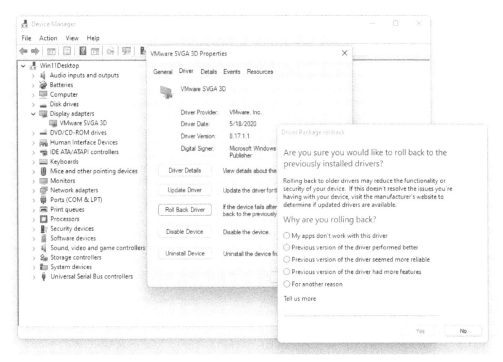

California at Berkeley (UC Berkeley) licensed UNIX from AT&T for its computer systems and expanded on the tools shipped in the original version of UNIX. These tools became the foundation of UNIX as it is today, but UC Berkeley only licensed the operating system for specific machines. The students quickly became upset and developed and released a version of UNIX called the Berkeley Software Distribution (BSD). The term *distribution* is used today with UNIX/Linux operating systems to define the operating system and its ecosystem for application management, patching, and upgrades.

Although it began with UNIX, BSD became very popular because it was an open-source license. This allowed everyone to use the operating system on any computer system they wished. In the mid-1980s, Steve Jobs created a company called NeXT and built computers that furnished the NeXTSTEP operating system. The NeXTSTEP operating system was originally built from BSD version 4.3. Unfortunately, the NeXT computer company never really took off. However, the NeXTSTEP operating system was acquired by Apple and eventually became the macOS we know today.

Linux has a very different origin story from macOS. Actually, Linux has nothing to do with the original codebase of UNIX. In the mid-1990s, a Finnish student named Linus Torvalds set out to create a completely open-source operating system for the world to use. Linux was the result of his efforts; it was designed from scratch, so it was completely free for anyone to use or incorporate into their own products. Today you can find a great number of Linux distributions, such as Ubuntu, Debian, Arch Linux, Gentoo, Red Hat … and the list goes on.

Although Linux has a completely different codebase from BSD and UNIX, the operating system itself functions similarly. Only the kernel and inner workings of the operating system are different. Many of the applications that were created by students on the BSD platform were ported over to Linux. Functionally, the operating systems are very similar in design and usability.

> The complete history of UNIX is vast and interesting; we have covered only the big events in the UNIX timeline. Many different organizations were involved, spanning all the way back to the 1960s. Learn more about the history of UNIX here: `https://unix.org/what_is_unix/history_timeline.html`.

System Updates/App Store

It is important to keep the operating system current and updated. Like Windows, many other operating systems include the ability to update automatically, and almost all can look for updates and tell you when they are available. In the Apple world, the *App Store* represents a location where you can also find updates.

For example, Figure 6.21 shows that a new version of the macOS is downloading and installing. You can obtain software updates by opening Settings, clicking on General, and then selecting Software Updates. If there is a software update, you will see it under the heading of Updates Available. You can then click Update Now, and the update will begin installing. This process can be automated by turning on Automatic Updates. Operating system updates are not the only thing that will install via the Software Update section; any applications downloaded from the App Store and security updates will install as well. In most cases, unless a production device would be negatively impacted, you should keep systems updated with the latest releases.

Patch Management

As a general rule, updates fix a lot of issues, and patches fix a few; multiple patches are rolled into updates. You can't always afford to wait for updates to be released and should install patches—particularly security-related patches—when they are released. Bear in mind that if all the security patches are not installed during the operating system installation, attackers can exploit the weaknesses and gain access to information.

A number of tools are available to help with patch management, although the intentions of some are better than others. For example, rather than probe a service remotely and attempt to find a vulnerability, the Nessus vulnerability scanner (`https://www.tenable.com/downloads/nessus`) will query the local host to see whether a patch for a given vulnerability

FIGURE 6.21   macOS update.

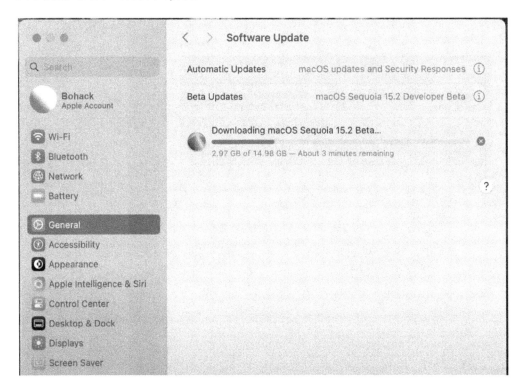

has been applied. This type of query is far more accurate (and safer) than running a remote check. Because remote checks actually send the exploit in order to check to see whether it is applicable, this can sometimes crash a service or process.

Depending on the variant of Linux you are running, APT (Advanced Package Tool) can be useful in getting the patches from a repository site and downloading them for installation on Debian and Ubuntu (just to name two). The most common command used with this tool is apt-get, which, as the name implies, gets the package for installation, as shown in Figure 6.22. The YUM (Yellowdog Updater, Modified) tool is used with RPM (Red Hat Package Manager)-based Linux distributions, such as CentOS, Fedora, and Red Hat, and works in a similar way to APT.

Firewall

Firewalls are also built into other operating systems, including Linux and macOS. Depending on the distribution of Linux or macOS, the firewall included will vary, as well as the way you configure it.

FIGURE 6.22 Ubuntu apt tool.

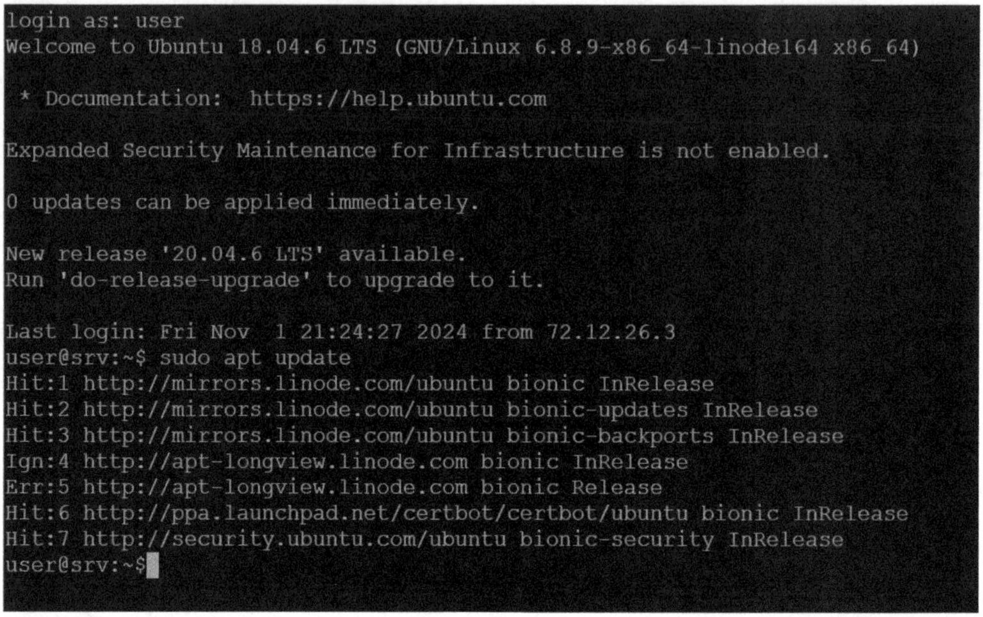

```
login as: user
Welcome to Ubuntu 18.04.6 LTS (GNU/Linux 6.8.9-x86_64-linode164 x86_64)

 * Documentation:  https://help.ubuntu.com

Expanded Security Maintenance for Infrastructure is not enabled.

0 updates can be applied immediately.

New release '20.04.6 LTS' available.
Run 'do-release-upgrade' to upgrade to it.

Last login: Fri Nov  1 21:24:27 2024 from 72.12.26.3
user@srv:~$ sudo apt update
Hit:1 http://mirrors.linode.com/ubuntu bionic InRelease
Hit:2 http://mirrors.linode.com/ubuntu bionic-updates InRelease
Hit:3 http://mirrors.linode.com/ubuntu bionic-backports InRelease
Ign:4 http://apt-longview.linode.com bionic InRelease
Err:5 http://apt-longview.linode.com bionic Release
Hit:6 http://ppa.launchpad.net/certbot/certbot/ubuntu bionic InRelease
Hit:7 http://security.ubuntu.com/ubuntu bionic-security InRelease
user@srv:~$
```

macOS

macOS comes with an application-based firewall, similar to Windows Defender Firewall. Unfortunately, the firewall on macOS is turned off by default. Because Apple does not ship with any high-risk services that listen for incoming requests, it is advisable to turn on the firewall and configure it properly.

You can turn on the firewall by selecting the Apple menu ➢ System Settings, clicking Network in the sidebar, then clicking Firewall, and then sliding the control on for the firewall. You should then click on Options and move the slider for Block All Incoming Connections; this will protect you similar to how the Windows Defender Firewall does, as shown in Figure 6.23. You can then exempt applications for inbound connectivity to the operating system.

If you prefer to manage the firewall via the command line, you can use sockfilterfw. The command sockfilterfw will allow you to view the status of the firewall and manage it. It is advisable to use the GUI for exempting applications, because it is just easier. The following shows how you can query the status of the firewall:

```
$ /usr/libexec/ApplicationFirewall/socketfilterfw --getglobalstate --getblockall
Firewall is DISABLED! (State = 0)
Block all DISABLED!
```

FIGURE 6.23   macOS firewall.

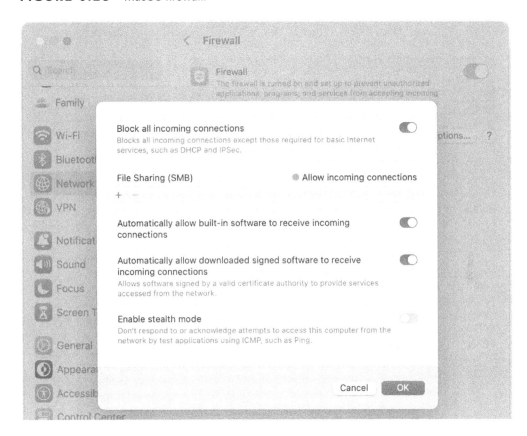

Linux

Most distributions of Linux, such as Ubuntu and Debian, come with the iptables firewall installed. CentOS and Fedora come with firewalld, which supports location-based firewall rules.

The iptables firewall is a really versatile firewall: you can create filters, NAT rules, route decisions, mangle packets, and marking packets, and these are just a few things you can do! It is very flexible, but there is a huge learning curve that requires a deep understanding of IP packets and iptables inner workings. Thankfully we just need to learn one aspect, which is the filtering capabilities in the filter table.

The filter table has two directions: inbound and outbound. Following the theme of the Windows Defender Firewall and macOS firewall, we just need to focus on blocking inbound traffic. However, like the other firewalls, you can block outbound traffic as well. Once we focus our attention on this aspect of iptables, it makes learning it much simpler.

If you want to view the current iptables filters, you can use the command `iptables -L`. This command will display the configured rules, as shown in the following example. We can see that TCP/22 for SSH, TCP/80 for HTTP, and ICMP/Echo-Requests are allowed:

```
user@srv:~$ sudo iptables -L
Chain INPUT (policy DROP)
target      prot opt source        destination
ACCEPT      tcp  --  anywhere      anywhere        tcp dpt:ssh
ACCEPT      tcp  --  anywhere      anywhere        tcp dpt:http
ACCEPT      icmp --  anywhere      anywhere        icmp echo-request

[ Output Cut ]
```

The rules are easy to read, and if we want to add a new rule, we can use the `iptables` command. In the following code, we will add a rule to accept TCP/443 for HTTPS. Then we will use the command `iptables -L -n` to see the protocol number in lieu of the friendly protocol names:

```
user@srv:~$ sudo iptables -A INPUT -p tcp --dport 443 -j ACCEPT
user@srv:~$ sudo iptables -L -n
Chain INPUT (policy DROP)
target      prot opt source        destination
ACCEPT      tcp  --  anywhere      anywhere        tcp dpt:22
ACCEPT      tcp  --  anywhere      anywhere        tcp dpt:80
ACCEPT      icmp --  anywhere      anywhere        icmp 8
ACCEPT      tcp  --  anywhere      anywhere        tcp dpt:443

[ Output Cut ]
```

You will notice that the new rule was added to the end of the filter list. By default, the new rule will be added to the end. If you want to add a rule in a specific place or delete a specific rule, you must use the command `iptables -L --line-numbers`, as shown in the following code. You can then use the command `iptables -D INPUT 4` to delete the line:

```
user@srv:~$ sudo iptables -L -n
Chain INPUT (policy DROP)
num target      prot opt source        destination
1   ACCEPT      tcp  --  anywhere      anywhere        tcp dpt:22
2   ACCEPT      tcp  --  anywhere      anywhere        tcp dpt:80
3   ACCEPT      icmp --  anywhere      anywhere        icmp 8
4   ACCEPT      tcp  --  anywhere      anywhere        tcp dpt:443

[ Output Cut ]

user@srv:~$ sudo iptables -D INPUT 4
```

Then use the command `iptables -I INPUT 3 -p tcp --dport 443 -j ACCEPT`. This will place the new rule between lines 2 and 3:

```
user@srv:~$ sudo iptables -I INPUT 3 -p tcp --dport 443 -j ACCEPT
user@srv:~$ sudo iptables -L -n
Chain INPUT (policy DROP)
num target prot opt source         destination
1   ACCEPT    tcp  -- anywhere     anywhere          tcp dpt:22
2   ACCEPT    tcp  -- anywhere     anywhere          tcp dpt:80
3   ACCEPT    tcp  -- anywhere     anywhere          tcp dpt:443
4   ACCEPT    icmp -- anywhere     anywhere          icmp 8

[ Output Cut ]
```

Regardless of which type of firewall an operating system comes preinstalled with, a third-party firewall can be installed. These firewalls can offer intrusion-detection capabilities that alert you when someone is attacking. In almost all cases, the firewall that comes with the operating system is more than adequate, but you have to keep it on at all times to prevent unwanted connections.

Permissions

You can get a directory listing by using the `ls` command. By default, the `ls` command, without any options, displays the contents of the current directory in a compact, multicolumn format. You can see even more detailed information about the files and directories with the `-l` (long format) option, as shown next. The rightmost column shows the name of the directory or file entry. The date and time before the name show when the last modifications to that file were made. To the left of the date and time is the size of the file in bytes. The file's group and owner appear to the left of the column that shows the file size. The next number to the left indicates the number of links to the file. (A *link* is like a shortcut in Windows.)

```
user@srv:/etc$ ls -l
total 184
-rw-r--r-- 1 root root      2981 Apr 16  2014 adduser.conf
drwxr-xr-x 2 root root      4096 Nov  1 23:14 alternatives
drwxr-xr-x 8 root root      4096 Nov  1 23:14 apache2
drwxr-xr-x 3 root root      4096 Apr 20  2014 apm
drwxr-xr-x 3 root root      4096 Nov  1 23:14 apparmor
drwxr-xr-x 8 root root      4096 Nov  1 23:14 apparmor.d
drwxr-xr-x 7 root root      4096 Feb 26  2021 apt
-rw-r----- 1 root daemon     144 Oct 21  2013 at.deny
-rw-r--r-- 1 root root      2319 Jun  6  2019 bash.bashrc
```

Finally, the leftmost column shows the file's permission settings, which determine who can read, write, or execute the file. This column shows a sequence of nine characters, which appear as `rwxrwxrwx` when each letter is present. Each letter indicates a specific permission.

A hyphen (-) in place of a letter indicates no permission for a specific operation on the file. Think of these nine letters as three groups of three letters (rwx), interpreted as follows:

Leftmost group   Controls the read, write, and execute permissions of the file's owner. In other words, if you see rwx in this position, the file's owner can read (r), write (w), and execute (x) the file. A hyphen in the place of a letter indicates no permission. Thus, the string rw- means that the owner has read and write permissions but not execute permission. Although executable programs (including shell programs) typically have execute permission, directories treat execute permission as equivalent to *use* permission: a user must have execute permission on a directory before they can open and read the contents of the directory.

Middle group   Controls the read, write, and execute permissions of any user belonging to that file's group.

Rightmost group   Controls the read, write, and execute permissions of all other users (collectively thought of as the world).

Thus, a file with the permission setting rwx------ is accessible only to the file's owner, whereas the permission setting rwxr--r-- makes the file readable by the world.

 An interesting feature of the ls command is that it doesn't list any file whose name begins with a period. To see these files, you must use the ls command with the -a option, as follows: ls -a.

Changing Permissions and Ownership

You may need to change a file's permission settings to protect it from others. Use the chmod command to change the permission settings of a file or a directory. To use chmod effectively, you have to specify the permission settings. A good way is to concatenate letters from the columns of Table 6.3 in the order shown (who/action/permission). You use only the single character from each column—the text in parentheses is for explanation only.

TABLE 6.3   Letter codes for file permissions.

Who	Action	Permission
u (user)	+ (add)	r (read)
g (group)	- (remove)	w (write)
o (others)	= (assign)	x (execute)
a (all)	s (set user ID)	

For example, to give everyone read access to all the files in a directory, pick a (for *all*) from the first column, + (for *add*) from the second column, and r (for *read*) from the third column, to come up with the permission setting a+r. Then use the set of options with chmod, as follows:

```
chmod a+r *
```

On the other hand, to permit everyone to execute one specific file, type the following:

```
chmod a+x filename
```

Use ls -l to verify that the change took place.

Sometimes you have to change a file's user or group ownership in order for everything to work correctly. For example, suppose you're instructed to create a directory named *cups* and give it the ownership of user ID *lp* and group ID *sys*. You can log in as root and create the cups directory with the command mkdir as follows:

```
mkdir cups
```

If you check the file's details with the ls -l command, you see that the user and group ownership are both assigned to root. To change the owner, use the chown command. For example, to change the ownership of the cups directory to user ID *lp* and group ID *sys*, type the following:

```
chown lp.sys cups
```

Driver/Firmware Updates

With any operating system, it is essential to keep the drivers and firmware updated. Always remember to back up your configurations (such as for routers) before making any significant changes—in particular, a firmware upgrade—in order to provide a fallback in case something goes awry.

Many network devices contain firmware with which you interact during configuration. For security purposes, you must authenticate in order to make configuration changes and do so initially by using the default account(s). Make sure that the default password is changed after the installation on any network device; otherwise, you are leaving that device open for anyone recognizing the hardware to access it using the known factory password.

Updating firmware for macOS is performed via software updates. During the software update process, the firmware and software that corresponds to it are updated. Updating firmware for the hardware installed on Linux computers will vary significantly, depending on the type of hardware. Many enterprise Linux vendors, such as Red Hat, include firmware updates in their software updates. As a rule, however, firmware is not part of the Linux software update process.

Operating System Life Cycle

All operating systems have a life cycle of release, support, and eventually end-of-life (EOL). When most operating systems reach their EOL, the vendor stops supplying security patches. The void of the most current patches creates a giant vulnerability for the organization, because the operating system is no longer protected from the latest vulnerabilities. To combat these vulnerabilities, it is recommended that you keep the operating system current. This is accomplished with continual upgrades to the operating system as new versions are released.

System Logs

This section will cover the system logs.

Event Viewer

Event Viewer (`eventvwr.msc`) is an MMC snap-in that shows a lot of detailed information about what is running on your operating system. You can start it in several different ways—for example, by clicking Start, typing **Event Viewer**, and selecting the Event Viewer app, or by right-clicking the Start button and selecting Event Viewer from the context menu. In addition, you can add it as a snap-in inside the MMC or press Windows key + R, type **eventvwr.msc**, and press Enter.

Event Viewer should be the first place you look when you are trying to solve a problem that is not evident. The system and applications will often create an entry in Event Viewer that can be used to verify operations or diagnose problems, as shown in Figure 6.24.

Table 6.4 highlights the three main event logs that you should be concerned with for the exam. Each feature in Windows has the ability to store its events in specific log files, in application and service logs.

Although you might think that all the security-related information is in the Security log, you're only half right. The Security log is used by the Security Reference Monitor inside the *Executive kernel*. It is responsible for reporting object audit attempts. Examples of object audit attempts include file access, group membership, and password changes.

Most of the useful security-related information will be in the Application and System logs. Using these logs, you can see errors and warnings that will alert you to potential security-related problems. When you suspect an issue with the operating system or an application that interacts with the operating system, you should check these logs for clues. The event log won't tell you exactly what is wrong and how to fix it, but it will tell you whether there is an issue that needs to be investigated.

FIGURE 6.24   Event Viewer.

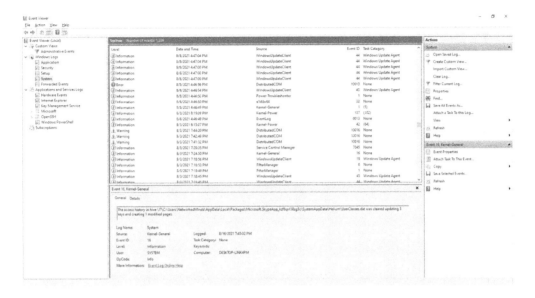

TABLE 6.4   Event Viewer logs.

Event log	Description
Application	Events generated by applications installed on the operating system
Security	Events generated by the Security Reference Monitor in the Executive kernel
System	Events generated by the operating system

Audit Logs

The most common method of tracking user actions is through the use of logs. Nearly all operating systems have built-in logs that track various actions. For example, Windows-based systems contain Windows Logs, which are part of Event Viewer. To open Event Viewer, click Start and type **Event**. Click Event Viewer in Best Matches when it appears. Windows has logs that track application events, security events, and system events. Figure 6.25 shows the Security log. In an environment where multiple users log in, those logins will be shown here.

FIGURE 6.25   Security log in Event Viewer.

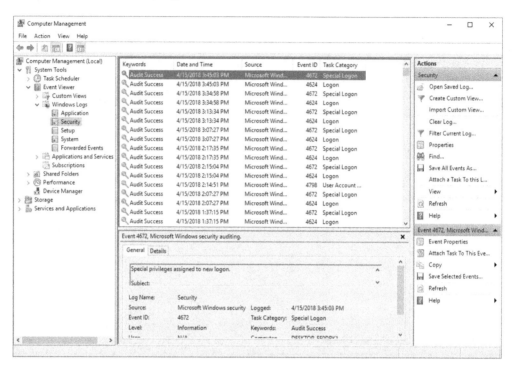

Syslog

Syslog is a client-server protocol that allows just about any device on the network to send logs as they happen. The protocol operates on UDP port 514, and it's considered a "fire-and-forget" type of protocol. This means that the device sending the message never receives an acknowledgment that the message was received. So you really need to make sure that the logs are being collected at the Syslog server, also known as the Syslog collector.

It is also important to note that by default, network devices and Linux/Unix operating systems will write a file called Syslog because it contains local events for the device. This comes in handy when troubleshooting, but it also causes challenges if the device completely fails. Therefore, it's always best to ship the logs off the network device or operating system with the Syslog protocol pointed to a Syslog collector.

Syslog Collector

The Syslog server is also called the Syslog collector. This is the server to which all log files are sent from the various servers, router, switches, and other devices that send logs. Figure 6.26 shows the data flow.

FIGURE 6.26 Syslog collector.

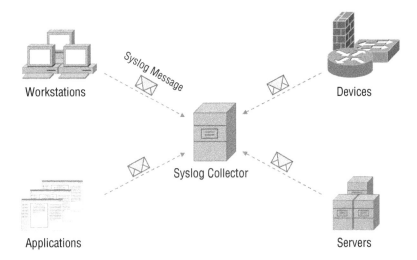

Workstations

Syslog Message

Devices

Syslog Collector

Applications

Servers

Network devices can be configured to generate a Syslog message and forward it to various destinations. These four examples are popular ways to gather messages from Cisco devices:

- Logging buffer (on by default)
- Console line (on by default)
- Terminal lines (using the terminal monitor command)
- Syslog server

Syslog Messages

The Syslog message format is standardized, as shown in Figure 6.27. The message will start with a timestamp so you know when it was created. On some network devices, sequence numbers can be used in lieu of timestamps. Sequence numbers are useful because some events can happen simultaneously, and the sequence number helps sort out which happened first. The next field, called the Device-id, is optional. By default, for most network devices, the Device-id is not sent. However, it's useful to send it if you are sending these messages to a centralized syslog server. The Device-id can be a hostname, an IP address, or any string that identifies the device. The next field actually comprises three different parts: the facility, severity, and mnemonic. The facility is the internal system inside the device that has generated the log message. The severity is standardized based upon a 0–7 severity level that we will cover in the next section. The mnemonic is nothing more than the action the facility took, and its value is a simple string. The last section of a Syslog message is the message text itself. This is what exactly happened to generate the Syslog message.

FIGURE 6.27   Anatomy of a Syslog message.

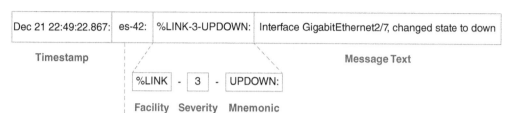

Logging Levels/Severity Levels

Most services such as DNS and DHCP have some sort of debug feature to help you diagnose problems. The debug feature will produce some form of logs, either on the screen or to a file. Keep in mind that when logs are produced, you will end up with a certain level of noise from normal events. So some services allow you to specify a logging level in an effort to reduce the noise or dive deeper into the problem. This of course all depends on what you specify, your mode of diagnostic, and your tolerance for the noise in the log file.

The Syslog protocol/service is used solely for logging events on network devices and operating systems. Therefore, it has a built-in logging level called a severity level. These severity levels range from the most critical level of 0 (emergency) to the least critical of 7 (debug). This gives you a total of eight levels to choose from, as shown in Table 6.5.

A level can be throttled back and forth depending on what you are trying to capture. The severity level is also inclusive of lower levels. This means that if you choose a level of 3, it will include the logging that would be produced at level 2 and level 1. For example, if you configure the severity level to the lowest value of 0, you will receive only the emergency messages. However, if you configure the severity level to 4, you will receive all of the warning (4), error (3), critical (2), alert (1), and emergency (0) messages.

Identifying Anomalies

Logging events is important for a number of reasons, such as post-mortem analysis and auditing as well as identifying what happened and who or what caused it in the event of a security breach. Most network devices and operating systems will log locally to a file, but this will cause a problem in the event of device failure because the log files will be inaccessible. The optimal strategy for logging is to point all of the network devices and operating systems to one centralized logging server. This centralized logging server will create a central repository of logs for the entire network. However, do not underestimate the massive amounts of logs that are collected daily. Depending on what exactly is being collected, these servers might require really big and very fast disks.

When reviewing logs, we must first isolate and drill down to the device we need to focus on. Most log management tools such as Splunk and Kibana, just to name a couple,

TABLE 6.5 Syslog severity levels.

Level	Severity	Description
0	Emergency	System is unusable.
1	Alert	Action must be taken immediately.
2	Critical	Critical conditions.
3	Error	Error conditions.
4	Warning	Warning conditions.
5	Notice	Normal, but significant conditions.
6	Informational	Informational messages.
7	Debug	Debug-level messages.

provide drill-down of log data for the system. After you isolate the device in the log, you then need to isolate the normal log data from the abnormal log data. This will allow you to find the root cause of a problem or identify a performance problem depending on the situation, as shown in Figure 6.28. In this particular example, a filter was created to remove anything that wasn't a normal log entry. This is called removing the noise in the logs. This is an art in itself because of the complexity of the data as well as the problem you are trying to solve.

All log viewing tools have a facility to filter log data—even the built-in Event Viewer in the Microsoft operating system has this functionality. In Figure 6.29, you can see that I filtered out everything in the application log except for Critical and Error levels. Every tool will have some method of removing the noise from the logs. I've only presented two tools here, but there are hundreds of tools on the market.

Something else that should be considered when viewing network logs is correlation. Correlation of data is a reason to use centralized log collection. This is because we can correlate events between devices for a given time period. For example, maybe you have a device that is rebooting for no reason. You may begin filtering out all of the noise in the logs to identify only shutdowns and startups for the device. You end up only finding startup events and nothing else for the device, which would mean the device doesn't know it is going to reboot. If you widen the scope of the search to include the networked UPS the device is plugged into, you might find that the UPS has issues that could lead to the mysterious reboots. If the times of the UPS error correlate to the device rebooting, you've solved the mystery. Of course, this correlation of data can be done in a decentralized fashion, but it often takes longer, and data is sometimes overlooked.

FIGURE 6.28   Example of an Elasticsearch with Kibana.

FIGURE 6.29   Event Viewer filtering.

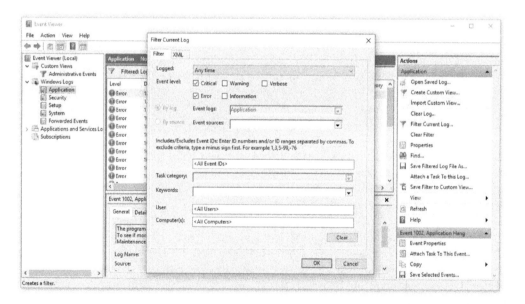

SIEM

Security information and event management (SIEM) is a term for software products and services combining security information management (SIM) and security event management (SEM). SIEM technology provides real-time analysis of security alerts generated by network hardware and applications. You can get this as a software solution or a hardware appliance, and some businesses sell managed services using SIEM. Any one of these solutions provides log security data and can generate reports for compliance purposes.

The acronyms SEM, SIM, and SIEM are used interchangeably; however, SEM is typically used to describe the management that deals with real-time monitoring and correlation of events, notifications, and console views.

 We will cover SIEM in further detail in Chapter 11, "Incident Handling."

Summary

We began this chapter by learning about the security features in the Microsoft Windows operating system. Windows Defender Firewall is the built-in firewall that is turned on right out of the box. PowerShell is the built-in scripting shell, as well as the native command shell. The scripting capability can allow an administrator to automate tasks, but it can also be used by threat actors. We then learned about NTFS permissions and share permissions and how they effectively secure the Windows operating system. We then learned about User Account Control (UAC) and how it protects the administrator form inadvertently installing malware. We then followed the section up by learning all about the Windows Update feature, application patching, and the importance of device driver updates.

The chapter continued to focus on operating system security features for the macOS and Linux operating systems. We learned how to keep the macOS and Linux operating systems up to date with the App Store and apt command, respectively. We then learned about the built-in firewall in macOS, how to turn it on, and how to manage it from the command line. We also learned how to manage the iptables Linux built-in firewall. The section followed up by learning how Linux permissions are configured and how they protect files in the Linux operating system.

The last section in this chapter covered system logs, detailing the importance of collecting and identifying security concerns. We learned that Event Viewer is the built-in Windows log viewer. We also learned how to filter events to remove the noise level in the logs to identify anomalies. The last topic covered in this section was the Syslog protocol and how entries are created.

Exam Essentials

Know how to manage Windows Defender Firewall.   You should know how to manage the Windows Defender Firewall through the basic interface, as well as the more advanced Microsoft Management Console called Windows Defender Firewall with Advance Security.

Know the basics of the PowerShell scripting language.   PowerShell introduced the concept of *cmdlets*. A cmdlet is simply a verb and noun separated by a dash.

Understand the NTFS permission structure and share permissions.   You should have a good understanding of the NTFS permissions of full control, modify, read & execute, list folder contents, read, and write. You should also understand the share permissions of full control, change, and read. You should be able to derive the effective permissions between the NTFS and share permissions.

Understand how User Account Control (UAC) protects the Windows OS.   The UAC was created to reduce the risk of running malware as the administrator account. It performs this function by removing the administrator security token and controlling its access.

Know the importance of updates for operating systems.   Windows Update, macOS App Store, and Linux updates keep the operating system secure by patching vulnerabilities.

Know how to control the macOS firewall and configure the Linux firewall.   The macOS firewall is not on by default, but you can turn it on through Settings or the command line. You should have a good knowledge of configuring rule for iptables in the Linux operating system.

Understand the Linux permission structure.   You should be able to read and configure the permission structure for the Linux file system.

Understand system logs and how they pertain to security.   You should have a good understanding of how system logs can help identify security concerns. You should also have a good understanding of filtering event logs and how removing noise in the logs allows you to identify anomalies.

Review Questions

The following questions are designed to test your understanding of this chapter's material. For more information on how to get additional questions, please see www.lammle.com/ccst.

You can find the answers to these questions in Appendix.

1. A user is in both the Sales group and the Marketing group. The Sales group has full permission at the share level, and the Marketing group has read-only permissions. The files on NTFS are secured with the Modify permission for the Sales group and the Read & Execute permission for the Marketing group. Which permissions will the user have?

   A. Full

   B. Modify

   C. Read-only

   D. Read & Execute

2. James just moved a folder on the same partition. What will happen with the permissions for the folder?

   A. The permissions will be the same as they were before the move.

   B. The permissions will be inherited from the new parent folder.

   C. The permissions will be configured as the root folder for the drive letter.

   D. The permissions will be blank until configured.

3. A user is in the Sales group. The Sales group has no permissions at the share level. The files on NTFS are secured with the Modify permission for the Sales group. What permissions will the user have?

   A. The user will have the Modify permission when connecting from the network.

   B. The user will have the Modify permission when logged in locally to the computer.

   C. The user will have no access when logged in locally to the computer.

   D. The user will have read-only permissions when connecting from the network.

4. Which statement about scripting languages is true?

   A. Scripting languages require a compiler.

   B. Scripting languages are strongly typed.

   C. Scripting languages are interpreted.

   D. Scripting languages have good memory management.

5. Which statement will load a PowerShell variable xvar with a value of 2?

   A. xvar = 2

   B. $xvar = 2

C. `xvar = 2;`

D. `set /a xvar=2`

6. Which of the following utilities can be used in Linux to download patches for installation on a workstation?

   A. `update`

   B. Shell/terminal

   C. `apt`

   D. `patch`

7. Which of the following commands can be used to change the owner of a file to a new owner in Linux?

   A. `cd`

   B. `chmod`

   C. `chown`

   D. `pwd`

8. If the permissions for a file are `rwxrw-r--`, what permissions apply for a user who is a member of the group to which the owner belongs?

   A. Read, write, and execute

   B. Read and write

   C. Read only

   D. No access

9. Which command will start the Event Viewer snap-in?

   A. `eventviewer.exe`

   B. `eventvwr.msc`

   C. `lusrmgr.msc`

   D. `devmgmt.msc`

10. Which event log should be checked if you suspect that the computer has rebooted unexpectedly?

    A. Application

    B. Boot

    C. Security

    D. System

Chapter

7

Endpoint Security

THE FOLLOWING CCST EXAM TOPIC IS COVERED IN THIS CHAPTER:

✔ **3.0 Endpoint Security**

  ▪ 3.2. Demonstrate familiarity with appropriate endpoint tools that gather security assessment information.

   netstat, nslookup, tcpdump

  ▪ 3.3. Verify that endpoint systems meet security policies and standards

   Hardware inventory (asset management), software inventory, program deployment, data backups, regulatory compliance (PCI DSS, HIPAA, GDPR), BYOD (device management, data encryption, app distribution, configuration management)

  ▪ 3.6. Demonstrate familiarity with malware removal

   Scanning systems, reviewing scan logs, malware remediation

It is arguable that the endpoints in our networks are the weakest links in our security. The endpoint is where the end user interfaces with the network, and that is why it is an optimal place for a threat actor to enter the network.

Therefore, our defenses need to be strong at the endpoint, and we need to know how to diagnosis endpoints.

In this chapter, we will explore the various endpoint tools that you can use to assess and explore your endpoints. We will then explore endpoint security and compliance and how each goes hand-in-hand. We will then conclude the chapter by learning how to recover from endpoint compromise.

To find your included bonus material, as well as Todd Lammle videos, practice questions, and hands-on labs, please see www.lammle.com/ccst.

Endpoint Tools

When an endpoint misbehaves, it can be caused by outside interference from threat actors or bad configuration. Typically, you will find that the endpoint is just misconfigured; at least, that's the best scenario. Fortunately, there are tools that can help diagnose a misconfigured endpoint. They come in the form of command-line tools and GUI (graphical user interface) tools. In the following section, we will learn about the most common tools to help you diagnose endpoints.

Command-Line Tools

On any given day at work, you will always find a command prompt open on one of my many monitors. Using a command line is just faster than a bunch of clicking. Some tools can only be accessed via a command line, as you'll see in the following sections. These command-line tools allow us to diagnose and troubleshoot network issues.

netstat

The `netstat` command allows you to view listening and established network connections for the operating system. Several switches can be used with the `netstat` command. One of the most useful is the `-b` switch, which displays the name of the application and its current established connections. Adding the `-a` switch displays all the listening connections in addition to the established connections. A basic example follows:

```
C:\Users\Sybex>netstat

Active Connections

   Proto  Local Address         Foreign Address         State
   TCP    127.0.0.1:49750       view-localhost:50912    ESTABLISHED
   TCP    127.0.0.1:50912       view-localhost:49751    ESTABLISHED
   TCP    172.16.1.181:49208    104.20.60.241:https     ESTABLISHED
   TCP    172.16.1.181:49599    172.67.181.149:https    ESTABLISHED
   TCP    172.16.1.181:49600    52.167.17.97:https      TIME_WAIT
   TCP    172.16.1.181:49602    20.50.80.210:https      ESTABLISHED
   TCP    172.16.1.181:49603    a104-75-163-105:http    TIME_WAIT
   TCP    172.16.1.181:56759    151.101.1.140:https     ESTABLISHED
   TCP    172.16.1.181:64151    iad23s96-in-f10:https   CLOSE_WAIT
   TCP    172.16.1.181:64152    iad66s01-in-f13:https   CLOSE_WAIT
   TCP    172.16.1.181:64154    iad23s96-in-f10:https   CLOSE_WAIT

C:\Users\Sybex>
```

nslookup

DNS is one of the most important network services that an operating system and user rely on for resolution of a domain name to an IP address. Without DNS, we just couldn't remember the millions of IP addresses; it would be like trying to remember the phone number of every person you've ever met or are going to meet.

When DNS problems arise, the `nslookup` command allows you to verify that DNS is working correctly and that the correct results are being returned. The simplest way to use DNS is to use an inline query, such as **nslookup**. This will return the IP address associated with the *fully qualified domain name (FQDN)* of a domain name. The `nslookup` command can also be used in the interactive mode by typing **nslookup** and pressing Enter. This mode allows you to query more than the associated IP address, depending on the type of DNS record you are trying to diagnose. By default, the record looked up with the `nslookup` command is the A or CNAME DNS records. These records are the most commonly looked-up DNS records for diagnosing connectivity issues. By specifying the `-type` argument, you can change the default record queried.

The following is an example of retrieving the IP address for the FQDN of the domain name, as well as the use of the `-type` argument:

```
C:\Users\Sybex>nslookup www.sybex.com
Server:  pfsense.wiley.local
Address:  172.16.1.1

Non-authoritative answer:
Name:    www.sybex.com
Address:  63.97.118.67

C:\Users\Sybex>nslookup -type=mx sybex.com
Server: pfSense.wiley.local
Address: 172.16.1.1

Non-authoritative answer:
sybex.com    MX preference = 20, mail exchanger = cluster1a.us.messagelabs.com
sybex.com    MX preference = 10, mail exchanger = cluster1.us.messagelabs.com

C:\Users\Sybex>
```

dig

The Domain Information Groper (dig) tool is almost identical to the `nslookup` tool and has become an adopted standard for name resolution testing on Linux/UNIX operating systems. The tool allows us to resolve any resource record for a given host and direct the query to a specific server.

The command does not offer an interactive mode like the `nslookup` command. The command by default queries A records for a given host, and the output has debugging turned on by default.

In the following example, we see a query being performed on the DNS server of 8.8.8.8 for an MX record for the domain of sybex.com. The debugging output shows that one query was given, two answers were retrieved, and nothing was authoritative (not the primary servers). The output also details the query made and the answers returned:

```
root@Sybex:~# dig @8.8.8.8 mx sybex.com

; <<>> DiG 9.9.5-3ubuntu0.13-Ubuntu <<>> @8.8.8.8 mx sybex.com
; (1 server found)
;; global options: +cmd
;; Got answer:
;; ->>HEADER<<- opcode: QUERY, status: NOERROR, id: 49694
;; flags: qr rd ra; QUERY: 1, ANSWER: 2, AUTHORITY: 0, ADDITIONAL: 1

;; OPT PSEUDOSECTION:
; EDNS: version: 0, flags:; udp: 512
;; QUESTION SECTION:
;sybex.com. IN MX
```

```
;; ANSWER SECTION:
sybex.com.        899   IN   MX    10 cluster1.us.messagelabs.com.
sybex.com.        899   IN   MX    20 cluster1a.us.messagelabs.com.

;; Query time: 76 msec
;; SERVER: 8.8.8.8#53(8.8.8.8)
;; WHEN: Wed Nov 01 21:43:32 EDT 2017
;; MSG SIZE rcvd: 104

root@Sybex:~#
```

ping

Next to the `ipconfig` command, the `ping` command is the runner-up as the network administrator's best friend. The `ping` command allows you to verify network connectivity via *Internet Control Message Protocol (ICMP)* packets. A common troubleshooting step used by network administrators is to ping the default gateway. If it returns a ping, then the network connectivity problem is probably beyond that device or your subnet mask is incorrect. However, after a successful ping, you can verify that your computer has basic connectivity to it. An example of a successful ping is as follows:

```
C:\Users\Sybex>ping 172.16.1.1

Pinging 172.16.1.1 with 32 bytes of data:
Reply from 172.16.1.1: bytes=32 time<1ms TTL=64
Reply from 172.16.1.1: bytes=32 time<1ms TTL=64
Reply from 172.16.1.1: bytes=32 time<1ms TTL=64
Reply from 172.16.1.1: bytes=32 time<1ms TTL=64

Ping statistics for 172.16.1.1:
    Packets: Sent = 4, Received = 4, Lost = 0 (0% loss),
Approximate round trip times in milli-seconds:
    Minimum = 0ms, Maximum = 0ms, Average = 0ms

C:\Users\Sybex>
```

tracert

The `tracert` command allows the network administrator to verify the path a network packet travels to its destination. As the diagnostic packet passes through the internetwork, each router responds with a response time. This enables you to locate a fault in an internetwork. Here's an example:

```
C:\Users\Sybex>tracert 8.8.8.8

Tracing route to google-public-dns-a.google.com      [8.8.8.8]
over a maximum of 30 hops:
  1    <1 ms    <1 ms    <1 ms   pfsense.Sybex.local  [172.16.1.1]
  2    13 ms    12 ms    17 ms   96.120.62.213
  3    15 ms    15 ms    12 ms   te04012.comcast.net  [68.86.101.141]
```

```
 4    13 ms    19 ms    12 ms   162.151.152.153
 5    12 ms    13 ms    20 ms   96.108.91.78
 6    22 ms    14 ms    20 ms   96.108.91.121
 7    21 ms    24 ms    20 ms   be-7016-cr02.comcast.net   [68.86.91.25]
 8    20 ms    20 ms    26 ms   be-10130-pe04.comcast.net  [68.86.82.214]
 9    20 ms    20 ms    21 ms   as040-2-c.comcast.net   [75.149.229.86]
10    22 ms    21 ms    20 ms   108.170.240.97
11    20 ms    23 ms    21 ms   108.170.226.85
12    20 ms    22 ms    18 ms   google-public-dns-a.google.com  [8.8.8.8]

Trace complete.

C:\Users\Sybex>
```

tcpdump

The tcpdump command is available only on Linux and UNIX operating systems. The command is used to dump network data to a file or the console of the host you are connected to. It is useful when we want to see the network packets either entering or leaving a host. The tcpdump command that follows will output all of the packets that match the port of SSH on interface eth0:

```
root@sybex:~# tcpdump -s 0 port ssh -i eth0
tcpdump: verbose output suppressed, use -v or -vv for full protocol decode
listening on eth0, link-type EN10MB (Ethernet), capture size 262144 bytes
22:17:59.829560 IP 172.16.1.161.ssh > 172.16.1.101.50703: Flags [P.], seq 32238
1889:322382097, ack 106937580, win 326, length 208
22:17:59.829719 IP 172.16.1.101.50703 > 172.16.1.161.ssh: Flags [.], ack 208, w
in 16121, length 0
22:17:59.831710 IP 172.16.1.161.ssh > 172.16.1.101.50703: Flags [P.], seq 208:4
96, ack 1, win 326, length 288
22:17:59.831782 IP 172.16.1.161.ssh > 172.16.1.101.50703: Flags [P.], seq 496:6
72, ack 1, win 326, length 176
22:17:59.831856 IP 172.16.1.101.50703 > 172.16.1.161.ssh: Flags [.], ack 672, w
in 16425, length 0
22:17:59.831863 IP 172.16.1.161.ssh > 172.16.1.101.50703: Flags [P.], seq 672:8
48, ack 1, win 326, length 176
22:17:59.831922 IP 172.16.1.161.ssh > 172.16.1.101.50703: Flags [P.], seq 848:1
120, ack 1, win 326, length 272

[Output cut]
```

The tcpdump command is so versatile that we can even capture traffic into a file and then pull up the file in Wireshark! The command tcpdump -s 0 port ssh -i eth0 -w capture.pcap will save all the packets that match a port of SSH to the file called capture.pcap. We can also omit the filter for SSH and capture any traffic to and from the system. If we wanted to be really creative, we could use ifconfig eth0 promisc to turn on promiscuous mode for the interface and capture any traffic seen by the host.

nmap

The nmap tool allows us to scan open and closed ports on remote systems for audit purposes. It can be used to validate that the firewall is open to accept requests for an application. The nmap tool is a Linux/UNIX-based tool that has been ported to Windows.

The nmap tool can scan all ports of a specific host or a range of hosts in the network. This allows for the discovery of a host that might not be known or protected with firewall rules. The nmap tool will also try to negotiate with Transport Layer Security (TLS) in an attempt to discover the encryption key strength being used. In addition to these features, it will try to predict the operating system the remote system is using.

In the following example, the nmap command was run with the -A argument that enables operating system detection, version detection, script scanning, and route tracing:

```
root@sybex:~# nmap -A scanme.nmap.org

Starting Nmap 6.40 (http://nmap.org) at 2017-10-31 21:34 EDT
Nmap scan report for scanme.nmap.org (45.33.32.156)
Host is up (0.094s latency).
Not shown: 993 closed ports
PORT    STATE   SERVICE   VERSION
22/tcp  open    ssh       (protocol 2.0)
| ssh-hostkey: 1024 ac:00:a0:1a:82:ff:cc:55:99:dc:67:2b:34:97:6b:75 (DSA)
| 2048 20:3d:2d:44:62:2a:b0:5a:9d:b5:b3:05:14:c2:a6:b2 (RSA)
|_256 96:02:bb:5e:57:54:1c:4e:45:2f:56:4c:4a:24:b2:57 (ECDSA)
25/tcp filtered smtp
80/tcp open     http      Apache httpd 2.4.7 ((Ubuntu))
|_http-title: Go ahead and ScanMe!
135/tcp  filtered msrpc
139/tcp  filtered netbios-ssn
445/tcp  filtered microsoft-ds
31337/tcp open    tcpwrapped
1 service unrecognized despite returning data. If you know the service/version,
please submit the following fingerprint at http://www.insecure.org/cgi-bin/ser
vicefp-submit.cgi:SF-Port22-TCP:V=6.40%I=7%D=10/31%Time=59F925EF%
P=x86_64-pc-linux-gnu%r(NUL
SF:L,2B, "SSH-2\.0-OpenSSH_6\.6\.1p1\x20Ubuntu-2ubuntu2\.8\r\n");
Device type: general purpose|firewall|WAP|terminal
Running (JUST GUESSING): Linux 3.X|2.6.X|2.4.X (92%), IPFire Linux 2.6.X (88%),
IGEL Linux 2.6.X (85%) OS CPE: cpe:/o:linux:linux_kernel:3 cpe:/o:linux:linux_k
ernel:2.6 cpe:/o:ipfire:linux:2.6.32 cpe:/o:linux:linux_kernel:2.4 cpe:/o:igel:
linux_kernel:2.6 Aggressive OS guesses: Linux 3.2 - 3.6 (92%), Linux 2.6.32 - 2
.6.39 (90%), Linux 2.6.32 - 3.0 (89%), Linux 3.5 (88%), Linux 2.6.32 (88%), IPF
ire firewall 2.11 (Linux 2.6.32) (88%), Linux 2.6.15 - 2.6.26 (likely embedded)
(86%), Linux 2.6.32 - 2.6.33(86%), Linux 2.6.32 - 2.6.35(86%),
Linux 2.6.18(86%)No exact OS matches for host (test conditions non-ideal).
Network Distance: 12 hops

[Output cut]
```

If we add the -v argument, we will be able to see the progress of nmap as the scan progresses. The problem with scanning a remote host is that closed ports do not always respond as they should, and some operating systems do not respond at all. This lack of response makes it difficult to know whether the service is running, firewalled, or just dead. There are many other arguments that we can include to change the behavior of the scan:

- Use -sN for a NULL scan in which no flags are set in the transport layer header. If the port is closed, then the destination operating system will send back an RST. If the port is open, then nothing is sent back.

- Use -sF for a FIN scan in which the FIN flag is set in an attempt to trick the operating system into responding to closed ports with an RST, similar to a NULL scan.

- Use -sX for an Xmas-Tree scan in which the URG, PSH, and FIN flags are set in an attempt to trick the operating system into sending an RST for closed ports.

gpresult

The gpresult command is used to show the Resultant Set of Policy (RSoP) report/values for a remote user and computer. Bear in mind that configuration settings occur in any number of places: they are set for a computer, a user, a local workstation, the domain, and so on. Often, one of the big unknowns is which set of configuration settings takes precedence and which is overridden. With gpresult, it is possible to ascertain which settings apply.

A number of switches can be used in conjunction with the gpresult command. The most useful switches are the /r and /z switches. The /r switch allows you to see the RSoP summary of GPOs applied. This allows you to quickly verify whether a policy is being applied. You can then use the /z switch to turn on super-verbosity, which allows the output to display the exact settings being applied.

Software Tools

Software tools are used to troubleshoot network problems and verify cause and validate effect. In the previous section, you learned about hardware tools that are used to repair network connections. You will now learn about the popular software tools that are used to detect the root cause of problems and troubleshoot networking issues.

Port Scanner

Port scanners are used for troubleshooting connectivity issues and security assessments. When the port scanner is used for troubleshooting, the tool will scan the remote server to identify open ports that respond to the tool's requests. This is useful to validate that a server is serving information on the port and a firewall is not blocking the request.

We also use a port scanner to perform a security assessment of our servers. The port scanner verifies the open ports and the ports that are closed (firewalled). This helps reduce the risk that a firewall is misconfigured and allowing unauthorized access to services on the remote server.

There are several different port scanners that can be downloaded for free. The most popular open-source port scanner is Nmap. Originally it was compiled for Linux and UNIX, but it has since been ported to the Windows platform. Microsoft also offers a free tool called PortQry, which is a command-line-based tool similar to Nmap.

iPerf

The iPerf tool is a software tool used to measure the performance of a network path. It measures performance by sending traffic from one end to the other. The tool requires a client and a server: the server sits and waits for an incoming connection from the client and reports back the speed of the incoming packets. The most useful feature of this tool is that it's compiled for many different devices such as firewalls, switches, and platforms such as Linux and Windows, just to name a few. The tool also works in two different modes, TCP and UDP. In TCP mode, the overhead of the acknowledgments and sequencing can be measured with overall traffic compared to UDP.

A typical application for iPerf is the measurement of bandwidth across a network path for Voice over IP (VoIP) applications. The iPerf tool acts as a stress test by sending large numbers of packets in an attempt to measure the overall throughput. Another application where iPerf is used is to benchmark the throughput for a router or firewall. In the following example, you will see the path across a network connection over an interval of 10 seconds:

```
C:\sys>iperf3.exe -c iperf.sybex.com
Connecting to host iperf.sybex.com, port 5201
[  4] local 172.16.1.181 port 58039 connected to 24.7.124.124 port 5201
[ ID] Interval           Transfer     Bandwidth
[  4]   0.00-1.00   sec  1.12 MBytes  9.43 Mbits/sec
[  4]   1.00-2.00   sec  1.38 MBytes  11.5 Mbits/sec
[  4]   2.00-3.00   sec   512 KBytes  4.19 Mbits/sec
[  4]   3.00-4.00   sec  1.38 MBytes  11.5 Mbits/sec
[  4]   4.00-5.00   sec  1.38 MBytes  11.5 Mbits/sec
[  4]   5.00-6.00   sec  1.38 MBytes  11.5 Mbits/sec
[  4]   6.00-7.00   sec  1.50 MBytes  12.6 Mbits/sec
[  4]   7.00-8.00   sec  1.38 MBytes  11.5 Mbits/sec
[  4]   8.00-9.00   sec  1.38 MBytes  11.5 Mbits/sec
[  4]   9.00-10.00  sec  1.38 MBytes  11.5 Mbits/sec
- - - - - - - - - - - - - - - - - - - - - - - - - - -
[ ID] Interval           Transfer     Bandwidth
[  4]   0.00-10.00  sec  12.8 MBytes  10.7 Mbits/sec                    sender
[  4]   0.00-10.00  sec  12.7 MBytes  10.6 Mbits/sec                    receiver

iperf Done.

C:\sys>
```

FIGURE 7.1   A typical IP scanner.

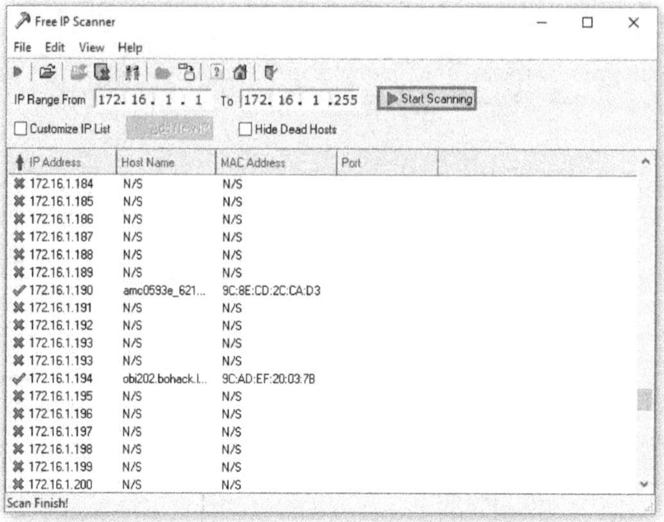

IP Scanner

An IP scanner is used to scan a range of IP addresses, as shown in Figure 7.1. The IP scanner software tool is extremely useful for finding free IP addresses in a particular IP address range. The tool is also useful for locating a host within an IP address range. The tool will first scan the IP address space and report back if the IP address responds to an ICMP ping request. Most tools will then reverse the DNS address of the IP address to display the host's friendly DNS name.

Although this tool is useful for quickly finding out whether an IP address is taken, many operating systems will not reply to a ping request by default. On many newer operating systems such as Windows 11 and Server 2022, the firewall is configured out of the box. So you should always use a more formal approach to IP address management (IPAM). With that being said, this tool does work in most situations.

Endpoint Security and Compliance

One of our primary responsibilities as security professionals is to ensure the security and compliance of all our endpoint systems. Before we can secure our systems, we need to know what systems we own and the various software packages installed on them. We need to ensure that these applications are up to date and that we have made proper backups of the data these applications maintain. Once we know what we need to protect, we need to know how to protect these systems. Fortunately, this is where compliance come to the rescue. In this section, we will learn the important of inventory, updates, and regulatory compliance.

Hardware Inventory

Keeping track of your hardware inventory is an important part of IT department's responsibilities. When equipment is initially purchased, the accounting department will record it as an asset on the company's general ledger because it adds to the value of the company. Over time, however, the asset will lose its initial value. The accounting department will depreciate the value of the asset based on its perceived lifespan.

As hardware ages, it doesn't just depreciate financially; it can also increase an organization's risk due to security vulnerabilities. Hardware typically contains firmware or an operating system that can become vulnerable to exploits as the device ages. An example of firmware might be something as simple as BIOS for a host, the code that makes a network, or a video card function, just to name a few. In addition, many different network devices such as switches and routers contain an operating system, such as Cisco IOS. These network device operating systems can contain vulnerabilities as well.

Therefore, we need to track hardware and its respective firmware or operating system versions. We can then assess our organization's risk due to outdated firmware or operating systems. Hardware inventory management also helps the IT department in forecasting upgrades. This in turn helps us gauge the work involved to patch the hardware. As hardware ages and reaches its end of life, it will eventually fall out of support for upgrades. Hardware inventory management will help plan for future expenditures for replacement of the equipment, in addition to the growth of the organization.

Asset Management Systems

There are a number of ways to manage assets for the organization. Choosing a way to manage assets depends on what needs to be done with the information. Asset management at an organization-wide level is often a module of an accounting package used by the company. This software allows an asset (equipment) to be tracked by associating a number on the asset tag with the condition, business unit, and perceived value of the equipment. These types of databases work well for reporting on the value of equipment that the organization owns to calculate a net worth for an organization, but they do very little in helping the IT department plan upgrades.

Laptops, desktops, and other devices have variables such as storage, RAM, operating system versions, and other unique variables to the hardware and software of the device. Asset management systems are databases that collect data from the operating system through the use of an agent. This type of asset management is more detailed than a purchasing record from the accounting department. Once the information is collected, reports can be created when upgrades are required. For example, a report you may compile in the asset management

FIGURE 7.2   An asset tag.

system might be all operating systems that match Windows 10 and that have less than 4 GB of RAM and hard drives smaller than 100 GB. You then have a report of what needs to be upgraded in terms of hardware for an upgrade of the operating system to Windows 11. When using asset management for an organization that spans a large geographic area, this is invaluable information that otherwise would have taken days to collect.

Asset Tags

All computer and network equipment should be tracked, from the cradle to the grave, by the IT department. When equipment enters the company, it should be labeled with an asset tag, as shown in Figure 7.2. The asset tag is often a permanent metallic sticker or metallic plate that is riveted to the equipment. The asset tag will often have a barcode, which defines the numeric number that identifies the asset. This asset tag should then be entered into the asset management software by either typing in the number or scanning the barcode.

Software Inventory

Whether the assets in your organization are hardware or software, the assets will at some point raise the organization's risk. All hardware and software at some point will contain a vulnerability that you need to patch. Collecting all the hardware and software inventory into a spreadsheet or database might be great for tracking the monetary value of an organization. However, it does very little to help you correlate versions of firmware and software that need to be patched.

Many popular endpoint detection and response (EDR) systems and vulnerability management systems will require the installation of an agent on the operating system. This agent will inventory all your attached hardware and installed software. The agent will report the hardware and software to a centralized server that is located either on-premises or in the cloud. This list will then be compared to current vulnerabilities, and a report can be generated to help you plan your upgrades.

One popular system for identifying vulnerabilities and collecting hardware and software components is the Microsoft Defender Security Center. Microsoft Defender Security Center will correlate current vulnerable to your current hardware and software inventory and produce a rolling security score. You can then drill down and find which hosts are affecting your overall score. An example of vulnerabilities on a specific host is shown in Figure 7.3.

FIGURE 7.3   Microsoft Defender Security Center.

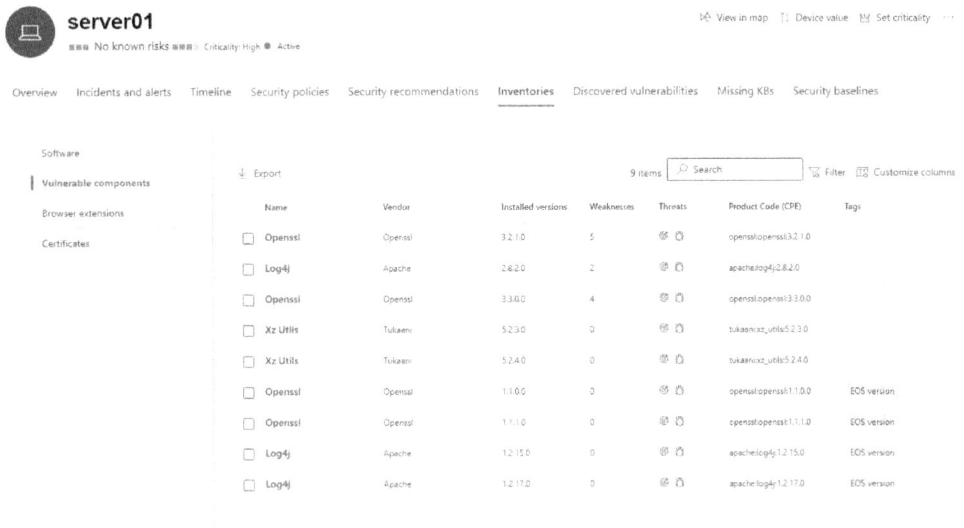

The mechanism that inventories the software is an agent installed in the operating system. With Microsoft Defender Security Center, this is performed by the Microsoft Defender client installed on all Windows operating systems. This works great for software inventory, but what if you want to inventory routers and switches? An agent can be installed on your network that can continually scan IP addresses and report back discovered hardware. Then the EDR or vulnerability management system can present you with vulnerabilities that might exist and need to be patched.

Although the prior example focused on Microsoft solutions, there are many other solutions on the market today. They all function similarly, requiring a software agent and a hardware scanning agent. The software inventory and protection at the host level is typically one agent, and the hardware scanning is another agent.

Remediation

Now we have an understanding of how we can inventory our vulnerable hardware and software. We also have a system that can identify the systems that need to be patched for vulnerabilities. The next question is, how do we remediate these hosts?

Unfortunately, there is no one answer for the remediation of vulnerabilities. Hardware vulnerabilities might require you to physically visit the hardware and upgrade the firmware or operating system. Hardware might even have a system that is proprietary to itself for updates, such as sever firmware upgrades. Software typically requires an update or reinstallation of the software, depending on the product.

The two most common methods for application deployment are on-premises and cloud-based. The on-premises system called Microsoft Endpoint Manager, formerly called System Center Configuration Manager (SCCM), can deploy applications to on-premises systems. The cloud-based system that is typically used with Microsoft products is Intune. Both solutions will accommodate different needs. The on-premises system works well when all your clients are fixed to an office location, such as desktop computers. The cloud-based solution excels when you have laptops and users who work from home.

Regardless of your preference of the method you might want to use to deploy updated software, the software vendor must support it. Most applications today support application deployments and upgrades. However, there are some vendors that might not support application deployments and upgrades. These vendors typically have their own patching methods. One example of this is Google Chrome, but there are many other vendors, such as server-based software. The underlying key is to get rid of vulnerabilities and drive your security score higher, no matter how you deploy your applications and patches.

Considerations

With every great plan, there are unplanned consequences; we call them *considerations*. When you upgrade an operating system, firmware, or application, you have the potential for data loss. Therefore, it is always advisable to back up files and user preferences before starting an upgrade. Depending on the device or user you are upgrading in your organization, if files are lost, it could cause catastrophic loss of sales, payments, and, most importantly, time. Whenever possible, perform a backup of the endpoint. A full-drive backup is advisable, because settings may be in a spot you wouldn't normally back up.

If you are upgrading the operating system, make sure that the applications are supported by the new operating system. You may think that if it runs, then it's supported, but you'd be wrong. Just because a program runs it doesn't mean that it was meant to be run on the operating system. It is up to the discretion of the software vendor if it will support you on the latest operating system. This is often discovered in the event you need help from the vendor. So always check whether the application is supported on the latest operating system before upgrading. In many cases, you'll find that software vendors require the latest version of their product purchased or installed for it to be supported on the latest operating system. Applications are also backward compatible with older operating systems because not everyone will be on the latest and greatest operating system.

Destruction and Disposal

Think of all the sensitive data written to a hard drive. The drive can contain information about students, clients, users—about anyone and anything. The hard drive can be in a desktop PC, in a laptop, or even in a printer. Many laser printers above consumer grade offer the ability to add a hard drive to store print jobs. If the drive falls into the wrong hands, you can not only lose valuable data but also risk a lawsuit for not properly protecting privacy. An appropriate data destruction/disposal plan should be in place to avoid any potential problems.

Because data on media holds great value and liability, that media should never simply be tossed away for prying eyes to stumble on. For the purpose of this objective, the media in question is hard drives, and there are three key concepts to understand with regard to them: formatting, sanitation, and destruction. Formatting prepares the drive to hold new information (which can include copying over data already there). Sanitation involves wiping the data off the drive, whereas destruction renders the drive no longer usable.

The following are best practices for recycling or repurposing.

Low-Level Format vs. Standard Format

There are multiple levels of formatting that can be done on a drive. A standard format, accomplished using the operating system's `format` utility (or similar), can mark space occupied by files as available for new files without truly deleting what was there. Such erasing—if you want to call it that—doesn't guarantee that the information isn't still on the disk and recoverable.

A low-level format (typically accomplished only in the factory) can be performed on the system, or a utility can be used to completely wipe the disk clean. This process helps to ensure that information doesn't fall into the wrong hands.

The manufacturer performs a low-level format on integrated device electronics (IDE) hard drives. Low-level formatting must be performed even before a drive can be partitioned. In low-level formatting, the drive controller chip and the drive meet for the very first time and learn to work together. Because controllers are integrated into Serial ATA (SATA) and IDE drives, low-level formatting is a factory process. Low-level formatting is not operating system dependent.

 WARNING   Never perform a low-level format on IDE or SCSI drives! These drives are formatted at the factory, and you may cause problems by using low-level utilities on them.

Hard Drive Sanitation and Sanitation Methods

A number of vendors offer hard drives with *Advanced Encryption Standard (AES)* cryptography built in. However, it's still better to keep these secure hard drives completely out of the hands of others than to trust their internal security mechanisms once their usable lifespan has passed for the client. Some vendors include freeware utilities to erase the hard drive. If it is a SATA drive, you can always run HDDErase, but you are still taking your chances.

Sanitation Utilities

HDDErase is a freeware utility that is included with many different boot images. HDDErase can be downloaded with Hiren's BootCD from www.hirensbootcd.org.

If you were to perform a web search, you would find several other sanitation utilities such as HDDErase, but it is important to recognize and acknowledge that many of these do not meet military or GSA specifications. Those specifications should be considered guidelines to which you must also adhere when dealing with your own, or a client's, data. The only surefire method of rendering the hard drive contents completely eradicated is physical destruction.

Solid-state drives (SSDs) pose a greater problem because the media is flash memory and not mechanical, such as conventional hard disk drives (HDDs). Low-level formats can be performed, as mentioned in the preceding section, but the 1s and 0s will still be technically on the flash memory. Therefore, many vendors have a sanitation utility for scrubbing information from SSDs. It is best to check with the vendor, as these tools are specific to the vendor and model of SSD.

Overwrite

Overwriting the drive entails copying over the data with new data. A common practice is to replace the data with 0s. A number of applications allow you to recover what was there before the last write operation, and for that reason, most overwrite software will write the same sequence and save it multiple times.

DBAN is a utility that comes with its own boot disk; it can be downloaded from https://dban.org. You can find a number of other software "shredders" by doing a quick web search.

Drive Wipe

If it's possible to verify beyond a reasonable doubt that a piece of hardware that's no longer being used doesn't contain any data of a sensitive or proprietary nature, then that hardware can be recycled (sold to employees, sold to a third party, donated to a school, and so on). That level of assurance can come from wiping a hard drive or using specialized utilities.

If you can't be assured that the hardware in question doesn't contain important data, then the hardware should be destroyed. You cannot, and should not, take a risk that the data your company depends on could fall into the wrong hands.

Physical Destruction

Physically destroying the drive involves rendering it no longer usable. Although the focus is on hard drives, you can also physically destroy other forms of media, such as flash drives and CD/DVDs.

Shredder   Many commercial paper shredders are also capable of destroying DVDs and CDs. Paper shredders, however, are not able to handle hard drives; you need a shredder created for just such a purpose. A low-volume hard drive shredder that will destroy eight drives per minute can carry a suggested list price of around $20,000.

Drill/Hammer   If you don't have the budget for a hard drive shredder, you can accomplish similar results in a much more time-consuming way with a power drill. The goal is to physically destroy the platters in the drive.

Electromagnet (degaussing)   A large electromagnet can be used to destroy any magnetic media, such as a hard drive or backup tape set. The most common of these is the degaussing tool. Degaussing involves applying a strong magnetic field to initialize the media. (This is also referred to as disk wiping.) This process helps ensure that information doesn't fall into the wrong hands.

Degaussing involves using a specifically designed electromagnet to eliminate all data on the drive, including the factory-prerecorded servo tracks. You can find wand model degaussers priced at just over $500 or desktop units that sell for up to $30,000.

Incineration   A form of destruction not to be overlooked is fire. It is possible to destroy most devices by burning them, using an accelerant such as gasoline or lighter fluid to aid the process.

Do You Really Want to Do It Yourself?

Even with practice, you will find that manually destroying a hard drive is time consuming. There are companies that specialize in this and can do it efficiently. One such company is Shred-it, which will pick up your hard drive and provide a chain-of-custody assurance and a certificate of destruction on completion. You can find out more about what the company offers at www.shredit.com.

Data Backups

You need to perform backups on the endpoints to safeguard against loss of data. You often need to restore files when users unintentionally write over them, delete them, or misplace them. Restoring from backups can also be useful when the fate of the file is out of your control—for example, when your operating system is struck with ransomware. One of the behaviors of ransomware is to dump all the restore points on your operating system before it starts to encrypt your files. The only way you can get your files back at that point is to pay the ransom or recover the files from a backup.

Now that you understand how important backups are in the wake of disaster, let's look at an option for backing up and restoring files with Windows 11. You can back up your files with OneDrive Folder Syncing. The Windows backup settings can be accessed by opening the Setting App ➤ Accounts ➤ Windows Backup, as shown in Figure 7.4.

Other third-party utilities, such as Carbonite and Backblaze, can also be used to back up and restore data. Some of these services have very unique features, such as locating a missing computer by its IP address if it is lost or stolen. You can even order a USB drive of your data so that the restoration of data is quicker, especially when the size of data to be restored is extremely large.

In Chapter 10, "Disaster Recovery," we will learn about the backup of hosts and servers in much greater detail.

FIGURE 7.4   Windows Backup.

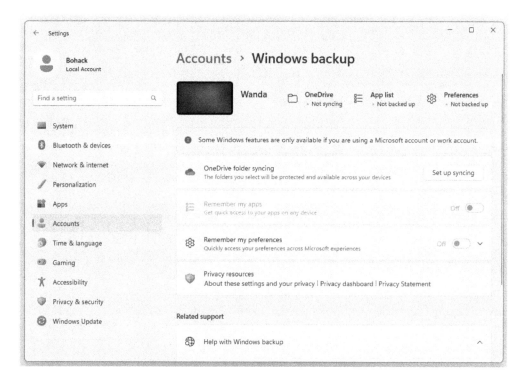

Regulatory Compliance

The concepts of security and compliance go hand and hand. When systems are compliant with security, they are secure. As a security professional, you will very likely have access to information that you will need to keep closely guarded. For example, you might have access to username and/or password lists, medical or educational records, addresses and phone numbers, or employee records. It's your responsibility to ensure that sensitive information does not get released into the wrong hands.

Much of the data you come into contact with could be regulated outside of the organization's internal policies. Regulated data must be identified as it enters your network, and the proper operating procedures should be followed. The operating procedures for such data should be constructed so that you can adhere to the data's regulatory compliance rules. The regulatory rules for compliance can be at any local, state, or federal level. Many of the regulations in the following sections are at a federal level of compliance.

The following are a few of the many regulatory standards you will encounter on endpoints in your organization.

Payment Card Industry Data Security Standard (PCI DSS).   PCI DSS is a standard of processes and procedures used to handle data related to transactions using payment cards. Any time there is a transfer of money for goods or services with a payment card or credit card, these regulations come into scope. You need to make sure that credit card information is not stored on endpoints. In addition, proper training of your users is required anytime a payment card of credit card is used.

Health Insurance Portability and Accountability Act.   The Health Insurance Portability and Accountability Act (HIPAA) affects health care providers and providers that process health records. It regulates how a patient's information is secured and processed during the patient's care. HIPPA regulations are imposed on health care providers to ensure patient privacy. The Department of Health & Human Services (HHS) enforces HIPAA compliance.

General Data Protection Regulation.   The General Data Protection Regulation (GDPR) is a European Union (EU) law. The regulation governs how consumer data can be used and protected. The GDPR was created primarily to protect citizens of the European Union.

In Chapter 11, "Incident Handling," we will learn more about regulatory standards.

BYOD vs. Organization-Owned

The traditional workforce is becoming a mobile workforce, with employees working from home, on the go, and in the office. These employees use laptops, tablets, and smartphones to connect their companies' cloud resources. Organizations have embraced BYOD initiatives as a strategy to alleviate the capital expense of equipment by allowing employees to use devices they already own.

Security is the biggest concern as it applies to BYOD devices. The biggest reason is that the organization has less control over BYOD devices than over devices it issues and owns. BYOD devices come with two inherent risks: data leakage and data portability. Data leakage happens when a device is lost or compromised in some way. There are tactics to mitigate this, such as full device encryption. However, the user's device is then forcefully encrypted by the organization, and there could be legal ramifications. Another common tactic is to use mobile device management (MDM) software that creates a partition for company data. This would allow the company to encrypt its data and not affect user data.

Data portability means that the user can cart away organizational data when they leave. Although most of the time this is not a risk, an unscrupulous salesperson may be a big risk to the organization. A line-of-business (LOB) application should be selected that displays only the data on a mobile device and does not allow data storage. Another tactic is to employ MDM software that allows remote wiping of the organization's data. When an employee leaves, the wipe is executed, and the organization's data is gone. This type of functionality is also useful if a device is lost, so it also mitigates the risk of data leakage.

Mobile Device Management (MDM)

Many organizations use MDM software, which helps enforce the requirements for the BYOD policy. MDM software helps organizations protect their data on devices that are personally owned by the employees. When employees are terminated or a device is lost, the MDM software allows a secure remote wipe of the company's data on the device. The MDM software can also set policies requiring passwords on the device. All of these requirements should be defined in the organization's BYOD policy.

Corporate-owned mobile devices are also of paramount concern when it comes to security. The equipment is mobile, so these devices sometimes travel and can disappear completely. Luckily, MDM software allows you to not only control the data on these devices but also in many instances even track it via a built-in Global Positioning System (GPS) sensor (if the device supports this functionality). When MDM software is implemented in the capacity of tracing assets, consideration must be given to privacy. Although it may be acceptable to track a corporate-owned mobile device, the end user must be made aware of this policy.

Configuration Management

When you implement an MDM solution to manage mobile devices, part of your implementation is the creation of profile security requirements for the mobile devices you will manage. The profile security requirements allow the management of the mobile devices in a uniform fashion. As an administrator, you can choose settings for mobile devices under your purview and enforce profiles security requirements in various ways. In a given scenario, you may want to enforce settings for the entire organization, whereas in other scenarios you may want to differ the settings based on organizational unit, role, or other group type. Among the settings you may want to enforce are those requiring the encryption of drives and the use of complex passwords.

App Distribution

Applications for mobile devices can be distributed through several different methods. There are three main methods you can distribute applications with: self-serve, enterprise distribution, and hybrid. The method is going to depend on the MDM and the device enrollment in the MDM software. In order to distribute software to the mobile device, you must have administrative access to the device. Most end users do not want to give the organization administrative access to their personal devices, whereas organization-owned devices are owned by the organization, and therefore this is a moot point.

The following are the three main methods for application distribution with mobile devices:

Self-serve.   The self-serve model is popular with BYOD deployments in which the organization does not have administrative access to the device. You can direct your end users to download applications from the official store associated with their device, such as the Google Play Store for Android, Apple App Store for iOS devices, or Microsoft Store for Windows. With the self-serve model, you cannot push configuration through the MDM.

Enterprise distribution.   Enterprise distribution is common when the device is owned by the organization. It is also common if the end user is required to enroll their device in the MDM platform. Enrollment in MDM can be a requirement for the use of BYOD outside of an end user's organization-issued devices. As an example, an organization might issue a laptop, but if you want email on your personal cell phone, then you must enroll it in MDM. When the device is enrolled, both applications and configuration can be distributed to the mobile device.

Hybrid.   This is the typical method that most organizations choose when deploying a BYOD strategy. The mobile device will still need to be enrolled in MDM. However, in lieu of distributing all the applications to the end user's device, the user can pick and choose from a company portal. This allows the end user to control the number of applications installed on their device. In this method, both the application and the configuration can be installed with the MDM software.

Data Encryption

To prevent the loss of data, data encryption should be considered—not that the data is really ever lost, but it's no longer within your control. Consider an example of a laptop with sensitive patient record information stored on it. If the laptop were to be stolen, there are a number of utilities that could provide unauthorized access. However, with encryption (such as BitLocker) enabled, both the operating system and the data would remain encrypted and inaccessible.

BitLocker

This tool allows you to use drive encryption to protect files—including those needed for startup and login. This is available only with more complete editions of Windows 10/11 Pro, Enterprise, Education, and Pro for Workstations.

Another requirement is the use of a Trusted Platform Module (TPM). The TPM is a chip on the motherboard that safely stores the encryption key so that the key is not stored on the encrypted disk. BitLocker can mitigate the risk of data loss, because if the disk is separated from the computer, it is still encrypted and only the TPM with the encryption/decrypting key can decrypt the disk. This prevents out-of-band attacks on the hard drive, where it would be mounted and examined on a second system. BitLocker can also sense tampering. If it senses tampering, the recovery key must be reentered. The recovery key is either entered from a printout, loaded from a USB drive in which it was originally saved, or recovered from your Microsoft account. An option of how the recovery key is stored is presented to you when you initially turn on BitLocker.

BitLocker to Go

You can also protect removable drives with BitLocker to Go. It provides the same encryption technology BitLocker uses to help prevent unauthorized access to the files stored on them. You can turn on BitLocker to Go by inserting a USB drive into the computer and opening the BitLocker Drive Encryption Control Panel applet, as shown in Figure 7.5. When a USB

FIGURE 7.5   BitLocker Drive Encryption applet.

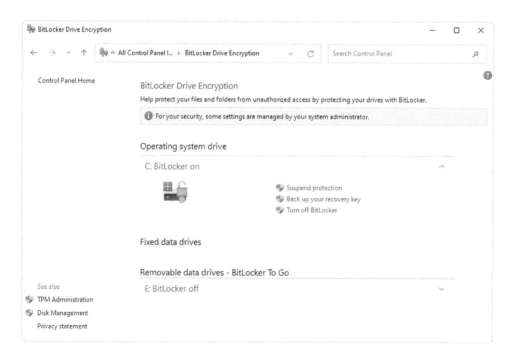

drive is inserted into a Windows computer that contains BitLocker to Go encryption, the operating system prompts you for the password to unlock the drive. This password is the one you used originally when you set up BitLocker to Go on the USB drive.

EFS

Encrypting File System (EFS), available in most editions of Windows, allows for the encryption/decryption of files stored in NTFS volumes. EFS uses certificates to encrypt the data, and the private certificate is stored in the user profile. When the first file is encrypted, the operating system automatically generates a key pair. If the computer were joined to an Active Directory domain and a certificate authority (CA) existed, the CA would create the key pair. You can encrypt a file or folder by right-clicking the object, selecting Properties, and then choosing Advanced, as shown in Figure 7.6.

All users can use EFS, whereas only administrators can turn on BitLocker. EFS does not require any special hardware, whereas BitLocker benefits from having the TPM. As an additional distinction, EFS can encrypt just one file, if so desired, whereas BitLocker encrypts the whole volume and whatever is stored on it. Finally, EFS can be used in conjunction with BitLocker to further increase security.

FIGURE 7.6   Encrypting a file in Windows.

Endpoint Recovery

To complement this chapter on endpoint security, we will learn how to protect against, identify, and recover from malware. It is inevitable that an end user is going to click on malware and compromise a device. It is important to understand the tools that you have at your disposal to recover from the compromise. In the following section, we will learn about some of the built-in tools in the Windows operating system. Keep in mind, there are far more tools available via third-party purchase and download, too many to cover and discuss in one book. The following are the most common as it pertains to the Windows operating system.

Endpoint Protection

Microsoft Defender, also known as Windows Defender Antivirus, was originally introduced with Windows XP as a downloadable antivirus product. It was later shipped with the Vista operating system, and it has become a pillar of security in the Windows 11 operating system. The addition of Microsoft Defender allows the Windows operating system to be protected right out of the box. A user never needs to install anything else to be protected from malware. That being said, there are lots of products on the market that provide security features above and beyond Microsoft Defender. You can view the Microsoft Defender settings in Windows 11 by navigating to Start ➢ Settings App ➢ Privacy & Security ➢ Windows Security ➢ Virus & Threat Protection, as shown in Figure 7.7.

On the Virus & Threat Protection screen, you can make a scan of the computer. In addition, the screen will detail how many threats have been found, when the computer was last scanned, how many files were scanned, and how long the scan lasted. By clicking Scan Options, you can select from Quick Scan, Full Scan, Custom Scan, and Microsoft Defender Offline Scan:

Quick Scan. This option will check folders in the system where threats are commonly found.

Full Scan. This option will perform a full scan of the entire operating system.

Custom Scan. This option will allow you to select the folders on the drive you want to scan.

Microsoft Defender Antivirus (Offline Scan). This option will restart the device, reboot into the Windows Recovery Environment (WinRE), and launch a full Microsoft Defender Scan. It is used to remove malware that is difficult to remove while the operating system is running.

You can also change the Microsoft Defender Virus & Threat Protection settings by clicking Manage Settings on the Virus & Threat Protection screen. This will allow you to manage a number of settings to change the way Microsoft Defender operates, as shown in Figure 7.8.

You can toggle off real-time protection when installing certain applications that require antivirus off during installation. However, the real-time protection will turn back on automatically after a period of time. You can also toggle Cloud-Delivered Protection, which provides cloud-based data on threats and ultimately faster protection. Turning this setting

FIGURE 7.7   Microsoft Defender settings.

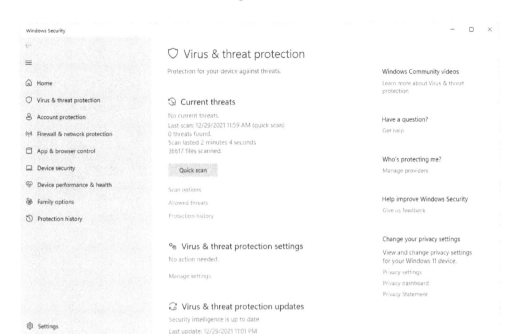

off might be required for certain regulatory requirements, because it automatically turns on cloud-based sample submission. Automatic Sample Submission can be controlled separately as well and toggled on and off. The Tamper Protection security setting prevents malicious applications from tampering with Microsoft Defender settings. Tamper Protection protects against tampering from third-party processes; even Group Policy settings cannot disable Microsoft Defender when Tamper Protection is turned on.

Controlled Folder Access.   The Controlled Folder Access feature can be accessed in the Virus & Threat Protection Settings. The feature is used to prevent ransomware from harming files, folders, and memory areas on the device. By default, it is turned off, but it can easily turned on by clicking the toggle. Once it is set to the default, folders protected are documents, pictures, videos, music, and favorites. Specific folders can be added, and the defaults can also be removed. You can also exempt an application so that it is allowed to modify the files.

Exclusions.   Although it is not common to need to exempt a folder from the antimalware engine, it can be configured from the Virus & Threat Protection Settings. This option allows you to exempt an entire folder from real-time protection and scans. One use may be performance-impacted applications such as games, but caution should be used.

Update Definitions.   An antimalware engine is only as good as its latest definitions, and Microsoft Defender is no different. Therefore, both the Microsoft Defender engine and its definitions are updated quite frequently. Both are updated through the Windows Update process.

FIGURE 7.8 Microsoft Defender Virus & Threat settings.

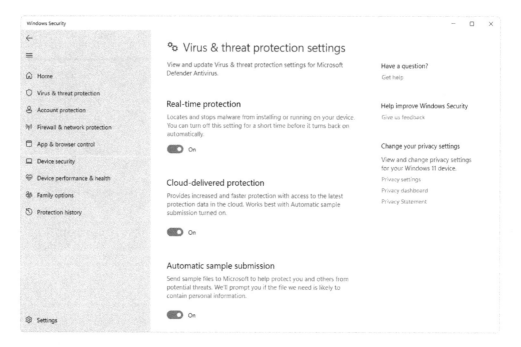

Cloud-Based Protection

It is rare for endpoints to be managed in a distributed model. Most endpoints are currently managed in a centralized fashion. When you combine the power of the cloud with endpoints, you can gain a "single pane of glass" to view and manage all your endpoint security. Microsoft Defender for Endpoint is a cloud-based subscription that brings the Microsoft Defender engine together with cloud-based management.

Within the Microsoft Defender Security Center, you can view and manage all of the devices in your organization. You can run antivirus scan, isolate the device from network activities, and even restrict app execution; all of this can be done remotely. You can see an example of some of the actions you can perform in Figure 7.9.

Reviewing Scan Logs

After a local scan on the Windows operating system, threats will appear in the Virus & Threat Protection Settings app. You can view the Virus & Threat Protection Settings in Windows 11 by navigating to Start ➢ Settings App ➢ Privacy & Security ➢ Windows Security ➢ Virus & Threat Protection ➢ Protection History. This will display the threat history, and you can open further details from here by clicking on the threat detected, as shown in Figure 7.10.

FIGURE 7.9   Microsoft Defender Security Center actions.

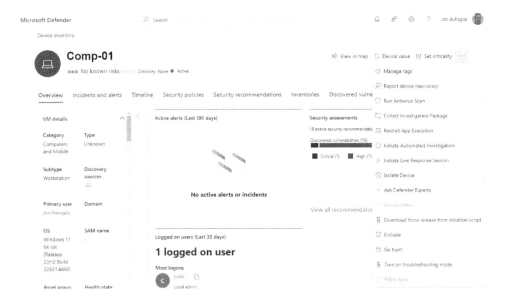

FIGURE 7.10   Detected threats.

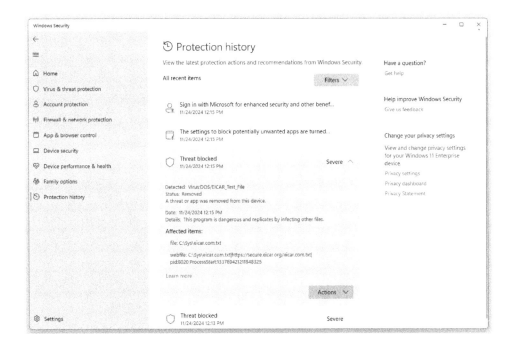

If you want a more detailed view, the Event Viewer MMC can provide a wealth of information. The Windows Defender logs can be opened by navigating to the log source of Windows Defender by clicking Applications and Service Logs ➤ Microsoft ➤ Windows ➤ Windows Defender ➤ Operational. From this view, you can see when the operating system has been scanned, when the configuration changed, antivirus updates, and what has been detected. The following are just a few of the informational items that can be found. The details from the prior threat initially displayed in Figure 7.10 can be seen in Figure 7.11 with much more detail.

FIGURE 7.11   Threat Event Viewer entry.

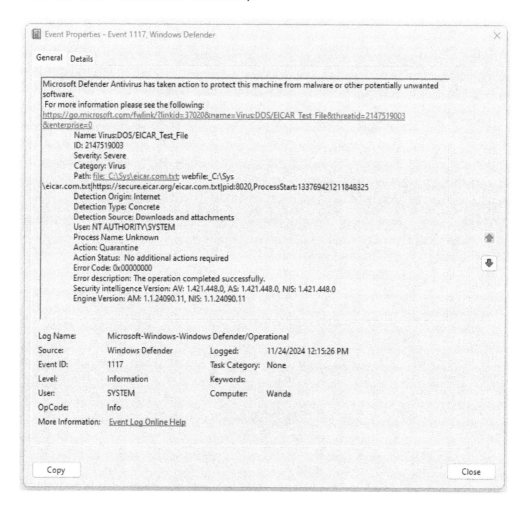

If you have a cloud-based instance of Microsoft Defender for Endpoint, you can view the overview of your organization's malware detections in the Intune portal. By opening the Intune Portal located at `https://intune.microsoft.com` and navigating Reports ➤ Microsoft Defender Antivirus, the Summary tab will display the number of scanned machines and pending scans, in addition to other pieces of high-level information. If you click the Reports tab and select Detected Malware, and then click Generate, you can view the detected malware on all of the organization's hosts.

The Microsoft Defender Security Center located at `http://security.microsoft.com` will give you a detailed look, and it places it in a timeline. The portal provides you a view of all the incidents in your organization by clicking on Incidents. You can then change the filters to see current and previous incidents. Then you can drill down to detailed information in the portal, as shown in Figure 7.12. You can even manage the event and add notes.

 The Microsoft Defender Security Center and Intune portals require a license subscription. The products can provide a wealth of protections and information, too much to include in one section. If you want to learn more about the Security Center portal, visit `https://learn.microsoft.com/en-us/defender-xdr/microsoft-365-defender-portal`. Also keep in mind that the Microsoft product is just one of many different products you can purchase; third-party providers pop up every day.

FIGURE 7.12   Security incident.

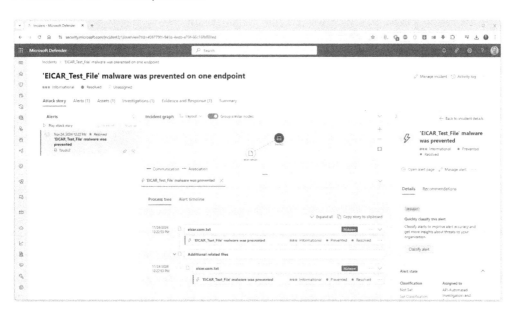

Malware Remediation

Best practices for malware removal are a key objective for the exam. The best way to think about this is as a seven-item list you should consider when approaching a possible malware infestation. The following discussion presents the information that you need to know.

Identify and Verify Malware Symptoms

Before doing anything major, it is imperative first to be sure that you are dealing with the right issue. If you suspect malware, try to identify the type (spyware, virus, and so on) and look for the proof needed to substantiate that it is indeed the culprit.

You first need to identify the problem. This can be done with a multitude of tools, but hopefully your antivirus/antimalware software will be the first tool that helps to identify the problem. If the antivirus/antimalware software fails to identify the problem, then other third-party tools must be used.

A great graphical tool called Process Explorer can be downloaded from Microsoft Sysinternals via `https://learn.microsoft.com/en-us/sysinternals/`. This tool allows a different visualization from what Resource Monitor provides, as shown in Figure 7.13. You can see the process list on the operating system; in this case, there is a process called `regsvr32.exe`. When you look closer, you can see that it is creating network traffic and is very active on the operating system. The process is actually a ransomware application calling out to command-and-control servers. It is sneakily disguising itself as the `regsvr32.exe` utility, which is normally used to register DLLs.

Unfortunately, this lone example will not give you the expertise of a professional virus/malware hunter. However, it provides just one of many examples of third-party software that can help you detect and identify viruses and malware running on a computer.

Many built-in tools, such as `netstat.exe`, can also provide assistance. For example, the `netstat -nab` command enables you to view all the processes on the operating system and their network connections. Using the `netstat -nab` command is how it was identified that something looked wrong with the `regsvr32.exe` process; otherwise, the command would have looked like any other process on the operating system.

In addition to applications that can identify viruses and malware, third-party websites can aid in detection. One such website is VirusTotal (`www.virustotal.com`). VirusTotal allows users to upload potentially unsafe applications. Their service will scan the applications against more than 70 antivirus engines and report if the signature is found. It's a valuable tool to validate that you've found an application on your operating system that is malicious. Many tools, such as Process Explorer, can even check against the VirusTotal database.

Quarantine Infected Systems

Once you have confirmed that a virus or malware is at hand, quarantine the infected system to prevent it from spreading the virus or malware to other systems. Bear in mind that the virus or malware can spread in any number of ways, including through a network connection, email, and so on. The quarantine needs to be complete enough to prevent any spread.

FIGURE 7.13   Process Explorer.

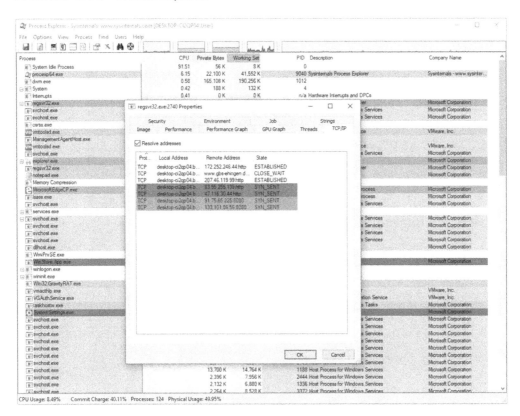

Ransomware is probably the biggest risk, because it will spread through a network rapidly and encrypt files in its path. The ransom is usually equivalent to the number of files or the total size of the files. In either case, over the past decade, ransomware has made headline news, as it has taken down extremely large companies. In one instance, the Petya ransomware even took down most of the computers in Ukraine, along with several other countries.

If an infected system is discovered and needs further analysis, it should be quarantined from the network and put into an isolated network. This hot network is a place where it can be studied further, without repercussions to the operational network.

Disable System Restore in Windows

This is a necessary step because you do not want to have the infected system create a restore point—or return to one—where the infection exists. System Protection in Windows 11 is turned off by default. You can disable System Protection with these steps:

1.   Click the Start menu.

2.   Type **Recovery** and select it from the results.

3. Choose Configure System Restore.

4. Select the system drive, and click Configure.

5. Disable System Protection.

6. Click Delete (Disk Space Usage).

7. Click Continue (confirmation), then Close, OK, and finally Yes (confirmation), as shown in Figure 7.14.

> Most ransomware will dump your restore points for you, because you could potentially recover the operating system and then recover files using your previous versions.

Remediate Infected Systems

The steps taken here depend on the type of virus or malware with which you're dealing, but they should include updating antivirus and antimalware software with the latest definitions and using the appropriate scan and removal techniques. You can update Microsoft Defender from the Settings app by clicking the task tray in the lower-right corner of the desktop, then right-clicking the Windows Security shield, and finally clicking Check For Updates, as shown in Figure 7.15.

FIGURE 7.14   System Protection.

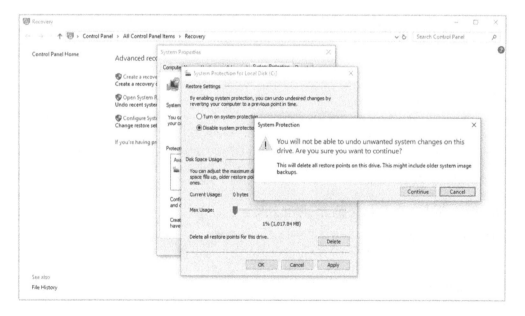

FIGURE 7.15   Microsoft Defender security updates.

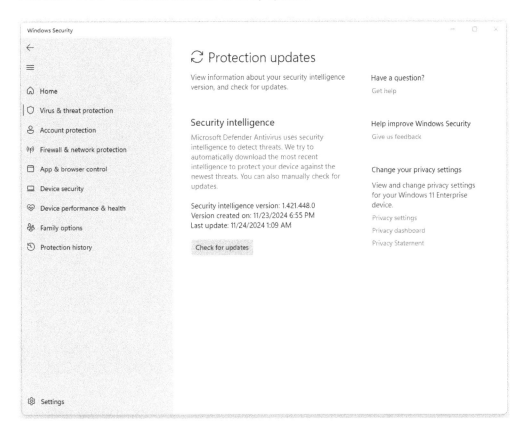

Depending on the type of virus or malware, you may need to boot into safe mode or the Windows Recovery Environment (as discussed earlier in this chapter). However, the remediation of the virus or malware will be different for each situation. Microsoft Defender Security can automatically perform an offline scan. To perform an offline scan, click the task tray in the lower-right corner, and then right-click the shield, select View Security Dashboard, click Virus & Threat Protection, click Scan Options, and select Microsoft Defender Offline Scan, as shown in Figure 7.16.

After you confirm that you will save your work by clicking Scan in the confirmation dialog box, the UAC will prompt you to answer Yes, and then Windows will reboot. The Windows Recovery Environment will boot, and Windows Defender Antivirus will run, as shown in Figure 7.17.

In some situations, such as in a ransomware attack, no remediation can be performed because the user files are encrypted. In these cases, the malware should be removed from the

FIGURE 7.16   Microsoft Defender offline scan.

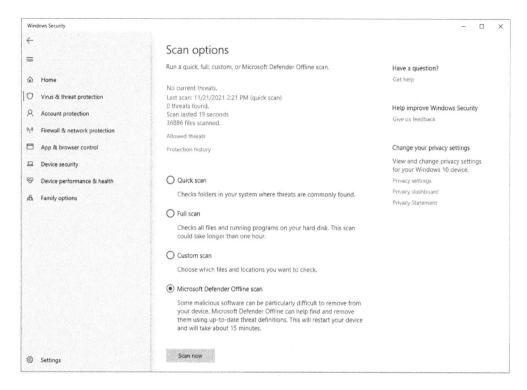

operating system, and then the user data must be restored from a backup. The unfortunate and terrifying fact when it comes to ransomware is that there will be loss of work.

In many instances, remediating the virus or malware is impossible because no one knows for sure what the virus or malware actually does. Antivirus researchers can document the delivery system that a virus or malware uses to enter your system. You can then patch the vulnerability, which is part of the remediation process. What antivirus research cannot do most of the time is document the payload of a virus or malware. This is because most of the time the payload is encrypted and changed, depending on the need of its creator. In these cases, the remediation might be to sanitize the drive and reinstall the operating system from an image or manually install it.

Schedule Scans and Run Updates

The odds of the system never being confronted by malware again are slim. To reduce the chances of it being infected again, schedule scans and updates to run regularly. Most antimalware programs can be configured to run automatically at specific intervals; however, should you encounter one that does not have such a feature, you can run it through Task Scheduler.

FIGURE 7.17 An offline Microsoft Defender Antivirus scan.

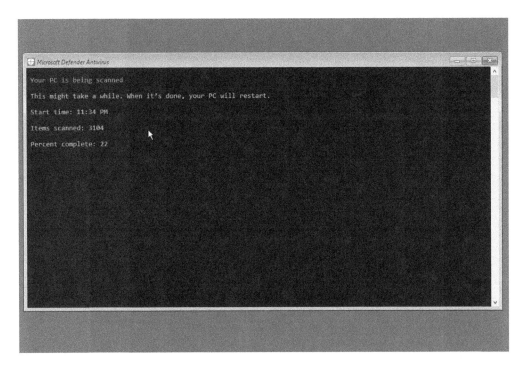

Microsoft Defender Security is scheduled to automatically scan the operating system during idle times. However, if you want to schedule a scan, you can use Task Scheduler:

1. Click the Start menu.

2. Type **Task Scheduler,** and then select Task Scheduler from the results.

3. Open the Task Scheduler Library.

4. Select Microsoft, and then select Windows.

5. Select Windows Defender, and double-click Windows Defender Scheduled Scan.

6. Select the Triggers tab.

7. Click New on the Triggers tab, and then select Weekly and choose the day of the week in the New Trigger dialog box.

8. Click OK, as shown in Figure 7.18. You'll need to click OK again after the New Trigger dialog box closes.

Windows Defender Security is scheduled to automatically download updates during the Windows Update check, which is daily. If you require the latest updates, use either the Check For Updates option in the Windows Update settings or the Check For Updates option in the Microsoft Defender Security Center.

FIGURE 7.18   Creating a Windows Defender Security scheduled scan.

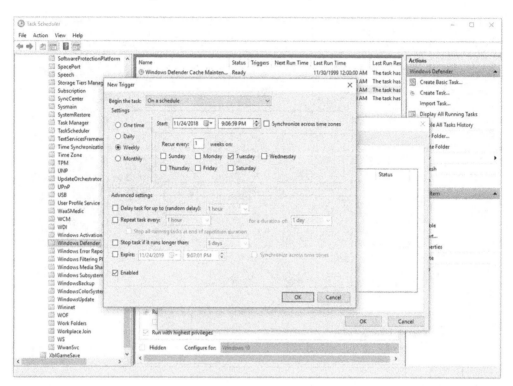

Microsoft is in the process of rebranding Windows Defender to Microsoft Defender. Some settings may be under Windows Defender, such as the scheduled tasks discussed in this section. Some settings may also be under Microsoft Defender. Keep this in mind when looking for settings such as scheduled tasks and GPOs.

Enable System Restore and Create a Restore Point in Windows

Once everything is working properly, it is important to create restore points again, should a future problem occur and you need to revert back. You can enable System Protection by following these steps:

1. Click the Start menu.
2. Type **Restore**, and select it from the results.
3. Click Create A Restore Point.
4. Select the System drive, and click Configure.
5. Click Turn On System Protection, and click OK.

You can then manually create a restore point by clicking Create in the System Protection dialog box, typing a description (such as **after remediation - date**), clicking Close (in the confirmation dialog box), and clicking OK to close the System Properties.

Educate the End User

Education should always be viewed as the final step. The end user needs to understand what led to the malware infestation and what to avoid, or look for, in the future to keep it from happening again. This training can be formal training in a classroom setting, or it can be an online training in which the user must participate and answer questions.

It is common for large companies to require annual or biannual end-user training for threats. It is becoming more common for training to be done online, and a number of companies offer this as a service. It is not uncommon for a company to send a phishing attempt to their employees. When an employee falls for the phishing attempt, they are automatically signed up for mandatory training. Incentives are also common, such as the first employee who notifies the IT department of the phishing attempt getting a gift card.

Summary

We began this chapter by learning about the various tools that you can use to validate your networking configurations. The tools also help you to verify that hosts are responding on the network and allow you to see open ports. The tools presented in this chapter are the bare minimum of what you should know as a security professional.

We then learned about all the various pieces of endpoint security. We learned why a hardware and software inventory is so important and how it can be combined with cloud services to identify vulnerabilities. We then learned the basics of how to remediate applications through both on-premises and cloud-based services. We learned about the proper disposal techniques for data drives. We followed this section by learning about how to manage BYOD and organization-owned devices.

In the last section in this chapter, we learned all about endpoint recovery. We began this section by learning about the various Microsoft Defender options we can employ to keep us malware free. We then learned the various ways we can read scan logs from Microsoft Defender for both local and cloud-based management. The last objective we learned about was how to properly remove malware.

Exam Essentials

Understand what each command-line tool does.   Many utilities allow you to perform various functions at the command line. These include `netstat`, `nslookup`, `dig`, `ping`, `tcpdump`, `nmap`, and `gpresult`. In addition, you should be familiar with port scanners, iPerf, and IP scanner utilities.

Understand how to implement appropriate data destruction and disposal methods. A hard drive can be destroyed by tossing it into a shredder designed for such a purpose, or it can be destroyed with an electromagnet in a process known as degaussing. You can also disassemble the drive and destroy the platters with a drill or other tool that renders the data irretrievable.

Understand the difference between standard and low-level formatting. Standard formatting uses operating system tools and marks the drive as available for holding data without truly removing what was on the drive (thus, the data can be recovered). A low-level format is operating system–independent and destroys any data that was on the drive.

Know the various regulatory compliance requirements. The Payment Card Industry Data Security Standard (PCI DSS) is a standard of policies and procedures used by the payment industry. The Health Insurance Portability and Accountability Act (HIPAA) regulates how a patient's information is secured and processed during the patient's care. The General Data Protection Regulation (GDPR) is a European Union (EU) law governing how EU citizen data is used.

Know the various components of a BYOD strategy. Mobile device management (MDM) is used to manage end-user devices. The MDM can deploy applications and configuration. The MDM can also require passwords, encryption, and an updated device.

Know the various ways that antivirus and antimalware protection can be deployed. The two common methods for antivirus and malware scanners to be deployed are locally and cloud-based. Locally is the default for Microsoft Defender. Cloud-based requires a license subscription and provides a single pane of glass to manage your organization's devices.

Know the process for removing malware. Know the seven steps to remove malware. Be able to identify how to perform these seven steps during the malware-removal process. You should be familiar with the various tools used to identify and remove malware.

Review Questions

 The following questions are designed to test your understanding of this chapter's material. For more information on how to get additional questions, please see www.lammle.com/ccst.

You can find the answers to these questions in Appendix.

1. Which software tool will allow you to check whether a web application running on a server is online?
    - **A.** ping
    - **B.** nslookup
    - **C.** tracert/traceroute
    - **D.** Port scanner

2. Which commands can be used to retrieve the A record for a domain? (Choose two.)
    - **A.** tracert/traceroute
    - **B.** ipconfig
    - **C.** nslookup
    - **D.** dig

3. You need to check the port an application is listening on; which command should you use to view the information?
    - **A.** portqry
    - **B.** ifconfig
    - **C.** netstat
    - **D.** iptables

4. Which policy would you create to define the minimum specification if an employee wanted to use their own device for email?
    - **A.** MDM
    - **B.** AUP
    - **C.** BYOD
    - **D.** NDA

5. You need to investigate how to protect credit card data on your network. Which information should you research?
    - **A.** PCI DSS
    - **B.** GDPR
    - **C.** PHI
    - **D.** PII

6. You need to encrypt a single file on a Windows desktop. Which technology should you use?

    A. EFS

    B. BitLocker

    C. NTFS

    D. BitLocker to Go

7. Which of the following is not a benefit of implementing asset tags for inventory management?

    A. Identifying vulnerabilities

    B. Scheduling the depreciation of the equipment

    C. Identifying assets

    D. Providing ownership of the equipment

8. You need to enforce profile security requirements on mobile devices. Which should you use to achieve this goal?

    A. AUP

    B. NDA

    C. BYOD

    D. MDM

9. Which of the following programs could be considered antimalware?

    A. Microsoft Defender Security

    B. MDM

    C. Windows Action Center

    D. VirusTotal

10. What is the first step in malware removal?

    A. Quarantine the infected system.

    B. Identify and verify the malware symptoms.

    C. Remediate the infected system.

    D. Educate the end user.

Chapter

8

Risk Management

THE FOLLOWING CCST EXAM TOPIC IS COVERED IN THIS CHAPTER:

✔ **4.0 Risk and Vulnerability Management**

   ▪ 4.3. Explain risk management

   Vulnerability vs risk, ranking risks, approaches to risk
   management, risk mitigation strategies, levels of risk
   (low, medium, high, extremely high), risks associated
   with specific types of data and data classifications,
   security assessments of IT systems (information security,
   change management, computer operations, information
   assurance)

The existence of risk can be found in any organization. When business processes change, there is a certain amount of risk that is inherited with the change. Typically, the business managers will manage the risk, and hopefully the change will have a positive impact on the organization.

Obviously, as security professionals, we can't assume all risk in the entire organization. However, we do assume a certain amount of technical risk from the information systems that have been put in place. In this chapter, we will cover the terminology used to identify these risks. We will also learn how to prioritize, mitigate, and manage the risks we identify throughout the process of risk management.

To find your included bonus material, as well as Todd Lammle videos, practice questions, and hands-on labs, please see `https://www.lammle.com/ccst`.

Risk Management

The information technology field is always changing, with new software, hardware, and business processes. As software changes with new feature updates and upgrades, we potentially introduce issues that affect the organization's day-to-day operation. This is inadvertent introduction of problems, and we also introduce these problems when hardware and business processes change. Unfortunately, new software, feature updates, upgrades to software and hardware, and changes to our business processes are inevitable for our business to evolve and stay on the cutting edge of technology.

Threat actors are another potential threat to our day-to-day operations. Threat actors look for weaknesses in our defense and attempt to exploit these weaknesses to gain a foothold in our systems. Threat actors also have a sinister motive and can cause an organization severe or even fatal financial harm.

All of these activities introduce the potential for catastrophe and ultimately introduce risk into our organization. Therefore, we must manage the risk and constantly evaluate the potential for risk. The risk management process is called the risk management lifecycle because it is a cyclical process that constantly needs to be evaluated. The simplified risk management lifecycle contains five steps, as shown in Figure 8.1. We will cover these steps in this chapter so you have a better understanding on how to manage risk.

FIGURE 8.1   Risk management lifecycle.

The overall process of risk management is as follows:

Risk Identification.   As new changes are proposed to take place, the identification of risk should begin.

Risk Analysis.   Once the risk is identified, the risk then needs to be analyzed. This step will prioritize the next steps the risk takes in the overall risk management process.

Risk Mitigation Planning.   The mitigation planning step is how the risk is mitigated from potentially happening. This planning step can introduce risk because it often requires other changes.

Risk Management Implementation.   The implementation step is where the rubber meets the road. This step is where the mitigation is actually applied.

Review and Tracking.   Once the mitigation is in place, monitoring the changes is the next logical step. We always want to make sure we didn't solve one problem and introduce a brand-new problem.

The simplified approach has been adopted from the NIST Risk Management Framework (RMF), which is a more comprehensive process. The RMF applies directly to the NIST 800–53 control. The simplified approach allows you to apply this process to more than just security controls. More information about the NIST RMF can be found at `https://csrc.nist.gov/projects/risk-management/about-rmf`.

Elements of Risk

In order to identify risk, we need to understand the elements that make up risk and their association with each other. There is a tight association with assets, vulnerabilities, and threats that make up risk. Let's see if you can identify each component of risk in the following analogy.

I will begin with a simple analogy for the potential of a bank robbery. Pretend you are the security person responsible for keeping the bank secure. The bank's risk is greatest when it has lots of money in the vaults, such as at the end of the month on pay day. The risk is lower when there is less money in the bank, such as the week before payday.

Let's explore the ways you can assure money is not stolen. The vault should be locked when not in use and full of money. The doors to sensitive areas should also be locked, such as the doors that lead to the areas behind the bulletproof glass. Does the bank even have strong defenses such as bulletproof glass and secure doors? Does the bank have biometric locks and retinal scanners? Armed guards and panic systems to alert authorities?

Enough of the anxiety; perhaps our bank is located in the middle of Pleasantville, USA, and there has never been a bank robbery or any crime. This would change the amount of risk we need to assume if we leave doors unlocked most of the time. Or maybe the bank really is in the worst part of a city with high crime and lots of robbery.

In the analogy, all the elements of risk were present. Were you able to identify them? Money is obviously the asset we are trying to protect. However, the asset could also be social security numbers or trade secrets for our organization. The vulnerabilities are the doors being left open, the lack of bulletproof glass, and even the lack of defenses such as armed guards. This element is similar to patches on applications and weak passwords, but the list goes on and on. The threat is the existence of a criminal entity, such as a bad neighborhood. The Internet allows for a certain amount of anonymity for threat actors. This unfortunately lowers the barrier to entry for a lot of threat actors. The threat actor no longer needs to pick up a gun and rob a bank; they can simply connect to your network and look for a vulnerability.

Figure 8.2 illustrates the association of assets, vulnerabilities, and threats. If one or more of the elements get bigger, then risk increases.

As security professionals, we can reduce the risk by reducing the vulnerabilities and threats that might exist. We can also take account of our assets and determine how sensitive they are to threats. In the following sections, we will learn more about the elements of risk.

FIGURE 8.2   Asset, vulnerability, and threat association.

Vulnerabilities

Vulnerabilities are weaknesses in the security of an organization. These weaknesses in security can be physical and network based. An example of physical vulnerabilities is often doors that are not locked to sensitive areas where data is accessible. Network vulnerabilities are often found in applications, operating systems, and network products.

Vulnerabilities are the reason we need to constantly patch network systems. However, even with constant patching, we can never be assured that we have eliminated all vulnerabilities. Some vulnerabilities will always exist and sometimes never be known by the owners of the system. The threat actors might not even be aware of some of these vulnerabilities, depending on their skill level. Patching does, however, lower our risk or potential for an attack through known vulnerabilities.

Zero-Day

All publicly known vulnerabilities usually have either a workaround or a patch. However, some vulnerabilities are discovered before a patch or workaround can be devised and made available. These are known as *zero-day vulnerabilities*, and they carry high risk because there is no way to defend from an attack. A zero-day vulnerability doesn't mean that the attack is imminent; some zero-day vulnerabilities are remediated the very next day. However, it does mean that until a patch or workaround is devised, you are vulnerable.

Other Vulnerabilities

Not all vulnerabilities hinge on an unpatched application or operating system. There are many other ways a system or process can be vulnerable to risk:

Physical. Systems can be open to physical vulnerabilities, such as theft or tampering with these systems. In many cases, the theft of a system can be just as damaging, such as if the system was compromised remotely. Therefore, locking of doors, surveillance systems, and overall physical security can mitigate these vulnerabilities.

Theft is not the only way a system can be vulnerable to physical attack. The system can also be vulnerable to hardware failure, such as a power supply, hard drive, or other electronic system that could cripple the device. Luckily, fault tolerance design and redundancy can be built into the system to prevent these vulnerabilities.

Configuration. The improper configuration of a system can lead to security vulnerabilities. Best practices and hardening of the system should always be performed before its deployment and operation. These best practices and hardening techniques might include changing default passwords, turning off unused services, and using supported configuration, just to name a few.

Training. The lack of training for people operating the systems can also be a vulnerability. For example, the lack of proper training for an email user can lead to a phishing attempt. Therefore, you should enforce security policies and employee training to make sure that your end users aren't your biggest vulnerability.

Threats

A *threat* is a potential danger to the network or the assets of the organization. When we think of threats, we tend to think of just cyberattack threats, where a bad actor uses the network to carry out an attack. However, threats can also be physical, such as weather or other environmental factors that have a potential to be dangerous.

As an oversimplified example, let's use a trip to the grocery store to set the stage in understanding threats. If we purchase groceries and place them in the car, there are all kinds of potential dangers (threats) to our groceries. We could get into an accident on the way home, they could be stolen, or our ice cream could melt. There is a certain amount of risk for each one of these threats, known as the likelihood it will happen. If you are a good driver, then the risk of an accident is low. If you live in a relatively safe neighborhood, then the risk that the groceries will be stolen is low. However, if it's a really hot day, there is a high risk of the ice cream melting.

Unfortunately, an organization's network is a lot more complicated than a grocery store visit. In most organizations, there are two types of threats, external and internal:

External Threats.   These types of threats are almost always carried out by an attacker with ill intent. The risk or potential of these threats is usually our connection to the outside world, such as the Internet, email, and our Internet-facing servers. If you mitigate the vulnerability, then the threat is less likely to occur.

Internal Threats.   These threats are also known as the threat from within and are potentially carried out by an employee. A disgruntled employee can compromise your organization's network by intentionally leaking the organization's data or intentionally running malicious code. Internal threats can be much more dangerous than external threats because employees often know exactly how systems are configured and how to circumvent controls.

Exploits

A vulnerability is a weakness in security, as you have learned. An *exploit* is a method that acts on a weakness (vulnerability). I will use a luggage lock as an example, mainly because they are notoriously weak security solutions. A simple paperclip bent appropriately could be used to exploit the weakness and open the lock. It would be nice if all problems were as simple as getting a better lock, but networks are complicated systems that can have many complex vulnerabilities as well as known exploits.

When we talk about exploits, we generally refer to scripts, software, or sequences of commands that exploit a known vulnerability. The CVE published against a vulnerability can be used to patch or block the exploit, depending on the vulnerability. Just like zero-day vulnerabilities, where there is a weakness that is not documented yet, there exist zero-day exploits, in which an attack is carried out without understanding the vulnerability it is carried out on.

Assets

An asset is something of value to your organization. When we discuss assets, we are talking about a monetary value that can be accounted as the worth of your organization. This is typically done on the general ledger for the organization by accountants. As an example, the router you purchase for the organization will have a monetary value attached. Depending on the class of the device, it can be very expensive. Typically, enterprise routers can cost upward of a quarter of a million dollars, because they include redundancy, high speed capacity, and fault tolerance in their design. This asset is something of monetary value to your company as tangible asset.

The router also has a worth as a digital asset to the organization, because it is essentially an information pump. When it goes down, your organization will come to a grinding halt. This is why we cover it with service contracts for hardware and software configuration and troubleshooting.

There are other non-tangible digital assets that will never make it to your general ledger. Such an asset might be the secret formula to the product your organization produces. It can also be the secret formula to the service your organization provides. The key here is that it is so special to your organization that it is secret.

Assets don't always need to be secret and behind armed guards to be worth something to an organization. The asset can also be your customer base, person health information (PHI), personal identifiable information (PII), or any other piece of information that your organization is entrusted to protect.

Digital assets are the hardest to protect because we must allow access to employees so our organization continues to function. At the same time, we must protect these digital assets from threat actors. Threat actors will have various motives in stealing your information, such as selling it to the highest bidder, ransoming it by preventing your access, or threatening to publish it to the public, or they might even change key information so your organization inevitably fails.

The key takeaway is that an asset is any data or system that attributes to your organization's data. Threat actors will attempt to affect the confidentiality, integrity, or availability of your organization's data. If this sounds familiar, it should; confidentiality, integrity, and availability are all parts of the CIA triad that is used for data protection.

Risk Analysis

Risk analysis is the process of determining the potential for a security event or failure that can negatively affect the organization. As we learned, risk is at the intersection of the asset, vulnerability, and threat. The process is a little subjective because there are not strong metrics to back up our analysis all the time. For example, you might do a risk analysis when you have a storm approaching, calculating whether it will cause a power outage based on past power outages in your area. That analysis is based on loose metrics, and it is somewhat subjective. There is no indication of how strong the storm will be in comparison to your surrounding infrastructure; you can only weigh the frequency of power outages in the past. It's enough of an analysis to determine risk, and it might make you reach for the candles just in case the power does go out.

Risk analysis for potential security events is a similar process. We need to analyze a few components such as the risk level to our data, and then the likelihood and impact to our organization in the event of a security event. In this section, we will look at several components that help us perform a risk analysis.

Risk Levels

Risk levels are used to communicate our perceived risk of failure or a security event. Risk levels can be simple, or we can make them very granular. For most purposes, the risk levels can be kept simple, such as a three-tier system of low, moderate, or high. You can build risk-level structures with more than three tiers of risk, such as the popular four-tier model of low, moderate, high, and extreme, or the six-tier model of very-low, low, medium, high, very-high, and extreme. The number of risk levels your organization will use to convey risk will be based on several factors, such as the typical audience and the amount of quantitative data used to determine the perceived risk.

If you are analyzing risk for a development department, you may want to use a granular system that has many tiers. Developers are accustomed to details, and they typically prioritize their work on a granular level. However, if you are presenting a C-suite level of individuals on a daily basis, a more simplistic system is preferred because executives drive their decisions based on the brevity of information and not always the finite details.

In most cases, a simple risk level model serves us well because most risk is subjective, although we can perform objective calculation, as we will learn later in this section. As stated before, risk analysis is the potential for failure and not a derived outcome. As you add tiers to the risk level system used, you imply the level of objective data used to calculate your risk. This is fine, as long as you have the objective data and metrics to back up your findings.

The three-tier model serves many organizations just fine when it comes to risk analysis. The risk levels when we classify data or systems are defined as such:

- Low Risk
    - The system processes or stores public data.
    - The system is easily recoverable and reproducible.
    - The system provides an informational (noncritical) service.
- Moderate Risk
    - The system processes or stores nonpublic or internal data.
    - The system is internally trusted by other networked systems.
    - The system provides a normal or important service.
- High Risk
    - The system processes or stores confidential data.
    - The system is highly trusted by networked systems.
    - The system provides a critical organization-wide service.

Risk Matrix

The relationship of likelihood and impact define the level of risk associated with an event. Hardware can typically be maintained to have a low-level of risk for security events if security updates and patches are consistently applied. Updates and patches lower the

FIGURE 8.3   Risk matrix.

	Negligible	Minor	Moderate	Significant	Severe
Very Likely	Low	Moderate	High	High	High
Likely	Low	Moderate	Moderate	High	High
Possible	Low	Low	Moderate	Moderate	High
Unlikely	Low	Low	Moderate	Moderate	Moderate
Very Unlikely	Low	Low	Low	Moderate	Moderate

Impact (horizontal axis, left to right)
Likelihood (vertical axis)

likelihood that a security event will happen because security issues are patched. However, if we don't update and patch, then the level of risk increases. The level of risk will also depend on the device's failure with respect to impact to the organization. As an example, if a router is maliciously taken offline at your main office, it has a high impact on the organization compared to a router maliciously taken offline at a small branch office.

In Figure 8.3, you will find a risk matrix that correlates the likelihood and impact to the associated risk level, using the prior example of a router that has not been patched and serves the main network for the organization. This scenario presents a high-risk level if it were to be compromised and maliciously taken offline. This is because it is possible to likely that it can be compromised, and the impact would be moderate to severe.

Up to this point, we have been applying the concept of risk analysis to the availability aspect for a piece of hardware. Data requires the calculation of risk for all three CIA triad elements: for the loss of confidentiality, integrity, and availability. The highest risk of any of the three becomes the overall risk level for the data. In Figure 8.4, you will see the risk analysis for an organization's internal list of customers. If the loss of confidentiality is possible and the impact would be severe, then the risk level is high. If the loss of integrity is likely and the impact would be minor, then the risk level is moderate. If the loss of availability is possible and the impact would be significant, then the risk level is moderate. The overall risk is high because that is the highest risk level for all three elements.

FIGURE 8.4 Risk analysis for organization's internal list of customers.

Threat Event	Likelihood	Impact	Risk Level
Loss of Confidentiality	Possible	Severe	High
Loss of Integrity	Likely	Minor	Moderate
Loss of Availability	Possible	Significant	Moderate
		Overall Risk:	High

Risk Prioritization

A risk analysis should be performed on every data type in the organization as well as hardware systems that serve IT functions. In our risk analysis process just described, we care about the highest risk from any of the three CIA triad elements to determine the overall risk. This analysis helps us identify data and hardware that serves the function with that of high risk. This analysis also serves a second function, and that is the prioritization of your efforts to lower risk overall. This process is called risk prioritization.

I'm sure that risk prioritization is a pretty obvious component of the risk analysis process. The goal is to fix the issues that pose our organization the highest risk because of the likelihood or impact from a potential event. However, I've seen many organizations waste time on low-risk items that do not really lower the overall risk. Therefore, you should always look for the immediate risk actions and be able to differentiate from the actionable items with lower value.

Quantitative vs. Qualitative Risk

For each of the CIA triad elements, starting with the highest or most immediate risk, you can apply some quantitative risk analysis techniques to obtain a much more objective view of the risks. Let's take a deeper look at the quantitative risk analysis technique and understand how it can be applied.

In this example, we will apply some objective values to the availability of your Internet connection using a service-level agreement (SLA) of 99.9% uptime. To apply the quantitative risk-analysis technique, you must first determine the single-loss expectation (SLE). The SLE is the expectation or anticipated financial impact for a single occurrence of that risk. Let's assume that the SLE for the loss of your Internet for one hour is that it would cost the organization $10,000 in productivity. We then need to determine the annualized rate of occurrence (ARO). The ARO is the number of losses you expect per year. In this example, the SLA of 99.9% calculates to the downtime of 8 hours and 46 minutes a year.

The quantitative risk is then calculated by multiplying the SLE by the ARO. For this example, we will round to 8 hours and 45 minutes to make the multiplier 8.75. With an SLE of $10,000 per hour and your ARO being 8.75 for the year, the estimated loss for a year is potentially $10,000 times 8.75, which is $87,500. The loss of Internet directly applies to the concept of availability, and you might have other risk factors for confidentiality and integrity of data. This same technique could also be applied to those other elements of risk. You then prioritize your risk by the potential it could cost your organization in dollars.

Quantitative risk is based on actual dollars and estimated occurrences, as we just learned. Not all risk can be boiled down to an objective dollar figure. Some risk, such as the loss of data or leak of a trade secret, can only be viewed as a subjective risk, also known as a qualitative risk. A qualitative risk can only be measured by the likelihood and impact that it may happen. These risks can only be gauged on the risk scale we set forth in the risk matrix.

Data Classifications

Data is classified with a level of risk depending on its sensitivity. This classification is referred to as data criticality to the organization. The terms *data classification* and *data criticality* mean basically the same thing. If the data were compromised or leaked, there would be a negative impact to the organization. Sensitive data has a higher level of risk than publicly available data. As an example, your organization's directory of employees has a low level of risk if it is compromised. The list of customers has a higher level of risk if it is compromised. Of course, the level of risk is also directly proportional to your organization's function. If you are a college, then the directory of employees being leaked is a low risk, but if you are a federal organization, then the directory of employees being leaked is a high risk. There are five common classifications for data types:

Public Data.   This data is important, but it is openly available to the public, which makes it public data. Some examples of public data are phone numbers, physical addresses, press release information and promotional material, job profiles, and organization positions. This list just scratches the surface of public data. Basically, anything on your organization's website or the Internet about your organization is public data.

Private Data.   The data is not public, but it might be open for customers and business partners. Examples of this data are direct-dial phone numbers, email addresses of associates, employee identification numbers, and personal emails sent to customers and partners, just to name a few. Much of this content is not published and might be protected by usernames and passwords.

Internal Data.   The data is internal to the organization and limited to use by its employees. Internal data can have a variety of security requirements that dictate who can use the data internally. Examples of the information are business strategies, sales information, internal organization websites, IP address information for various systems, and financial data and revenue forecasts, just to name a few.

Confidential Data.   This data classification is confidential data and typically limited to a small group of individuals inside your organization. Examples of confidential data are credit card and banking information, employee records, biometric information, Social Security numbers, driver licenses, and other personal identifiable information (PII), just to name a few.

Restricted Data.   This data classification contains the most sensitive information in the organization. This data should be encrypted to provide additional protection. If this data were to be leaked, it would lead to a high impact on the organization. Examples of restricted data are protected health information (PHI), trade secrets, intellectual property (IP), financial and tax information, and other highly regulated data that should be protected, just to name a few.

> Confidential and restricted data is typically treated with the same level of protection because it is typically hard to differentiate and therefore treated as highly sensitive information by the organization.
>
> In addition to the five common data types, an organization might adopt other data-type classifications.

Private organizations typically use the five common classification types previously described. Government organizations will typically use classifications for materials and information as they are related to the potential damage to national security. The three data classifications used by the United States Department of Defense (DoD) are as follows:

Confidential.   This data is information that, if it were disclosed in an unauthorized manner, could reasonably be expected to cause damage to national security.

Secret.   This data is information that, if it were disclosed in an unauthorized manner, could reasonably be expected to cause serious damage to national security.

Top Secret.   This data is information that, if it were disclosed in an unauthorized manner, could reasonably be expected to cause exceptionally grave damage to national security.

In an effort to maintain confidentiality and integrity of sensitive information, data encryption should be employed. Information assurance in the form of data encryption ensures that data loss to an unauthorized user will not occur. Although the term *data loss* might be construed as the actual loss of data in the form of availability, the term actually means that you have lost control of the data. Without encryption, a threat actor can obtain a copy of the data, the data could be sent unintentionally to an unauthorized user, or it could be modified in an unauthorized manner.

Consider an example of a laptop with sensitive patient record information stored on it. If the laptop were to be stolen, the threat actor could use a number of utilities that could provide unauthorized access to the patient records. However, with encryption (such as BitLocker) enabled, both the operating system and the data would remain encrypted and inaccessible to unauthorized users.

There are three concepts associated with information assurance – data in transit, data at rest, and data in use, as shown in Figure 8.5:

Data in Transit.   Encryption of data in transit refers to information traversing the network; it should always be encrypted so that it is not decipherable if intercepted. Over the past decade, just about every website and application has adopted some form of encryption, so there is no reason not to use encryption in transit.

FIGURE 8.5   Data and encryption.

Data at Rest.   Data at rest refers to data that is written out to disk. This concept is a point of contention, because it is believed that once the data hits the server, it's safe. However, the data is more vulnerable because it's in one spot. If a drive needs to be replaced because it went bad, outside of physical destruction, there is no way to assure the data is inaccessible. When backup tapes are used, it is not only a good idea but should be a requirement.

Data in Use.   Encryption of data in use refers to data that is in an inconsistent state and/or currently resident in memory. Most of the time, you don't need to be too concerned with data in memory, because that is normally a function of the operating system. However, when data is written to virtual memory such as the pagefile or swap file, it is considered data in use and therefore it could be intercepted.

The use of encryption is not just a good idea; in a lot of information sectors, the use of encryption is a regulatory requirement. Most regulatory requirements only define that data must be transmitted and stored with strong encryption. Data-in-use encryption is not typically defined, simply because network administrators use off-the-shelf products such as Windows, Linux, and SQL, just to name a few. These products typically adhere to standards that make them secure for data that resides in memory. However, some regulatory requirements might require you to crank the security down on the operating system or application. One such regulatory requirement is the Federal Information Processing Standard (FIPS), but there are many others.

Risk Mitigation

Now that you have learned how to identify and analyze the risk to your organization, it's time to mitigate the risk. Risk mitigation is the process in which you plan how to lessen the risk that you may have identified. In almost all cases, you can't totally remove the risk identified, but you can lessen the potential for the risk. If we use the analogy of a bank, the risk identified might be a bank robbery. We can plan to mitigate the risk by placing armed guards in the lobby and bulletproof glass on the teller windows. All of these mitigation tactics will effectively lower the risk of a bank robbery, but the risk of robbery is still there regardless.

To effectively lessen the risk involved, we need to develop a mitigation plan. The mitigation plan allows all of the stakeholders and team members to align with the goal of mitigating the risk. The mitigation plan allows for everyone involved to understand the tasks involved to effectively mitigate the risk. Planning also allows for everyone involved to be clear about their tasks for the implementation of the plan.

Introduction

Now that we understand the expectations for the risk mitigation plan, let's discuss the elements we should include in the introduction of the risk mitigation plan. The most important element is the clarification of the risk. This should be done by clearly stating what the risk is to your organization. If this risk is a security concern, such as a vulnerability that has a published CVE, then this should be included in the risk mitigation plan.

In addition, you should describe any exploits that might be known that can exploit the vulnerability. This will help you develop the second element, which is how likely the event is to happen to your organization. Although there might be a vulnerability that has been disclosed, it may not actively be exploited. Always remember that risk is the potential for a threat to be executed, so the likelihood is an important element of the risk mitigation plan. Understanding whether there are known exploits allows us to have objective data to back up our findings.

The last element in the introduction is the proximity of the event; this is also known as the urgency. It describes how likely the event is to happen to the organization in terms of time. The proximity will then of course drive your urgency to mitigate the risk. So the introduction should clearly state the risk is, the likelihood of the risk being realized, and what the organization's timeline should be.

In the following, I will show you a specific vulnerability published around the writing of this book. I have separated out the various elements of the introduction, but you may want to write the introduction as a paragraph in your mitigation plan:

Impact.   We have determined our organization has FortiOS installed on several FortiNet devices throughout our network. Currently there is CVE 2024-21762 published that affects FortiOS. The vulnerability allows a remote unauthenticated attacker to execute arbitrary code or command via a specially crafted HTTP request. This would allow a threat actor to gain control of the device for passive monitoring of conversations or disruption of service.

Likelihood.   There are multiple articles published on the Internet that explain the exploit against this vulnerability. The CVE has a score of 9.6 out of 10 and has classified this CVE as a critical severity. Therefore, it is extremely likely that this particular vulnerability could be realized by our organization.

Proximity.   This is a risk because of an outdated FortiOS version. The vulnerability is being exploited currently on the Internet, and it should be assumed that our organization will realize this impact within a few weeks, if it is left unpatched.

Strategic Response

Now that we have the introduction to the mitigation plan, we can concentrate on a strategic response to mitigate the risk. Keep in mind, the goal is to minimize the risk or eliminate the risk—that is, if it is possible, but typically we can't completely get rid of the risk. There are several different strategies to minimize the risk, as follows. They will range from completely removing the risk to accepting it and bracing for the impact:

Eliminate.   This option is probably the most sought after, because no one wants to deal with risk, now or in the future. Elimination of the risk is not always feasible. For example, using the prior scenario of FortiOS, the elimination of risk could be attained by upgrading to the latest version of operating system. This would eliminate the foreseen risk, but it would not prevent it in the future.

Reduce Likelihood.   Reducing the likelihood is often the fastest alternative when responding to the risk. For example, we can reduce the likelihood of the risk by firewalling access to the device. This would reduce the likelihood that someone from the Internet could exploit the vulnerability. Only trusted IP addresses and networks could then manage the FortiOS device.

Reduce Impact.   Reducing the impact is another quick way to get results in lowering the risk. For example, we can move the FortiOS devices to branch offices where they would make a smaller impact than serving our main office. This would reduce the impact if someone exploited the vulnerability.

Transfer.   Another useful tactic is to transfer the risk to another organization. This might be a vendor that maintains the devices for you. You could ask that they come up with a solution. This transference often works really well with business processes. For example, human resources (HR) might have third parties perform a background check on a new hire. Or one business manager might require a certain process to be performed outside of their business unit because of the direct risk.

Contingency Plan.   This is a good tactic if the risk is low and the work involved to reduce or eliminate the risk is too high. We can create a contingency plan in the event the risk is realized. This is often done with business processes where changing something might mean retooling the entire procedure. However, as it is applied to the example we have been working through, the contingency plan might detail that if the device is compromised, it should be replaced with a newer unit.

Accept.   The acceptance of risk is basically doing nothing about it. There are different scenarios where the risk is too small and the work to be done to mitigate it is far too much. So the organization just accepts the risk.

Action Plan

The action plan is how you are going to carry out your response to the risk with the strategic response. The action plan is a part of the risk mitigation step, but you might also hear the action plan referred to as the risk management plan. Regardless, the action plan helps convey all of the details to the rest of your team. Whenever you think about the action plan, think what, when, who, how, cost, and review. The sections of the action plan are as follows:

What.   This section is what we are going to carry out in the action plan to deliver the strategic response. This section will detail the steps to mitigating the risk, and it should not lack details. The action plan should be written to convey the intended steps of the mitigation process to the rest of the team.

Timing.   The timing of the events is basically when you intend to carry out the plan. All times and dates should be detailed in this section, along with their respective key action items. Any milestones should also be outlined and communicated so that everyone knows how to evaluate the progress of the overall plan.

Responsibility.   This section will detail who is responsible for which actions. The responsibility section can be created in two ways: assigning action items to the responsible parties, or assigning responsible parties to each action item. It does not matter which style you prefer, as long as everyone knows what is expected.

Resources.   The resources section of the action plan will detail all of the tools, data, hardware, and third parties, just to name a few. The resources are all of the required resources to complete the action plan, outside of the expected team members.

Budget.   In many cases, the mitigation action plan is going to cost the organization time, money, or both; this section is where the cost is conveyed. Sometimes, when the action plan is carried out, it will delay other projects in the organization. This section is where those project delays will also be explained.

Review.   The last and most important section in the action plan is the review. This section will explain to the rest of the team how success is evaluated. Without the review of the successful mitigation of risk, the team will have no way of knowing whether the risk is mitigated. Specific tests should be developed and written into the review section.

The action plan is the schematic to carrying the plan forward to mitigate the risk. Everything in the action plan should be very well detailed, and the preceding list is not everything; it is just the most common elements. You may want to include supporting data, or even case histories of other organizations and their mitigation successes.

Implementation and Tracking

Planning without execution is just simply planning. The implementation of your plan is one of the final steps in the process of mitigating risk. Getting ready for this step should be easy because the action plan should detail the step-by-step instructions, timeline, and team members responsible for execution.

Depending on the complexity of the action plan, completing it may be something you can do before lunch, or it could require further planning. If mitigating the risk gets to be really complex, this is where you can employ project management software such as Microsoft Project or Smartsheet, just to name two. Project management software will help you to prioritize the steps involved in the implementation. It will also allow you to track project completion and milestones, as well as keep your team members assigned to the various tasks. In many cases, the action plan can be transferred directly to the software because almost all of the details of time and dates are in the action plan already.

Once the project is detailed out, the next step is a kick-off meeting. The kick-off meeting allows everyone to understand the start of the project, milestones, and their individual contribution, as well as the expected completion. In addition, the kick-off meeting helps to notify affected groups about any related downtime during the remediation. The actual start of the project should be relatively soon after the kick-off meeting.

Tracking and review of the goals should be done as often as needed, depending on the pace of the project. In addition, weekly or biweekly meetings to keep everyone on task should also be considered. These periodic meetings ensure there is cadence to the project and keep everyone engaged. The weekly cadence meeting also allows for the evaluation of a rollback or backout plan in the event that there is extended downtime or unforeseen effects.

When the project of risk mitigation ends, you should conduct a debriefing meeting. The debriefing meeting, often called a hot wash, allows the team to review what went wrong and what could be done better next time. The hot wash is not just to evaluate the team's execution; it should help evaluate any residual risk. Any residual risk should then be placed back into the cyclical process of risk management to further whittle it down.

Security Assessments

A security assessment is typically performed by a third party to assess the overall security preparedness of your organization. The security assessment is also a review of the risk your organization might have and not realize it. The methods of a security assessment can include a number of different tactics that will be covered in the following sections. Each method will generate a report that will be included in the overall security assessment. The key goal of the security assessment is to report the current security of the organization in an effort to tighten security, thus reducing overall risk.

A security assessment should be performed quarterly, and the findings of the security assessment should be addressed promptly. Some cyber-insurance companies require an annual third-party security assessment as a prerequisite to a cyber-insurance policy. Security assessments can also be required by compliance regulations that apply to an organization's industry sector, such as the financial sector or health care sector, just to name two.

Vulnerability Assessment

A vulnerability assessment is critical to identifying risk in your network. A vulnerability scan is normally completed on the external and internal network ranges of the organization. The first tactic is to identify the open services by using a port scanning tool such as Nmap. The next tactic performed after the port scan is complete and services are identified is a vulnerability scan. The vulnerability scan will interrogate the services in an effort to identify their weakness. There are many different tools out there to scan network vulnerabilities. The

Nessus vulnerability scanner is the most popular, and it requires a subscription for large scans. The tactics of port scanning and identifying vulnerabilities are the same methods a bad actor will follow in an effort to compromise your organization.

Penetration Testing

A penetration test, also known as a pen test, will take the vulnerability assessment one step further by executing the vulnerabilities found in the vulnerability assessment. The penetration tester will attempt to circumvent security and penetrate the network by using the known vulnerabilities. A penetration test is the racy part of the security assessment, because there is no script that the penetration tester follows, just wits and tradecraft.

When a penetration test is being performed, there should not be a heightened security posture where the employees are expecting something to happen. You want to prevent a red team vs. blue team circumstance unless it is normal operating procedure. Many times, the penetration tester will use any means to penetrate the network, such as physical access or a phishing email with a payload that beacons back to a command-and-control server.

 Real World Scenario

It is best to perform a vulnerability scan three times a year (quarterly) and a full penetration test annually. This is the perfect mix of identifying vulnerabilities so they can be patched and an independent test of the overall security. In some high-risk organizations, it is now common to have monthly or even weekly assessments. The key difference between a vulnerability assessment and a penetration test is that the penetration test is driven by a capture the flag (CTF) goal, whereas a vulnerability assessment is driven by findings that could lead to a compromise. The penetration testers will act on the most common vulnerabilities to get into your network. How they got access to the network is disclosed in the final report. However, many other potential entry points (vulnerabilities) could exist. This is where a comprehensive vulnerability assessment is beneficial to the organization's security.

Posture Assessment

A security posture assessment is the assessment of how an organization handles a breach or threat and the risk associated with it. One of the goals of the security posture assessment is to establish a benchmark. This benchmark should then be improved on in an ongoing effort to heighten your security posture.

Fortunately, there are some objective guidelines that can be applied to network security and how network security is handled. The National Institute of Standards and Technology (NIST) Cyber Security Framework (CSF) and the International Organization for Standardization (ISO)

FIGURE 8.6   NIST CSF process.

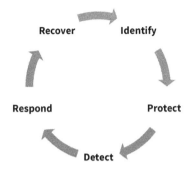

standards 27001 specification both outline frameworks and standards for network security. The NIST CSF describes a cyclical process of Identify, Protect, Detect, Respond, and Recover, as shown in Figure 8.6. Each item in the NIST CSF process should be carried out when a threat is identified. The threat should then be protected, and a system should be implemented to detect further threats. A response-and-recover plan should then be followed or outlined, depending on the circumstances. The ISO 27001 standard is for the management of information security that an organization should follow and can be certified as practicing.

Change Management Best Practices

When you implement a new system or change an existing system, you affect a lot of people. You also affect business processes and other business units with these changes and introduce risk. Don't underestimate the power of the documentation you will produce as a technician. It can and often will be used by change management groups to review the impact of your proposed changes.

Change management is a process often found in large corporations, publicly held corporations, and industries such as financial services that have regulatory requirements. However, change management is not exclusive to these types of organizations. The main purpose of change management is to standardize the methods and procedures used to handle changes in the company. These changes can be soft changes of personnel or processes, or hard changes of network services and systems.

When changes are proposed to a process or set of processes, a document is drafted called the *change management plan document*. Applications such as ServiceNow are commonly used in change management. This document is used throughout the change management process to evaluate the impact to the business continuity of the organization. In the following section, we will discuss the elements of a change management plan document.

The change management process can be accelerated with applications such as ServiceNow. This new generation of applications allow for faster deployment of the change management process and can be customized for various workflows. This reduces the time spent on development of the change management plan document, which in turn speeds up the overall process.

Documented Business Processes

The documented business process is incorporated into the change management plan document. It provides an overview of the business process that the changes are expected to affect. It allows everyone involved in the process both directly and indirectly to understand the entire process.

The documentation specifically defines who interacts with, how they interact with, why they interact with, and when they interact with the process. For example, if your company created widgets, your documentation might detail the process of manufacturing the widget. The document would describe the following:

- How the raw components enter the production line
- Who delivers the raw materials
- When they deliver the raw materials
- Who assembles the raw materials to create a finished product
- Who inspects the finished product
- When and how the product is shipped

Change Rollback Plan (Backout Plan)

The *rollback plan*, also called the backout plan, describes the steps to roll back from a failed primary plan. If it were determined that the primary plan could not be completed, you would implement either an alternate (secondary) plan or a rollback plan, depending on the changes proposed in the change management plan document. Like the primary and alternate plans, the rollback plan should contain the steps to be taken in the event the rollback plan must be executed. The rollback plan should also document any changes to configuration so that it can be reverted back. Most of the rollback plan will consist of the original configuration, with any additional steps to revert it back.

Sandbox Testing

Sandbox testing is extremely useful when you want to test a change before placing it into production. A sandbox can be constructed to match your environment; you can then implement the change and fine-tune your primary plan. The use of a sandbox testing environment allows you to hone your process for the proposed change while observing any potential issues.

The introduction of virtual machines makes it very easy to set up a sandbox for testing. You can clone production servers into an isolated network and then create snapshots on the server in the sandbox and test over and over again, until all the bugs are worked out of the primary plan.

Responsible Staff Member

Every process in the organization must have a person who is assigned to be the *responsible staff member*. This person oversees the process and can answer questions about the process. If there are any changes to the process or changes that can affect the process, this person acts as the main point of contact. They can then facilitate any changes to the process.

As an example, you may assign a person to be the responsible party for the electronics decommissioning process. Any questions about disposal of electronics should be directed to this person. If your organization is choosing a new e-waste company, it will affect the decommissioning process. Therefore, this person should be included in the decision as a stakeholder. Any changes can then be adjusted or integrated into the decommissioning process, and this person can facilitate the changes.

Request Forms

The change management process often begins with a *request form* that details the proposed change. The exact elements in the request form will differ slightly depending on your organization's requirements. The following lists the most common elements found on the change management request form. Some of the information found on the request form is preliminary; the information will be expanded on as the request form transitions into the change control document:

Item to be Changed.   This is the item that is being requested for a change. Examples are software, hardware, firmware, configuration, or documentation.

Reason.   The reason the item is being submitted for a change. Examples are legal, marketing, performance, software bug, or process problem.

Priority.   The urgency, or priority, of the change is documented in this section of the form, although this should also be conveyed in the reason for the change. The priority is often a separate field on the change control form. Examples are emergency, urgent, routine, or a specific date.

Change Description/Plan.   The description or plan for the change is documented in this section. For changes in configuration, you would detail the changes to the configuration and why each part of the configuration is being changed. Firmware changes would list the version being upgraded from and the version being upgraded to.

Change Rollback Plan.   The rollback plan describes the steps to roll back from a failed primary plan. If it was determined that the primary plan could not be completed, you would implement either an alternate plan or a rollback plan, depending on the changes proposed.

Technical Evaluation.   In this section of the form, you document why the primary plan will succeed. The changes should be tested in a lab environment closest to the production environment and documented in this section. When you're creating the technical evaluation, outline specific objective goals along with the metrics with which they can be measured.

Duration of Changes.   Here, you document the estimated duration of the change process. Any service outages will be documented in this section.

Purpose of Change

The *purpose of change* is the reason the change management process starts. Either your business unit requires a change that will affect others, or another business unit requires a change that can affect your business unit indirectly. A change to any part of the process, such as the intake of raw materials, could affect the end result. Change is an essential component of a business, and it should be expected. If your company only created widgets and never evolved, you would eventually be out of business.

Unfortunately, not all changes support the company's product line directly. Some changes are imposed on the company, because IT systems are constantly changing. As a technician, you are constantly upgrading and patching systems and equipment. These upgrades and patches are considered changes that can affect the entire business process.

This section of the change management plan document should explain why the change is necessary. It needs to include any vendor documentation explaining the change to the product. For example, if the proposed change were to install a Microsoft Windows security patch, the purpose of the change would be the security of the Windows operating system. The vendor documentation in this example would be the knowledge base article that normally accompanies Windows security patches. Other examples of purposes of change might be legal, marketing, performance, capacity, a software bug, or a process problem that requires a change.

Scope of Change

The *scope of change* details how many systems the proposed change will affect. The scope could involve only one system, or it could be all the systems in an entire enterprise. The scope of change is not limited to the number of systems that will be changed. The scope can also describe how many people a proposed change will affect. For example, if you propose to change lines of code in an ordering system, the change could affect your salespeople, customers, and delivery of the products. The scope of this change could impact the business continuity directly if something goes wrong during the change.

When creating this section of the change management plan documentation, be sure to document which systems the proposed change will affect, the number of systems the proposed change will affect, the number of people the proposed change will affect, as well as whether anyone will be directly or indirectly affected. In addition, you should include the proposed date and time of the change and how long the change will take. Keep in mind that this section allows the change management team to evaluate how big the proposed change is. The scope should answer the following questions:

- Who will the change affect?
    - IT resources
    - Other departments
    - Business units
    - Partners
    - Customers
- What will the change affect?
    - IT systems
    - Sites/locations
    - Processes/procedures
    - Availability of systems
    - Outage duration
- What will be affected?
    - Other proposed changes
    - System performance
    - System capacity
    - Other resources (personnel, security, etc.)
- When is the proposed change?
    - Date and time of the change
    - Duration of the change

Risk Review

Whenever a change is made to a system or equipment, there is the potential for the system or equipment to fail. The change could even cause another system or piece of equipment to fail. In some circumstances, the change might be successful but inadvertently cause problems elsewhere in the business process. For example, if a change to an ordering system causes confusion in the ordering process, sales might be inadvertently lost. This is where changes should be identified for risk and introduced into the risk management process. This process is also commonly known as a peer review.

Plan for Change

The plan for change section of the change management plan document explains how the proposed change will be executed. Steps should be detailed on the changes and the order of the changes. If changes were to be made in configuration files, switches, or routers, you would document the changes to the configuration and why each part of the configuration was being changed. Firmware changes would list the version being upgraded from and the version being upgraded to. The idea is to provide as much detail as possible about the documented changes to be made to the systems or equipment.

When a change is implemented or planned, there is always the potential for problems, or you may identify a consideration in the execution of the plan. The plan-for-change section should detail those considerations. It's common for a primary plan to be drafted as well as an alternate plan in the event the primary plan cannot be executed. For example, if the primary plan were to move a server from one rack to another so that it could be connected to a particular switch, the alternate plan could be to leave it in the rack and use longer cables. Be sure to have multiple plans; once the change is approved, the plan(s) outlined in this document must be executed closely.

You should also document why the primary plan will succeed. The changes should be tested in a lab environment closest to the production environment (if possible) and documented in this section as well. When creating the plan, you should outline specific, objective goals, along with the metrics with which they can be measured. For example, if you were planning to make a change because there is a high error rate on an interface, then the metric measure to be compared would be the error rate on the interface. You would document what you expect the error rate to be after the change is made so that you could measure the success of the change.

Change Board

The change board, also known as the *change advisory board*, is the body of users who will ultimately evaluate and then approve or deny the change you propose. This group of people often meets weekly to discuss the changes detailed in the change management plan documents. The goal of the change advisory board is to evaluate the proposed changes in order to reduce the impact on day-to-day operations of the organization.

It is common practice for the meetings of the change advisory board to be held via a conference call at a set time every week. This allows key stakeholders in an organization to be available regardless of where they are in the world. Because it's at a set time every week, there are no excuses for not being available during the change-control meetings.

It is likely that if you are the technician proposing the change, you will be on the call for questions or clarification. The key to getting a change approved is to know your audience and communicate clearly in the change-control plan document. Remember, the change advisory board is often composed of various stakeholders from the entire organization, not just IT. You should not assume that the change you are proposing is as clear to them as it is to you. Some change advisory boards are made up strictly of IT stakeholders, so you must understand who will review the proposed changes and choose your wording appropriately.

The change management document must be approved by the majority of change advisory board members or by specific board members. The approval of the proposed change should be documented in the change-control policy for the organization. Only approved changes can be executed. If other changes need to be made outside of the original submission, additional approvals must be acquired.

 Each organization is different, and each change management documentation process will be slightly different. However, the sections described here are the most common elements found in these documents.

User Acceptance

Although the exam does not focus on application development testing and approval, *user acceptance* is an integral piece the change management process. It should be noted that user acceptance is not solely used for application development; it is also used when there is a significant update to an interface or a process, such as a service pack or upgrade to an operating system.

When a change is to be made in which the user's interaction will be affected, it is common practice to beta-test the change. This is also known as user testing or just plain application testing. You can achieve user acceptance two different ways:

In-Person Testing.   The person responsible for testing dedicates time and performs testing in person with the developer.

Self-Paced Testing.   This has its advantages because the user will be relaxed in their own environment during testing.

Regardless of which method of testing you choose, a strict time frame must be communicated to the user testing the change.

Once user acceptance is obtained, it should be documented in the user acceptance section of the change management documentation. The methods of testing, the users and groups involved in testing, and the time invested in testing should be included in this section as well. Remember that the goal is the approval and successful implementation of the changes, so it is important that you are convincing and, more importantly, convinced that the change will succeed without repercussions.

Summary

In this chapter, we learned about the cyclical risk management process, in which you must constantly identify risks in your environment, analyze risk, plan risk mitigation, implement the mitigation, and review and track changes. The process begins with risk identification by examining the vulnerabilities, threats, and assets. Then you analyze the risk and prioritize the mitigation in the form of a strategic response. Once a strategic response is selected, an action plan can be created. The action plan is a detailed schematic of how to mitigate the risk, and once it is created, the mitigation can be implemented. The final step is to review and track the mitigation of the risk. Then the cycle begins all over again.

We also learned about the various security assessments that help identify security risks in the network. There are three main assessments that should be done periodically. There are vulnerability assessments that help uncover vulnerabilities in the network. Then there are penetration tests that show how the network can be penetrated by a threat actor. Last but not least is the posture assessment that details how your organization handles breaches and security events.

The last topic we learned about was the change management process, which is aimed at avoiding risk from changes in the network. The change management process helps avoidance by assembling a team of people in the organization so that everyone has an opportunity to see how the change will affect their department.

Exam Essentials

Know the elements of risk.   Risk is the intersection of vulnerabilities, threats, and assets.

Understand the various risk levels.   The most common risk tier levels are low, moderate, and high. The various risk levels derived from the risk matrix will dictate the priority for the mitigation of the risk.

Understand the various strategic responses to risk.   The various strategic response are eliminate, reduce likelihood, reduce impact, transfer, contingency plan, and acceptance of the risk.

Know the various components of a security assessment.   A security assessment is the final product from a number of other assessments, such as the vulnerability assessment, penetration testing, risk assessment, and security-posture assessment.

Know the elements of the change management process.   Change management is adopted by organizations to standardize the methods and procedures for any changes in the organization. Change management documentation is an integral part of this process. It is used to document a change so that it does not impede the organization's operations.

Review Questions

 The following questions are designed to test your understanding of this chapter's material. For more information on how to get additional questions, please see www.lammle.com/ccst.

You can find the answers to these questions in Appendix.

1. Which is a vulnerability that no patch or workaround is available for at the time of its disclosure?

   A. Exploit

   B. Asset

   C. Zero-day

   D. Training

2. You have found that a number of devices on your network have default credentials still configured. Which type of vulnerability is this?

   A. Training

   B. Physical

   C. Zero-day

   D. Configuration

3. Which is not an element of risk?

   A. Network

   B. Vulnerability

   C. Threat

   D. Asset

4. You have a large proprietary database of users. Which would these be considered in relation to risk?

   A. Vulnerable

   B. Asset

   C. Exploitable

   D. Configuration

5. Which is not a component of the risk analysis calculation to derive an outcome?

   A. Likelihood

   B. Availability

   C. Level

   D. Impact

6. With a three-tier risk rating, if the impact of a risk is significant but the likelihood is low, what is the expected risk level?

    A. Extreme

    B. High

    C. Moderate

    D. Low

7. Which risk prioritization approach uses objective data to prioritize risk?

    A. Qualitative

    B. Confidential

    C. Subjective

    D. Quantitative

8. Your organization uses a third party to vet employees. Which risk mitigation strategy is this an example of?

    A. Transference

    B. Elimination

    C. Acceptance

    D. Contingency plan

9. Which element of the risk mitigation plan is the urgency of the mitigation?

    A. Impact

    B. Proximity

    C. Resources

    D. Budget

10. Which section of the change management documentation contains whom the change will affect?

    A. Business processes

    B. Scope of change

    C. User acceptance

    D. Plan for change

Chapter

9

Vulnerability Management

THE FOLLOWING CCST EXAM TOPIC IS COVERED IN THIS CHAPTER:

✔ **4.0 Vulnerability Assessment and Risk Management**

- ▪ 4.1. Explain vulnerability management

  Vulnerability identification, management, and mitigation; active and passive reconnaissance; testing (port scanning, automation)

- ▪ 4.2. Use threat intelligence techniques to identify potential network vulnerabilities

  Uses and limitations of vulnerability databases; industry-standard tools used to assess vulnerabilities and make recommendations, policies, and reports; Common Vulnerabilities and Exposures (CVEs), cybersecurity reports, cybersecurity news, subscription services, and collective intelligence; ad hoc and automated threat intelligence; the importance of updating documentation and other forms of communication proactively before, during, and after cybersecurity incidents; how to secure, share and update documentation

Vulnerabilities can be found in any system that handles or protects something valuable. Information systems are no different than a safe that protect something precious. Threat actors will find a vulnerability in the system and work to exploit that flaw. This chapter will teach you how to identify vulnerabilities in your network, to thwart threat actors before they can be exploited. The systematic approach to identifying vulnerabilities is called vulnerability management.

To find your included bonus material, as well as Todd Lammle videos, practice questions, and hands-on labs, please see www.lammle.com/ccst.

Vulnerabilities

Finding the vulnerabilities in your network and mitigating or eliminating them is your best defense from being compromised by a threat actor. Unfortunately, finding vulnerabilities is harder than it sounds. Threat actors are constantly finding new vulnerabilities to exploit in our networks, software, and security systems. This is literally a full-time position for a security professional in any organization. Many organizations outsource this task to vendors that identify vulnerabilities as their main business.

The good news is that once you know the vulnerability exists, you can typically mitigate it and thwart the threat actor. As a matter of fact, a good defense is to not be the low hanging fruit. If you make it hard to exploit your network, the threat actor will likely move on to another network that is easier to exploit.

This section will discuss the tactic you can use in your organization to find vulnerabilities.

Vulnerability Identification

Common Vulnerabilities and Exposures (CVE) is a system that provides a reference-method for publicly known vulnerabilities and exposures. The CVE system was originally created in 1999 by a working group based on a white paper published by David E. Mann and Steven M. Christey of the MITRE Corporation. The purpose of the CVE system is to create a common naming scheme for vulnerabilities while reducing any overlaps in documentation from varying agencies documenting the same vulnerability.

A typical CVE will look similar to this common nomenclature of CVE-2020-17084. This particular CVE details a buffer overflow in Microsoft Exchange Server that was discovered in 2020. By investigating this CVE on the Internet, you can see that regardless of who hosts the information, it pertains to the same vulnerability. For example, Microsoft refers to the same vulnerability the National Institute of Standards and Technology (NIST) refers using this CVE number. All sources have the same relative information about the vulnerability, such as affected versions, a score that explains the associated risk, the impact, and references.

Keep in mind that the CVE is not a database. It is a numbering system for tracking vulnerabilities. The numbering and characterization of a CVE is up to the CVE Numbering Authority (CNA). As in the previous example, Microsoft is CNA and therefore created the initial CVE-2020-17084 document that all other CVE repositories must reference similarly. There are CNAs all around the world, and most of them are software manufacturers such as IBM, Microsoft, and VMware. However, some of the CNAs are security organizations. The underlying theme is not who creates the CVE, but that once it is created, the CVE should be consistent across all references.

Management

The management of vulnerabilities and the management of risk have an inseparable relationship. This is because risk is produced when vulnerabilities exist in our network. Therefore, many of the concepts associated with risk management are similar when compared to vulnerability management. The first familiar concept is the cyclical process of vulnerability management, as shown in Figure 9.1. This process is known as the vulnerability management life cycle.

The vulnerability management lifecycle starts with the discovery of vulnerabilities and ends with the verification and monitoring of vulnerabilities. The following explains each of the various stages of the vulnerability management lifecycle.

Discovery.   The discovery phase in the vulnerability management lifecycle starts with knowing what you have. You should have a comprehensive list of all hardware and software in the organization. Then a baseline should be created by identifying all of the vulnerabilities that exist in the hardware and software. Since the vulnerability management lifecycle is a cyclical process, this step will need to be completed on a periodic basis. Therefore, if it can be automated to run daily, weekly, or monthly, it should be done so that you can have an up-to-date list of all vulnerabilities in the organization's hardware and software.

Prioritization.   The hardware and software in the organization will have varied importance and impact; this is also known as criticality. The hardware or software should be grouped together based on their criticality; this is often known as an asset group. By creating assets grouped based on their criticality, it will help in the decision-making process when you need

FIGURE 9.1 Vulnerability management lifecycle.

to allocate resources to remediate a vulnerability. For example, you probably would not want to dedicate half of your IT team to updating firmware on a device that has little or no impact to the organization.

Assessment. As discussed in the prioritization phase, some hardware and software will have a greater impact to the organization if it is compromised. For example, domain controllers (DCs) should have the highest importance to patching vulnerabilities, because they hold all the accounts in the organization. Low-impact items might be the time-clock, projector, or software that does not attribute to line-of-business applications, just to name a few. These devices or software applications would still need to be patched, as they can be used as an initial access point or elevation of privilege in the network. The assessment phase allows for you to assess the order in which you patch the vulnerabilities.

Reporting. The reporting phase is pretty similar to the risk mitigation phase from the risk management process. This is mainly because you are evaluating and reporting on the associated risk for each asset that has a vulnerability. In this phase a security plan should be created that details the vulnerability, the impact to the organization, and the remediation steps to mitigate the vulnerability.

Remediation. The remediation phase is where the rubber meets the road. In this phase the step to remediate the vulnerability should be executed. Of course, you will want to start with the assets that pose the greatest risk to the organization. You also want to allocate the appropriate amount of resources to mitigate the vulnerability.

Verification and Monitoring.   In this final phase, you will want to verify that the devices and applications patched are no longer vulnerable. This phase will ensure that the vulnerabilities that were previously discovered in the organization will not reoccur due to misconfiguration or an errant change. This phase is also known as the audit phase, since you are regularly auditing the network for previously known vulnerabilities. This is one of the key differentiators between this phase and the discovery phase. The discover phase finds new vulnerabilities, and this phase verifies and monitors previously known vulnerabilities.

These six phases are the most commonly found in most vulnerability management lifecycles. The key is to find the right combination of these phases to keep security moving forward. As your security team matures, you can condense several of these steps to streamline the mitigation of vulnerabilities.

Mitigation

Patching is probably the most common method to mitigate a vulnerability, but it is only one of many different ways to mitigate a vulnerability. There are many instances where the patch might change the functionality of the hardware or software. This change in functionality might be undesirable by the organization. As an example, a certain protocol might be too old for the vendor to fix the vulnerability, and the patch might just disable the protocol. In these cases, an alternate method to mitigate the vulnerabilities would be desirable. Many of the vendors will give you a guide on workarounds for a vulnerability; they might include several different workarounds. The following section details all the possible ways to mitigate a vulnerability without using a patch. This is not a complete list, since ever vendor and situation will have a unique method to mitigate a vulnerability.

Configuration Management.   Some mitigation can be done via a specific configuration detailed by the vendor. This configuration might require turning on another security protocol to protect the primary protocol, such as DHCP snooping to protect from DHCP spoofing. The configuration might also harden the operating system or service, such as requiring 2048 bit RSA keys for SSH, when the default is 768 bits; a special configuration would force the 2048 bit RSA key generation. These are just a few examples of configuration management to mitigate a vulnerability. The key takeaway is some mitigations of vulnerabilities might require configuration changes.

Access Controls.   A very common way to mitigate a vulnerability is to fence it in with an access control list. This is a common workaround when protocol and services not meant for Internet access contain a vulnerability. An access control list will protect the protocol or service by limiting access to only trusted or privileged computer accounts. A classic example is administrative pages on a device that is typically configured from a web browser. This strategy is also an operating system hardening technique, but when a vulnerability exists and the default is to allow access, this becomes a mitigation technique.

Network Security.   Although adding a layer of network security to another vendor's product might not seem like a mitigation technique, this technique might be in the admin's best interest. Adding firewalls, intrusion detection and intrusion preventions systems (IDS/IPS), and implementing virtual private network (VPNs) are all examples of mitigation through network security. They are often employed when a line-of-business application is too old to be patched or there is no workaround other than to security the service, device, or application externally.

Encryption. Implementing encryption helps to protect data in transit, data at rest, and data in use. It is typically used as a mitigation technique when a protocol, storage system, or hardware device is too weak or the potential for data leakage exists without encryption. Implementing encryption is a best practice when hardening operating systems, but it is used as a mitigation technique when a vulnerability is found and no other workaround is available. A typical example is a configuration file that stores a password in clear text and can be exploited. Encrypting the password will protect the password and mitigate the vulnerability.

Training. In rare instances training employees might be the only mitigation to a vulnerability. These instances are rare but happen from time to time, and vendors choose education over patching an old protocol or system. The training might be as simple as never turn on this protocol, as it will degrade the security of a previous patch. As stated throughout this section, training is another best practice. However, when it is used in response to a vulnerability, it is a mitigation technique.

Active and Passive Reconnaissance

Active reconnaissance techniques are used to find vulnerabilities in an organization's network attack or probe security, whereas passive reconnaissance is the collection of data or development of intelligence to assess the security posture. The differences might seem insignificant as we learn the various techniques, and in many cases, there is a fine line between active and passive reconnaissance.

Active reconnaissance techniques are typically intrusive and potentially disruptive. Since scans often require connecting to the network system and in some cases testing a vulnerability to see if the vulnerability exists, this can of course crash a system. The following sections explain the common active reconnaissance techniques used today.

Passive reconnaissance techniques are performed without any connection to the victim. Passive recognizance tactics are typically performed by a threat actor or pen tester in an attempt to collect and analyze the information

If you are still confused about the differences between an active or passive reconnaissance, always remember that active reconnaissance techniques interact directly with the unit being observed, while passive reconnaissance techniques do not interact (even in an indirect manner) and only receive data to be further analyzed.

Port Scanning

A port scan is an active reconnaissance tactic used to probe the open ports on a destination host or entire network of hosts. These open ports could have potential vulnerabilities attached to the listening daemon, such as an Apache web listening on TCP port 80 or TCP port 443. If it was unpatched and contained vulnerabilities, it could be exploited. A port scanner works by attempting to connect to a port and if the connection is successful and a response is received, then the port is reported to be open.

There are several different tactics used when port scanning a remote system. The most common used to scan Transmission Control Protocol (TCP) is the completion of the three-way handshake. When probing User Datagram Protocol (UDP) the tools will wait for an ICMP message from the remote system signaling a port is closed; if none are received, the port is assumed open. The following is the output from an nmap port scanning. The nmap utility is a popular port scanning utility that can be used to scan remote hosts for open ports and even finger print operating systems, based on their response.

```
c:\Sys\nmap-7.70>nmap www.wiley.com
Starting Nmap 7.70 ( https://nmap.org ) at 2023-02-22 00:04 Eastern
Daylight Time
Nmap scan report for www.wiley.com (172.64.145.177)
Host is up (0.025s latency).
Other addresses for www.wiley.com (not scanned): 104.18.42.79
Not shown: 996 filtered ports
PORT        STATE SERVICE
80/tcp      open  http
443/tcp     open  https
8080/tcp    open  http-proxy
8443/tcp    open  https-alt

Nmap done: 1 IP address (1 host up) scanned in 4.37 seconds

c:\Sys\nmap-7.70>
```

Vulnerability Scanning

A vulnerability scan is an active reconnaissance tactic, and it is one of the best defense tools an administrator can use. It will report all of the active vulnerabilities in your network so you can patch them before they are exploited by a threat actor.

The vulnerability scanner works in two basic modes: inventory and analysis. In inventory, also known as discovery mode, the scanner will scan the entire network for software and devices in use. The scanner will attempt to identify operating system and service version numbers by enumerating each IP address it scans. In analysis mode, the scanner will take that information and apply it to known vulnerabilities in its database to compile a report. This functionality was adopted from the original Nessus project back in 1998. Today Tenable Nessus Professional is a popular vulnerability scanner used by penetration testers.

Some scanners will actively test vulnerabilities against the host to see whether the host is vulnerable. These types of aggressive scans are dangerous, because they could cause a segmentation fault or blue screen on a system and take it offline.

Some vulnerabilities scanners will allow for data collection with an agent installed on each machine. These is the most accurate and safest way to scan hosts in a network.

FIGURE 9.2   Microsoft endpoint protection report.

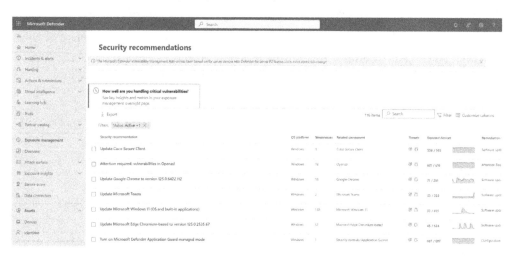

These are often scheduled weekly or even daily to produce an up-to-date report on the health of the network. Microsoft 365 E5/A5 Endpoint Security will inventory and analyze software discovered on every workstation and server endpoint protection is installed on. It will then produce an up-to-the-minute report, as shown in Figure 9.2.

Packet Sniffing/Network Traffic Analysis

Packet sniffing is considered both an active and passive reconnaissance tactic. It is considered an active reconnaissance tactic because you must actively sniff traffic on the network; this means that you must be connected to the network. There are two ways to sniff network traffic: direct and indirectly. A direct approach to packet sniffing might involve a utility such as tcpdump to be installed on a server, or an agent-based installation such as the libpcap capture utility. An indirect approach typically uses sensors to collect the traffic and send it to a centralized spot for analysis.

Traffic analysis is a passive reconnaissance tactic typically performed with the open-source Wireshark packet sniffer utility after packet sniffing is performed. You don't need to capture with Wireshark to analyze traffic with Wireshark. You can use any packet sniffer to capture network traffic such as third-party built-in capture utilities, tcpdump, or dumpcap, just to name a few. Regardless of how you have captured the packets, the Wireshark utility can be used to view the contents of a packet capture, and it will display the analysis, as shown in Figure 9.3. The Wireshark utility can also perform other complex analysis, such as a distribution of protocol graphing. The Wireshark utility can even piece a VoIP call back together into a WAV file so you can hear a VoIP call.

Wireshark isn't the only utility that can perform network traffic analysis. nTop, Suricata, Bandwidthd, and Darkstat are other popular network traffic analysis utilities that can

FIGURE 9.3   Wireshark packet analysis.

analyze information collected. These utilities are installed services that run as dedicated analyzers. Packets are collected from nTop sensors, the Cisco Netflow protocol, or the Internet Engineering Task Force (IETF) IPFIX protocol, just to name a few.

Brute-Force Attacks

A brute-force attack of any sort is the epitome of active reconnaissance tactic. Typically, brute-force attacks are used to obtain passwords, passphrases, usernames, just to name a few. This will be done by either running through a password list or by trying every variation of letters, numbers, and symbols until the username or password is guessed. Common utilities used to brute-force attack passwords are Jack the Ripper and Hydra, just to name a few. These attacks are typically referred to as online brute-force attacks, as they attack a working authentication system.

Passwords are not the only information that is brute-force attacked. Wireless access can also be brute-force attacked. Aircrack-ng is a popular utility used to brute-force attack SSIDs in an attempt to crack their passphrase. The attack method is a bit different than rolling through variations of letters, numbers, and symbols. Aircrack-ng uses a voting system to crack WPA and WPA2 in which chunks of data are analyzed, guessed, and tallied.

If the passwords have been dumped out into a hash file, then they can be brought offline and brute-force attacked with an application such as L0phtCrack and Hashcat, just to name a few. These type of attacks are considered offline brute-force attacks.

Rainbow tables are precalculated hashes used for brute-force attacks; these types of attacks are typically referred to as reverse brute-force attacks. This tactic involved sending the hash to a database of previously hashed passwords in an attempt to reverse the password. These tables can be terabyte large, even petabytes! Access to them is typically allowed for a fee, or you can buy a copy, which ships on a physical hard drive because of the size.

Open-Source Intelligence (OSINT)

Open-source intelligence (OSINT) is a passive reconnaissance tactic. If you ever searched someone's name on social media, then you used open-source intelligence. You probably learned what their interests are, who their friends are, and what they look like now, without the fear of the person knowing you peeked. We are all guilty at some point of having curiosity.

Threat actors are not curious; they are motivated! Using OSINT is trade craft for them. They will figure out what you do, where you do it, and who you do it with. Then they will use this information to exploit you. Do you have a pet, what are the chances that your pet's name is a security question?

OSINT is not limited to people; there are applications that can use OSINT to glean information on an organization. Applications such as Maltego, Spinderfoot, and Intelligence X are just some of the many different sites that allow you to search OSINT information. Other sites such as Shodan, Fofa, and ZoomEye allow you to search for Internet-enabled devices that have been found on the Internet. All of these tools can be used to research an organization's external network and the devices that are connected to the organization. These tools even show firmware versions that have been discovered!

DNS Enumeration

DNS enumeration is a passive reconnaissance tactic that is used to collect DNS information about an organization. With simple queries to public DNS you can actually learn a lot about a target network, such as the public IP address space that the target network uses, the applications in use, and other various intelligence items. For example, in the following, we can see that networkedminds.com uses the Microsoft 365 Office suite from the Sender Policy Framework (SPF) record. We can also see that this organization uses the Smartsheet and Atlassian applications. We now have some items that can be used for phishing the victim, such as a well-crafted email from Microsoft stating that the victim's account will be terminated unless they log in and pay the bill. Of course the link will go to our threat actor's server to harvest the credentials.

```
Microsoft Windows [Version 10.0.17763.5830]
(c) 2018 Microsoft Corporation. All rights reserved.

C:\Users\bohack>nslookup
Default Server:   dns.google
Address:   8.8.8.8

> set type=txt
> networkedminds.com.
Server:   dns.google
Address:   8.8.8.8

Non-authoritative answer:
networkedminds.com text = "MS=ms62370523"
networkedminds.com text = "v=spf1 include:spf.protection.outlook.com -all"
networkedminds.com text = "smartsheet-site-validation=M8qZCn2Bchk"
networkedminds.com text = "atlassian-domain-verification=H926DUsYI"
>
```

Other records can be queried to discover even more information about the organization, such as A and CNAME records to identify hosts and NS records to identify the name servers serving the DNS records, the start of authority (SOA) record to reveal the administrator's email address, or the mail exchanger (MX) records to reveal the organization's mail servers. There are many other records that can be queried to uncover information about an organization. With a little searching on the Internet, you can even find scripts that will automate the discovery process.

Social Engineering

Social engineering is the art of using manipulative conversation to obtain information that would not normally be obtained. Social engineering tactics are considered passive because no direct connection is made to systems. A threat actor will just gather information about a target, by typically calling and engaging the person into a conversation.

You've probably used these tactics in real life, when you've called to see whether a toy is in stock at a store and the sales person says there is one left. You might say, "Can you please put it aside? I live an hour away, and I don't want to disappoint my kids if it gets sold." This manipulation works on the good nature of people, and it typically works.

A threat actor might call a help desk and explain they can't log in. When the help desk person asks then to elaborate, they might explain that they entered their password, then the computer prompts them to enter the Google Authenticator code. There are two possible outcomes; the first is the help desk person explaining how to use the Google Authenticator app. The second outcome is the help desk support person explaining the use of the app they should be using. The second option is always preferred since people share more when they believe they are teaching you something. In either case the threat actor will know what multifactor authentication (MFA) system is in use.

Testing

As we progress though this section and learn about the vulnerability management process, we've covered the initial findings of vulnerabilities. Vulnerabilities eventually get mitigated, and as we learned, some require the implementation of access control lists or some other workaround. Eventually, we forget why a rule was put in place or a configuration change was made, and the changes could get reverted. This is the reason we should test periodically for the same vulnerability, in addition to new vulnerabilities. The following are two common methods for testing, but there are many other types of testing outside of the objectives.

Port Scanning

As we learned earlier in the chapter, port scanning test open ports on hosts in your network by attempting a connection. Although the way it tests the connection might differ between UDP and TCP, if the port is open, the application is considered to be available. Periodic testing of open ports should be performed on all hosts in your network. This will ensure that network applications don't pop up on your network without your knowledge. It will also validate that ports have been firewalled, or the applications have been uninstalled. If new open ports pop up on the report, you can investigate and mitigate.

External port scans of your network are equally valuable to your security since threat actors are constantly testing your network defenses. Therefore, you should proactively mitigate unknown open ports. There are services for little or no money that will scan your external network for open ports and provide a report via email.

Automation

We should block off an hour or two in our schedules every week. Then we will have plenty of time to test our network's security and its defenses. I'm sure that tactic would work for about a week, before something else would interrupt our schedule. This is the reason we should employ testing automation.

There are two main types of testing automation that you can use to test security. The first type is internal testing, which is where your internal network hosts and devices are tested for vulnerabilities. Internal testing is typically performed by utilizing an agent installed on the internal network. The agents are often installed on each individual host so each host can be scanned. The agent will then report back to a central host or a cloud service. Then a report will be generated on a schedule and sent to an email address.

Another type of testing automation is the external type. This is the most common type of testing automation because it can be performed without the installation of agents. There are even free testing automation services, such as the Department of Homeland Security (DHS) Cyber Hygiene Services. The service will provide an automated vulnerability scan of your external network and produce a report on a weekly basis. There are countless other paid-for or semi-free services that can perform test automation on your external network.

Threat Intelligence

We have learned about the management of vulnerabilities to this point in the chapter. We have assumed that the information on threats and vulnerabilities are just available in a database for the asking. This is actually the case for most threats and vulnerabilities.

As a refresher, vulnerabilities are weaknesses in security, and threats are the potential for the vulnerability to be exploited. The third component of risk is the asset that you are trying to protect. So threats are constantly changing as new vulnerabilities and assets are targeted. This might seem overwhelming, and it might be without threat intelligence.

Threat intelligence is the way we can defend our assets from the threats that are looking to exploit vulnerabilities. Threat intelligence helps us understand how threat actors look to control our assets or steal our intellectual property. Understanding how threat actors can control or steal assets helps us better understand how we can protect them. The quote "If you know the enemy and know yourself, you need not fear the result of a hundred battles," from Sun Tzu's *The Art of War*, is very relevant today when it comes to cybersecurity. Threat intelligence at every level will help us understand the threat actors (enemy) and assets (yourself), so we can protect ourselves. If we have a clean knowledge, we survive hundreds, thousands, or even hundreds of thousand of attacks every day from the threat actors on the Internet.

You might see parallels with central intelligence and governments as we learn about threat intelligence. This is intentional; the tactics we use to prevent invasion of a territory are the same tactics we us to prevent threat actors invading our digital assets. Threat intelligence is typically broken down into the following quadrants, as shown in Figure 9.4.

Looking at threat intelligence, there are two main priorities and two different approaches. There are low-level priorities, which are either tactical or technical. There are also high-level priorities, which are either strategic or operational. These priorities are divided by their

FIGURE 9.4   Threat intelligence quadrants.

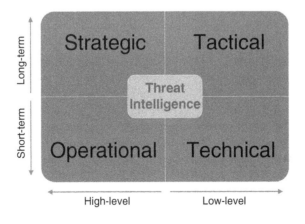

approaches, of either long-term or short-term. Long-term approaches are strategic or tactical, whereas short-term approaches are operational or technical. The following are explanations of each of the quadrants:

Technical.   The technical quadrant of threat intelligence is low in the weeds and constantly changing. The technical aspect of tools used by both threat actors and security professionals change by the minute and are very detailed in nature. Therefore, they are very low-level in respect to security; they are also considered very short-term in their approach as new tactics are being used continually. A malicious URL being actively blocked or a spam email being recalled are all examples of technical threat intelligence.

Tactical.   The tactical quadrant of threat intelligence is also low-level and in the weeds. The information caters to technically focused security analysts. However, it is using a long-term adopted approach to security defense tactics and operates based on the strategy of cybersecurity. An example of tactical threat intelligence is tactic, techniques, and procedures (TTPs) a threat actor might use. These threats are more complicated that a simple spam message coming into your organizations. They involve multiple tactics to compromise your network.

Operational.   The operational quadrant of threat intelligence is high-level in priority and short-term in approach. The information in this quadrant is aimed at managers that have a working knowledge of the various TTPs a threat actor might use. The intelligence in this quadrant are how cybercriminals infiltrate an organization, such as the TTPs used to gather information on the dark web by cybercriminals.

Strategic.   The strategic quadrant of threat intelligence is also high-level in priority, but it is a much more long-term approach. The information in this quadrant is aimed at less technical people and more toward decision makers and C-suite-level people in the organization. The intelligence in this quadrant explain how the organization can be impacted by general threats and overall risk. The information is typically based on case studies, trends, and real-life factors. Some real-life factors might include political climate, economics, and geopolitical events, just to name a few.

Threat intelligence use cases will vary depending on the quadrant you need to serve. Let's look at a number of ways we can employ threat intelligence to identify potential network vulnerabilities. We will start at a very high level with strategic and gradually learn about some of the technical threat intelligence tactics.

Risk Analysis.   Risk analysis is a tactic often used to survey the current threat landscape. Threat intelligence at a strategic level will be used to create threat models for each of the risks. For example, an emerging threat is artificial intelligence being used for nefarious purposes. One such purpose is creating a custom-tailored email to launch a business email compromise (BEC) attack on your organization. Another emerging risk is vishing attacks in which someone calls in via a VoIP call to social engineer a password from your help desk. Or smishing, in which a test is sent via SMS asking an employee to perform a task, such as buying iTunes gift cards. There are so many current threats it would take an entire book to list them. The theme is capture the most prevalent and emerging to your organization and model the risk.

Monitoring of Executives.   This might seem like a strategic tactic, but it tends to be more operational. The executives in your organization are what make up the moral integrity of the organization. Therefore, executives should be monitored with the use of third parties that can identify compromise. They should be monitored not just of information on the dark web, but also anything that could impact the safety, reputation, and security of the organization.

Collaborative Sharing.   The collaborative sharing of information with the sector your organization functions within is a tactic of operational threat intelligence. Typically, the information gathered from a compromise should be shared with an information sharing and analysis center (ISAC) to that it can be passed along to other organizations. The Department of Homeland Security (DHS) has many different working groups; also the Federal Bureau of Investigation has a private-sector organization called Infragard. However, there are many other ISACs and working groups sponsored by every federal government.

Fraud Prevention.   Fraud prevention is an operational tactic that is used for the monitoring of leaked credentials on the dark web for an organization's employees and customers. There are third-party services that will monitor the dark web and initial access brokers for email domains; the services are relatively inexpensive and alerts you when credentials are found. Another popular tactic to prevent fraud is running your organization's name through a domain spinner. The domain spinner will show you alternate ways in which your domain name can be typo-ed. You can then purchase or research alternate domain names further.

Endpoint Detection and Response (EDR).   Endpoint detection and response (EDR) is one of the most clear-cut examples of threat intelligence. It tends to be more technical in nature, as it looks for malicious signatures. However, EDR can spring into tactical mode when it sees a chain of events, also known as TTPs, that are malicious in nature. Extended detection and response (XDR) takes detection to another level bringing in monitoring from the cloud and networked devices.

Malware and Forensic Analysis.   Malware and forensic analysis reports are very technical in nature and help educate us on how malware operates. This type of threat intelligence is very low level and constantly changing. Much of what comes from these reports attributes to the indicators of compromise (IoCs) that our EDR, XDR, and antimalware applications use on daily.

These are just a few of the most common examples of threat intelligence. The threat intelligence industry is constantly growing, and new products and tactics are delivered to market every day. Artificial intelligence (AI) and machine learning are rapidly adding to this market. Newer tools can utilize AI and machine learning to remove bogus entries from log files and zone in on the relevant notifications in a log file.

For an organization to properly use threat intelligence, it must employ every quadrant. This means that upper management must align with cybersecurity goals and adopt strategies to protect the organization from threat actors. Some organizations facilitate the other three quadrants in-house or they might hire contractors, such as a security operation center (SOC), to watch over the technical and tactical issues day-to-day. The organization might also contract out a virtual chief information and security officer (CISO). The virtual CISO is responsible for setting policy and assuming the operational tactics of threat intelligence. Contracting these functions out is something smaller organizations might tend to do. For larger organizations, the CISO role and security personnel will be hired in-house.

Vulnerability Databases

As we learned earlier in this chapter, each vulnerability is given a Common Vulnerabilities and Exposures (CVE) number. Once a CVE number is associated with a vulnerability, it will exist for that specific vulnerability in all the databases. The vulnerability is then described by its number in the security community and in assessment reports.

The CVE vulnerability database is probably the most important threat intelligence tool you can employ to identify security weaknesses. The CVE vulnerability database allows for the centralization of information related to vulnerabilities. The most common public databases to access CVE information are the National Vulnerability Database (NVD) hosted by the National Institute of Standards and Technology (NIST) https://nvd.nist.gov/, MITRE https://cve.mitre.org/, and CVE Details https://cvedetails.com. This list is just the most popular; there are countless other CVE databases out there, and you can even download the CVE database and host your own from http://cve.org!

When a vulnerability database, such as the CVE database, is married with a vulnerability scanner you can get a detailed report of vulnerable hosts. The details will typically include the CVE the host is vulnerable for, and the list is commonly sorted by the CVE severity rating. The CVE severity rating, also known as the Common Vulnerability Scoring System (CVSS), is based on a scale of 0 to 10; 0 is low or not affected, and 10 is high or critical. The following table, Table 9.1, shows the CVSS 2.0 severity rating range, and Table 9.2 shows the most current CVSS 3.x severity rating range.

You may see the CVSS version of 2.0, 3.0, or 3.1 in the CVE entry depending which site you obtain the entry from. The CVSS difference is the scoring system used to calculate the CVSS severity rating that correlates to the severity. There is also a CVSS version of 4.0, which is not popular as of the writing of this book. On each CVE entry you will find the vector, which looks like a string of letters and symbols, also containing the CVSS version

TABLE 9.1   CVSS 2.0 Severity Rating Scale.

Severity	Severity Score Range
Low	0.0–3.9
Medium	4.0–6.9
High	7.0–10.0

https://nvd.nist.gov/vuln-metrics/cvss

TABLE 9.2   CVSS 3.x Severity Rating Scale.

Severity	Severity Score Range
None	0.0
Low	0.1–3.9
Medium	4.0–6.9
High	7.0–8.9
Critical	9.0–10.0

https://nvd.nist.gov/vuln-metrics/cvss

FIGURE 9.5   CVSS scoring.

CVSS 3.x Severity and Metrics:

CNA: Microsoft Corporation   Base Score: 8.8 HIGH   Vector: CVSS:3.1/AV:N/AC:L/PR:L/UI:N/S:U/C:H/I:H/A:H

number itself. Each component of the string means explains the attack vector used to calculate the severity score, as shown in Figure 9.5.

Limitations

The CVE database by itself is incomplete as a vulnerability database because it lacks details of the vulnerability. The CVE entry typically only contains a brief description of the vulnerability. If you want a more complete understanding of how to mitigate the vulnerability, the vendor will typically have a more detailed article. The vendor article will typically detail a patch or security update to mitigate the vulnerability. The article might also contain a workaround if the patch or security update can't be installed due to compatibility issues.

One other significant limitation of the CVE vulnerability database is it only reflects the unpatched software as a vulnerability. The CVE vulnerability database does not reflect other security concerns that could be considered a vulnerability. This is one of the benefits of coupling a vulnerability scanner with the CVE database. The CVE provides information for the unpatched software, along with other security concerns that would not be listed in the CVE vulnerability database. One such example might be a weak password or password that has not been changed in a while. This particular example would not have an associated CVE entry, but it's a best practice to have secure and current passwords.

CVE vulnerability databases are not the only vulnerability databases available. There are many other types of vulnerability databases available on the Internet. However, the CVE is the most commonly integrated because the format is universal between all vendors. Other vulnerability databases on the Internet have much more detail, such as the Exploit Database (`https://www.exploit-db.com`) that has references to proof of concept code. Many of the databases available will reference CVE entries in some fashion.

Assessment Tools

There are countless vulnerability assessment tools that are free open-source software (FOSS), as well as commercial products. Some of the tools might be free but require a subscription for the latest vulnerabilities. The following is a list of the most common tools used to assess the security posture of a network. This list is in no way complete and grows every day.

Cisco Secure Endpoint.   Cisco Secure Endpoint, formerly known as Cisco AMP for Endpoints, is an Endpoint Detection and Response (EDR) security solution. Secure Endpoint is used to protect endpoints, such as laptops, desktops, and mobile devices, from advanced cyber threats. Secure Endpoint leverages Cisco Talos threat intelligence to provide real-time threat analysis and continuous monitoring, ensuring rapid detection of suspicious activities. Secure Endpoint uses behavioral analytics, machine learning, and file reputation to identify and block threats proactively. The platform also includes built-in tools for incident response and remediation, allowing security teams to efficiently investigate and address threats.

Cisco XDR.   Cisco XDR (Extended Detection and Response) is a security solution aimed at delivering integrated threat detection, investigation, and response across diverse domains such as endpoints, networks, email, and cloud environments. The Cisco XDR security solution integrates data from various security layers. Because Cisco XDR can extend across all the different domains, it eliminates silos and enhances visibility into an organization's security posture. It utilizes automated analytics, machine learning, and threat intelligence to analyze data, rank alerts by priority, and deliver actionable insights to security teams.

Cisco Talos.   Cisco Talos is a threat intelligence organization and research team that contributes to Cisco security product and services. Cisco Talos's mission is to identify, analyze, and mitigate emerging cyber threats globally. They leverage advanced analytics, machine learning, and a team of expert researchers. Their data comes from extensive telemetry data from Cisco's global network. Talos also plays a vital role in the cybersecurity community by publishing in-depth research, disclosing vulnerabilities, and offering tools designed to fortify defenses against evolving cyber threats.

Nessus.   The Nessus vulnerability scanner is considered the original security tool for assessing the security posture of a network or system. Nessus uses a scanning engine that checks a system against the CVE database as well as scanning a list of common vulnerabilities. Nessus is most effective when used with an agent that is installed on each host. Nessus can also be used without installing the agent, but the results are limited because of the lack of details such as version numbers.

Microsoft Defender for Endpoint.   The Microsoft Defender for Endpoint is typically bundled with A3/E3 and A5/E5 subscriptions or separately as an add-on to your Microsoft 365 plan. The Microsoft Defender for Endpoint has two components: The first component is the software built into each Windows operating system that provides the protection. The second component is the Microsoft Defender Vulnerability Management dashboard. The dashboard provides the analytics reported back from the Windows operating system. This produces an up-to-the-minute vulnerability report for each client and aggregates the overall score for your organization's security.

OWASP Tools.   The Open Worldwide Application Security Project (OWASP) is a community of security professionals that provide articles on web-based security. They are best known for their testing guides related to web-based applications, as well as their best practices penetration testing framework. The OWASP Tool Project contains many different tools that can scan an application from code-related vulnerabilities, to functionality. They have a very comprehensive list of tools that are freely available to perform web application vulnerability assessments. The complete list OWASP tools are available via `https://owasp.org/www-community/Free_for_Open_Source_Application_Security_Tools`.

Burp Suite.   The Burp Suite is another very popular penetration testing software for web applications. There are two versions, a free community edition and a paid version. The Burp suite contains a number of tools, too many to list. However, some of the more notable tools are the Burp Proxy, which allows a man-in-the-middle, also known as an on-path attack; the Repeater app, which allows for fuzzing of data; and the Inspector app, which allows for analysis and editing of HTTP and WebSockets data. The paid-for, professional version includes a vulnerability scanner and Collaborator app, which allows for identifying out-of-band vulnerabilities. A full list of apps can be found on PortSwigger, the vendor of Burp Suite, via `https://portswigger.net`.

Nmap.   The nmap tool allows us to scan open and closed ports on remote systems for audit purposes. It can be used to validate that the firewall is open to accept requests for an application.

The nmap tool can scan all ports of a specific host or a range of hosts in the network. This allows for the discovery of a host that might not be known or protected with firewall rules. The nmap tool will also try to negotiate with Transport Layer Security (TLS) in an attempt to discover the encryption key strength being used. In addition to these features, it will try to predict the operating system the remote system is using.

Protocol Analyzer.   Protocol analyzers, also called sniffers or network monitors, are used to capture packets in their raw format as they cross the network. Windows desktop operating systems before Windows Vista came with a built-in protocol analyzer called Network Monitor, but that is no longer the case, although you can download one for free that will work with the newer operating systems.

The Network Monitor tool that comes with these operating systems will capture only packets that are sourced from or destined to the computer on which the tool is running. Commercial sniffers such as Wireshark and Omnipeek can capture any packets because they set the NIC to operate in promiscuous mode, which means the NIC processes all packets that it sees.

Protocol analyzers can be used to determine the type of traffic that you have in your network, and depending on the product and the bells and whistles contained therein, you may be able to sort the results based on port numbers, protocols, and so on. Another use of a sniffer is to examine the traffic that should be occurring on the network when something is not working to aid in troubleshooting. These devices can capture and display all packets involved in the connection setup, including, for example, request and response headers to a web server.

Kali Linux.   The Kali Linux distribution is used by just about all penetration testers and security professionals. The Linux distribution can be booted from a USB drive or installed as a virtual machine. Just about every tool mentioned in this section is available on the Linux distribution. In addition, there are several other tools preinstalled, such as the Impacket application suite of tools. The Impacket tools allows you to exploit a number of Microsoft protocols such as SMB, NTLM, LDAP, and MSSQL, just to name a few. The Linux distribution also contains a number of password cracking programs such as John The Ripper, Hashcat, Hydra, and Ophcrack, just to name a few. A complete list of applications can be found on `https://www.kali.org/tools`, but keep in mind that you can download a number of other application not listed on that page.

Recommendations

Not every security concern is in the form of a vulnerability and can be cataloged by the CVE vulnerability database. This is one of the weaknesses of using a vulnerability database. There are many security recommendations that can be overlooked if you only focus on CVE vulnerabilities. Security recommendations are typically a product of vulnerability scanners, such as Nessus or Microsoft Defender for Endpoint, just to name a few.

Security recommendations are best practices that help you reduce the surface area of attack for the operating system. An example of a simple security recommendation might be to turn on password complexity for end users. A vulnerability scanner can obtain this information by checking the default security policies for the local operating system or domain. Another security recommendation might be to turn on SMB signing and turning off weak protocols such as SMBv1. Turning on SMB signing prevents SMB replay attacks and turning off weak protocols such as SMBv1 prevents the hash from being easily cracked.

Security recommendations will typically refer to a security policy that can be used to secure the operating system. This is particularly common in the Windows environment, but it is not limited to Windows. The UNIX and Linux operating systems have security policies that can be turned on to secure it from security concerns. As an example, the Windows operating system contains several policies that can be adjusted for SMB signing. The policies can be applied either locally to a specific computer or more commonly deployed to a group of computers through a Group Policy Object (GPO). The local Group Policy for Windows security options is shown in Figure 9.6.

Not all Windows security policies have to be controlled through Group Policy; some security policies might require a registry edit for them to be turned on. This is especially true for newer security policies that have not been fully vetted by the Windows quality assurance team. Group Policy is typically updated in feature releases and major/minor releases of the Windows operating system. In the interim, Windows security updates will deliver security policies that can be controlled though the registry. The most relevant or common security policies are found in Group Policy.

Security policies can be found in just about any operating system. Red Hat–based Linux distributions contain a feature called SELinux mode that assists in hardening the operating system. In addition, there are several policies that can be adjusted to set system-wide cryptographic policies. This is just the tip of the iceberg when it comes to security policies. Red Hat does not have an exclusive on security policies; Debian-based Linux distributions contain a feature equivalent to SELinux called AppArmor. Both SELinux and AppArmor perform

FIGURE 9.6   Windows Group Policy.

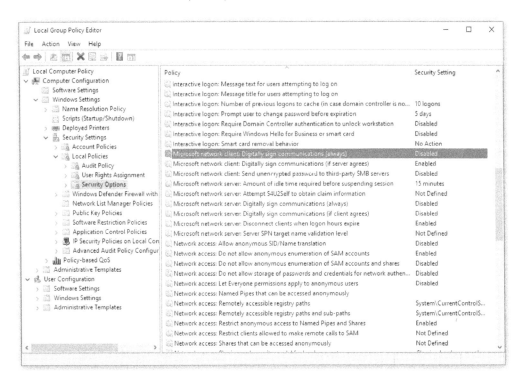

similar functions in applying security policies to the operating system to harden it from security concerns. There are also several other open-source applications such as Samba that have their own security policies, which can be found on both Linux distributions, including UNIX.

Reports

The last category of threat intelligence that we learn about is the countless number of reports on security readily available and how they can help us protect systems. Reports are probably the most important piece of threat intelligence that help us protect our systems; they are also the most underrated. Security reports educate us on the current threats, emerging threats, as well as help us understand how they are carried out and how we can protect ourselves.

We've already learned about the CVE vulnerability database. A function of the CVE database is the live data feed that many make available. The data feed can come in many different formats, such as Really Simple Syndicate (RSS), JSON, and even an API, just to name a few formats. The feed will produce an up-to-the-minute report of released CVEs. This data feed is typically digested into vulnerability scanners by the vendor of the scanner. However, if you choose to read each CVE, many CVE databases will share their data feed.

Security Reports

Reading every CVE article is a daunting task, unless you are looking from something specific. Therefore, a better approach is to subscribe to cybersecurity reports from the specific vendor of software you employ in your network. Many vendors will send security reports based on their product or services when a security concern is discovered. The security report will typically contain the associated CVE, a synopsis of the security concern, and an explanation on how to remediate the security concern.

You can sign up for security reports from the Microsoft Security Response Center (MSRC). The MSRC sends out a daily report that details the current vulnerabilities in Microsoft products, along with the correlating CVE. In addition to daily security reports on vulnerabilities, you can access release notes for patches. The MSRC can be access through the URL of `https://msrc.microsoft.com/update-guide/`. Red Hat Linux also offers a security report through the Red Hat Customer Portal, accessed via `https://access.redhat.com/`. Just like the Microsoft security reports, you can receive daily reports that detail vulnerabilities in the Red Hat Linux product, along with their corresponding CVE. Just about every vendor has a similar reports for applications and services that you can sign up for.

Cybersecurity News

At some point, you will conclude that you need to stay ahead of security trends that affect our industry; this is where cybersecurity news comes in handy. Subscribing to a news feed that details the latest security or insecurity news can help you stay ahead of threat actors. I can't count how many times a news article in my RSS feed sparked my interest, only to find out later that the security concern in the article turned into the next big thing that affected our industry. I came away feeling lucky that I learned about it, and I was able to make decisions based on my newfound knowledge. Therefore, we consider cybersecurity news a form of threat intelligence.

We also need to value that we have a limited amount of time in each day to read the headlines and stay ahead of the security curve. So choosing the news source is paramount in respect to your time vs. value. Typically, tech-focused news sources are unbiased and have current technical articles, such as Wired, SANS, or Krebs on Security, just to name a few. There are countless security news sites out on the Internet. As for mass media cybersecurity news sources, they are fine for the masses, but they are also written for the masses. So mass media will often lack the detail our industry requires.

Another overlooked source for cybersecurity news is social media aggregation sites such as Reddit, Slashdot, and Hacker News (Y Combinator), just to name a few. These sites allow you to see emerging articles and problems that make it to the top of the feed based on the collective intelligence of the users to promote and comment on articles. The comments on many of these thread posts serve as an ad hoc threat intelligence and helps you understand different aspects of a particular threat. However, if it is on the top of the RSS feed then it is probably a current security concern and you can dive deeper to stay ahead of it.

Subscription-based

There is a wealth of subscription-based threat intelligence feeds that you can purchase and some that are totally free of charge. Every endpoint detection and response (EDR) platform is typically sold as a subscription model. They typically include a report of malicious URLs, IP addresses, and malware signatures. The URLs, IP addresses, and malware signatures are typically produced from automated threat intelligence from deployed sensors on the Internet. These subscription-based services are extremely useful in providing an up-to-the-minute list of threats for your endpoints.

Subscription-based reports in the form of a list for your EDR are not the only subscription-based reports you can use. There are countless other subscription-based reports that can provide you an analysis of malware or threats. For example, the Department of Homeland Security (DHS) CyberSecurity and Infrastructure Security Agency (CISA) provides a free list of known threats, to include the latest indicators of compromise (IoC).

 More information on the DHS CISA subscription can be found via the URL `https://www.cisa.gov/about/contact-us/ subscribe-updates-cisa`.

There are many other subscription-based reports you can find for free. Some of them are custom for your particular industry, and some are offered by the vendors of EDR products to establish they are the best in class. In addition to the free subscription-based reports, there are some reports that you can purchase from industry leaders that provide a custom-tailored report. Vendors such as NSFocus, Keysight, and IBM, just to name a few, can produce custom reports to detail threats to your organization.

Documentation

Creating documentation of the network, system, or security you work on is the last step to many projects. However, it is the most overlooked, or it is considered secondary to fixing new problems, upgrading to the next system, or strengthening security. The documentation produced in the end has positive effects on procedure, production, and problem solving. It is used so that you don't need to redo the step of discovery the next time you have a problem. Documentation also allows you to have others work on a problem with the same distinctive view you had at the time of documentation.

Some of the documentation you create will help to create policies and procedures that others will need to follow. Throughout this book, we have discussed the hard controls of these policies. For example, when you implement a password policy, you can dictate that a password be complex and of a certain length. A written policy is a soft control that might detail how to create a complex password.

Updating Documentation

The inevitable fact and reality is that your network, security, and policies evolve with the threat every changing landscape and maturity of the organization. Therefore, constant updating of documentation is critical for the health of the organization. As new threats come into focus, new modification to the network could be required, and this requires documentation. If you don't keep up with the documentation, you could find that someone has reverted a change required for security. And if you discover one or more setting required for security have been changed, the documentation becomes the source of truth for reverting the settings back.

A best practice to keeping documentation up to date is to review the documentation during a periodic audit of your security standards. This is typically performed during the periodic audit or recertification of SOC2, ISO 27001, NIST, or CIS controls, just to name a few. During the audit or recertification process you will typically check your security control to attest you are still compliant with security outlined. This is when you should reread your documentation and make any necessary updates to reflect changes.

Another outcome from updating your documentation is the refinement of the documents themselves. When the documentation is first written, it is typically brief mainly because it's the last piece to a project. There are always new projects waiting to be queued up, waiting for you to finish the projects before them. Therefore, when you revisit the document during an audit or periodic review, you might question your wording, instructions, or just want to introduce relevant additions. Updating the documentation will make a periodic audit that much easier to complete because you build on the prior work. Good documentation can also make for a speedy audit!

Security Incident Documentation

An incident is any event that is unusual or outside of the normal processes. You may encounter many different types of incidents as a technician: network security incidents, network outage incidents, and even customer service incidents. Regardless of which type of incident transpires, an incident document should be completed so that there is a record of the event. A record of the incident allows for further review after the incident has subsided so that it is not repeated.

The incident document should be completed as soon as possible so that key details are not forgotten. This document is often used as an executive brief for key *stakeholders* in the company, such as C-level people—for example, the *chief information officer (CIO)*. The incident document can also be public-facing and used to inform customers of the incident. When used in this fashion, the incident document allows the organization to communicate with transparency about a major incident they may or may have not experienced. Here are common elements of a security incident document:

Date and Time.   The date and time of the incident is probably the most important element because several incidents could happen on the same day. The date and time allows you to distinguish between various incidents. The date and time should use the *Universal Time Code (UTC)* so that someone anywhere in the world does not need to calculate the time offset.

Summary.   The *incident summary* is another important piece of information that should be documented. It will often be the first thing that is looked at because it describes the summary of what happened during the incident.

Root Cause.   The *root cause* is the reason the incident occurred. Every incident needs to have a root cause defined; otherwise, the incident could happen over and over again. The network team's first responsibility is to identify the root cause.

Actions Taken.   The actions taken are the actions that transpired during the incident to rectify the situation. Most of the time, they are temporary actions so that business can resume.

Remediation.   The *remediation* is the ultimate fix that will repair the root cause of the incident. This could be as simple as installing a patch, or it could be as complex as redesigning a network component.

Services Impacted.   The services impacted section details all the network systems and business units that were affected during the incident. This section defines the severity of the incident.

Recommendations.   The recommendations section details the next steps to take to remediate the issue. It also explains how to avoid similar incidents in the future.

Although these are the most common elements of an incident document, the document is not limited to these elements. Each organization will have different needs for the process of reviewing network incidents. A template should be created so that there is consistency in the reporting of incidents.

Documenting the Incident

Once an incident is detected using the methods mentioned in the preceding section (passive, active, or proactive), or it's detected through dumb luck, it's time to spring into action and document the incident. The person responding to the incident, called the *first responder*, should be versed in how to collect and document evidence in the *order of volatility*. If the evidence is not collected, for example, from a computer's RAM, and the computer reboots, the evidence will be gone. The *order of volatility* is as follows:

Memory Contents.   Evidence of the incident located in the RAM of the computer or system. This evidence can be a file that has not been saved to the filesystem. It can also be a process running in RAM that requires a memory dump for further analysis.

Swap Files/Virtual Memory.   Evidence that has been saved out to a swap file/virtual memory, because the process has been backgrounded or is no longer in foreground RAM. The swap file/paging file should be copied to removable media.

Network Processes.   Evidence that is part of a network process, such as a browser redirection or spam or active network communications. This is where most of the incidents occur on a network. This information should be saved to removable media.

System Processes.   Evidence that is part of a system, such as an exploit that has been rooted into the operating system. This is also a common place for incidents to occur. The information should be separated out of the system and saved to removable media.

Filesystem Information.   This evidence is in the form of files on a hard drive. An example of filesystem information is illegal content that has been saved to the filesystem. This information must be preserved in its original form but also copied for evidence purposes.

Raw Disk Blocks.   This evidence is in the form of a block-level copy of the data. Once an incident is discovered and all the other volatile evidence has been collected, the last step is to create an image of the affected system. This can be done with a tool called a *write-blocker* (which makes the media read-only) and specialized software that copies data at the block level.

The preceding evidence can be collected with the sophisticated tools that only a highly trained first responder might have on hand. However, not all the tools need to be complex tools. A simple camera can preserve information. For example, if you walk up to a system that displays a ransomware screen, your first reaction should be to take a photo of the screen. If you press a key, the ransomware could crash and disappear. Photo evidence of data and processes that are loaded in RAM is a good alternative to not having any evidence, but having a digital copy of the evidence is preferred.

The act of photographing the scene should not be limited to just the computer screen; anything relevant to the incident should be photographed as evidence. Time and date stamps should be overlaid onto the image. This is normally a function of any camera. However, if you can't digitally record the time stamps, a simple alternative is to include a watch in the frame of the photo.

You should take notes with a pad and pen, recording the initial scene, including time and date, and create a chronology of the discovery and collection of the evidence. Remember, any of this could potentially be used in a court of law. The underlying premise is to record as much evidence as possible before the crime scene is tainted by others.

Following the Right Chain of Custody

The removed materials should be secured and turned over to the proper authorities. Depending on the situation, materials may be held in a safe, locked location at the office, or they may need to be turned over to local authorities. Have a documented procedure in place to follow, given a situation.

The materials that are deemed as evidence should be well documented as to why they are considered evidence. The *chain of custody* documentation should define the following:

- Who obtained the evidence
- Who secured the evidence
- Who controlled the evidence during the entire process

If the evidence is moved, the chain of custody documentation should reflect the following:

- The reasons it was moved
- Who moved it
- How it was secured
- Who controlled it

The chain of custody must be maintained at all times. If a chain of custody of the evidence is not maintained, the evidence may not be admissible in a court of law.

Securing and Sharing of Documentation

The documentation for a security incident will often identify a weakness in network security. This is potentially dangerous because a threat actor will have a road map into your network, if the vulnerability is not patched right away. Therefore, it is important to properly secure the documentation from the security incident. Documentation should be secured like any other sensitive information, both in transit and at rest with encryption.

When documentation about an incident is created, sharing the documentation with others should be a normal expectation. To keep the documentation secure, proper role-based access controls (RBAC) should be employed. The roles might be something like first-responders, investigators, reviewers, C-level staff, just to name a few. Of course, each role will have its own varying permissions to the documentation, and a rights management system (RMS) such as Azure Rights Managements can be used to enforce these permissions. The RMS will also allow secure sharing of the documentation so that it is not forwarded and printed. Microsoft Azure Rights Management is not your only option to share and secure documentation. Other proprietary document management solutions (DMS) exist, such as Adobe and NetDocuments, just to name a few.

In some cases, the documentation created will be given to your legal counsel for prosecution of the threat actors or other legal reasons. In these cases, you should make sure the that the legal counsel has a means to secure the documentation at rest and in transit. You should also consider how they will securely share the documentation that you provide them. In some cases, you may elect to create an executive briefing and remove the specific technical details and evidence. At some point you will need to furnish this information if the threat actors are prosecuted and there is a court date. However, in many cases the executive brief is enough to get the process started.

Reporting the Incident

Once you've collected the initial set of evidence and in the order of volatility, it's time to report the incident. The incident should be reported to management, and a decision should be made to involve law enforcement. Involving law enforcement is of course dependent on the severity of the incident. A piece of malware that has infected a single machine is a bit different than malware that has infected an entire network. Your management might elect not to involve law enforcement at all. However, some incidents must be reported depending on regulations that the organization must adhere to.

 You will learn about the various regulations that might be applicable to an organization in Chapter 11, "Incident Handling."

Regardless of the direction management takes, the evidence collected, as well as notes taken during the collection, will help an escalation team or law enforcement to proceed in building a case. The goal of the first responder is to collect evidence that answers the following questions:

- What happened?
- When did it happen?
- How did it happen?
- Who made it happen?
- Why did it happen?

An escalation team or law enforcement's job is to fill in the blanks by using the evidence. If the evidence is complete and concise, it will be used to build a case against the threat agent. The ultimate goal is to stop a future incident from happening.

Recovering from the Incident

Your most important task is to recover from the incident. If your critical ordering system was affected during the incident, it's your job to get it back online. If the incident involved one computer that is used by a task worker, then it's your job to get it back up and running. You might notice a common theme here: it's your job to get things back to normal after the incident. Once you can get the flow of information flowing again, you can move on to remediating the incident.

During the recovery from the incident, you may have to make changes to the network or systems that support the clients. Any changes during the recovery process should be documented thoroughly. Documenting these changes is important if you are submitting claims to insurance, assessing damages, or looking for future reparations.

Documenting the Incident

Before, during, and after the incident, the documentation process should begin. You should collect as much information as possible as a formal incident report will eventually be formulated defining the following key elements.

- Date and time
- Summary
- Root cause
- Actions taken
- Remediation
- Services impacted
- Recommendations

It really doesn't matter how you collect information for documentation purposes. It can be pad and pen or something more elaborate. The only stipulation is that the documentation should not be on a system that can be affected by the incident. An offline laptop is fine, as long as the laptop is never introduced to the affected network with the ongoing incident. This could jeopardize all of the documentation efforts and hinder the outcome.

Reviewing the Incident

The final step in an response to an incident is to review all the documentation and findings of the incident—a process often called a hot-wash meeting. During a hot-wash meeting, the incident response team should talk about what has been done properly during the incident and what procedures should be changed for future incidents. These meetings should be constructive and support standards of excellence for the incident response team.

Another key goal of the review process is to identify threats similar to the characteristics of the incident. If an employee entered credentials into a phishing page, what measures are in place to prevent this from happening to others in the organization? You may have rules in place for this particular phishing email, but are your employees trained for future incidents similar to this? If not, end-user training may be required.

Documentation Best Practices for Incident Response

Now that you have a good understanding of how documentation can be used in response to an incident, let's look at some of the best practices. The following best practices should be applied to all elements of the incident response process:

Follow your policies exactly as they are written.   Yes, we've already said this several times. It's crucial that you do this. Not following the policies and procedures can derail your case against the offender and possibly set you up for problems as well.

If you are the first responder, get a verifier.   Your first priority as the first responder is to identify the improper activity or content. Then you should always get someone else to verify the material or action so that it doesn't turn into a situation of your word against someone else's. Report the situation immediately through the proper channels.

Preserve the data or device.   The data or device should immediately be removed from the possession of the offending party and preserved. This will ensure that the data doesn't mysteriously disappear before the proper parties are notified.

Use documentation.   Document everything that could be relevant to the situation. Many companies have standard documentation that is used in incident response in order to be sure that the responder captures important information and does not forget to ask critical questions or look for vital clues.

Summary

Vulnerability management is broken down into three distinctive components of identification, prevention, and documentation. In this chapter we covered the basics of vulnerabilities and the phases of vulnerability management. We also learned how to identify vulnerabilities existing in our network through active/passive reconnaissance.

We learned in this chapter how to prevent exploitation of vulnerabilities with threat intelligence. We also learned how vulnerability databases are structured, and their limitations. We then focused on the various assessment tools used in industry today to identify vulnerabilities in your network. We finished learning about threat intelligence and how we can prevent exploits with the various security reports, cybersecurity news, and subscription services.

In the last section of this chapter, we learned about the various documentation processes we should use before, during, and after a breach of security. We learned the importance of updating our internal documentation and how it can help us during our periodic audit. We also learned the proper handling, sharing, and securing of documentation.

Exam Essentials

Know the phases of vulnerability management lifecycle.   Vulnerability management lifecycle is typically comprised of six different phases: discovery, prioritization, assessment, reporting, remediation, and verification and monitoring.

Know the various mitigation tactics for vulnerabilities.   Vulnerabilities can be mitigated with configuration management, access controls, network security, encryption, and training

Understand the difference between active and passive reconnaissance.   Active reconnaissance requires interacting with the network in which the reconnaissance is intrusive and potentially disruptive. Passive reconnaissance collects information without being intrusive or information is gathered with other means, such as profiling a target.

Know the various reconnaissance techniques.   The most common reconnaissance techniques used are: port scanning, vulnerability scanning, packet sniffing/network traffic analysis, brute force attacks, open source intelligence (OSINT), DNS enumeration, social engineering.

Understand how vulnerability databases are structured.   Vulnerability databases such as the CVE vulnerability database contains a CVE identifier, short description, a score, and at least one external reference. In addition, it will also reflect the scoring rubric, as well as the attack vectors that comprise the score.

Know the various security reports used with threat intelligence.   The various reports you will use for threat intelligence include security reports, cybersecurity news, and subscription-based reports.

Understand why documentation is important and why it is important to update documentation.   Documentation is a road map to how to complete certain tasks, why you are compliant, and you have secured your network. Updating documentation is required as changes are made, so that you do not inadvertently create a vulnerability.

Review Questions

The following questions are designed to test your understanding of this chapter's material. For more information on how to get additional questions, please see www.lammle.com/ccst.

You can find the answers to these questions in Appendix.

1. What system is used for the classification of vulnerabilities?

    A. OSINT

    B. CVE

    C. DNS

    D. NMAP

2. Which step of the vulnerability lifecycle is responsible for detecting if a vulnerability has resurfaced?

    A. Discovery

    B. Prioritization

    C. Reporting

    D. Verification and Monitoring

3. You recently found out that there is a critical vulnerability in a line-of-business application that is no longer supported. What is an acceptable remediation?

    A. Uninstalling the application

    B. Training the end-users

    C. Requiring strong encryption

    D. Adding a firewall

4. Which is an example of active reconnaissance?

    A. Traffic analysis

    B. Port scanning

    C. OSINT

    D. DNS enumeration

5. You found a vulnerability referenced to a CVE of CVE-2018-8033. What can't be derived from looking up the CVE in the CVE vulnerability database?

    A. The scoring of the vulnerability

    B. Affected software versions

    C. How to remediate the vulnerability

    D. A description of the vulnerability

6. Which testing technique can help you verify that proper firewalling of services has been performed?

    A. Port scanning

    B. Vulnerability scanning

    C. OSINT

    D. Brute force attack

7. How is the CVE score derived for a particular CVE?

    A. It is assigned based on the impact of a vulnerability

    B. It is assigned by the CVE vulnerability database

    C. It is based on the probability or likelihood it can be exploited

    D. It is calculated from the attack vector associated with the CVE

8. Which assessment tool be used to find vulnerabilities in applications and services?

    A. Nessus

    B. A Protocol Analyzer

    C. Burp Suite

    D. Nmap

9. Which typically contains URL, IP addresses and malware signatures to keep your EDR up to date?

    A. Cybersecurity news

    B. Security reports

    C. Subscription-based reports

    D. RSS feeds

10. Which documentation type allows you to track the entire evidence process?

    A. Chain of custody

    B. Incident document

    C. Order of volatility

    D. Root cause document

Chapter

10

Disaster Recovery

THE FOLLOWING CCST EXAM TOPIC IS COVERED IN THIS CHAPTER:

✔ **4.0 Vulnerability Assessment and Risk Management**

  ▪ 4.4. Explain the importance of disaster recovery and business continuity planning

    Natural and human-caused disasters, features of disaster recovery plans (DRP) and business continuity plans (BCP), backup, disaster recovery controls (detective, preventive, and corrective)

Disaster can happen at any time and for a myriad of reasons. Threat actors can be the cause, human error, or just plain old dumb luck. In any case your organization should have a solid disaster recovery process to bounce back. This chapter will teach you how to construct a strategy for disaster recover.

To find your included bonus material, as well as Todd Lammle videos, practice questions, and hands-on labs, please see www.lammle.com/ccst.

Disaster Prevention and Recovery

As a cyber security professional, you'll be responsible identifying risk and preventing disasters that could impact the organization. You're also responsible for recovering from uncontrolled disasters. Luckily, you can prevent disasters by taking the proper precautions, as we will discuss in the following sections.

When you take steps to prevent disaster, you'll find that you're prepared when disaster strikes and can restore business continuity that much quicker. This section discusses the following types of disasters:

- Data loss
- Power-related issue
- Facility-related issue
- Infrastructure-related issue
- HVAC
- Fire suppression
- Human error
- Threat actors

All of these types of disasters have the potential for data loss and work stoppage.

Data Loss

When we think of data backups, we usually relate them to disasters. However, data backups are not just used to restore from disaster; we often use data backups when a user inadvertently deletes files they shouldn't have deleted. Data backups are also used when users overwrite files or just plain forget where they put them in the first place. Regardless of how the data was lost, the underlying reason we create data backups is to recover from data loss.

Because you can't choose the disaster or situation that causes the loss of data, you should adopt a layered strategy, starting with the user and expanding outward to the infrastructure. The following sections cover several different types of strategies that can protect you from data loss.

File Level Backups

Most of the time, your users will need to restore a single file or perhaps a few files, but definitely not the entire server or server farm. Therefore, you should make sure that one of the layers of protection allows for the restoration of individual files. You can implement this type of strategy several different ways. Depending on your resources, you should use them all.

Volume Shadow Copy

Volume Shadow Copy, also known as the Volume Snapshot Service (VSS), has been an integral part of the Windows Server operating system since the release of Windows 2000. Volume Shadow Copy can be enabled on a volume-by-volume basis. Once it's turned on, all the shares on the volume are protected. You can access Volume Shadow Copy by right-clicking a volume and selecting Properties. You can then configure it by using the Shadow Copies tab, as shown in Figure 10.1.

Volume Shadow Copy has one amazing advantage: it empowers the user to restore their own files. All the user needs to do is right-click the file or empty space in the shared folder, select Properties, and then in the Properties window, select the Previous Versions tab. This will open a list of snapshots, as shown in Figure 10.2. The user can then double-click the snapshots to open them as if they were currently on the filesystem. This allows the user to evaluate what they are looking for. Once they find what they are looking for, they can either click the Restore button or drag the files over to the current folder.

One limitation to Volume Shadow Copies is the number of snapshots that can be active. Only 64 snapshots can be active at one time. The oldest snapshot is deleted when a new snapshot is created to maintain a running total of 64 snapshots. By default, Volume Shadow Copy is not enabled. When it is enabled, the default schedule creates a snapshot twice a day, at 7 a.m. and 12 p.m. It's advisable to set a schedule that creates a snapshot every hour during normal business hours. This will give the user the last 64 hours of work, which could be well over a week and a half, if you were open nine to five.

FIGURE 10.1   The Shadow Copies tab.

FIGURE 10.2   The Previous Versions tab.

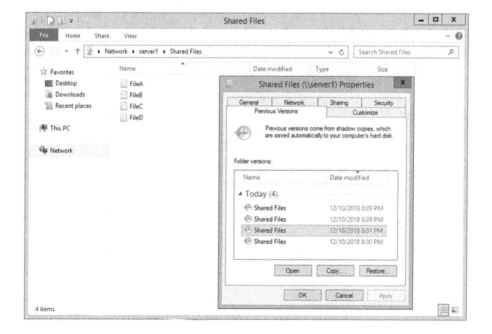

File-Based Backups

File-based backups are a common type of backup in organizations today and have been since the introduction of backup software. The Windows Server operating system includes a backup program capable of protecting the local server, as shown in Figure 10.3. It is somewhat limited, because it only supports a file-based destination and does not offer options for data tapes. It also only allows for the management of the local server. However, the product is free and is included with the Server operating system, so there is no reason not to have some type of backup.

Advanced backup software, such as Veeam Backup & Replication and Veritas Backup Exec, allows for the centralized management of all backups. Multiple backup jobs can be created for various groups of servers and can be directed to various destinations. For example, the accounting servers might back up to a tape library unit, whereas the sales servers back up to a disk storage unit. We'll discuss media type later in this chapter, but the key takeaway is that multiple jobs can be created and executed at the same time.

Advanced backup software often requires a licensed agent to be installed on each server. Depending on the type of agent purchased, the agent might just allow for a simple backup of files, or it might allow for open files to be backed up while they are in use. Some agents even allow for the snapshot of all files so that a point-in-time image can be made of the filesystem. The backup is then created from the snapshot. This type of backup is common in financial institutions, where an end-of-day cutoff needs to be created.

Advanced backup software normally performs a pull of files from the selected source server and directs the information to the selected media. This is called the pull backup method, and it is probably the most common type of backup you will encounter. However, there are also push backup methods, in which the backup software directs the selected source server to push the files to the destination media using the backup server. This reduces the utilization on the backup server and speeds up the backup process, also known as the backup window.

FIGURE 10.3   Windows Server Backup.

Image-Based Backups

Image-based backups allow for a complete server to be backed up. This type of backup is also called a *bare-metal backup*. It's called a bare-metal backup because if the server hardware were to fail, you would restore the backup to a new server (bare-metal) and restore it completely. The inherent problem with these types of restorations is that they require administrator intervention. However, the technology is impressive and spares you from reinstalling the server from scratch.

Virtualized environments are where image-based backups really add value. Virtualization is changing the landscape of IT, and the area of backups is no different. When a server is virtualized, the guest virtual machine consists of configuration files, a virtual filesystem file, and other supporting files. When access is given to the underlying filesystem where the files can be directly accessed, they can be backed up. This allows for an image to be created for the current state of an operating system—files and all.

Most enterprise backup software supports image-based backups for an additional license fee. It normally requires an agent to be installed on the host operating system, such as Microsoft Hyper-V. In VMware environments, a VMware Consolidated Backup (VCB) proxy is required. This application proxy allows the backup software to create snapshots for the guest virtual machines and assists in backing up the virtual machine files.

Critical Applications

So far, we've discussed how to use file server backups to protect an organization. However, an organization does not rely solely on file servers; there are many other types of servers in an organization. Examples include Microsoft SQL, for databases, and Microsoft Exchange, for email. In addition, there are several other types of applications that might be custom to an organization.

Just like file servers, Microsoft SQL and Microsoft Exchange have custom agents that are licensed. These agents allow for the data contained in the proprietary data stores to be backed up to your backup media. In addition to the backup of data, the agent will start a maintenance process at the end of a backup. This maintenance process will check the consistency of the current data store by replaying transaction logs, also called *tlogs*.

Critical applications for an organization do not have to be on site. As organizations adopt a cloud-based approach to IT, they push critical applications out of the network and into the cloud. Providers such as Amazon Web Service (AWS) and Microsoft Azure can provide not only the critical applications but also backup services that are contained in the cloud.

Network Device Backup/Restore

Files are not the only thing that should be backed up on the network. Network devices should be backed up as well, since their configuration is usually completely unique. Configurations such as the various port configurations on a network switch can be a nightmare to reconfigure. Configurations can be lost because they were erased by accident or overwritten or due to just plain failure of the equipment. There are automated appliances and software that can automatically back up configuration of switches on a daily basis. Many vendors also have mechanisms so that the equipment can back itself up to a TFTP, FTP, SFTP server, or even a flash card.

In the case of a cluster host or virtualization host, configuration is not the only thing you will need to back up in the event of failure. The overall state of the device should be saved as well, in the event the device needs to be completely replaced. The software installed on the device expects MAC addresses and disk configuration to be the same when it is moved to new hardware. Otherwise, the software could need to be completely reinstalled. Thankfully, many vendors allow for the state to be saved. This allows a complete forklift of the operating system and data without reinstalling.

Data Restoration Characteristics

When discussing the restoration of data, two characteristics dictate when you back up and how you back up. The concept of the *recovery point objective (RPO)* defines the point in time that you can restore to in the event of a disaster. The RPO is often the night before, since backup windows are often scheduled at night. The concept of the *recovery time objective (RTO)* defines how fast you can restore the data.

In this section I discuss backup methods, some of which can speed up the process. However, the disadvantage is that these methods will increase the recovery time, as I will explain. You will also learn how the RPO and RTO apply to the disaster recovery plan, later in this chapter.

Backup Media

When creating a backup job, you choose what you want to back up (source) and a destination where it is to be stored. Depending on the backup software, you may have several different destinations to select from. Examples include iSCSI storage area networks (SANs), network-attached storage (NAS), tape library units (TLUs), or even cloud-based storage, such as Amazon S3. These are just some examples; there are many different media options for storing backups. Each backup media option uses a specific media type, and each media type has unique advantages and disadvantages. Here are the three media types commonly used for backups:

Disk-to-Tape.   Disk-to-tape backups have evolved quite a bit throughout the years. Today, Linear Tape-Open (LTO) technology has become the successor for backups. LTO can provide 6 TB of raw capacity per tape, with plans for 48 TB per tape in the near future. Tapes are portable enough to rotate off-site for safekeeping. However, they require time to record the data, resulting in lengthy overall backup time. Restore requires time to tension the tape, locate the data, and restore the data, making the RTO a lengthy process.

Disk-to-Disk.   Disk-to-disk backups have become a standard in data centers as well because of the proximity of the data and the short RTO. This type of media is usually based on-site and then it is used to create an off-site copy. They can record the data quicker than traditional tape, thus shortening overall backup time. They also do not require tensioning and seeking for the data, like a tape requires.

The capacity of a disk, however, is much smaller than a tape because the drives remain in the backup unit. Data deduplication can provide a nominal 10:1 compression ratio, depending on the data. This means that 10 TB of data can be compressed on 1 TB of disk storage. So, a 10 TB storage unit could potentially back up 100 TB of data. Again, this depends on the types of files you are backing up. The more similar the data, the better the compression ratio.

Disk-to-Cloud.   Disk-to-cloud is another popular and emerging backup technology. It is often used with disk-to-disk backups to provide an off-site storage location for end-of-week backups or monthly backups. The two disadvantages of a disk-to-cloud backup is the ongoing cost and the lengthy RTO. Anytime you want to restore data, you must download the data from the cloud. Depending on your Internet connection speeds, this could require some time. The advantage is that expensive backup equipment does not need to be purchased along with the ongoing purchase of tapes. However, it is typical for the cloud vendor to charge for the amount of data restored or read from the cloud. Hopefully, you don't need to do many restores.

Media Rotation

Administrators will adopt a rotation schedule for long-term archiving of data. The most popular backup rotation in grandfather, father, son (GFS). The GFS rotation defines; the daily backup will be rotated on a first-in, first-out (FIFO) basis. One of the daily backups will become the weekly backup on a FIFO basis. And lastly, one of the weekly backups will become the month-end backup. Policies should be created such as retaining 6 daily backups, 4 weekly backups, and 12 monthly backups. As you progress further away from the first six days, the RPO jumps to a weekly basis, then to a monthly basis. The benefit is that you can retain data over a longer period of time with the same number of tapes.

Backups are created for one of two main reasons: accidental deletion and disaster. Therefore, it makes sense that a disaster that could potentially destroy your data center could also destroy the backup media. For this reason, media should be rotated off-site from the on-site presence of the original media.

The *3-2-1 backup rule* method is a common method for maintaining both on-site and off-site backups. The 3-2-1 method works like this: Three instances of the data should exist at all times. The original copy of the files and a backup of the file should be on-site, and the third copy of the data should be off-site in the event of tragedy at the site. Here's an example: You create a business proposal on your computer (first instance), and nightly your files are backed up (second instance). You know have two instances local to your immediate site (on-site) in the event of an accidental deletion. A second backup job then backs the file up to the cloud. This provides a third instance of the file, one of which is off-site.

There are a number of ways you can achieve this method of disaster recovery. For instance, you create the file, Volume Shadow Copy snapshots the drive on the hour, and a nightly backup copies the file to the cloud for off-site storage.

Backup Methods

There are several options for creating file-based backup jobs. Each backup method has advantages and disadvantages, depending on the media you are using and the amount of time in your backup window. The following are several of the backup methods you will find primarily with file-based backups:

Full. A full backup is just that: a full backup of the entire dataset. A full backup requires the longest backup window of all the methods, because it is the slowest. Therefore, full backups are generally performed on weekends, when you have a lengthy window. All files are backed up, regardless of the state of the archive bit. The archive bit is an attribute of each file; when a file is created or modified, the archive bit is turned on. When a full backup is performed, all the archive bits are reset on the files in the dataset. A full backup is not sustainable through the week because it backs up all the files, regardless of whether they have been modified.

Incremental. An incremental backup is used to speed up backups through the week when backup windows are short. An incremental backup will back up all files with the archive bit set. After the files are backed up, the archive bit will be reset. Only the files that were created and modified from the last full or prior incremental backup are backed up, so backups are small. If you need to restore from an incremental, however, you will need to restore the full backup as well as all of the incremental backup files up to the RPO required. This type of restore will create a longer RTO because of the multiple backups that are required.

Differential. A differential backup is also used to speed up backups through the week. It will back up all the files with the archive bit set as well, but it will not reset the archive bit after it has done so. A differential will create a gradually larger backup until a full backup is completed and the archive bits are reset again. This type of backup will have a shorter RTO than incremental backups, because only the full and the last differential are needed to restore to the RPO required.

Copy. A copy backup is used when you want to make an exact copy of the server. This backup method is identical to a full backup, with the exception that it does not reset archive bits. This backup method is often used when you want to make a copy of a server before a major upgrade. This backup method allows you to create a backup without affecting an ongoing nightly backup.

Synthetic. A synthetic backup is a full backup without the overhead of performing a full backup on the entire dataset. A synthetic backup is performed by the backup software. The software will take the latest full backups and apply the differential backups or incremental backups up to the desired date the job runs. For example, if you create a full backup once a month but want weekly full backups, a synthetic full backup can be created by taking the last full backup and applying the changes up to the current date. The synthetic full will now serve as a full backup in the event a restore is required, thus lowering the RTO.

Backup Testing

Over the years, we've seen fellow administrators rely on their backups—up to the point they try to restore them. It's a very different story when they fail during a critical moment. Fortunately, this only happens to you once, and then you adopt testing strategies. You should not consider data on a backup to be safe until you have proven that it has been restored successfully. There are so many things that can go wrong with a restore, the most common being media failure.

We recommend that you perform a restore of your backup at least once a month. This will allow you to verify that you actually have data that is restorable in the event of an emergency. Many backup products will allow you to schedule a test restore. The test restore will actually restore the data and compare it to what is on the backup media. When it's done testing the restore, it will delete the restored data and notify you of any discrepancies.

Account Recovery Options

Disaster can strike in several different ways and is not limited to data loss or power problems. A critical admin or user account can be inadvertently deleted or you may simply forget the password. Fortunately, there are several different options, depending on the type of account involved.

Online Accounts

Starting with Windows 8, the push to use Microsoft accounts as your primary login has been emphasized by Microsoft. When you set up Windows for the first time, the default is to use a Microsoft online account. A Microsoft account allows you to download content and applications from the Microsoft Store. It also allows you to recover your account by using Microsoft services. When you sign up for a Microsoft account, you're asked for backup email accounts and even your cell phone number for text messages. All these alternate methods of contact make it easier to recover your account if you lose your password.

Local Accounts

If you are using a local account to log into the operating system, your options will be slightly limited. Fortunately, starting with Windows 10 version 1803, there is a built-in option to recover a password for a local account. During the setup of the administrator account, the operating system will ask you three security questions. If you forget the password, you simply need to answer the security questions you provided during setup to reset the password, as shown in Figure 10.4.

If the local account is deleted or the password is forgotten and you are not running Windows 10 version 1803 or later, then your only option is to perform a System Restore on

FIGURE 10.4   Windows 10 security questions.

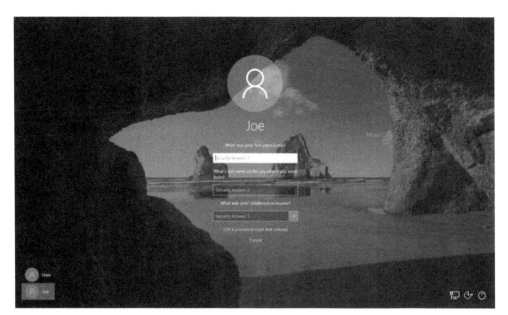

the operating system to restore the affected account. Unfortunately, if the user account is completely deleted, a System Restore will not bring back the user files. It will, however, restore the local user account, after which a traditional restore from it can be performed.

Domain Accounts

You have several options with domain accounts versus local accounts. The first and most obvious option is that with domain accounts you have other privileged accounts. These other privileged accounts can reset passwords if they are forgotten or locked out after too many unsuccessful attempts.

If an account is deleted, you have several options as well, but they require that you've taken preventive measures before the account is deleted. The first option for account recovery with domains is the use of the *Active Directory Recycle Bin*. The Recycle Bin feature first appeared in Windows Server 2008 R2, so you must be running this version of Windows Server or later. A second requirement is having the Recycle Bin enabled, since it is not enabled by default. Once the Recycle Bin is enabled, if an Active Directory user account is deleted, it will show up in the Deleted Objects container. All you need to do is right-click the object and choose Restore.

Another way to restore Active Directory objects is from backup. Almost all Windows backup utilities have a provision for the backup of Active Directory. Even the Windows Backup utility allows for the backup of Active Directory by selecting the backup of the

System State data on the domain controller. In the event that an object is deleted, most backup products will allow you to restore the individual user account with a few clicks.

If you are using the Windows Backup utility, you must perform an authoritative restore, which is a little more complicated than a few clicks. The following is an overview of the steps to perform an authoritative restore with a backup program that supports only the restore of System State, such as the Windows Backup utility:

1. Stop the Active Directory Domain service by using the command `net stop ntds`.

2. Restore the latest System State backup.

3. Use the `ntdsutil` utility to update the object you need to restore.

4. Reboot the server.

Facilities and Infrastructure Support

When infrastructure equipment is purchased and deployed, the ultimate success of the deployment can depend on selecting the proper equipment, determining its proper location in the facility, and installing it correctly. Let's look at some common data center and server room equipment and a few best practices for managing these facilities.

Battery Backup/UPS

An uninterruptible power supply (UPS) is a battery backup system that allows for power conditioning during power sags, power surges, and power outages. A UPS should be used only until a power generator can start supplying a steady source of power. For workstations and server installations where backup generators are not available, the UPS allows enough time for systems to shut down gracefully.

UPSs are most often used incorrectly as a source of power generation during a power outage. The problem with this scenario is that there is a finite amount of power in the battery system. It may allow you some time to stay running, but if the power is out for too long, the UPS will shut down when its batteries are depleted.

UPS systems should be used to supply power while a power generator is starting up. This protects the equipment during the power sag that a generator creates during its start-up after a power outage has triggered it.

There are several types of UPS systems. The main types are as follows:

Standby UPS.   This is the most common UPS that you find under a desk protecting a personal computer. It operates by transferring the load from the AC line to the battery-supplied inverter. Capacitors in the unit help to keep the power sag to a minimum. These units work well, but they are not generally found in server rooms.

Line-Interactive UPS.   This is commonly used for small server rooms and racks of networking equipment. It operates by supplying power from the AC line to the inverter. When a power failure occurs, the line signals the inverter to draw power from the batteries. This might seem similar to a standby UPS, but the difference is that the load is not shifted. In a standby UPS, the load must shift from AC to a completely different circuit (the inverter), whereas on a line-interactive UPS, the inverter is always wired to the load, but only during the power outage is the inverter running on batteries. This shift in power allows for a much smoother transition of power.

Online UPS.   An online UPS is the standard for data centers. It operates by supplying AC power to a rectifier/charging circuit, which maintains a charge for the batteries. The batteries then supply the inverter with a constant DC power source. The inverter converts the DC power source back into an AC power circuit again, which supplies the load. The benefit of an online UPS is that the power is constantly supplied from the batteries. When there is a power loss, the unit maintains a constant supply of power to the load. The other benefit is that the online UPS always supplies a perfect AC signal.

Power Generators

Power generators supply a constant source of power during a power outage. Power generators consist of three major components: fuel, an engine, and a generator. The engine burns the fuel to turn the generator and create power. The three common sources of fuel are natural gas, gasoline, and diesel. Diesel fuel generators are the most common type of generator supplying data centers around the world. However, natural gas generators are common for small businesses and home installation.

As mentioned in the previous section, generators require a start-up period before they can supply a constant source of electricity. In addition to the start-up period, there is also a switchover lag. When a power outage occurs, the transfer switch moves the load from the street power to the generator circuit. UPSs help to bridge both the lag and sag in electricity supply during the switchover and start-up periods.

Surge Protection

The power specification in North America is around 120 volts 60 Hz alternating current (AC). Normally, your voltage will be plus or minus 10 volts from 120 volts. Most equipment is rated for this variance in electricity. A power surge, however, can be upward of 500 volts for a split second, which is where damage to your equipment occurs.

A power surge can happen for a number of reasons. Two common reasons are lightning strikes and power company grid switches. A lightning strike is probably the most common reason for power surges during a storm. When the lightning hits near an electrical line, it will induce a higher voltage, which causes the surge. After a storm is over, you are still not safe from power surges. When the electrical company transfers a load back on with the power grid switches, a brief surge can sometimes be seen.

Luckily, you can protect yourself from power surges with surge protection. Surge protection can be implemented two different ways: point-of-use and service entrance surge

FIGURE 10.5   A common surge protector.

protection. Surge protectors, UPSs, and power conditioners are all point-of-use devices, with surge protectors being the most common and obvious point-of-use device used for protection. Surge protectors look like common power strips but have protection circuits built in that can suppress up to 600 joules of energy. Many of them have coaxial protection for cable modems and telephone jacks, as shown in Figure 10.5. Some surge protectors even have RJ-45 network jacks, to protect your network equipment.

Service entrance surge protection, also called a *transient voltage surge suppressor (TVSS)*, is normally installed by your electric company. It is commonly installed between the electrical meter and the circuit breaker box, to protect you from any surges from the power grid. Most of these devices can handle over 1,000 joules of surge. These devices often come with a type of insurance from the electric company. In the event you suffer a power surge and your electronics are damaged in the process, you can submit a claim for reimbursement of the damaged equipment. Every electric company is different, so you should check before you contract these services. Figure 10.6 shows an example of a large, industrial service entrance surge protection unit.

A single joule is equal to the energy required to produce 1 watt of electricity continuously for 1 second. Ohm's law states that a watt is equal to voltage multiplied by amperage. During a power surge, voltage can exceed 700 joules.

HVAC

Like any device with a CPU, infrastructure devices such as routers, switches, and specialty appliances must have a cool area to operate. When temperatures rise, servers start rebooting and appliance CPUs start overworking as well.

The room(s) where these devices are located should be provided with heavy-duty heating, ventilation, and air conditioning (HVAC) systems and ample ventilation. It is advisable to dedicate a suite for this purpose and put the entire system on a UPS with a backup generator in the case of a loss of power.

FIGURE 10.6 An industrial service entrance surge protection unit.

The heating and air-conditioning systems must support the massive amounts of computing equipment most enterprises deploy. Computing equipment and infrastructure devices such as routers and switches do not like the following conditions:

- **Heat:** Excessive heat causes reboots and crashes.
- **High humidity:** It causes corrosion problems with connections.
- **Low humidity:** Dry conditions encourage static electricity, which can damage equipment.

The American Society of Heating, Refrigerating and Air-Conditioning Engineers (ASHRAE) publishes standards for indoor air quality and humidity. Their latest recommendations are as follows:

- A class A1 data center
- Can range in temperature from 59°F to 89.6°F
- Can range in relative humidity from 20 percent to 80 percent.

Also keep in mind:

- At 175 degrees, damage starts occurring to computers and peripherals.
- At 350 degrees, damage starts occurring to paper products.

Fire Suppression

While fire extinguishers are important and should be placed throughout a facility, when large numbers of computing devices are present, it is worth the money to protect them with a fire-suppression system. There are five basic types of fire suppression you may find in a facility:

Wet Pipe System.   This is the most common fire suppression system found in facilities such as office complexes and even residential buildings. The wet pipe system is constantly charged with water from a holding tank or the city water supply. The sprinkler head contains a small glass capsule that holds a glycerin-based liquid that keeps the valve shut. When the glass capsule is heated between 135°F and 165°F, the liquid expands, breaking the glass and opening the value. Gallons of water will dump in that area until either the fire is extinguished or another head opens from excessive heat.

Dry Pipe System.   Although the name is deceiving, a dry pipe system uses water, similar to a wet pipe system. The difference is that a dry pipe system does not initially contain water. The pipes in a dry pipe system are charged with air or nitrogen. When a pressure drop occurs because a sprinkler head is heated between 135°F and 165°F, the air escapes out of the sprinkler head. The water is then released behind the initial air charge and the system will operate similarly to a wet pipe system.

Preaction Systems.   The preaction system is identical to the dry pipe system in operations. The preaction system employs an additional mechanism of an independent thermal link that pre-charges the system with water. The system will not dump water unless the sprinkler head is heated between 135°F and 165°F and the thermal link is tripped by smoke or fire. This is an additional factor of safety for the equipment, so a sprinkler head is not tripped by an accident such as a ladder banging into it.

Deluge Systems.   The deluge systems are some of the simplest systems, and they are often used in factory settings. They do not contain a valve in the sprinkler head, just a deflector for the water. When a fire breaks out, the entire system dumps water from all of the sprinkler heads.

Clean Agent.   There are many different clean agents available on the market today. These systems are deployed in data centers worldwide because they do not damage equipment in the event of a fire. The principle of operation is simple: the system displaces oxygen in the air below 15% to contain the fire. The clean agent is always a gas, and these systems are often mislabeled as halon systems. At one time, fire suppression systems used halon gas, which works well by suppressing combustion through a chemical reaction. However, the US Environmental Protection Agency (EPA) banned halon manufacturing in 1994 as it has been found to damage the ozone layer.

The EPA has approved the following replacements for halon:

- Water
- Argon
- NAF-S-III
- FM-200
- Or mixture of gases

Redundancy and High Availability Concepts

By now it must be clear that redundancy is a good thing. While this concept can be applied to network connections, it can also be applied to hardware components and even complete servers. In the following sections, you'll learn how this concept is applied to severs servers and infrastructure devices.

All organizations should identify and analyze the risks they face. This is called risk management. In the following sections, you'll find a survey of topics that all relate in some way to addressing risks that can be mitigated with redundancy and high availability techniques.

Switch Clustering

A switch cluster is a set of connected and cluster-capable switches that are managed as a single entity without interconnecting stack cables. This is possible by using Cluster Management Protocol (CMP). The switches in the cluster use the switch clustering technology so that you can configure and troubleshoot a group of different switch platforms through a single IP address. In those switches, one switch plays the role of cluster command switch, and the other switches are cluster member switches that are managed by the command switch.

Figure 10.7 shows a switch cluster.

Notice that the cluster is managed by using the CMP address of the cluster commander.

FIGURE 10.7   Switch cluster.

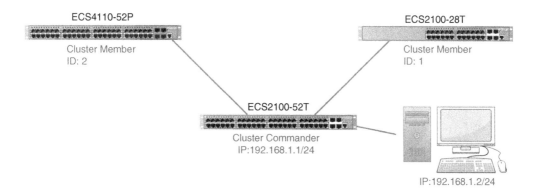

Routers

Routers can also be set up in a redundant fashion. When we provide router redundancy, we call it providing first-hop redundancy since the router will be the first hop from any system to get to a destination. Accomplishing first-hop redundancy requires an FHRP protocol.

First-hop redundancy protocols (FHRPs) work by giving you a way to configure more than one physical router to appear as if they were only a single logical one. This makes client configuration and communication easier because you can configure a single default gateway and the host machine can use its standard protocols to communicate.

First hop is a reference to the default router being the first router, or first router hop, through which a packet must pass.

So, how does a redundancy protocol accomplish this? The protocols I'm going to describe to you do this basically by presenting a virtual router to all of the clients. The virtual router has its own IP and MAC addresses. The virtual IP address is the address that's configured on each of the host machines as the default gateway. The virtual MAC address is the address that will be returned when an ARP request is sent by a host. The hosts don't know or care which physical router is actually forwarding the traffic, as you can see in Figure 10.8.

It's the responsibility of the redundancy protocol to decide which physical router will actively forward traffic and which one will be placed in standby in case the active router

FIGURE 10.8 FHRPs use a virtual router with a virtual IP address and virtual MAC address.

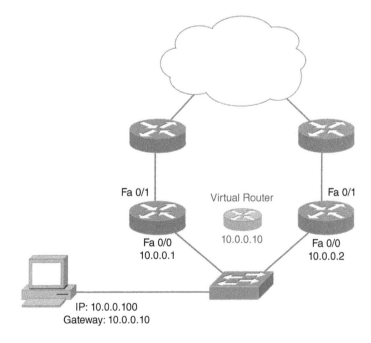

fails. Even if the active router fails, the transition to the standby router will be transparent to the hosts because the virtual router, identified by the virtual IP and MAC addresses, is now used by the standby router. The hosts never change default gateway information, so traffic keeps flowing.

Fault-tolerant solutions provide continued operation in the event of a device failure, and load-balancing solutions distribute the workload over multiple devices. Later in this chapter you will learn about the two most common FHRPs.

Firewalls

Firewalls can also be clustered, and some can also use FHRPs. A firewall cluster is a group of firewall nodes that work as a single logical entity to share the load of traffic processing and provide redundancy. Clustering guarantees the availability of network services to the users.

Cisco Adaptive Security Appliance (ASA) and Cisco Firepower next-generation firewall (NGFW) clustering allow you to group multiple ASA nodes as a single logical device to provide high availability and scalability. The two main clustering options discussed in this chapter are active/standby and active/active. In both cases, the firewall cluster looks like a single logical device (a single MAC/IP address) to the network.

Later in this chapter, you will learn more about active/active and active/standby operations.

Servers

Fault tolerance is the ability of a system to remain running after a component failure. Redundancy is the key to fault tolerance. When systems are built with redundancy, a component can suffer a failure and an identical component will resume its functionality. Systems should be designed with fault tolerance from the ground up.

Disaster Recovery Sites

Although a secondary site that is identical in every way to the main site with data kept synchronized up to the minute would be ideal, the cost cannot be justified for most organizations. Cost-benefit analysis must be applied to every business issue, even disaster recovery. Thankfully, not all secondary sites are created equally. They can vary in functionality and cost. We're going to explore four types of sites: cold sites, warm sites, hot sites, and cloud sites.

Cold Site

A cold site is a leased facility that contains only electrical and communications wiring, air conditioning, plumbing, and raised flooring. No communications equipment, networking hardware, or computers are installed at a cold site until it is necessary to bring the site to full operation. For this reason, a cold site takes much longer to restore than a hot or warm site.

A cold site provides the slowest recovery, but it is the least expensive to maintain. It is also the most difficult to test.

Warm Site

The restoration time and cost of a warm site is somewhere between that of a hot site and a cold site. It is the most widely implemented alternate leased location. Although it is easier to test a warm site than a cold site, a warm site requires much more effort for testing than a hot site.

A warm site is a leased facility that contains electrical and communications wiring, full utilities, and networking equipment. In most cases, the only thing that needs to be restored is the software and the data. A warm site takes longer to restore than a hot site but less than a cold site.

Hot Site

A hot site is a leased facility that contains all the resources needed for full operation. This environment includes computers, raised flooring, full utilities, electrical and communications wiring, networking equipment, and uninterruptible power supplies. The only resource that must be restored at a hot site is the organization's data, usually only partially. It should take only a few minutes to bring a hot site to full operation.

Although a hot site provides the quickest recovery, it is the most expensive to maintain. In addition, it can be administratively hard to manage if the organization requires proprietary hardware or software. A hot site requires the same security controls as the primary facility and full redundancy, including hardware, software, and communication wiring.

Cloud Site

A cloud recovery site is an extension of the cloud backup services that have developed over the years. These are sites that, while mimicking your on-premises network, are totally virtual, as shown in Figure 10.9.

Organizations that lack the expertise to develop even a cold site may benefit from engaging with a cloud vendor of these services.

Active/Active vs. Active/Passive

When systems are arranged for fault tolerance or high availability, they can be set up in either an active/active arrangement or an active/passive configuration. Earlier in this chapter you learned that when set to active/active state, both or all devices (servers, routers, switches, etc.) are performing work, and when set to active/passive, at least one device is on standby in case a working device fails. Active/active increases availability by providing more systems for work, while active/passive provides fault tolerance by holding at least one system in reserve in case of a system failure.

FIGURE 10.9   Cloud recovery site.

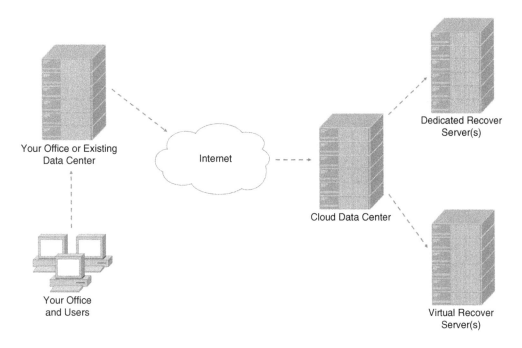

FIGURE 10.10   Path redundancy.

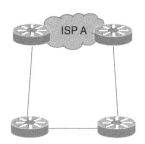

Multiple Internet Service Providers/Diverse Paths

Redundancy may also be beneficial when it comes to your Internet connection. There are two types of redundancy that can be implemented.

Path redundancy is accomplished by configuring paths to the Internet service provider (ISP), as shown in Figure 10.10. There is a single ISP with two paths extending to the ISP from two different routers.

That's great, but what if the ISP suffers a failure (it does happen)? To protect against that you could engage two different ISPs with a path to each from a single router, as shown in Figure 10.11.

For complete protection you could combine the two by using a separate router connection to each ISP, thus protecting against an issue with a single router or path in your network, as shown in Figure 10.12.

Testing

When discussing testing, you must understand that your network plan needs testing. To do that, the industry uses what is called tabletop exercises.

Tabletop exercises are cost-effective to test and validate your plan, procedure, network, and security policies. This can also be called walk-throughs or table-top exercises (TTXs).

This exercise is a discussion-based event where staff or personnel with roles and responsibilities in a particular IT plan meet in a classroom setting or breakout groups to discuss their roles during an emergency and their responses to a particular emergency.

These are meant to be a very informal environment, with an open discussion, guided by an administrator, through a discussion designed to meet predefined objectives.

FIGURE 10.11   ISP redundancy.

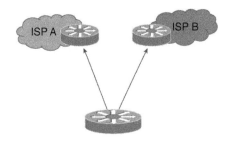

FIGURE 10.12   Path and ISP redundancy.

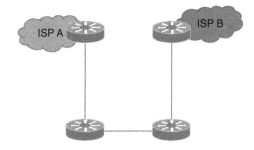

These can be a cost-effective tool to validate the plans of IT, such as backups, contingency plans, and incident response plans. This ensures the plan content is viable and implementable in an emergency.

Tabletop Exercises

TTXs exercises, also called play, are a great way to test processes and plans. By communicating with the group members, you can stress test all the procedures and other processes.

You can use a TTX play to perform a tabletop exercise, verify the existing integration plane, and identify areas that would break if you were to implement the plans.

Tabletop exercises can do the following:

- Help assess plans, policies, and procedures

- Identify gaps and challenges

- Clarify roles and responsibilities

- Identify additional mitigation and preparedness needs

- Provide hands-on training

- Highlight flaws in incident response planning

Validation Tests

Once your plan is in place, next comes the validation.

Validation of the plan comes from listening or reading all group and group participants' feedback. These sessions allow for the plan, procedures, and policies to be revised.

Before you design and execute any exercise, you must clearly understand what you want to achieve and plan your testing methods.

Consider these questions: What are the specific goals and outcomes? What are the potential threats and risks that could disrupt your operations? How will you measure and evaluate your performance and improvement? You can focus your exercise on the most relevant and essential aspects by identifying your objectives first.

Here is a list to use well-validating and tabletop tests:

Set Up the Initial Meeting.   Gather all cross-functional leads and domain experts and lay out the scenario. Provide all the facts regarding the deal for evaluation and input for the next meeting.

Listen to Feedback.   In this second meeting, listen to the cross-functional teams. They will be able to provide good insights into how the integration will affect their respective function. If it's too complicated, a third meeting might be required.

Conclusion.   Come up with conclusions on the things that are possible. Everyone should be clear on what can be safely integrated, the risks that come with it, and mitigation plans.

Document the Process.   A new practice, process, or function should be generated at the end of these exercises. Document them for future reference.

Disaster Recovery Plan

A disaster is an emergency that goes beyond the normal response of resources. The causes of disasters are categorized into three main areas according to origin:

- Technological disasters (device failures)
- Manmade disasters (arson, terrorism, sabotage)
- Natural disasters (hurricanes, floods, earthquakes)

The severity of financial and reputational damage to an organization is largely determined by the amount of time it takes the organization to recover from the disaster. A properly designed disaster recovery plan (DRP) minimizes the effect of a disaster. The DRP is implemented when the emergency occurs and includes the steps to restore systems so the organization can resume normal operations. The goal of a DRP is to minimize or prevent property damage and prevent loss of life.

All companies rely on network services in some way for their day-to-day operations. These companies use network services for the storage of internal financial data, communications, client records, and so forth. Many companies such as online retailers and service providers can lose money by the second when there is an outage.

The disaster recovery plan is how the company transitions from a disaster back to normal operations. If the disaster was the sales database getting completely wiped out, the business continuity plan would detail how to continue business during the outage. The disaster recovery plan would detail how to restore systems so that business functions normally.

Disasters can be critical files deleted by accident, files destroyed or lost because of a virus or ransomware, or unexpected events such as fire and flooding.

The network administrator is responsible for the recovery of IT systems during a disaster. Therefore, a disaster recovery plan should be prepared for high risk disasters. If your server room is on the bottom floor of a building, then the server room flooding is a high risk. The business continuity plan for each of the departments would detail how they would function while the servers were down. However, your responsibility is to get them back up and running and this is the purpose of a disaster recovery plan. Although there are many different types of disasters, the disaster recovery plan should outline the following:

Responsibilities of Personnel. A detailed list of who is responsible for each system involved in the disaster recovery effort. This should also include scheduling, since a disaster can span longer than an eight-hour work shift and you will probably need a second team for the next shift or two.

Processes and Procedures. The processes used to recover from the disaster should be detailed in the document as well as the procedures to perform the tasks to recover the organization.

Systems Involved in Recovery. Documentation should outline each of the systems that are involved in the recovery effort. This list should coincide with the list of responsible personnel for each system.

Recover Point Objective (RPO).   The RPO is the point in time to which you can recover the organization. It is commonly used to describe the restoration of files from a backup restore. If the recovery effort requires the restoration of data from the prior backup, then the expectation for RPO should be the point in time when the backup initially ran. Having the RPO documented allows for everyone involved to have an adequate expectation.

Recovery Time Objective (RTO).   The RTO is the time it will take to recover the from the disaster. This is really subjective because it depends on the scope of the recovery effort. The term is also commonly used with backup and restoration of files. However, if it is simple recovery of files, an approximate time can be documented. If the recovery is getting a new server because the old one is under water, then the time it takes to purchase, install, and configure a new server is the RTO. The documentation of the RTO allows everyone involved to have an expectation of when the organization can recover from a disaster.

I have been in many network outages where the information about the network was on the network and only on the network. This creates a chicken-and-egg scenario that you don't want to find yourself in during a panic situation. It is a best practice to create hard copies of key information about your network and compile it into a binder. Articles to be included are network diagrams, IP addresses of vital equipment, support numbers, and account information. Back in the mainframe days, we called this collection of documents "crash books." If and when the system crashed, it was the first book you would grab. Additionally, configuration backups should be external of the network as well.

Real Life Lesson

The 2020 COVID-19 pandemic was unexpected and unprecedented in many organizations. Many organizations shut down for several months, and in some cases, organizations continued to operate. It was all dependent on their product or service. Regardless of the product or service, some organizations supplied back-office functions needed to continue, such as accounts payable, payroll, and bookkeeping, just to name a few.

Many organizations quickly reacted to the disaster of the pandemic and formed a business continuity plan. A lot of these plans directly involved technology and the IT departments. The disaster recovery effort IT faced was bringing these back-office functions online virtually with a work-from-home strategy. The COVID-19 pandemic was unforeseen, but was your organization ready to launch a work-from-home strategy? Was there a plan in place for an event such as the pandemic?

Business Continuity Plan

One of the parts of a DRP is a plan to keep the business operational while the organization recovers from the disaster; this is known as a business continuity plan (BCP). Continuity planning deals with identifying the impact of any disaster and ensuring that a viable recovery plan for each function and system is implemented. By prioritizing each process and its supporting technologies, the company can ensure that mission-critical systems are recovered first and systems that are considered luxuries can be recovered as time allows.

One document that should be created to drive this prioritization is the business impact analysis (BIA). In this document, the impact each system has on the ability of the organization to stay operational is determined. The results list the critical and necessary business functions, their resource dependencies, and their level of criticality to the overall organization.

It is important for an organization to have both a business continuity plan and a disaster recovery plan. The two go hand in hand with each other. The business continuity plan will outline how an organization will continue to function during a disastrous event. The business continuity plan cannot account for every disaster, but each critical sub-organization in the organization should have a contingency plan if their function is affected by disaster. As an example, if a company derived their business from online sales and the risk is the servers failing, the company should have an alternate method of completing sales detailed in the business continuity plan.

Summary

In this chapter, you learned the importance of preparing for disasters by performing backups. You also learned how to ensure systems can be restored in the event of disaster. In addition, to a myriad of disaster recovery concepts.

We learned the importance of good facility design to support our organization during a disaster. These design components consist of UPS systems, generators, HVAC systems, and fire suppression systems.

We then learned about redundant systems and how they can keep operations up during a disaster by providing fault tolerance. The redundant systems in this chapter are clusters of routers, switches, and firewalls, but the list doesn't stop there. Many other systems can support or be built to support fault tolerance. In addition, we learned about disaster recovery for our sites by providing hot, cold, warm, and cloud sites.

Last we learned how all these components fit into a disaster recovery plan, as well as our business continuity plan.

Exam Essentials

Understand how to prevent disasters and recover from data loss.　Data loss is the most common disaster an organization can suffer from on a day-to-day basis. You should understand how to prevent data loss with the implementation of data backups and other prevention methods. You should also understand how to protect an organization from power-related problems using uninterruptible power supplies and surge protection.

Describe facilities and infrastructure redundancy techniques.　Among these are uninterruptible power supplies (UPSs), power distribution units (PDUs), generators, HVAC systems, fire suppression, and multiple Internet service providers (ISPs)/diverse paths.

Utilize disaster recovery techniques.　These include physical cold sites, warm sites, hot sites, and cloud sites. It also requires an understanding of RPO, MTTR, MTBF, and RTO.

Identify applications of active/active and active/passive configurations.　These include switch clusters, Routers with FHRP, and firewall clusters.

Know the various components of the disaster recovery plan and the considerations.　The disaster recovery plan will define the key people that are needed to recover from a disaster, as well as the system, and the RPO and RTO to recover the systems. In addition, a key consideration is the work shifts to cover round the clock recovery. There are many other considerations as you develop the disaster recovery plan and business continuity plan.

Review Questions

You can find the answers to these questions in Appendix.

1. Which backup media is the fastest from which to recover?

   A. Disk-to-tape

   B. Disk-to-disk

   C. Disk-to-flash

   D. Disk-to-cloud

2. You need to upgrade a server and want to make a backup of the data before you begin. Which backup method should you choose so that your normal backups are not affected?

   A. Full

   B. Copy

   C. Incremental

   D. Differential

3. Which type of power protection is used between the electricity coming into the premises and the power meter, to protect from surges in electric?

   A. Surge protector strip

   B. Uninterruptible power supply

   C. Service entrance surge protection

   D. Generator

4. Which of the following is a measure back in time to when your data was preserved in a usable format, usually to the most recent backup?

   A. RTO

   B. MTBF

   C. RPO

   D. MTTR

5. Which of the following provides only fault tolerance?

   A. Two servers in an active/active configuration

   B. Three servers in an active/passive configuration with one on standby

   C. Three servers in an active/passive configuration with two on standby

   D. Three servers in an active/active configuration

6. Which site type mimics your on-premises network yet is totally virtual?

    A. Cold site

    B. Cloud site

    C. Warm site

    D. Hot site

7. Which of the following fire suppression systems is not a good choice where computing equipment will be located?

    A. Deluge

    B. CO2

    C. Argon

    D. NAF-S-III

8. Which type of recovery is the least expensive to maintain over time?

    A. Cold site recovery

    B. Warm site recovery

    C. Hot site recovery

    D. Cloud site recovery

9. A recovery from tape will take 4 hours; what is this an example of?

    A. The recovery point objective (RPO)

    B. The recovery time objective (RTO)

    C. GFS rotation

    D. Backup window

10. You need to purchase a power backup system for a mission critical data center. Which combination of backup systems will ensure long-term power that has a flawless AC signal? (Choose two.)

    A. Standby UPS

    B. Line interactive UPS

    C. Online UPS

    D. Generator

Chapter

11

Incident Handling

THE FOLLOWING CCST EXAM TOPIC IS COVERED IN THIS CHAPTER:

✔ **5.0 Incident Handling**

- 5.1. Monitor security events and know when escalation is required

    Role of SIEM and SOAR, monitoring network data to identify security incidents (packet captures, various log file entries, etc.), identifying suspicious events as they occur

- 5.3. Explain the impact of compliance frameworks on incident handling

    Compliance frameworks (GDPR, HIPAA, PCI-DSS, FERPA, FISMA), reporting and notification requirements

It's inevitable that at some point you will have an incident that you must deal with. It might be a slight incident of data loss or something much more severe that requires authorities. As a security professional, you must be ready to handle the incident according to the law and regulatory sector applicable to your organization. This chapter will teach you how incidents are detected and handled and the requirements of regulations for your business sector.

To find your included bonus material, as well as Todd Lammle videos, practice questions, and hands-on labs, please see www.lammle.com/ccst.

Security Monitoring

Security monitoring helps us thwart intrusion into our organization's network and prevent threat actors from entering. This is an easy statement to make, but in practice there is a vast array of security monitoring techniques. Each of the following security monitoring techniques allows us to get a clearer picture of our blind spots in our organization's network. The following isn't even a complete list of all the different security monitoring techniques. You will notice that a lot of these techniques were already covered in parts of this book:

- Intrusion Detection and Prevention Systems (IDPS)
- Log Management and Analysis
- Network Traffic Monitoring
- Endpoint Detection and Response (EDR)
- Threat Intelligence Integration
- Cloud Security Monitoring
- Vulnerability Management
- Penetration Testing and Red Teaming
- Compliance Monitoring

Security Information and Event Management (SIEM)

Today we need to be equally talented with all of these security techniques to keep up with threat actors that threaten our network. Unfortunately, this presents a few problems because many of the techniques are siloed from one another, and the log files generated by each of the monitoring techniques can reach thousands per minute. Some organizations outsource the task to security operation centers (SOCs), and some create custom tools to query the most important events. If the organization doesn't optimize its monitoring techniques, staff burnout is inevitable.

Luckily, a security information and event management (SIEM) system can solve a lot of common problems with security monitoring. Modern SIEM systems can combine log files from several different security monitoring services to produce high-fidelity alerts. There are a few decisions when choosing SIEM system.

Hosting Model

A major first decision is where you will host it. Many SIEM systems can be hosted on-premises or in the cloud. Although, this might seem like a straightforward decision based on your organization's initiative to the cloud, it requires much more consideration. The amount of log traffic leaving your network is one of the major considerations when choosing a hosted model. If the application is hosted in the cloud, there may be charges for incoming network activity into the cloud service. You might also purchase a SIEM as a service (SIEMaaS) that makes it impossible to self-host the SIEM system. Cloud-based SIEMaaS is an emerging technology that allows anyone with a credit card to set up a SIEM instance.

Detection Methods

The detection engine is probably the most important decision you can make. The SIEM system will offer a few different detection methods. The most basic detection method is called baseline analysis. This type of detection is dependent on a baseline of captured log activity. This initial capture will train the SIEM detection engine as to what is normal and what is not.

The next detection method is called anomaly detection, and it works by detecting anomalies in activity. This method uses machine learning to detect anomalies in user and entity behavior, to generate alerts. Both baseline analysis and anomaly detection are typically used in conjunction with one another, and they are classified as user and entity behavior analytics (UEBA). The baseline trains the machine learning algorithm, and the anomaly detection uses machine learning to detect an event.

Another detection method is artificial intelligence (AI), and when it comes to detection, it is not just a buzzword. Unlike other uses of AI in society today, this method really complements detection analytics. AI can identify a series of events that are suspect by comparing them to an internal model, based on network activity and the activity of other networks being monitored. As an example, the AI might see a string of login attempts for a user who does not normally log in from a certain area at a certain time and create an alert. AI might also see certain network activity that is from or to a source that it deems suspected of risky activities. With more advanced AI models, it might even be a series of events that leads to an alert.

The single most important detection method that any SIEM will use is threat intelligence data. The threat intelligence that the vendor adopts into the product is typically the main detection method, and it's considered the vendor's "secret sauce." Threat intelligence that is integrated into the SIEM is typically in the form of a constant update stream of indicators of compromise (IoC). These IOCs might be uniform resource locators (URLs), IP addresses, file signatures, and many other telltale signs that have been identified as being used by threat actors.

Integration

Another area to concentrate on when selecting a SIEM is the level of integration that you can adopt. Every SIEM should be able to collect basic logs such as the audit log, service log, and custom logs. These are the primary logs you should be collecting for post-mortem analysis in the event of a breach or failure of a system. These basic logs are typically generated from the servers in your network, and any SIEM worth its weight should be able to collect them. However, your SIEM system should also be able to collect cloud-generated logs, such as AWS and Azure events and login audits.

In addition to cloud-generated logs, some other log sources that should be integrated into the SIEM system are as follows:

- Endpoint detection and response (EDR)
- Network devices
- Security devices
- Applications
- Phone system
- IDS sensors

This list just scratches the surface of what should be collected. The rule of thumb is, anything that can be logged should be consumed into the SIEM system. The more data that is consumed into the SIEM, the better insight you have on the activities in your network.

Cost

The cost of the SIEM system is of course going to be a major decision factor in selection. Some factors to consider when you are pricing the SIEM are the cost of the infrastructure to operate the SIEM, such as the servers and storage, and the licensing costs. Where you host the system, on-premises versus the cloud, will also be a determining factor.

If you choose an on-premises solution, then you just need to select a server and storage solutions that can accommodate the expected size of your logs. These systems are always best as stand-alone servers, so if your private cloud is compromised or has issues, your logging will remain intact for post-mortem analysis.

If you choose a cloud-based system or SIEMaaS, then storage and the size of your logs will be the primary determination. Some vendors will pass the storage costs on to their customer with a nominal markup. And some vendors' storage could be half the annual cost of the product. In either case, storage of logs and the amount of logs will be a major factor in cost. You can always shorten the retention of logs to alleviate some of the storage costs. However, the consideration is the sacrifice of historical logs that could be critical in the event of a breach or incident.

Security Orchestration, Automation, and Response (SOAR)

A SIEM system can manage events and alert you to the most important events you should pay attention to. SIEM systems can email you and let you know something is happening, and they use all the techniques discussed in this chapter. However, SIEM lacks a systematic way to intervene and automate or orchestrate a countermeasure to the threat actor. This is where security orchestration, automation, and response (SOAR) complements SIEM.

SIEM systems collect, correlates, analyzes log data among other data sources, and, most importantly, it can produce alerts. SOAR systems work hand in hand with SIER by creating a decision path for events produced or collection data so a decision can be made. SOAR systems help security personnel investigate events and utilize the information collected, correlated, and analyzed by the SIEM system. This close relationship between SIEM and SOAR can be seen in Figure 11.1.

SOAR systems assist with the investigation of alerts by creating a case for the alert. After a case is created, all evidence pertaining to the alert is compiled and stored in the case. This allows security personnel to review the case or intervene and ultimately remediate the security concern. A SOAR system is really valuable when you have repeated security events that can be automated. A case will automatically be created, logs and data are collected, and then the system can automate a response to the event and automatically close the case. If something need to be investigated after the case is closed, all the information will remain, so the case can be reviewed.

FIGURE 11.1   SIEM vs. SOAR.

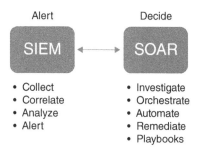

Sometime a case is too complex to automate a response or an automation cannot be configured. In situations like these, security personnel can intervene, review the case, and either close the case or orchestrate a response. You should see a common theme with SIEM producing an alert and SOAR providing a response to the alert in the form of remediation. The remediation to the security alert is the ultimate goal, and that is one major benefit of SOAR systems.

Orchestration vs. Automation

The difference between orchestration and automation is the level of autonomous actions. Automation is typically an automated action based on an event, whereas orchestration is a guided action based on an event. The automation can be triggered by an event, or it can be triggered by security personnel.

As an example, let's say a user logs in from a suspicious IP address, maybe a private VPN. This sort of thing happens all the time. The SOAR system will open a case and start collection logs, such as access, firewall, and audit logs. These logs will be attached to the case for a security person to review. An organization might have an automated response to this type of event to automatically lock the account out. In comparison, an orchestrated action might require a security person to start the process of logging the user out of everything and then requiring sign-in with multifactor authentication.

The difference is that in an automated event, there is a conditional: if this condition exists, then do this. And automation typically works great when it's a simple event. However, it fails when a black swan appears, and this is where user intervention and orchestration is required. The black swan theory is that most swans are white, and you threaten every event when those conditions exist. Automation breaks down when a black swan appears simply because the conditions are not met. When a security person intervenes, they can take the logs attached to the case and orchestrate actions appropriate for the situation.

Regulations and Compliance

Regulations are rules imposed on your organization by an outside agency, such as a certifying board or a government entity, and they're usually totally rigid and immutable. The list of possible regulations that your organization could be subjected to is so exhaustively long, there's no way I can include them all in this book. Different regulations exist for different types of organizations, depending on whether they're corporate, nonprofit, scientific, educational, legal, governmental, and so on, and they also vary by where the organization is located.

For instance, US governmental regulations vary by county and state, federal regulations are piled on top of those, and many other countries have multiple regulatory bodies as well. The Sarbanes-Oxley Act of 2002 (SOX) is an example of a regulation system imposed on all publicly traded companies in the United States. Its main goal was to ensure corporate responsibility and sound accounting practices, and although that may not sound like it would have much of an effect on your IT department, it does because a lot of the provisions in this act target the retention and protection of data. Believe me, something as innocent sounding as deleting old emails could get you in trouble—if any of them could've remotely had a material impact on the organization's financial disclosures, deleting them could actually be breaking the law. All good to know, so be aware, and be careful!

The penalties of noncompliance with regulations can be in the form of financial penalties, reputation damage, loss of services, loss of licensing, and ultimately disruptions to operations. Therefore, it is paramount to the continued operation of our organizations that we comply with safeguarding the data entrusted to our companies.

Common Regulations

One of the most commonly applied regulations is the ISO/IEC 27002 standard for information security, previously known as ISO 17799, renamed in 2007 and updated in 2013. It was developed by the International Organization for Standardization (ISO) and the International Electrotechnical Commission (IEC), and it is based on British Standard (BS) 7799-1:1999.

The official title of ISO/IEC 27002 is *Information technology - Security techniques - Code of practice for information security controls*. Although it's beyond our scope to get into the details of this standard, know that the following items are among the topics it covers:

- Risk assessment
- Security policy
- Organization of information security
- Asset management
- Human-resources security
- Physical and environmental security
- Communications and operations management
- Access control
- Information systems acquisition, development, and maintenance
- Information security incident management
- Business-continuity management
- Compliance

The following are various regulations you may encounter while working in the IT field. This is in no way a complete list of regulations, just the most common.

Data Locality

The adoption of cloud computing by private and government entities has created new challenges for the collection, processing, and storage of information about citizens or residents. Data locality, also known as data localization laws, requires data of a citizen be collected, processed, and stored within the same country before being transferred to other countries. This ensures that local laws related to privacy can be applied to the information of the country's citizens. In certain situations, specific data about a citizen might even need to be removed from the dataset before it can be transferred. Once these requirements are met, then the governed data can be moved outside of the country.

Data locality does not fit into a specific regulatory compliance framework. Instead, it is a concept that binds local regulations focusing on what can be done with citizen or resident data. The local regulations that might apply can vary greatly and pertain to different aspects of the citizen or resident data. The following is a short list of some common regulations or laws that might pertain to data locality for a country's citizens or residents. In no way is the following list exhaustive:

- National security
- Tax or financial records
- Employment
- Export controls
- Investment
- Education

 Each of the applicable regulatory compliance rules will have a different reporting requirement and notification requirement.

Family Educational Rights and Privacy Act (FERPA)

The Family Educational Rights and Privacy Act (FERPA) is a federal law that protects the privacy of student education records. The federal law imposes regulations on education providers and organizations that process student records. It regulates the handling of student records, such as grades, report cards, and disciplinary records. It was created to protect the rights of both students and parents for educational privacy.

FERPA provides specific rights to parents for their children's education records. However, when a child turns 18 or begins a postsecondary education at any age, the rights are transferred from the parents to the student. This means that a parent would not be able to see grades, attendance, or other specific records without the student's permission.

The Department of Education enforces FERPA compliance under Title 34, Subtitle A, Part 99 of the Code of Federal Regulations (CFM). If a provider or organization is out of compliance, their federal funding could be revoked. In addition, penalties could be applied to the provider or organization.

The federal regulations under Title 34, Subtitle A, Part 99 of the CFM cover the following criteria:

§ 99.1 To which educational agencies or institutions do these regulations apply?

§ 99.2 What is the purpose of these regulations?

§ 99.3 What definitions apply to these regulations?

§ 99.4 What are the rights of parents?

§ 99.5 What are the rights of students?

§ 99.5 Reserved

§ 99.7 What must an educational agency or institution include in its annual notification?

§ 99.8 What provisions apply to records of a law enforcement unit?

§ 99.10 What rights exist for a parent or eligible student to inspect and review education records?

§ 99.11 May an educational agency or institution charge a fee for copies of education records?

§ 99.12 What limitations exist on the right to inspect and review records?

§ 99.20 How can a parent or eligible student request amendment of the student's education records?

§ 99.21 Under what conditions does a parent or eligible student have the right to a hearing?

§ 99.22 What minimum requirements exist for the conduct of a hearing?

In addition to the various sections, there are complete subparts that handle the following:

- What Are the Procedures for Amending Education Records?

- May an Educational Agency or Institution Disclose Personally Identifiable Information From Education Records?

- What Are the Enforcement Procedures?

To learn more about FERPA regulations, the full regulation is located in the electronic Code of Federal Regulations (eCFM) via `https://stud entprivacy.ed.gov/ferpa`.

Federal Information Security Modernization Act (FISMA)

The Federal Information Security Modernization Act (FISMA) of 2014 amends the Federal Information Security Management Act of 2002 (FISMA). The current FISMA was developed by the Cybersecurity & Infrastructure Security Agency (CISA), a division of the Department of Homeland Security (DHS). The goal of FISMA is to enhance the security of the federal information systems. It does this by creating standards and guidelines for federal agencies to follow so they can protect their information.

FISMA establishes roles and responsibilities for the Office of Management and Budget (OMB), DHS, and other agency CIOs to provide accountability over information security capabilities for their respective agencies. FISMA does this by simplifying reporting to eliminate inefficient or wasteful reporting by agencies. One way FISMA simplifies reporting is by defining reporting requirements for information security incidents. These requirements require agencies to clearly report in a uniform manner when a major security incident occurs.

FISMA has created a standard by which each head of each federal agency is to provide a definition of the information security protection policies in place. The policies for each agency are required to be realistic compared to the risk and degree of harm resulting from unauthorized access, use, disclosure, disruption, modification, or destruction of information and information systems. In addition, FISMA requires each agency head to furnish a report on the adequacy and effectiveness of the information security policies, procedures, and practices for their respective agency.

Reporting is not the only major changes to FISMA; the regulations also require each agency to use a unified risk management framework (RMF). This requirement means that each agency is required to identify, evaluate, and mitigate risks to information systems. In addition, agencies must regularly test and articulate the effectiveness of security controls. This monitoring is to be continuous for each agency; this means that each agency must detect vulnerabilities, threats, and breaches in real time.

FISMA applies to all organizations that work in accordance with the federal government and all federal agencies. Every organization and federal agency must adhere to the National Institute of Standards and Technology (NIST) 800-53 compliance framework. The NIST 800-53 compliance framework defines security controls and the respective requirements for compliance and reporting.

The penalties for not adhering to FISMA regulations could land a federal agency department head in a congressional hearing. As FISMA pertains to organizations that work in accordance with the federal government, it could result in heavy fines, government contracts being canceled, or in extreme cases jail time, depending on the severity.

More information on FISMA can be found on the CISA/DHS website located at https://www.cisa.gov/topics/cyber-threats-and-advisories/federal-information-security-modernization-actor https://www.congress.gov/bill/113th-congress/senate-bill/2521.

Gramm–Leach–Bliley Act

The Gramm–Leach–Bliley Act (GLBA) affects providers of financial services. GLBA requires financial institutions that offer products and services, such as loans, investment advice, or insurance, to safeguard customer information and detail the practices for sharing consumer information. It was created to protect consumer information and avoid the loss of consumer information.

The GLBA regulations are detail in Title V, subtitle A of the Act (15 U.S.C. §6801 to §6809) and Subtitle B of Title V (15 U.S.C. § 6821 to §6827) of the federal legal code.

Subtitle A states that the Federal Trace Commission (FTC), federal banking agencies, and other regulators are to enforce GLBA compliance. Institutions that work with such federal entities must ensure that the institution protects the privacy of consumers' personal financial information. Institutions must furnish their privacy policies to their customers annually, or as they change. The privacy policies must be disclosed before any consumer's data is disclosed to a third party. The institution must also give notice and an opportunity for that consumer to opt out from the disclosure. You probably got handed a piece of paper the last time you applied for a loan and were told briefly that it was a disclosure because you were applying for a loan; this is GLBA compliance at work. You of course have the option to opt out and not apply for the loan, but you probably wanted the item to be purchased with the loan.

The GLBA also requires the institution to safeguard personal financial information from being leaked to other institutions or malicious individuals. This is to include safeguarding data to be used for marketing purposes. The regulations prohibit obtaining customer information from a financial institution by false pretenses.

The underlying theme is that your financial data is to be kept safe and not used against you for marketing purposes or nefarious reasons. The penalties for an institution not complying could be crippling for the institution, as fines and even criminal charges could be brought upon the people responsible for the transgressions.

The federal regulations under the GLBA, Title V, subtitles A and B are as follows:

§6801. Protection of nonpublic personal information
- **(a)** Privacy obligation policy
- **(b)** Financial institutions safeguards

§6821. Privacy protection for customer information of financial institutions
- **(a)** Prohibition on obtaining customer information by false pretenses
- **(b)** Prohibition on solicitation of a person to obtain customer information from financial institution under false pretenses
- **(c)** Nonapplicability to law enforcement agencies
- **(d)** Nonapplicability to financial institutions in certain cases
- **(e)** Nonapplicability to insurance institutions for investigation of insurance fraud
- **(f)** Nonapplicability to certain types of customer information of financial institutions
- **(g)** Nonapplicability to collection of child support judgments

To learn more about GLBA regulations, the full regulation is located at `https://www.ftc.gov/legal-library/browse/statutes/gramm-leach-bliley-act`.

General Data Protection Regulation (GDPR)

The General Data Protection Regulation (GDPR) is a European Union (EU) law governing how consumer data can be used and protected. The GDPR went into effect and became applicable as of May 5, 2018. It was created primarily to protect citizens of the EU, as well as standardize data privacy laws across the EU. It applies to anyone involved in the processing of data based upon the citizens of the European Union, regardless of where the organization is located.

There are 11 chapters to the GDPR regulations of the (EU) 2016/679 (General Data Protection Regulation) that separate the 99 articles that detail the regulation. The current version of the OJ L 119, 04.05.2016; cor. OJ L 127, 23.5.2018 is neatly arranged as a website located at `https://gdpr-info.eu/`. The chapters that are applicable to the GDPR are as follows:

Chapter 1 (Article 1–4) General provisions
Chapter 2 (Article 5–11) Principles
Chapter 3 (Article 12–23) Rights of the data subject
Chapter 4 (Article 24–43) Controller and processor
Chapter 5 (Article 44–50) Transfers of personal data to third countries or international organizations
Chapter 6 (Article 51–59) Independent supervisory authorities
Chapter 7 (Article 60–76) Cooperation and consistency
Chapter 8 (Article 77–84) Remedies, liability and penalties
Chapter 9 (Article 85–91) Provisions relating to specific processing situations
Chapter 10 (Article 92–93) Delegated acts and implementing acts
Chapter 11 (Article 94–99) Final provisions

The 99 articles that detail the GDPR are extremely in depth and require some interpretation for your individual organization. Therefore, the GDPR recommends that organizations hire a data protection officer (DPO). This person is the point of contact for all compliance for GDPR, as well as any other compliances your organization falls under.

The underlying goal is to achieve consent from the end user of your product or service. Consent to collect information must be proven by an organization beyond a shadow of doubt. This means that if someone visits your website from the EU, you must receive consent in clear language to even place a cookie in their web browser. The DPO is responsible for coordinating this language, as well as the life cycle of any data that is collected.

The penalties for not complying with the GDPR are heavy fines and being barred from doing business in the EU. United States (US) organizations need to follow the GDPR regulations if they are collecting data, using data, monitoring data, and storing data of EU citizens. Therefore, many websites must now comply with EU laws because there is a bit of data collection that a website will perform.

Although the GDPR is neatly arranged as a website, you can download a PDF version from the main web page, `https://gdpr-info.eu/`.

Health Insurance Portability and Accountability Act

The Health Insurance Portability and Accountability Act (HIPAA) of 1996 was created to protect health information for patient care. HIPPA is regulated by the US Department of Health and Human Services (HHS). HIPPA regulates how a patient's health information is secured and processed before, during, and after the patient's care. HIPPA applies to health care providers, insurers, and business associates that provide services such as prescriptions and other health services; these organizations are typically referred to as covered entities.

There are three main elements to HIPPA: privacy, security, and breach notification.

Privacy.   The privacy of element of HIPPA defines the standards to protect individuals' medical records and personal health information (PHI). A few examples of the various ways privacy might be implemented are as follows:

- Verifying a patient's information before proceeding with treatment
- Using sound barriers so patient information is not overheard
- Using security filters on laptops so patient information cannot be seen

The underlying theme of privacy defines who can access the PHI and under which circumstances.

Security.   The security of PHI is pretty evident because HIPAA is a regulation we are covering in a security book. However, the security of patient information is extremely important beyond the scope of information security.

A patient's health could be affected if the electronic PHI (ePHI) is not secured properly. For example, if patient's health insurance was used to obtain a diagnosis or if a diagnosis was mis-associated with a patient's information, the diagnosis would impact future treatments. If the patient were to need emergency services, their medical record would help providers deliver the proper medical services. However, if the record was wrong due to a lack of security, it could affect the outcome of treatment and the ultimate health of the patient.

HIPAA requires a degree of protection for ePHI through administrative, physical, and technical safeguards. Proper training for administrative personnel should be performed periodically so staff are aware of potential situations where security should be adhered to. Records and systems should have a physical security measure, such as locked doors, cabinets, and access controls. Finally, as security professionals, we should exercise every possible information security technique to safeguard patient data.

Breach Notification Rule. HIPPA mandates that individuals, the government (HHS), business associates, and the media (press release) are notified with 60 days of a breach of PHI. HHS defines a breach as follows:

> an impermissible use or disclosure of protected health information is presumed to be a breach unless the covered entity or business associate, as applicable, demonstrates that there is a low probability that the protected health information has been compromised based on a risk assessment of at least the following factors:
>
> The nature and extent of the protected health information involved, including the types of identifiers and the likelihood of re-identification;
>
> The unauthorized person who used the protected health information or to whom the disclosure was made;
>
> Whether the protected health information was actually acquired or viewed; and
>
> The extent to which the risk to the protected health information has been mitigated.

The penalties for noncompliance with HIPPA regulations range from criminal penalties to civil penalties in the form of lawsuits. Fines can also be imposed on the organization from $100 to $50,000 per violation, obviously depending on the severity.

For more information on HIPPA you can visit `https://www.hhs.gov/hipaa/index.html`. HHS has guidelines for individuals and health care professionals and posts the latest information on HIPPA changes.

Payment Card Industry Data Security Standard (PCI-DSS)

The Payment Card Industry Data Security Standard (PCI-DSS) is a set of regulations created by the credit card industry to protect cardholder data and secure payment systems. The PCI-DSS regulations define the processes and procedures used to handle data related to transactions using payment cards. A payment card is any card that allows the transfer of money for goods or services. Types of payment cards include credit cards, debit cards, and even store gift cards.

PCI-DSS compliance is not enforced by government entities. PCI-DSS compliance is actually enforced by banks and creditors. It applies to all entities that store, process, and transmit credit payment cards. These entities include merchants, payment processors, service providers, and any organization that accepts a payment for goods or services with a payment card.

The PCI-DSS core requirements comprise six controls as follows:

- Maintain a secure network.
- Protect cardholder data (in transit and at rest).

- Perform vulnerability assessments.

- Implement strong access controls.

- Monitor and test network security.

- Maintain an information security policy.

Merchants are assigned a level of 1 through 4 that is based on their transaction level. Merchants are required to comply to more stringent requirements as their transaction level increases. The assessment methods for compliance are self-assessment questionnaires (SAQ) for lower levels and qualified security assessor (QSA) audits for higher levels.

If a merchant does not comply with PCI-DSS standards and a breach occurs, the merchant can be fined by the banks. A merchant can also lose customer trust due to larger data breaches. If a breach of PCI data occurs, then local, state, and federal laws can require the merchant to pay for credit-monitoring services for victims of the breach.

 To learn more about PCI-DSS, you can visit `https://www.pcisecur itystandards.org/standards/pci-dss/`. The PCI Security Standards Council is the governing body that maintains the PCI-DSS regulations.

Reporting

Let's assume that we comply with the working sector regulations and we pass regular audits as part of the compliance. If an incident occurs, we need to be attentive to the regulatory compliance that binds us. Each applicable regulatory compliance will have different reporting and notification requirements. This means that we must file a report with the regulatory body within a specific time frame if we are compromised. Not following through has the same devastating effects as not complying in the first place.

Many different regulations have reporting requirements as a component of their compliance. The reporting requirements fall into two categories, routine reporting and breach reporting. Routine reporting is typically required by many government agencies as a requirement to remain compliant. The routine reports may need to be submitted to the government office, or they might be as simple as a self-assessment. In some circumstances, if your organization participates in certain activities, you may be required to file a report with a local or federal agency routinely. This routine reporting is often required when pharmacies dispense controlled substances, for example.

FISMA also has many different routine reporting requirements for agency heads and organizations working with the government. Routine reports must be submitted on the feasibility of their data being used in an unauthorized manner and how they will safeguard the data.

A breach reports only needs to be filed in the event of a breach. This is the type of report nobody wants to file. As an example, HHS requires breached organizations to submit reports on behalf of their HIPPA compliance regulations. FERPA has similar reporting requirement that need to be followed in the event of a breach: a report must be submitted to the Department of Education detailing the breach.

Notifications

In addition to reporting requirements, a regulation may also have an obligation to send notifications to customers who have had their data compromised. Regulations might also require an organization to create a press release for the media. This is the case with HIPPA regulations when the number of compromised individuals is over 500 patients. The HIPPA regulations require a press release within 60 days of the breach.

The requirement to provide customer notifications is a large part of any breach. There are two main reasons why it's a lot of work and costly. The first reason is that notifications may have different requirements depending on where the customer is located. Some states have their own requirements to notify customers, including the time frame. The state might even require special credit monitoring.

The second reason, and the most impactful to the organization, is the loss of trust by the consumer. When an organization has a breach, customers typically move to another vendor. Many cyber insurance policies can cover you for notification services, but no insurance policy can get trust back from the consumer.

The most important notification is the notification to the regulatory body that a breach has been made. This type of notification is typically required by all regulations. There is typically a window of time from the initial discovery of the breach to the time you notify the regulatory body. Always keep in mind that the lack of reporting and notifications is just as bad as not complying in the first place. It typically carries heavy penalties.

Summary

This chapter focused on the software tools used in incident handling. It covered SIEM systems that are used to collect, aggregate, and analyze log files. The log files that are fed to the SIEM system come from network devices, firewalls, VoIP systems, and EDR systems. In addition, analysis algorithms are used as well as AI to create high-fidelity alerts. SOAR systems work in conjunction with SIEM systems to collect relevant information about a case raised from an alert. They rapidly speed up investigations by security personnel. SOAR systems can also incorporate automation and orchestration to automatically respond to a security concern.

The chapter then focused on regulations and compliance. There are many different regulations that organizations must comply with on a daily basis. If they fail to comply, there are strict consequences, including, in extreme cases, jail time. We covered the most common regulations for the CCST exam, but in no way is this a complete list. In addition to complying with the regulations, reporting must be completed if there is a breach. Furthermore, you may have to notify the public if the breach is large enough.

Exam Essentials

Know the function of a SIEM system.   SIEM systems collect, correlate, and analyze log data, among other data sources, and, most importantly, produce high-fidelity security alerts.

Know the function of a SOAR system.   SOAR systems create cases and collect the relevant logs and supporting data. SOAR then automates or orchestrates a response with the help of security personnel.

Understand the difference between SIEM and SOAR.   SIEM and SOAR systems work together to identify security concerns and respond to them. SIEM systems identify security alerts and send them to the SOAR system. SOAR is then responsible for responding to the security concern.

Know the common regulations covered on the exam.   The FERPA regulation requires compliance with the protection of student records. FISMA regulations require compliance for government agencies and organizations that work with the government. The GDPR protects the information of EU citizens and residents. HIPPA is a federal law that protects the privacy and security of health information. PCI-DSS is a set of regulations that merchants and organizations that process credit cards must adhere to.

Understand the importance of reporting and notifications.   Routine reporting is sometimes required by regulations that an organization must comply with. Almost all require reporting in the event of a breach or security incident. All regulations have a requirement to notify customers when their information is breached; some even require notifying the press.

Review Questions

The following questions are designed to test your understanding of this chapter's material. For more information on how to get additional questions, please see www.lammle.com/ccst.

You can find the answers to these questions in Appendix.

1. Which system is cloud-based and can create alerts based on security logs?
    A. Vulnerability management
    B. Compliance monitoring
    C. SIEMaaS
    D. IDPS

2. Which action often requires security personnel intervention?
    A. Automation
    B. Creation of cases
    C. Orchestration
    D. Alert generation

3. What is the first action that happens after a SOAR system receives an alert?
    A. Response
    B. Logging
    C. Email alerting
    D. Case creation

4. Which type of SIEM analytics is used with UEBA to aid in the training of machine learning?
    A. Anomaly detection
    B. Baseline detection
    C. AI
    D. IoC

5. Which detection method alerts on known malicious URLs or IP addresses?
    A. IoC
    B. AI
    C. UEBA
    D. EDR

6. Which system is responsible for remediation of security events?

A. SIEM

B. SOAR

C. IDS

D. AI

7. If you are a merchant and process credit cards, which regulation do you need to comply with?

A. FIMSA

B. FERPA

C. PCI-DSS

D. GDPR

8. Which is not a main element of HIPPA compliance?

A. Privacy

B. Breach notification

C. Security

D. Portability

9. Which regulation must you comply with if you are a government contractor?

A. FIMSA

B. FERPA

C. PCI-DSS

D. GDPR

10. If you work for a hospital and have a breach of patient information, which entity must you notify?

A. HHS

B. EU

C. QSA

D. DPO

Chapter

12

Digital Forensics

THE FOLLOWING CCST EXAM TOPIC IS COVERED IN THIS CHAPTER:

✔ **5.0 Incident Handling**

- 5.2. Explain digital forensics and attack attribution processes

    Cyber Kill Chain

    MITRE ATT&CK Matrix

    Diamond Model

    Tactics, Techniques, and Procedures (TTP)

    Sources of evidence (artifacts)

    Evidence handling (preserving digital evidence, chain of custody)

Introduction

The process of investigating and recovering assets from criminal activity is referred to as *digital forensics*. This process is used to determine the motives, methods, and impact of cyber threats and security. It is also used to prevent future attacks and prosecute cybercriminals.

You will learn in this chapter the primary processes and models used in digital forensics and how to maintain a chain of custody, which is the formal process of tracking how evidence is gathered and tracked. We will also investigate the different types of models used in digital forensics and how to preserve the evidence.

Forensic Incident Response

The US National Institute of Standards and Technology (NIST) uses the *Forensic Incident Response* model in forensic investigations. It consists of the following four steps:

Collection   After a breach, forensic investigators collect data from affected systems, which may include operating systems, user accounts, mobile devices, storage systems, and other assets the attackers may have accessed.

Preservation.   Forensic investigators make copies of data to preserve the evidence before processing it. They keep a copy of the originals so they cannot be altered and use copies to carry out the investigation.

Analysis.   Forensic investigators analyze the data for any signs of criminal activity. They use standard forensic techniques to process, correlate, and extract insights from digital evidence. Proprietary and open-source threat intelligence feeds can also link the findings to specific threat actors.

Reporting.   Investigators compile a report that explains what happened during the breach and identifies suspects or culprits if possible. The report should also contain recommendations for preventing future attacks. The report can be shared with law enforcement, insurers, regulators, and other authorities.

The NIST SP 800-86 Guide to Integrating Forensic Techniques into Incident Response is at `https://nvlpubs.nist.gov/nistpubs/Legacy/SP/nistspecialpublication800-86.pdf`.

Attack Attribution

Cyberattack attribution is the process of determining who is behind a cyberattack. Attribution is like solving a digital mystery where investigators analyze technical clues, contextual information, and intelligence sources to identify the responsible party. Attack attribution can be performed with different levels of complexity and detail. The three primary approaches—technical, operational, and strategic attribution—each contribute to piecing together the puzzle:

- *Technical attribution* is the analysis of technical indicators of compromise, which includes the attacker's source IP addresses, DNS domain names, malware signatures, toolkits used, and the tactics, techniques, and procedures used during the attack. By using technical attribution procedures, you can group multiple intrusions and identify hostile groups or global attacks. The attackers may use spoofed infrastructure or copy the fingerprints of other bad actors. This makes it hard to identify the actual identity of the attackers.

- The *operational attribution* method analyzes information including the timing, target, motive, and impact of the attack. Operational attribution can help you understand the intent and objectives of the attackers. It may be also possible to identify likely attack sponsors or beneficiaries. Since operational attribution often relies on assumptions, hypotheses, or circumstantial evidence, the information may not be conclusive or definitive.

- The *strategic attribution* approach uses intelligence sources of information, such as human signals, or geospatial intelligence, to attempt to corroborate and validate the findings of technical and operational attribution. This approach can often help confirm or disprove the identity of the attackers and their relationship with other actors or entities. However, since strategic attribution may include classified or sensitive information, it may not be possible to publicly disclose the findings.

Digital forensics and attack attribution are complementary disciplines that enable cybersecurity professionals to respond to and learn from cyberattacks. The analysts can collect, preserve, analyze, and report digital evidence, as well as attribute attacks to their perpetrators. It is important to keep in mind that digital forensics and attack attribution do have limitations. Your organization should avoid quickly making conclusions or false accusations.

Cyber Kill Chain

The *Cyber Kill Chain* model was developed by Lockheed Martin, a major US defense contractor, to provide a framework to identify and prevent cyber intrusions. The model breaks down the stages of a cyberattack, providing a systematic approach to network defense. The Cyber Kill Chain consists of seven stages, as shown in Figure 12.1.

These are the seven stages:

1. Reconnaissance is the first stage, when the attacker gathers information about the target. This includes identifying vulnerabilities, mapping the network architecture, and gathering information about employees.

2. The weaponization stage is when the attacker creates a malicious tool or malware to exploit the vulnerabilities identified in the reconnaissance stage.

3. In the delivery stage, the attacker delivers the weaponized bundle to the victim via various means such as application vulnerabilities, email attachments, websites, unpatched servers, or USB drives.

4. The attacker exploits a vulnerability to execute code on the victim's system.

5. Installation is next, when the attacker installs malware on the victim's system to gain control.

6. Command and control, also known as C2, is when the attacker establishes a command-and-control channel to remotely manipulate the victim's system.

7. The final stage is called actions on objectives and is when the attacker takes actions to achieve their goals, such as stealing data, data destruction, or encryption for ransom.

Your organization can implement the Cyber Kill Chain model as a framework to detect and prevent cyberattacks. By understanding each stage of the attack, defenders can implement appropriate countermeasures at each step to disrupt the attack chain.

FIGURE 12.1   Stages of the Cyber Kill Chain.

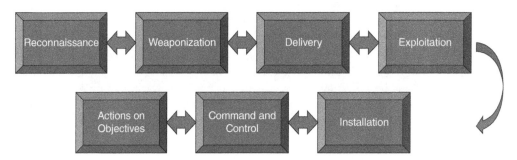

For example, during the reconnaissance stage, organizations can employ threat intelligence solutions to detect potential threats. In the weaponization and delivery stages, email filters and firewalls can be used to block malicious content. Regular patching and updating of systems can prevent exploitation of known vulnerabilities.

Understanding and applying the Cyber Kill Chain provides a framework for your organization to prevent cyberattacks. By breaking down an attack into stages, your organization can better defend against and respond to cyber threats.

MITRE ATT&CK Matrix

The *MITRE ATT&CK Matrix*, developed by Mitre Corporation, includes a global knowledge base of adversary tactics and techniques discovered with real-world observations. The ATT&CK knowledge base is used for the development of specific threat models and methodologies in the private sector, in government, and in the cybersecurity community.

The matrix is organized into tactics and techniques:

- Tactics are the *why*: the adversary's objective. There are categories that describe the adversary's intent, such as Initial Access, Execution, Persistence, Privilege Escalation, Defense Evasion, Credential Access, Discovery, Lateral Movement, Collection, Exfiltration, and Command and Control.

- Techniques are the *how* of an attack. These are the actions that adversaries use to achieve their objectives. Each technique comes with a detailed description, including how it works, how to detect it, and how to mitigate the attack.

The MITRE ATT&CK Matrix can be used to protect your organization from cyberattacks with improved threat intelligence, enhanced incident response, and stronger defenses, as well as to educate your staff. The matrix also provides a framework for testing your organization's defenses, called the *red team*, and improving detection and prevention capabilities, known as the *blue team*.

The ATT&CK Matrix is used for various purposes in cybersecurity:

- Threat intelligence helps to understand the behavior of threat actors and may help predict their next moves.

- Incident response identifies the techniques used in an attack and helps your organization in planning your response.

- The red team is the group authorized and organized to emulate a potential adversary's attack or exploitation capabilities against an enterprise's security defenses.

- The blue team is the group responsible for protecting the organization against simulated or real-world attacks. This is typically your organization's in-house security team, but it may also include outside teams to provide guidance or monitor processes during certain types of cybersecurity engagements.

For more detailed information on the MITRE ATT&CK Matrix, go to `https://attack.mitre.org/matrices/enterprise`.

The MITRE ATT&CK Matrix provides a common language to describe cyber adversary behavior. This improves threat intelligence sharing, enhances your detection and response capabilities, and strengthens your company's cybersecurity defenses.

Diamond Model

The *Diamond Model* is used for incident analysis and maps out the components of an intrusion. Threat intelligence shows the tactics, techniques, and procedures used by the adversaries, and strategic planning helps you to understand your organization's vulnerabilities.

The Diamond Model is a structured method for analyzing and understanding cyber intrusions and provides a graphical representation of the relationships between different elements of an intrusion.

The model consists of four core features, described here:

- Adversary is the individual or group that is responsible for the intrusion.
- Capability refers to the tools or methods used by the adversary to carry out the intrusion.
- Infrastructure includes the systems and networks used by the adversary to launch and manage the intrusion.
- The victim is the target of the intrusion.

These four components form the vertices of a diamond, as shown in in Figure 12.2.

The Diamond Model is a powerful tool for analyzing and understanding cyber intrusions. By providing a structured approach to intrusion analysis, it allows organizations to respond more effectively to cyber threats.

FIGURE 12.2   The Diamond Model.

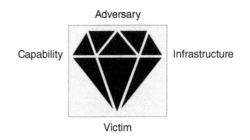

Tactics, Techniques, and Procedures

In cybersecurity, *tactics, techniques, and procedures* (TTPs) is the term used to describe the behavior and strategies of your adversaries. TTPs help you to understand how threat actors, the "who," conduct their operations, the *how*, to achieve their objectives, the *why*.

Tactics are high-level objectives or goals of an adversary. Tactics would include gaining initial access to a network or maintaining connections inside of it. Tactics answer the question of why an adversary is conducting an operation. Techniques are the methods used by adversaries to achieve their tactical objectives. Techniques answer the question of how an adversary intends to achieve their goals. Procedures are the granular details and steps that an adversary takes while executing a technique. Procedures provide a detailed answer to the how.

When you are able to determine your adversary's TTPs, you gain insights into the attack that includes Threat Intelligence, which helps organizations anticipate and prepare for potential attacks. Incident Response used during a security incident, understanding the TTPs used can aid in swift and effective response and remediation. The Security Strategy knowledge of potential TTPs helps you develop of effective security strategies and defenses.

TTPs offer a window into an adversary's intent, capabilities, and methods. By studying and understanding TTPs, organizations can enhance their ability to predict, prevent, detect, and respond to cyber threats.

Artifacts and Sources of Evidence

Artifacts, or sources of evidence, are digital traces left behind by activities on a system or network. This data can be used to understand the actions taken by an attacker during a cyber intrusion.

Artifacts can come from various sources including the following:

- Logging data that records events occurring in operating systems, applications, networking equipment or any other piece of IT hardware or software. This includes data such as IP addresses, API calls, system operations, timestamps, and user actions, to name a few different types.
- Network traffic, including data packets that are sent over a network, can be captured and analyzed to reveal information about the source, destination, and content of the communication.
- In Windows systems, the registry contains settings and options for the operating system. Changes to the registry can provide clues about an attacker's actions.
- File Systems stores and organizes a computer's files and directories. It can contain artifacts such as modified files, created/deleted files, metadata, and timestamps.
- Memory holds stored data stored that can be analyzed to uncover evidence that may not be found on disk. This includes data about running processes, network connections, and loaded modules.

Artifacts are important to cybersecurity, including operations such as incident response that help identify the nature of an incident, understand how it occurred, and determine its impact. Forensic analysis uses artifacts to reconstruct events and find evidence. Threat hunting is the proactive searching for artifacts that can help identify threats before they cause damage.

Understanding and analyzing artifacts is important to your cybersecurity operations. By studying these sources of evidence, organizations gain insights into potential threats and enhance their security measures.

Evidence Handling

Cybersecurity evidence handling is a very important component of incident response and forensics. Evidence handling is the identification, collection, preservation, analysis, and presentation of digital artifacts related to a cybersecurity incident.

Proper evidence handling helps to ensure that the digital artifacts maintain their integrity and are admissible in a court of law if necessary. It also helps in the accurate reconstruction of cybersecurity incidents, helping organizations understand how the incident occurred and how similar incidents can be prevented in the future.

The key steps in evidence handling include the following:

1. Identification, which involves recognizing potential sources of evidence and understanding their relevance to the incident.

2. Collection involves gathering digital artifacts using appropriate tools and methods to ensure data integrity.

3. Preservation preserves evidence in its original state to prevent data corruption or loss. This usually involves creating copies or images of the data.

4. The Analysis step involves examining the collected evidence to draw conclusions about the incident. It often requires specialized tools and expertise.

5. The final stage, Presentation, is when the results of the analysis are compiled into a format suitable for reporting or legal proceedings.

Cybersecurity evidence handling is a process that requires a high level of expertise and precision. When done correctly, it can provide valuable insights into cybersecurity incidents and form the basis for legal proceedings and policy development.

Preserving Digital Evidence

The preservation of digital evidence is critical to both cybersecurity and legal proceedings. Digital evidence is the information stored or transmitted in binary form that may be relied on in court. Digital evidence can be collected from many sources, including computers, virtual machines, cell phones, network equipment, and applications such as emails, DNS, databases, stored documents, photos, and any other source of information.

Preserving digital evidence is the practice of protecting it from accidental or intentional alteration or destruction. The process begins from the moment an incident is identified. The evidence must be carefully collected and stored in a way that maintains its original state.

Whether you are a cybersecurity professional, law enforcement officer, legal professional, or part of other interested groups, an in-depth understanding of how to handle and preserve digital evidence effectively is important to understand.

Chain of Custody

The *chain of custody* processes ensures the integrity and admissibility of digital evidence in legal proceedings.

Chain of custody in cybersecurity is the process of maintaining and documenting the handling of digital evidence from the moment it is collected until it is presented in a court of law. It ensures that the evidence remains in its original state and is admissible in court.

A well-maintained chain of custody is crucial to ensure the integrity of the digital evidence, proving that it has not been tampered with. It establishes the authenticity of the evidence, linking it to the incident, and maintains the continuity of the evidence, showing who had access to it and when.

The steps to be aware of when maintaining a chain of custody include the collection of digital evidence, which should be collected by trained professionals using forensically sound methods to avoid altering the data; and maintaining the documentation of every action taken with the evidence, including who collected it, when and where it was collected, and any actions taken with it. The preservation of the evidence, data should be stored in a secure manner to prevent unauthorized access or accidental alteration. Transportation of the evidence must be done in a secure manner, with documentation of who transported it where and when. Finally, when presenting digital evidence in court, the chain of custody proves that the evidence is reliable and relevant to the case.

Maintaining a proper chain of custody is a critical aspect of cybersecurity incident response and digital forensics. It ensures that digital evidence can be relied on in investigations and legal proceedings.

Summary

In this chapter, you learned about digital forensics and how to collect and handle evidence from a cyberattack.

We started by introducing what digital forensics is and defined it as the process used to determine the motives, methods used, and impact of cyber threats and security. It is also used to prevent future attacks and prosecute cybercriminals.

We then explained the NIST incident response model, which consists of four steps used in a forensic investigation, including the collection, preservation, analysis, and reporting of findings.

Cyberattack attribution is the process of determining who is behind a cyberattack. Attribution is when investigators analyze technical clues, contextual information, and intelligence sources to identify the responsible party. The three primary approaches of attack attribution include technical, operational, and strategic attribution.

There are multiple models available to analyze a cyberattack, including the Cyber Kill Chain, which provides a framework used to identify and prevent cyber intrusions. The model breaks down the stages of a cyberattack, providing a systematic approach to network defense.

The Mitre ATT&CK Matrix includes a global knowledge base of adversary tactics and techniques discovered with real-world observations.

The Diamond Model is a structured method for analyzing and understanding cyber intrusions and provides a graphical representation of the relationships between different elements of an intrusion. The model consists of four core features: the adversary, capabilities, infrastructure, and victim.

Next you learned about tactics, techniques, and procedures, which are the behavior and strategies of your adversaries. TTPs help you to understand how threat actors, the *who*, conduct their operations, the how, to achieve their objectives, the why.

We then discussed artifacts, or sources of evidence, which are digital traces left behind by activities on a system or network. This data can be used to understand the actions taken by an attacker during a cyber intrusion.

Next you learned about evidence handling, which is the identification, collection, preservation, analysis, and presentation of digital artifacts related to a cybersecurity incident. Proper evidence handling helps to ensure that the digital artifacts maintain their integrity and are admissible in a court of law if necessary. It also helps in the accurate reconstruction of cybersecurity incidents, helping organizations understand how the incident occurred and how similar incidents can be prevented in the future.

Preserving digital evidence is the practice of protecting it from accidental or intentional alteration or destruction. The process begins from the moment an incident is identified. The evidence must be carefully collected and stored in a way that maintains its original state.

Finally, we covered the chain of custody in cybersecurity and defined it as the process of maintaining and documenting the handling of digital evidence from the moment it is collected until it is presented in a court of law. A well-maintained chain of custody is crucial to ensure the integrity of the digital evidence, proving that it has not been tampered with. It establishes the authenticity of the evidence, linking it to the incident, and maintains the continuity of the evidence, showing who had access to it and when.

Exam Essentials

Know what digital forensics is.   Digital forensics is the process used to determine the motives, methods used, and impact of cyber threats and cybersecurity. It is also used to prevent future attacks and prosecute cybercriminals.

Understand what a digital forensic response is.   The digital forensic response model was developed by the National Institute of Standards and Technology in the United States and is a model consisting of four steps use in forensic investigations. It is composed of collection, preservation, analysis, and reporting of findings.

Know what attack attribution is.   Attribution is where investigators analyze technical clues, contextual information, and intelligence sources to identify the responsible party. The three primary approaches of attack attribution include technical, operational, and strategic attribution.

Be able to identify attack models.   Know what the Cyber Kill Chain, Mitre ATT&CK, and Diamond Model are and what their characteristics are.

Remember the components of tactics, techniques, and procedures.   TTP is the term used to describe the behavior and strategies of your adversaries. TTPs help you to understand how threat actors, the "who," conduct their operations, the *how*, to achieve their objectives, the why.

Understand artifacts and evidence sources.   These are digital traces left behind by activities on a system or network. This data can be used to understand the actions taken by an attacker during a cyber intrusion.

Be able to answer questions about evidence handling, preservation, and custody.   Evidence handling is the identification, collection, preservation, analysis, and presentation of digital artifacts related to a cybersecurity incident. Preserving digital evidence is the practice of protecting it from accidental or intentional alteration or destruction. Chain of custody in cybersecurity is the process of maintaining and documenting the handling of digital evidence from the moment it is collected until it is presented in a court of law.

Review Questions

You can find the answers to these questions in Appendix.

1. You are a digital forensics investigator working for a private company. You have been asked to investigate a case of data theft. An employee has been accused of stealing confidential company data and selling it to a competitor. What is the first step in your investigation?

    A. Obtain a search warrant and seize the employee's computer.

    B. Interview the employee and ask them to provide you with any information they may have about the data theft.

    C. Contact the competitor and ask them if they have received any confidential company data.

    D. Contact the company's IT department and ask them to provide you with a list of employees who have access to the confidential data.

    E. None of the above.

2. You are a cybersecurity analyst working for a financial institution. You have been notified of a data breach that has occurred on one of the institution's servers. You have been tasked with investigating the breach. What is the first step in your investigation?

    A. Contact the affected customers and inform them of the breach.

    B. Collect data from the affected server and preserve the evidence.

    C. Analyze the data for any signs of criminal activity.

    D. Compile a report that explains what happened during the breach.

    E. None of the above.

3. You are a cybersecurity analyst working for a health care organization. You have been notified of a data breach that has occurred on one of the organization's servers. You have been tasked with investigating the breach. What is the final step in your investigation?

    A. Contact the affected customers and inform them of the breach.

    B. Collect data from the affected server and preserve the evidence.

    C. Analyze the data for any signs of criminal activity.

    D. Compile a report that explains what happened during the breach.

    E. None of the above.

4. Your cybersecurity team is performing attack attribution research. What part of this process covers intelligence sources such as human signals and geospatial intelligence?

    A. Technical

    B. Operational

    C. Strategic

D. Tactical

E. All of the above

5. You are a cybersecurity analyst working for a financial institution. You have been notified of a cyberattack that has occurred on one of the institution's servers. You have been tasked with investigating the attack. What is the first stage of the Cyber Kill Chain model?

A. Collection

B. Preservation

C. Analysis

D. Reporting

E. None of the above

6. You are a cybersecurity analyst working for a government agency. You have been tasked with developing a threat model for your organization. What is the purpose of the Mitre ATT&CK knowledge base?

A. To provide a framework used to identify and prevent cyber intrusions

B. To provide a systematic approach to network defense

C. To provide a taxonomy of adversarial actions across their life cycle

D. To provide a list of common tactics, techniques, and procedures (TTPs) that advanced persistent threats use against Windows enterprise networks

E. None of the above

7. You have been tasked with developing a threat model for your organization. What is the purpose of the Diamond Model?

A. To provide a framework used to identify and prevent cyber intrusions

B. To provide a systematic approach to network defense

C. To provide a taxonomy of adversarial actions across their life cycle

D. To provide a list of common tactics, techniques, and procedures (TTPs) that advanced persistent threats use against Windows enterprise networks

E. None of the above

8. You are a cybersecurity analyst working for a private company. You have been tasked with developing a methodology for incident response. How can TTPs be used to support your work?

A. To provide a list of common tactics, techniques, and procedures (TTPs) that advanced persistent threats use against Windows enterprise networks

B. To provide a taxonomy of adversarial actions across their life cycle

C. To provide a framework used to identify and prevent cyber intrusions

D. To describe the behavior and strategies of your adversaries

E. None of the above

9. What are artifacts in cybersecurity?
   A. Digital traces left behind by activities on a system or network
   B. A list of common tactics, techniques, and procedures (TTPs) that advanced persistent threats use against Windows enterprise networks
   C. A listing of adversarial actions across their life cycle
   D. A framework used to identify and prevent cyber intrusions

10. What is the process of chain of custody in cybersecurity?
    A. The process of maintaining and documenting the handling of digital evidence from the moment it is collected until it is presented in a court of law
    B. A list of common tactics, techniques, and procedures (TTPs) that advanced persistent threats use against Windows enterprise networks
    C. A list of adversarial actions across their life cycle
    D. A framework used to identify and prevent cyber intrusions

Chapter

13

Incident Response

THE FOLLOWING CCST EXAM TOPIC IS COVERED IN THIS CHAPTER:

✔ **5.0 Incident Handling**

    ■ 5.4. Describe the elements of cybersecurity incident response.

        Policy, plan, and procedure elements; incident response lifecycle stages (NIST Special Publication 800-61 sections 2.3, 3.1–3.4)

Incident Handling

When there is a breach or cyberattack, your organization must be prepared to act quickly and take the correct steps to resolve the issue. Incident response is the process to effectively handle any security incident or situation. The incident response outlines the steps your organization takes to prepare, detect, contain, and recover from a cyberattack or data breach.

A well-planned incident response plan or, as it is sometime called, a cybersecurity incident response, should detail how to quickly identify the attack and what steps to take to minimize the impact, contain the blast radius, and finally to remediate the cause to reduce exposure to future incidents.

Incident handling refers to an organization's processes, procedures, tools, and technologies for detecting and responding to threats, breaches, or cyberattacks.

The incident response plan is a document internal to your organization that is used to detail your organization's processes, steps, and responsibilities in its incident response plans.

The primary goal of the incident response plan is to prevent cyberattacks before they happen and to minimize the cost and disruption resulting from any attacks that do occur.

A well-organized IT operation will have a prepared and well-defined incident response plan that details the processes and technologies available and exactly how different types of cyberattacks should be identified, contained, and resolved.

A properly designed incident response plan assists cybersecurity teams in determining what is occurring, containing the cyber threats, and finally quickly restoring affected systems. The incident response plan will decrease response times, limit the impact on your organization, and reduce the lost revenue, regulatory fines, and other costs associated with a security incident.

The National Institute for Standards and Technology Computer Security Resource Center is at `https://csrc.nist.gov/topics/laws-and-regulations/laws/fisma`.

What Are Security Incidents?

A security incident, or security event, is any digital or physical breach that threatens the confidentiality, integrity, or availability of an organization's information systems or sensitive data. Security incidents can range from intentional cyberattacks by hackers or unauthorized users to unintentional violations of security policy by legitimate authorized users.

Before we deep dive into how deal with an incident response, let's review some of the most common security incidents.

Ransomware

Ransomware locks or encrypts the victim's data or computing device and threatens to keep or destroy the data unless the victim pays the attacker a ransom.

Social Engineering

Social engineering is a class of attack that hacks human nature, rather than digital security vulnerabilities, to gain unauthorized access to your data and assets. Social engineering is the most common type of attack and the costliest. The cyber bad guy uses human nature to get around all the hard work of doing reconnaissance, penetrating your network, sneaking through misconfigured firewalls, navigating though cybersecurity controls, and many other roadblocks to steal your data.

The social engineering attack manipulates people to get them to share information that they should keep confidential, such as passwords and other authentication methods. It also includes having them install software that they should not install, visiting malicious websites, sending money to the bad guys, and many other mistakes based on human nature. We also call this human hacking because it uses psychological manipulation and exploits human weakness rather than technological vulnerabilities.

Some examples of social engineering include a threatening voicemail claiming to be from the IRS and a call informing you that you were last night's Powerball Lottery winner. Your personal data, financial information, login credentials, credit card numbers, bank account numbers, and Social Security numbers are then used for identity theft, enabling the hackers to make purchases with your stolen information.

Phishing

Phishing attacks are digital or voice messages that attempt to manipulate recipients into sharing sensitive information, downloading malicious software, or transferring money or assets to their accounts. Scammers are very good at craft phishing messages to look identical to the real information of a trusted or credible organization or individual.

DDoS Attacks

The distributed denial-of-service or, as it is commonly called, DDoS attack is used by hackers to gain remote control of large numbers of computers and use them to flood and overwhelm a target organization's network and servers with traffic, making those resources unavailable to legitimate users.

Supply Chain Attacks

Supply chain attacks infiltrate the target organization by first attacking its partners, vendors, and contractors and stealing sensitive data from a supplier's systems, using a vendor's services to distribute malware, or accessing your network over remote connections such as VPNs.

Insider Threats

Malicious insiders are employees, partners, or other authorized users who intentionally compromise an organization's information security.

Negligent insiders are legitimate users who, without malice, unintentionally compromise your company's security by failing to follow your organization's security practices: for example, storing sensitive data in insecure places or posting their password on the side of their monitor with a sticky note.

Incident Response Planning

Your organization's incident response efforts are defined in your internal incident response plan. In this section, we will take a close look at preparing and planning for a cyberattack. By having a plan in place, your organization will be better prepared to react.

Incident response plans are created and executed by what is commonly called the computer security incident response team; of course there is an acronym for this: CSIRT. The team usually consists of corporate stakeholders from across the organization. This would include the chief information security officer (CISO), members from the security operations center (SOC), and IT staff, including the server, application, and networking teams. Representation from executive leadership, legal, human resources, regulatory compliance, and risk management would also be part of the CSIRT.

Incident Response Plans

Each member of the CSIRT team should have their roles and responsibilities well defined.

Identify your organization's security solutions. These include software, hardware, and other technologies installed across your operations.

FIGURE 13.1   Incident response life cycle.

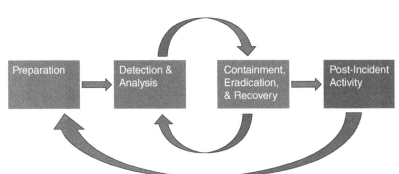

Include your business continuity plan, which outlines the procedures for restoring critical affected systems and data as quickly possible in the event of an outage.

The incident response methodology lays out the specific steps to be taken at each phase of the incident response process in detail, and which members are responsible for each step. A communications plan for informing company leaders, employees, customers, and even law enforcement and the media about the incident should be included. Detailed instructions on how to document, collect information, maintain a chain of custody, and collect data for the post-mortem review and, if required, any legal proceedings should also be included.

It's not uncommon to draft different CSIRT incident response plans for different scenarios. Many organizations, for example, have specific incident response plans pertaining to DDoS attacks, malware, ransomware, phishing, and insider threats.

Larger enterprises may partner with external professional services firms that specialize in responding to cyberattacks. This is important if there is a concern that the attack was an inside job and those individuals are on the response team. Retainer agreements are arranged for the partners to assist with various aspects of the incident management life cycle shown in Figure 13.1 as required by the organization.

In addition to detailing the steps CSIRTs should take in the event of a security incident, your incident response plans should outline the security solutions that you may need to have in place to carry out or automate key incident response workflows, such as gathering and correlating security data, how to detect incidents as they are occurring, and how to respond to in-progress attacks.

Incident Response Frameworks

Most incident response plans follow very similar frameworks based on incident response models developed by the SANS Institute, the National Institute of Standards and Technology (NIST), and the Cybersecurity and Infrastructure Agency (CISA). These are excellent reference documents to leverage when creating your incident response plans to make sure you are not missing any critical steps and to help you create an effective logic flow.

Cisco recommends using the NIST Special Publication 800-61 Computer Security Incident handling guide that documents the planning for an effective Incident handling process.

National Institute of Standards and Technology (NIST): `https://www.hhs.gov/sites/default/files/cybersecurity-incident-response-plans.pdf`

UC Berkeley Security Incident Response Plan Template: `https://security.berkeley.edu/incident-response-planning-guideline`

California Department of Technology's Incident Response plan example: `https://cdt.ca.gov/wp-content/uploads/2017/03/templates_incident_response_plan.doc`

Carnegie Melon's Computer Security Incident Response Plan: `https://www.cmu.edu/iso/governance/procedures/incidentresponseplanv1.6.pdf`

Michigan Incident Response Plan Template: `https://www.michigan.gov/msp/-/media/Project/Websites/msp/cjic/pdfs6/Sample_Incident_Response_Plan_IR_Policy.docx`

NIST states in its abstract that incident response planning is an important component of your organization's information technology operations.

Executing an incident response effectively is a complex undertaking; establishing a successful incident response capability requires substantial planning and resources. The NIST 800-61 publication assists organizations in establishing computer security incident response capabilities and handling incidents efficiently and effectively. The document provides guidelines for incident handling, particularly for analyzing incident-related data and determining the appropriate response to each incident. The guidelines can be followed independently of hardware platforms, operating systems, protocols, and applications.

Incident Preparation

This first phase of incident response is proper preparation; this will be a continuous undertaking that your organization should constantly review and update to make sure it is current with your ongoing IT operations. Your organization must ensure that the CSIRT is always up to date with the most current procedures and tools in place for your team to respond to identify, contain, and recover from an incident as quickly as possible to minimize business disruption.

Risk Assessments

By following ongoing risk assessments, the CSIRT document will identify vulnerabilities and the various types of security incidents that pose a risk to your organization and prioritize each type by its potential impact. Based on this risk assessment, the CSIRT may need to be updated or new incident response plans drafted.

Detection and Analysis

The detection and analysis phase is when the security and operations teams monitor the network for suspicious activity and potential threats.

Modern tools such as artificial intelligence, in particular machine learning, and analytics are used to analyze the data, notifications, and alerts gathered from device logs and from various security tools such as antivirus software firewalls and intrusion detection/prevention systems installed in the network. The tools will filter false positives and prioritize the actual alerts in order of severity.

Having a communication plan in place is helpful once the breach has been detected and analyzed. After the CSIRT has been used to identify what kind of threat or breach occurred, you can notify the appropriate personnel before moving to the next stage of the incident response process.

Containment

Containment planning helps the incident response team define the steps to prevent the breach from doing further damage to the network. Containment activities can be split into two categories:

- The *short-term containment* measures' primary concern is to prevent the threat from spreading by isolating the affected systems, such as by taking infected devices offline.

- *Long-term containment measures* should focus on protecting unaffected systems by placing stronger security measures. For example, this may include segmenting sensitive applications or databases from the rest of the network.

At this stage, the CSIRT should define the process to preserve the data by creating backups of the affected and unaffected systems to prevent additional data loss, and to capture forensic evidence of the incident for future study.

Eradication

After you have contained the threat, your focus should move to the remediation steps to completely remove the threat from the infected systems. This involves actively eradicating the threat itself, such as removing a virus or disabling a user's account, and reviewing both affected and unaffected systems to ensure that no traces of the breach are left behind.

Recovery

After your incident response team is confident that the threat has been entirely eradicated, you may need to restore affected systems back to normal operations. This includes deploying patches and hotfixes, rebuilding systems from backups, and bringing remediated systems and devices back online.

Post-incident Review

During each phase of the incident response process, the CSIRT collects evidence of the breach and documents the steps it takes to contain and eradicate the threat. Your incident response team should review the information in the CSIRT to better understand the incident and the steps taken to mitigate the breach.

   You should use the CSIRT to determine the root cause of the incident, to identify how successful the attack was in breaching the network and the attack vectors used, and to resolve your vulnerabilities so that future incidents of this type don't occur.

   The CSIRT can be used to identify what steps went well and areas that need review and improvement. This could include tools and processes that can be used to strengthen your incident response plan against future attacks. Depending on the circumstances of the breach, law enforcement may also be involved in the post-incident investigation.

Lessons Learned

After the incident has subsided, it is always a good idea to go back and review how effective your planning was. You can review the details of the incident and its severity. Review how effective your remediation methods and procedures were. Are there any steps that can be improved? Did the process flow evenly, or were there gaps in your incident planning? Did the remediation methods meet the needs of your organization?

   Have everyone in the incident response team identify areas that can be improved on, and use the feedback to update your incident response plans.

   The lessons learned report should include the details of the incident, its severity and impact on your organization, the remediation methods implemented, and how effective your response was. Finally, it should provide recommendations for improvements in the future.

The incident response plan's value doesn't end when a cybersecurity event is over; it will continue to provide supporting data for successful litigation, documentation to show auditors, and lessons learned to add to your risk assessment process and improve your organization's incident response.

Creating an Incident Response Policy

Incident response documents are customized to the specific requirements of each organization. However, they tend to follow a similar list of key elements. It is desirable to use the NIST framework and a template when creating your internal incident response plans. Refer to sections 2.3 Incident Response Policy, Plan, and Procedure Creation and 2.3.2 Plan Elements of the NIST 800-61 document.

The key elements of an incident response policy are as follows:

- A brief statement from management committing to the incident response documents.

- Purpose and objectives of the policy.

- The policy scope, which includes to whom and what it applies and under what circumstances.

- Definition of key terms, including defining computer security incidents and related terms.

- Your organization's structure and definition of roles, responsibilities, and levels of authority. This should include the authority of the incident response team to confiscate or disconnect equipment and to monitor suspicious activity.

- The reporting requirements for the different types of events. These include guidelines for external communications and information sharing that define what can be shared with whom, when, and over what channels, and the handoff and escalation points in the incident management process.

- The prioritization or severity ratings of incidents.

- Detailed reporting and contact documentation.

The incident response plan needs to be a focused and coordinated approach that your organization takes when responding to incidents. The incident response plan is your flow when implementing incident responses. Every company will have different, and often unique, requirements, and the plan should take this into account.

The incident response plan should include the following elements:

- A mission statement

- Strategies and goals

- Senior management approval

- Organizational approach to incident response

- How the incident response team will communicate with the rest of the organization and with other organizations

- Metrics for measuring the incident response capability and its effectiveness

- Road map for maturing the incident response capability
- How the program fits into the overall organization

The definitions in the document will include any standard operating procedures (SOPs) that your organization has implemented and that apply to the incident and document any applicable processes, techniques, checklists, and forms used by the incident response team. SOPs should be reasonably comprehensive and detailed to ensure that the priorities of the organization are implemented into the response operations.

Document How You Plan to Share Information with Outside Parties

Your organization needs to be prepared to contact outside entities such as law enforcement, your hardware and software vendors, regulatory agencies, the media, business partners, and others.

You need to have plans in place for how you want to communicate with your organization's public relations staff, your legal department, and corporate management ahead of time and follow that plan closely to minimize risk to your organization.

You must document all contacts and communications that have been made with all organizations for legal protection. When communicating with the media, it is important to have a designated internal person, with a good backup, who acts as a single point of contact.

A current document showing the status of the incident that is accessible to all incident response members will provide everyone, including the media team, with consistent and up-to-date information. Figure 13.2 shows a basic workflow of the different outside agencies that you may need to contact.

FIGURE 13.2   Contacting outside entities.

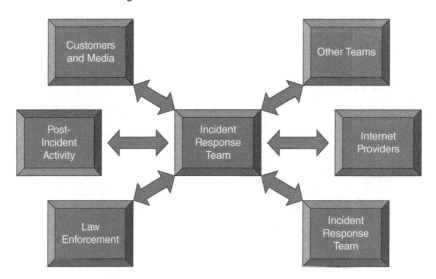

Interfacing with Law Enforcement

To effectively prosecute security breaches, it is critical that you know how and when to work with law enforcement. As part of your incident response planning, list the agencies you may need to work with and how to contact them. You may need to contact global, federal, state, local, or any other country-specific organizations.

Incident Reporting Organizations

Your planning documents should include any governmental reporting requirements including in the United States Federal Information Security Management Act (FISMA), which requires federal agencies to report incidents to the United States Computer Emergency Readiness Team or US-CERT. US-CERT can act focal point for dealing with incidents.

 In the United States, the Cybersecurity and Infrastructure Security Agency posts the notification guidelines at `https://www.cisa.gov/federal-incident-notification-guidelines`.

Other outside parties to consider the need to contact may include Internet service providers and carriers, the owner of the IP address blocks that originated the attack, and your hardware and software vendors. Also, you may work with other incident response organizations that would need contacting during a breach. Consider that if there are other affected organizations, you need to know how to contact them.

Handling an Incident

Executing the incident response process has several phases. The initial phase involves preparation that requires your organization to establish and prepare an incident response team. To accomplish this, you must acquire all the needed tools and resources. Your organization attempts to limit the number of incidents that will occur by selecting and implementing a set of processes based on the findings in the risk assessments.

There will always be some residual risk even after all your preventative measures and controls have been deployed. You must deploy detection methods to alert your organization when a breach occurs.

Preparation

You response to an incident relies on your preparation, which includes preparing your capabilities, system hardening, monitoring tools, and other identified preparation steps.

In this section, we will review the basics of how to handle and prevent incidents.

The Computer Security Incident Handling Guide provides a list of tools to collect when preparing for an incident, including the following:

- Contact information for team members and others within and outside the organization

- On-call information for other teams within the organization, including escalation information

- Incident reporting mechanisms, such as phone numbers, email addresses, online forms, and secure instant messaging systems

- Issue tracking system for tracking incident information, status, etc.

- Smartphones to be carried by team members for off-hour support and onsite communications

- Encryption software to be used for communications among team members, within the organization and with external parties

- A war room for central communication and coordination

- Secure storage facility for securing evidence and other sensitive materials

From FIPS 140-2, create a forensic workstation or laptop that is designed to assist incident handlers in acquiring and analyzing data including the following:

- Laptops and backup devices are used to create disk images, preserve log files, and save other incident data

- Laptops for activities such as analyzing data, sniffing packets, and writing reports

- Spare workstations, servers, and networking equipment, or the virtualized equivalents, which may be used for many purposes, such as restoring backups and trying out malware

- Blank removable media

- Portable printer to print copies of log files and other evidence from non-networked systems

- Packet sniffers and protocol analyzers to capture and analyze network traffic

- Digital forensic software to analyze disk images

- Removable media with trusted versions of programs to be used to gather evidence from systems

- Evidence gathering accessories, including hard-bound notebooks, digital cameras, audio recorders, chain of custody forms, evidence storage bags and tags, and evidence tape, to preserve evidence for possible legal actions

- Port lists, including commonly used ports and Trojan horse ports

- Documentation for operating systems, applications, protocols, and intrusion detection and antivirus products

- Network diagrams and lists of critical assets, such as database servers

- Current baselines of expected network, system, and application activity

- Crypto hashes of critical files to speed incident analysis, verification, and eradication

- Copies of images of clean operating system and application installations for restoration and recovery purposes

 A good reference is the Guide to Test, Training, and Exercise Programs for IT Plans and Capabilities, which can be found at `http://csrc.nist.gov/publications/PubsSPs.html#800-84`.

Many incident response teams create a jump kit, which is a portable case that contains materials that may be needed during an investigation. The jump kit should always be ready to go. Jump kits contain many of the same items listed in the previous bulleted lists. For example, each jump kit typically includes a laptop loaded with appropriate software (e.g., packet sniffers, digital forensics). Other important materials include backup devices, blank media, and basic networking equipment and cables. Because the purpose of having a jump kit is to facilitate faster responses, the team should avoid borrowing items from the jump kit.

Each incident handler should have access to at least two computing devices (e.g., laptops). One, such as the one from the jump kit, should be used to perform packet sniffing, malware analysis, and all other actions that risk contaminating the laptop that performs them. This laptop should be scrubbed and all software reinstalled before it is used for another incident. Note that because this laptop is special purpose, it is likely to use software other than the standard enterprise tools and configurations, and whenever possible the incident handlers should be allowed to specify basic technical requirements for these special-purpose investigative laptops. In addition to an investigative laptop, each incident handler should also have a standard laptop, smart phone, or other computing device for writing reports, reading email, and performing other duties unrelated to the hands-on incident analysis.

Exercises involving simulated incidents can also be very useful for preparing for incident handling; see NIST SP 800-84 for more information.

Preventing Incidents

Keeping the number of incidents reasonably low is very important to protect the business processes of the organization. If security controls are insufficient, higher volumes of incidents may occur, overwhelming the incident response team. This can lead to slow and incomplete responses, which translate to a larger negative business impact (e.g., more extensive damage, longer periods of service and data unavailability).

It is outside the scope of this chapter to provide specific advice on securing networks, systems, and applications. Although incident response teams are generally not responsible for securing resources, they can be advocates of sound security practices. An incident response team may be able to identify problems that the organization is otherwise not aware of; the team can play a key role in risk assessment and training by identifying gaps.

The following are recommended practices for securing networks, systems, and applications:

▪ Perform risk assessments of systems and applications to identify the risks posed by combinations of threats and vulnerabilities.

▪ Each risk should be prioritized, and the risks can be mitigated, transferred, or accepted until a reasonable overall level of risk is reached.

▪ All servers must be hardened using recommended configurations. The hosts should be configured to follow the principle of least privilege, have auditing enabled, and should log significant security-related events.

▪ The network perimeter should be configured to block all traffic that is not expressly permitted.

▪ Malware detection software should be deployed throughout the organization. Malware protection should be deployed at the host level, the application server, web proxies, and the application client level.

▪ Users should be made aware of policies and procedures regarding appropriate use of networks, systems, and applications. Applicable lessons learned from previous incidents should also be shared with users so they can see how their actions could affect the organization.

Detection and Analysis

In this section, you will learn about the process of detecting the different attack vectors, what the signs of an attack might look like, and what precursors and sources are.

Attack Vectors

There are so many different attack vectors that it is almost impossible to prepare plans to detect and respond to each individual attack scenario. The common approach to this issue is to prepare for the more common types of attacks.

Here are some of the more common types of attacks that can be used as a reference when creating your own planning documents:

Attrition.   Uses brute force to gain access, degrade, or destroy systems, networks, or services. Examples of attrition-based attacks include DDoS, which will degrade or deny access to a service or application; and a brute-force attack against an authentication mechanism, such as passwords, CAPTCHAS, or digital signatures.

Email.   Email messages and attachments that exploit code disguised as an attached document or a link to a malicious website contained in the email message.

External and removable media.   This type of attack is executed from removable media or a peripheral device that can inject malicious code into a system from an infected USB or external HDD storage drive.

Impersonation.   An attack that replaces existing code or communications with malicious attacks. Spoofing, man-in-the-middle, rogue wireless access points, and SQL injection attacks are examples of impersonation attacks.

Improper usage.   This type of attack originates from a violation of an organization's acceptable usage policies by an authorized user: for example, a user installs file sharing software, leading to the loss of sensitive data; or a user performs illegal activities on a system.

Loss and theft.   The loss or theft of a computing device or media used by the organization, such as a laptop, smartphone, or multifactor authentication token.

Web.   An attack executed from a website or web-based application such as cross-site scripting that is used to steal credentials or a redirect to a site that exploits a browser vulnerability and installs malware.

Signs of an Incident

Accurately determining whether an incident has occurred and the type, extent, and magnitude of the problem is a real challenge. This is due to the following factors:

- There are many ways that an incident may be identified. This leads to a situation where the details may vary in specificity and accuracy. The ideal method to detect a breach is to deploy automated systems such as network-based and host-based intrusion detection and prevention systems, antivirus software, and log analyzers.

- Incidents may also be detected through user reports at the support desk. Some of these attacks can be obvious, whereas others may be very difficult to detect.

- The volume of incidents is elevated in your reporting systems, such as the intrusion detection sensor or the firewall logs. A steady stream of intrusion data is common in most networks; however, if it all of a sudden spikes to a much higher volume, it may be an indication of an attack that is underway. Your staff should have a deep understanding of their operations and be able to identify anomalies.

Signs of an incident include precursors and indicators. Precursors are data an incident might occur, and an indicator is a sign that the breach is currently underway or has occurred in the past:

- Examples of precursors are web server logs that show scanning activity, zero-day vulnerabilities that may be exploited, and bad actor threats to your organization that they are targeting you for an attack.

- Indicators are much more common than precursors and come in many forms. Some examples would include IDS sensor alerts, buffer overflows, antivirus alerts, application audit and reporting logs, a large number of failed login attempts, suspicious or bounced emails, and network traffic with a large deviation for the baseline flows.

Precursor and Indicator Sources

There are many different methods used to identify precursors and indicators, including security software, logs, publicly available information, and reports from users and administrators:

Alerts

- Intrusion detection and protection products (IDPSs)
- Security information and event management (SIEM) products
- Antivirus and antispam software
- File integrity checking software
- Third-party monitoring services

Logs

- Operating system, service, and application logs
- Network device logs

Containment, Eradication, and Recovery

The NIST Incident Handling Guide section 3.3 of the NIST 800-61 publication details containment, eradication, and recovery operations and techniques. In this section, you will learn the basics of these operations.

Choosing a Containment Strategy

To prevent a breach from quickly taking over your operations, it must be contained. Containment takes place at the beginning of the incident, as shown in Figure 13.3, to prevent further damage and give you time to develop and implement a remediation.

FIGURE 13.3 Containment, eradication, and recovery.

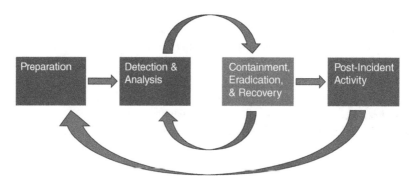

By containing the breach, you will have time to deploy your incident response strategy. Containment responses will depend on the type of attack and your specific architecture. You may decide to power off systems, isolate network segments, or disable services and applications.

Your containment decisions are determined by the type of incident. Email attacks are different than database breaches, for example, and the strategy for containing an email-borne malware infection is quite different from that of a network-based DDoS attack.

Your company needs to define containment strategies for each of these incident types, with clearly documented steps to take.

The following are issues to consider when developing your containment strategy:

- Damage or theft of resources

- Evidence preservation

- Operational availability such as network connections, services, servers, and storage systems

- Resources needed to implement the strategy.

- Effectiveness of your strategy, such as whether it will result in partial or full containment

- The duration of your solution: is it an emergency workaround for a few hours, a temporary workaround to be removed in two weeks, or a permanent solution?

If your company is aware that a system has been compromised and allows the compromise to continue while gathering data, the company can be liable if the attacker uses the compromised system to attack other systems. The delayed containment strategy is dangerous because an attacker could escalate unauthorized access or compromise other systems.

Another potential issue regarding containment is that some attacks may cause additional damage when they are contained. For example, a compromised host may run a malicious process that pings another host periodically. When the incident handler attempts to contain the incident by disconnecting the compromised host from the network, the subsequent pings will fail. As a result of the failure, the malicious process may overwrite or encrypt all the data on the host's hard drive. Handlers should not assume that just because a host has been disconnected from the network, further damage to the host has been prevented.

Evidence Gathering and Handling

Although the primary reason for gathering evidence during an incident is to resolve the incident, it may also be needed for legal proceedings. If this is the case, it is critical to clearly document how all evidence, including compromised systems, has been preserved. Evidence should be collected according to procedures that meet all applicable laws and regulations that have been developed from previous discussions with legal staff and law enforcement agencies so that any evidence can be admissible in court. In addition, evidence should be always accounted for; whenever evidence is transferred from person

FIGURE 13.4   Post-Incident Activity.

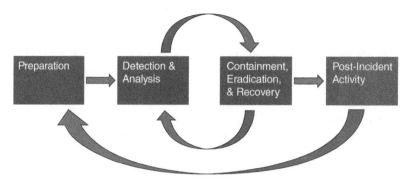

to person, chain of custody forms should detail the transfer and include each party's signature. Figure 13.4 shows the workflow for an incident response life cycle post-incident activity plan.

NIST SP 800-86, Guide to Integrating Forensic Techniques into Incident Response, provides detailed Information on establishing a forensic capability. It focuses on forensic techniques for PCs, but much of the material is applicable to other systems. The document can be found at `http://csrc.nist.gov/publications/PubsSPs.html#800-86`.

Searching and Seizing Computers and Obtaining Electronic Evidence in Criminal Investigations, from the Computer Crime and Intellectual Property Section (CCIPS) of the Department of Justice, provides legal guidance on evidence gathering. The document is available at `http://www.cybercrime.gov/ssmanual/index.html`.

A detailed log should be kept for all evidence, including the following:

- Identifying information such as location, serial number, model number, hostname, media access control (MAC) addresses, and IP addresses of a computer
- Name, title, and phone number of each individual who collected or handled the evidence during the investigation
- Time and date (including time zone) of each occurrence of evidence handling
- Locations where the evidence was stored

When you collect evidence from servers and other resources, you should do so as soon as possible. This is because there may be changes made post incident that will modify the state of the systems when the event occurred. Collect your snapshots early to better assist you in identifying the attack data.

Attack Sources

There is often a need to determine the source of the attack during an incident response. However, it is usually much more important to contain the attack and work to stop it, and then recover from it, than to identify the source.

If the attacker is sophisticated enough, they will cover their tracks, and it may be very difficult to trace the attack to its source.

Steps that you can take to identify the attacker are as follows:

- Identify the attacker's IP address. This can vary in its usefulness as the attacker can be sitting behind a jump box or intermediate systems. Also, dynamic IP addresses are often used that will go away after they are used for the attack.

- Researching the attacking host through internet search engines or tracking sites. This approach may turn up information on email lists that are reporting similar attacks.

- Searching incident tracking databases. Many security companies track, record, and publish data in real time that can be used to identify the source of your attacker.

- Monitoring attacker communications. Bots may use IRC as a communication channel. Attackers will use IRC channels to brag about their compromises and share information.

Eradication and Recovery

After an incident has been contained, eradication will be needed to eliminate remnants of the incident; this would include items such as removing malware and disabling compromised user accounts, and the identification of the vulnerabilities that were exploited followed by mitigation. During eradication, you must identify all affected hosts, devices, or services so that they can be remediated. There may be incidents where the eradication step may not be necessary or is performed during recovery.

Restoring systems to normal operation is performed as part of the recovery step. The recovery steps include confirmation that the systems are functioning normally and, if needed, to remediate vulnerabilities to prevent future incidents. Performing recovery operations involves restoring systems from clean backups, rebuilding systems, restoring backup files to replace compromised files, installing patches, changing passwords, and reviewing your network perimeter security to add additional protection such as modifying firewall rules or router access control lists. Increasing the levels of system logging or network monitoring can be included in the recovery process to collect more detailed event information.

If an attacker can gain access to your system, there is a good probability that there will be future attempts to breach your network. It is a good practice to use a phased approach to eradication and recovery with a review of which steps should take priority over less critical steps.

Post-Incident Activity

After the incident has concluded, it a best practice to review and learn from the events. This enables you to improve your response strategy. As we discussed earlier in the chapter, you should meet as a group and discuss any lessons that were learned and update your planning documents.

Multiple incidents can be covered in a single lessons-learned meeting. This meeting provides a chance to achieve closure with respect to an incident by reviewing what occurred, what was done to intervene, and how well the intervention worked. The meeting should be held within several days of the end of the incident. Questions to be answered in the meeting include

- Exactly what happened, and at what times?
- How well did staff and management perform in dealing with the incident? Were the documented procedures followed? Were they adequate?
- What information was needed sooner?
- Were any steps or actions taken that might have inhibited the recovery?
- What would the staff and management do differently the next time a similar incident occurs?
- How could information sharing with other organizations have been improved?
- What corrective actions can prevent similar incidents in the future?
- What precursors or indicators should be watched for in the future to detect similar incidents?
- What additional tools or resources are needed to detect, analyze, and mitigate future incidents?

Small incidents may only need a short post-incident analysis, except for incidents performed through new attack methods that are of widespread concern and interest. After serious attacks have occurred, it is important to hold post-mortem meetings that cross team and organizational boundaries to enable information sharing. It's important to invite people who have been involved in the incident that is being analyzed, but also to invite those who may be involved in future incidents.

Reports from the lessons-learned meetings are often good training material for new team members by showing them how more experienced team members respond to incidents.

Another important part of the lessons-learned process is seeing if the incident response policies and procedures need to be updated. The post-mortem analysis of the way an incident was handled can help identify missing steps or an inaccurate procedure.

Due to the changes in your IT environment and personnel, the incident response team should review all related documentation and procedures for handling incidents at designated intervals.

Finally, a good action to take is to create a report on each incident, for future reference. This report can be used to assist in handling similar incidents. By creating a formal chronology of events that includes timestamped information such as logging data, this data can be used for any possible legal actions that may be taken and used for calculating the financial impact of the damage the incident caused. This estimate may become the basis for subsequent prosecution activity.

> The General Records Schedule (GRS), *Information Technology Operations and Management Records*, specifies that "computer security incident handling, reporting and follow-up records" should be destroyed 3 years after all necessary follow-up actions have been completed. GRS 24 is available from the National Archives and Records Administration at `http://www.archives.gov/records-mgmt/grs/grs24.html`.

Using Collected Incident Data

The lessons-learned activities produce the data collected on each incident. Over time, the collected incident data may be needed to determine the total hours of involvement, and the cost to the organization might be used to justify additional funding of the incident response team. A review of the incident characteristics may help you identify security weaknesses and threats as well as changes in incident trends. This data can be used to update the risk assessment process, which will allow you to update your processes as needed. You can also use this data to see how effective your response team was and where there are areas for improvement.

Collecting incident-related data may include the number of incidents handled, time per incident, and an assessment for each incident.

To perform an objective assessment of an incident, follow these steps:

- Review logs, forms, reports, and other incident documentation for compliance to your incident response plan.
- Identify how indicators of the incident were recorded to determine how quickly and effectively the incident was logged and identified.
- Identify whether the incident caused damage before it was detected.
- Determine and document the root cause of the incident, the attack vector, and which, if any, vulnerabilities were exploited.

- Determine whether the incident had occurred previously.

- Estimate monetary damage from the incident.

- Measure the difference between the initial impact assessment and the final impact assessment.

- Identify steps that could have been taken, if any, and whether they could have reduced the impact or prevented the incident from occurring.

Evidence Retention

Your organization should have a policy that details how long evidence from an incident should be retained. It is common for an organization to retain all evidence for months or even years after the incident ends.

When creating a retention policy, it is helpful to take into consideration the future possibility of legal prosecution that would require you to present evidence of the incident. This evidence will need to be retained until all legal actions have been completed. This may take several years. Keep in mind that evidence that seems insignificant today may become more important in the future.

Companies should have data retention policies in place that state how long certain types of data may be kept. For example, an organization may state that email messages should be retained for only 180 days. GRS 24 specifies that incident handling records should be kept for 3 years. You may decide to have different policies for email, chat, databases, and other types of data.

Summary

In this chapter, you learned about the different types of security incidents, how to respond to a breach, and the planning process to prepare for an incident.

We began with the basic question of what security incidents are and then reviewed the more common types such as ransomware, social engineering, phishing, denial of service, supply chain attacks, and insider threats.

Finally, we covered how to learn from the incident and plan for future incidents.

Exam Essentials

Identify the incident planning process.   Know where to get frameworks to use as templates when creating your own incident response plan.

Know what security incidents are.   Be able to identify some of the more common types such as DDoS, social engineering, ransomware, social engineering, supply chain, and insider threats.

Know the steps contained in the incident planning process. The incident response methodology lays out the specific steps to be taken at each phase of the incident response process in detail and which members are responsible for each step.

Remember the different types of frameworks. Most incident response plans follow very similar frameworks based on incident response models developed by the SANS Institute, the National Institute of Standards and Technology (NIST), and the Cybersecurity and Infrastructure Agency (CISA).

Understand the different types of attack vectors. There are so many different attack vectors that it is almost impossible to prepare plans to detect and respond to each individual attack scenario. The common approach to this issue is to prepare for the more common types of attacks such as attrition, email, media, impersonation attacks, and improper usage.

Understand evident gathering and handling. Read the sections on gathering and handling of data and the appropriate NIST documentation for greater detail.

Understand containment, eradication, and recovery. Read the sections on containment, eradication and recovery and review the appropriate NIST documentation for greater detail.

Understand the post-incident review process and lessons learned. Review the section on incident reviews and lessons learned to better prepare for any future incidents. on containment, eradication and recovery and review the appropriate NIST documentation for greater detail.

Review Questions

The following questions are designed to test your understanding of this chapter's material. For more information on how to get additional questions, please see www.lammle.com/ccst.

You can find the answers to these questions in Appendix.

1. Which of the following are security incidents? (Select three.)

    A. DDoS

    B. Supply chain

    C. Block encryption

    D. PKI

    E. Phishing

2. Which document details how to quickly identify an attack, what are the steps to take to minimize the impact, contain the blast radius, and finally to remediate the cause to reduce exposure to future?

    A. Network benchmark

    B. Eradication and recovery plan

    C. Containment plan

    D. Incident response plan

3. Which document details your business continuity plan?

    A. Eradication and recovery plan

    B. Incident response plan

    C. Incident response policy

    D. Incident handling plan

4. Which process is used to identify vulnerabilities and the various types of security incidents that pose a risk to your organization and prioritize each type by its potential impact?

    A. Risk assessments

    B. Detection and analysis

    C. Incident handling

    D. Identifying attack sources

5. Most incident response plans follow very similar frameworks based on incident response models developed by the SANS Institute, the National Institute of Standards and Technology (NIST), and the Cybersecurity and Infrastructure Agency (CISA). Question? (Choose three.)

    A. CISA

    B. NIST

   C.   SANS

   D.   Cisco

   E.   Homeland Security

6.   Which document reviews how effective your remediation methods and procedures were and identifies steps that can be improved?

   A.   Chain of custody

   B.   Lessons learned

   C.   CSIRT

   D.   Eradication and recovery

7.   What is the process that takes place at the beginning of an incident to prevent further damage and give you time to develop and implement a remediation?

   A.   Containment strategy

   B.   Evidence gathering

   C.   Identify incident precursors

   D.   Incident preparation

8.   What are sources of precursors? (Choose three.)

   A.   Intrusion detection and protection products (IDPSs)

   B.   GitHub

   C.   Security information and event management (SIEM) products

   D.   Antivirus and antispam software

   E.   Incident response team

9.   Which document details how well the staff performed in dealing with an incident, whether documented procedures were followed, whether they were adequate, and what information was needed sooner?

   A.   Eradication and recovery

   B.   Lessons learned

   C.   Incident handling

   D.   Precursors and indicators

10.   Theft of a computing device, an attack executed from a website or web-based application, brute force, and impersonation are all examples of?

   A.   Social engineering

   B.   Ransomware

   C.   Attack vectors

   D.   Insider threats

   E.   Phishing

Appendix A

Answers to Review Questions

Chapter 1: Security Concepts

1. **Answer: C**

    Explanation: Shoulder surfing is NOT a technology-based attack. It is a social engineering attack.

2. **Answer: A**

    Explanation: The command and control server is used to control the zombies in the Botnet, which a part of a DDoS attack.

3. **Answer: B**

    Explanation: Here's how a smurf attack works: The bad guy spoofs the intended victim's IP address and then sends a large number of pings (IP echo requests) to IP broadcast addresses. The receiving router responds by delivering the broadcast to all hosts in the subnet, and all the hosts respond with an IP echo reply—all of them at the same time.

4. **Answer: D**

    Explanation: In the SYN flood, the attacker sends a SYN, the victim sends back a SYN-ACK, and the attacker leaves the victim waiting for the final ACK. While the server is waiting for the response, a small part of memory is reserved for it. As the SYNs continue to arrive, memory is gradually consumed.

5. **Answer: B**

    Explanation: The attackers use the monlist command, a remote command in older versions of NTP, that sends the requester a list of the last 600 hosts who have connected to that server. This attack can be prevented by using at least NTP version 4.2.7 (which was released in 2010).

6. **Answer: B**

    Explanation: A man-in-the-middle attack (also known as an on-path attack) happens when someone intercepts packets intended for one computer and reads the data.

7. **Answer: A**

    Explanation: A VLAN hopping attack results in traffic from one VLAN being sent to the wrong VLAN. Normally, this is prevented by the trunking protocol placing a VLAN tag in the packet to identify the VLAN to which the traffic belongs. The attacker can circumvent this by a process called double tagging, which is placing a fake VLAN tag into the packet along with the real tag. When the frame goes through multiple switches, the real tag is taken off by the first switch, leaving the fake tag. When the frame reaches the second switch, the fake tag is read and the frame is sent to the VLAN to which the hacker intended the frame to go.

8. **Answer: B**

    Explanation: ARP spoofing is the process of adopting another systems MAC address for the purpose of receiving data meant for that system. It usually also entails ARP cache poisoning.

9. Answer: A

Explanation: These are APs that have been connected to your wired infrastructure without your knowledge. The rogue may have been placed there by a determined hacker who snuck into your facility and put it in an out-of-the-way location or, more innocently, by an employee who just wants wireless access and doesn't get just how dangerous doing this is.

10. Answer: C

Explanation: This ugly trick is achieved by placing their AP on a different channel from your legitimate APs and then setting its SSID in accordance with your SSID.

Chapter 2: Network Security Devices

1. Answer: A

Explanation: An accidental file deletion by an employee is an example of an internal threat.

2. Answer: D

Explanation: To ensure confidentiality, you must prevent the disclosure of data or information to unauthorized entities.

3. Answer: D

Explanation: The Zero Trust concept supports least privilege. It prescribes that when a resource is created, the default permission should be No Access. It also means that when ACLs are configured on routers, all traffic should be blocked by default and only specific traffic allowed.

4. Answer: A

Explanation: A defense-in-depth strategy refers to the practice of using multiple layers of security between data and the resources on which it resides and possible attackers.

5. Answer: A

Explanation: Network Access Control (NAC) systems examine the state of a computer's operating system updates and antimalware updates before allowing access, and in some cases they can even remediate the devices prior to permitting access.

6. Answer: B

Explanation: WPA3 Enterprise uses GCMP-256 for encryption; WPA2 uses AES-CCMP for encryption; and WPA uses TKIP.

7. Answer: C

Explanation: The IEEE 802.11b and IEEE 802.11g standards both run in the 2.4 GHz RF range.

8. Answer: D

Explanation: The IEEE 802.11a standard runs in the 5 GHz RF range.

9. Answer: C

Explanation: The IEEE 802.11b and IEEE 802.11g standards both run in the 2.4 GHz RF range.

10. Answer: C

Explanation: The minimum parameter configured on an AP for a simple WLAN installation is the SSID, although you should set the channel and authentication method as well.

11. Answer: A

Explanation: WPA3 Enterprise uses GCMP-256 for encryption; WPA2 uses AES-CCMP for encryption; and WPA uses TKIP.

12. Answer: A

Explanation: The IEEE 802.11b standard provides three nonoverlapping channels.

13. Answer: C

WPA3 is resistant to offline dictionary attacks where an attacker attempts to determine a network password by trying possible passwords without further network interaction.

14. Answer: D

Explanation: The IEEE 802.11a standard provides a maximum data rate of up to 54 Mbps.

15. Answer: D

Explanation: The IEEE 802.11g standard provides a maximum data rate of up to 54 Mbps.

Chapter 3: IP, IPv6, and NAT

1. Answer: B

Secure Shell (SSH) protocol sets up a secure session that's similar to Telnet over a standard TCP/IP connection and is employed for doing things like logging into systems, running programs on remote systems, and moving files from one system to another.

2. Answer: B

Address Resolution Protocol (ARP) is used to find the hardware address from a known IP address.

3. Answer: A, C, D

The listed answers are from the OSI model and the question asked about the TCP/ IP protocol stack (DoD model). Yes, it is normal for the objectives to have this type of question. However, let's just look for what is wrong. First, the Session layer is not in the TCP/IP model; neither are the Data Link and Physical layers. This leaves us with the Transport layer (Host-to-Host in the DoD model), Internet layer (Network layer in the OSI), and Application layer (Application/Process in the DoD). Remember, the CCENT objectives can list the layers as OSI layers or DoD layers at any time, regardless of what the question is asking.

4.   Answer: C

A Class C network address has only 8 bits for defining hosts: $2^8 - 2 = 254$.

5.   Answer: A, B

A client that sends out a DHCP Discover message in order to receive an IP address sends out a broadcast at both layer 2 and layer 3. The layer 2 broadcast is all Fs in hex, or FF:FF:FF:FF:FF:FF. The layer 3 broadcast is 255.255.255.255, which means any networks and all hosts. DHCP is connectionless, which means it uses User Datagram Protocol (UDP) at the Transport layer, also called the Host-to-Host layer.

6.   Answer: B

Although Telnet does use TCP and IP (TCP/IP), the question specifically asks about layer 4, and IP works at layer 3. Telnet uses TCP at layer 4.

7.   Answer: RFC 1918. These addresses can be used on a private network, but they're not routable through the Internet.

8.   Answer: B, D, E

SMTP, FTP, and HTTP use TCP.

9.   Answer: C

The range of multicast addresses starts with 224.0.0.0 and goes through 239.255.255.255.

10.   Answer: A

Both FTP and Telnet use TCP at the Transport layer; however, they both are Application layer protocols, so the Application layer is the best answer for this question.

11.   Answer: C

The four layers of the DoD model are Application/Process, Host-to-Host, Internet, and Network Access. The Internet layer is equivalent to the Network layer of the OSI model.

12.   Answer: C, E

The Class A private address range is 10.0.0.0 through 10.255.255.255. The Class B private address range is 172.16.0.0 through 172.31.255.255, and the Class C private address range is 192.168.0.0 through 192.168.255.255.

13.   Answer: B

The four layers of the TCP/IP stack (also called the DoD model) are Application/Process, Host-to-Host (also called Transport on the objectives), Internet, and Network Access/ Link. The Host-to-Host layer is equivalent to the Transport layer of the OSI model.

14.   Answer: B, C

ICMP is used for diagnostics and destination unreachable messages. ICMP is encapsulated within IP datagrams, and because it is used for diagnostics, it will provide hosts with information about network problems.

15. Answer: C

The range of a Class B network address is 128–191. This makes our binary range 10*xxxxxx*.

16. Answer: D

An IPv6 address is represented as eight groups of four hexadecimal digits, each group representing 16 bits (two octets). The groups are separated by colons (:). Option A has two double colons, B doesn't have 8 fields, and option C has invalid hex characters.

17. Answer: A, B, C

This question is easier to answer if you just take out the wrong options. First, the loopback is only::1, so that makes option D wrong. Link local is FE80::/10, not /8 and there are no broadcasts..

18. Answer: A, B

ICMPv6 router advertisements use type 134 and must be at least 64 bits in length.

19. Answer: B, D, F

NAT is not perfect, but there are some advantages. It conserves global addresses, which allow us to add millions of hosts to the Internet without "real" IP addresses. This provides flexibility in our corporate networks. NAT can also allow you to use the same subnet more than once in the same network without overlapping networks.

20. Answer: C

Another term for Port Address Translation is *NAT Overload* because that is the keyword used to enable port address translation.

21. Answer: A

An inside local address is considered to be the IP address of the host on the private network before translation.

Chapter 4: Network Device Access

1. Answer: A

The Cisco Identity Services Engine (ISE) is a complete Network Access Control (NAC) system. The Cisco ISE will use 802.1X to control access, but the Cisco ISE is the authentication server in the 802.1X model. The authenticator will be the switch, wireless access point, or router, as it will facilitate authentications of the user or computer. Identity and Access Management (IAM) is a security framework used for the authentication and authorization of users.

2. Answer: C

A captive portal will capture the users' first web page request and redirect them to either a login page or an AUP. Access control lists (ACLs) and MAC filtering restrict specific traffic. The 802.1X protocol is used to authenticate users and devices to control a layer 2 switchport.

3. Answer: C

The principle of least privilege dictates that a user be given the least permission to perform their job. Zero trust is a method of requiring the user to authenticate for each resource they access, regardless of where the asset is located. Role-based access is a method of granting permissions based upon a role in the organization. The defense in depth security concept is a layered approach to security, where several layers are used to protect the organization.

4. Answer: A

Remote Authentication Dial-In User Service (RADIUS) was originally proposed by the IETF and became an open standard for authentication, often used with wireless. TACACS+ is a Cisco technology that became an open standard. The Cisco Identity Services Engine (ISE) is a Network Access Control (NAC) system. Identity and Access Management (IAM) is a security framework used for the authentication and authorization of users, but it is not a standard from the IEEE.

5. Answer: D

The RADIUS protocol uses the UDP protocol for both authentication and accounting. The port numbers used for accounting is 1813/UDP. Port number 1812/UDP is for authentication. All of the other answers are incorrect.

6. Answer: C

Your fingerprint is an example of something that you are, because it is unique to you. A password is something that you know. A signature is something that you do, as it is unique to how you sign and can be forged. A location is somewhere you are, according to you GPS location.

7. Answer: C

Role-based access control (RBAC) is a strategy where you grant roles to users that contain the various permissions. Another admin simply needs to place the user into the role to grant permissions. Terminal Access Controller Access-Control System + (TACACS+) and Remote Authentication Dial-In User Service (RADIUS) are authentication/authorization server used for wired and wireless access. Public Key Infrastructure (PKI) is a system that is used for encryption and signing.

8. Answer: B

The local second method should always be configured. This will ensure that if the router's connection to the AAA server is down, you can still gain access to diagnose or repair. If properly secured, a second method of local authentication does not create a backdoor because it creates a backup of authentication. The local second method is not required, but it is a good idea so that you can log in during outages of the AAA server.

9. Answer: A

A captive portal will allow you to require all guests to register for wireless Internet access before granting them access. A AAA server is required if you have a list of already established users and want to authenticate them via the AAA server. 802.1X is a control protocol that will help you implement a captive portal and AAA server, but by itself it will not register guests. Role-based access control (RBAC) helps remove the complex granularity by creating roles for users who accumulate specific rights.

10. Answer: C

The AAA server listens for requests on UDP port 1812 for authentication of credentials. UDP port 49 is not correct and is not associated with a popular protocol. UDP port 1821 is not correct and is also not associated with a popular protocol. UDP port 1813 is used for AAA servers listening for accounting in-formation.

Chapter 5: Secure Access Technology

1. Answer: D

It's compared with lines of the access list only until a match is made. Once the packet matches the condition on a line of the access list, the packet is acted upon and no further comparisons take place.

2. Answer: C

The range of 192.168.160.0 to 192.168.191.0 is a block size of 32. The network address is 192.168.160.0 and the mask would be 255.255.224.0, which for an access list must be a wildcard format of 0.0.31.255. The 31 is used for a block size of 32. The wildcard is always one less than the block size.

3. Answer: C

Using a named access list just replaces the number used when applying the list to the router's interface. `ip access-group Blocksales` in is correct.

4. Answer: B

The list must specify TCP as the Transport layer protocol and use a correct wildcard mask (in this case 0.0.0.255), and it must specify the destination port (80). It also should specify any as the set of computers allowed to have this access.

5. Answer: D

IPsec is an industry-wide standard suite of protocols and algorithms that allows for secure data transmission over an IP-based network that functions at the layer 3 Network layer of the OSI model.

6. Answer: C

A VPN allows or describes the creation of private networks across the Internet, enabling privacy and tunneling of TCP/IP protocols. A VPN can be set up across any type of link.

7. Answer: A

DES was compromised a long time ago and should never be used in production.

8. Answer: D

SHA is the preferred hash algorithm these days.

9. Answer: B

A Certificate Authority issues certificates.

10. Answer: C

Intermediate Certificate Authority is what we call CAs after the Root.

Chapter 6: OS Basics and Security

1. Answer: B

Because the user is in both groups and the Sales group has full share permissions and the Sales group has modify NTFS permissions, the most restrictive of the two is Modify, so that will be the effective permission for the user. All of the other answers are incorrect.

2. Answer: A

The permissions will be the same as before the move, since you are just moving the files and not creating a new entity. The permissions will not be inherited from the parent folder. The permissions will not be configured the same as the root folder. The permissions will not be blank.

3. Answer: B

The user will have only the Modify permission when logged in locally to the computer, since the filesystem is not shared with the appropriate permissions. The user will not have the Modify permission when connecting from the network. The user will still have the Modify permission when logged in locally, because of the NTFS permissions. The user will not have read-only permissions when connecting from the network.

4. Answer: C

Scripting languages are interpreted languages that run on top of a runtime environment. Programming languages, not scripting languages, require a compiler. Scripting languages are not strongly typed; programming languages are strongly typed. Scripting languages have bad memory management because of loosely typed variables.

5. Answer: B

The statement `$xvar = 2` is a PowerShell statement that will load the variable `xvar` with a value of 2. The statement `xvar = 2` is Bash syntax. The statement `xvar = 2;` is JavaScript syntax. The statement `set /a xvar=2` is Windows batch script syntax.

6. Answer: C

The `apt` utility can be used to download and apply patches to a Linux installation. The `update` command is not a utility. Shell/terminal is an interface for interacting with the operating system with the command line. The `patch` command is not a utility.

7. Answer: C

The chown command is used to change ownership of a file. The cd command changes the working directory. The chmod command changes permissions on files. The pwd command displays the current working directory.

8. Answer: B

The effective permissions are read and write. From left to right, the permissions are rwx for the user, rw- for the group, and r-- for everyone else. Since the user is only a member of the group applied to the file, they will have read and write permissions.

9. Answer: B

The command eventvwr.msc will start the Event Viewer snap-in. The command eventviewer.exe is not a valid command. The command lusrmgr.msc will start the Local Users and Group snap-in. The command devmgmt.msc will start the Device Manager snap-in.

10. Answer: D

The System event log would contain an entry when the operating system reboots. The Application log is used to log applications installed on the system. The boot log is not a valid log. The Security log contains log information pertaining to the security of objects and files.

Chapter 7: Endpoint Security

1. Answer: D

A port scanner will allow you to check if an application is accepting connections. The port will return an open status, and most port scanners will check for an HTTP response. The ping utility will only check if the server is online. The nslookup utility will allow you to resolve a domain name to an IP address and vice versa. The tracert/traceroute command will allow you to watch a packet as it traverses a network path to its destination.

2. Answer: C, D

The nslookup and dig commands can be used to retrieve the A record for a domain name, such as www.wiley.com. The tracert/traceroute command is used to find problems in the routing path for a destination. The ipconfig command is used to view the IP address information on the Windows operating system.

3. Answer: C

The netstat command will allow you to see layer 4 binding between applications and the TCP/UDP ports. On Windows, the netstat -ab command will display listening ports. On Linux/Unix, the netstat -ap command will perform the same function. The portqry and iptables commands are not valid answers. The ifconfig command is used to view the interface configuration for Linux and Unix operating systems.

4. Answer: C

A bring your own device (BYOD) policy defines the minimum specifications for an employee's device used for work-related access. The mobile device management (MDM) software would usually police these specifications, but it would not define them. The acceptable use policy (AUP) is a code of conduct when dealing with organization resources. The nondisclosure agreement (NDA) is an agreement used when dealing with intellectual property.

5. Answer: A

You should research information on the Payment Card Industry Data Security Standard (PCI DSS) standard. The General Data Protection Regulation (GDPR) is used for protecting EU citizens. Protected health information (PHI) is any data that defines a patient or an ailment of a patient. Personally identifiable information (PII) is any information that can be used to identify a person.

6. Answer: A

The Encrypted File System (EFS) is a functionality of the Windows NTFS filesystem. EFS can encrypt individual files and folders. BitLocker is a full-device encryption technology. NTFS is a filesystem that supports encryption and security, among other functionality. BitLocker to Go is used for full-device encryption of removable drives.

7. Answer: B

Scheduling of the depreciation of the equipment is performed in accounting software. Identifying vulnerabilities is a benefit of inventory management. Identifying assets is a direct benefit of asset tags. An asset tag provides a proof of ownership.

8. Answer: D

Mobile device management (MDM) software enables you to enforce profile security requirements on mobile devices. The acceptable use policy (AUP) is a code of ethics your users should follow when dealing with organizational resources. A nondisclosure agreement (NDA) is an agreement between an employee and the organization to protect intellectual property. A bring your own device (BYOD) policy explains how devices should be secured but provides no enforcement.

9. Answer: A

Microsoft Defender Security is considered antimalware and antivirus protection for the Windows operating system. Mobile device management (MDM) software is used to manage mobile devices. Windows Action Center is a notification center for action to be taken in the operating system. VirusTotal is a third-party site that analyzes virus signatures, but it does not protect you from them.

10. Answer: B

The most important first step is to identify and verify the malware symptoms. You should quarantine the infected system once you have verified it is infected. Remediating the infected system happens after you disable System Restore. Education of the end user is the last step to malware removal.

Chapter 8: Risk Management

1. Answer: C

    A zero-day is a vulnerability in which there is no known patch or workaround available at the time of the vulnerability's disclosure. An exploit is a method of using a vulnerability typically for malicious purposes. An asset is the element in which the organization hold value upon, such as data or a computer system. The lack of end-user training is a vulnerability in which a threat actor can exploit by outsmarting the end-user, such as a phishing attempt.

2. Answer: D

    Default credentials configured on network devices on the network is a configuration vulnerability. Since these defaults should have been changed in the configuration. Training vulnerabilities allow for phishing attacks on unknowledgeable employees in the organization. Physical vulnerabilities are vulnerabilities in which physical mechanisms like lock are not used. A zero-day is a vulnerability in which no patch or workaround is known at the time of its disclosure.

3. Answer: A

    The elements are vulnerabilities, threats, and assets. The network itself is not a component of risk.

4. Answer: B

    The database of users should be considered the asset as a component of risk. The database should not be vulnerable or exploitable, as the test question didn't give any further information on the security posture of the database. The data would not be considered configuration or a vulnerable configuration, as the question did not state any vulnerabilities.

5. Answer: C

    The level of risk is the outcome of the risk analysis calculation and not a component of the calculation itself. The likelihood and impact of the loss of confidentiality, integrity, or availability are the main components of the risk analysis calculation.

6. Answer: B

    If the impact of the risk is significant or higher, then the risk will be high; regardless of what the likelihood is perceived to be. Conversely, if the likelihood of a risk is likely or very likely, then the risk will be moderate or high depending on the impact. All other answers are incorrect.

7. Answer: D

    A quantitative approach uses objective data, evaluating the loss. It is calculation of a single instance of realized risk multiplied by the number of expected occurrences during a year. A qualitative approach is used when the value of a loss is unknown. Confidentiality is not a prioritization approach, it is typically used in the risk level calculation. A subjective approach is when a lack of data exists, but a case can be made on what the potential impact could be.

8. Answer: A

If your organization uses a third-party to vet employees, it is a classic example of transference of risk. Since your organization is contractually transferring risk to the third-party. Risk elimination is a strategy where you are completely eliminating the risk which is rare, and in most cases you can only reduce the likelihood. Acceptance of risk would assume your organization has accepted the risk, and continued to do business. A contingency plan allows your organization to continue, if the risk is realized.

9. Answer: B

The element of proximity is the urgency of completion for the mitigation of the risk. The proximity is directly linked to the impact and the likelihood of the risk. The impact is how the risk will effect your organization if the risk is realized. Resources involved, refers to any outside tools or third-party help to mitigate the risk. The budget, of course refers to the money allocated to the risk mitigation, as well as other effected projects.

10. Answer: B

The scope of change section details whom the change will affect. The business processes section details the current business processes the change will affect. The user acceptance section details how the changes were tested and accepted by the users. The plan for change contains the primary and alternate plans for the proposed change.

Chapter 9: Vulnerability Management

1. Answer: B

Common Vulnerabilities and Exposures (CVE) is a system that provides a reference-method for publicly known vulnerabilities and exposures. Open source intelligence (OSINT) is a form of reconnaissance that use public information.

2. Answer: D

The verification and monitoring stage of vulnerability management is responsible for verifying that a vulnerability has been patched and not resurfaced. The discovery phase is the initial phase of detecting a vulnerability. The prioritization phase is responsible for defining the criticality of vulnerability. The reporting phase is responsible for reporting on the remediation steps and impact to the organization.

3. Answer: D

Adding a firewall around the application is the most acceptable remediation for a critical vulnerability in a line-of-business application that is no longer supported. Uninstalling a line-of-business application could have a high-impact to the organization and should be avoided. Training of end-users will not secure the application and threat actors could still potentially exploit the vulnerability. Although requiring strong encryption is a best practice, most vulnerabilities cannot be secured with encryption alone.

4. Answer: B

Port scanning is an active reconnaissance tactic, because you are directly interacting with the hosts and probing them. Traffic analysis is a passive tactic, assuming you have previously sniffed traffic in a passive manner. Open source intelligence (OSINT) and DNS enumeration are both passive reconnaissance tactic, because you are not directly interacting with the network.

5. Answer: C

Outside of upgrading to a version of the software that is not affected, there is no direction as to how to remediate the vulnerability. The scoring, affected versions, and a brief description of the vulnerability can all be found in the CVE vulnerability database.

6. Answer: A

Periodic port scanning as a testing technique can identify open ports that are not properly firewalled. Vulnerability scanning is a test that can be automated for periodic or continuous checking for vulnerabilities in software, but does not directly detect improper firewalling. Open source intelligence (OSINT) is a form of reconnaissance that use public information. A Brute force attack is an active reconnaissance tactic that attempts to brute force passwords.

7. Answer: D

The CVE score is derived from the attack vector associated with the CVE. Each CVE is scored based upon version 2.0, 3.0, 3.1 of the scoring systems; with a version 4.0 to be released soon. Since the impact of a vulnerability will vary, it is impossible to create a score based upon the impact or probability of a vulnerability. The CVE vulnerability database does not assign a CVE score, they only report the score.

8. Answer: A

Nessus is a popular vulnerability scanner that is used to find vulnerabilities in applications and services. A protocol analyzer is used to analyze network activity that has been captured by a network sniffer. The Burp Suite is a collection of web penetration tools used to test a web application. The Nmap utility scans IP addresses of network ranges for open ports.

9. Answer: C

When you purchase an endpoint detection and response (EDR) platform it is in the form of a subscription. Subscription-based reports are delivered to the EDR to keep security up to date. Cybersecurity news helps you stay on top of emerging threats. Security reports are typically delivered from vendors, to keep you aware of current vulnerabilities in their products. Really Simple Syndicate (RSS) feeds help you display a list of topics from a security report or cybersecurity news site.

10. Answer: A

The chain of custody defines who obtained the evidence, who secured the evidence, and who controlled the evidence during the entire process. In addition to documenting if and when the evidence is moved. The incident document reports the details of the incident. The order of volatility is the order in which evidence should be collected, based on the volatility of information. A root cause document is used to detail the root cause of a network issue or security event that has caused a disruption.

Chapter 10: Disaster Recovery

1. Answer: B

    Disk-to-disk is the fastest recovery method and backup method as well, because you are backing up from a disk to another disk attached via the network. Disk-to-tape is slower because you must re-tension the tape and then locate the data on the tape to recover it. Disk-to-flash is not a backup method, because of the price of flash. Disk-to-cloud is the slowest recovery method because you must recover from the cloud over a network connection.

2. Answer: B

    You should use the copy backup method, since it will perform a full backup of the files without resetting the archive bits. A full backup makes a full backup and resets all the archive bits affecting the normal backups. An incremental backup copies only the files that have changed since the last backup and leaves the archive bits unchanged. A differential backup backs up only the files that have changed since the last backup and then resets all the archive bits.

3. Answer: C

    A service entrance surge protection is used between the power meter and the main breakers, to protect from electrical surges. A surge protector strip is found under desks to protect from electrical surges. An uninterruptable power supply (UPS) is used as a backup power source until power is restored or conditioned properly. A generator is used during power outages to sustain power.

4. Answer: C

    The recovery point objective (RPO) is a measurement of time from a failure, disaster, or comparable loss-causing event. RPOs measure back in time to when your data was preserved in a usable format, usually to the most recent backup. The recovery time objective (RTO) is how long it takes to recover your data back to the RPO. The mean time between failures (MTBF) is an average time between failures. The mean time to repair (MTTR) is the average time it takes for a vendor to repair a failure.

5. Answer: C

    With three servers in an active/passive configuration with two on standby, only one is doing work. Therefore, it does not provide load balancing, only fault tolerance. Having two servers in an active/active configuration provides scale-out of services. Having three servers in an active/passive configuration with one in standby does not provide fault tolerance because it requires two in standby to match the active count. Having three servers in an active/active configuration does not allow for any failure.

6. Answer: B

    A cloud recovery site is an extension of the cloud backup services that have developed over the years. These are sites that while mimicking your on-premises network are totally virtual. Cold sites require equipment to be installed and configured. Warm sites are between cold and hot sites and require some intervention. Hot sites typically do not require any intervention, except for organizational data restoration.

7. Answer: A

Deluge systems allow large amounts of water to be released into the room, which obviously makes this not a good choice where computing equipment will be located. CO_2, argon, and NAF-S-III systems use heavy gases to extinguish a fire.

8. Answer: A

A cold site is the least expensive to maintain over time because very little or no hardware is at the site. If a disaster occurs, it will take time to acquire hardware and configure it. A warm site contains equipment but requires intervention to bring it online. A host site or cloud site contains a replica of the organization's servers and is probably the most expensive. The difference between a hot and cloud site is where the servers are running.

9. Answer: B

The recovery time objective (RTO) is a measurement of how quickly you can recover from data loss using backup. The recovery point objective (RPO) is the point in time to which you can recover in the event of a disaster. The grandfather, father, son (GFS) rotation is a systematic way to archive backup media. The backup window is the window of time in which a backup can be performed.

10. Answer: C, D

An online UPS will supply a flawless AC signal since the DC power source is fed into the rectifier and the AC power only charges the DC batteries. However, batteries are finite in their charge; therefore, you need a generator to supply long-term AC power to charge the DC batteries in the event of a power failure. A line interactive and standby UPS does not supply flawless power because the load is shifted during a power outage.

Chapter 11: Incident Handling

1. Answer: C

A Security Information and Event Management as a Service (SIEMaaS) is a cloud-based service that can create alerts based upon security logs. Vulnerability management uses scanning of the network to identify vulnerabilities. Compliance monitoring actively scans your network to make sure that you adhere to regulatory requirements. Intrusion detection and prevention systems (IDPS) detect intrusions and prevent the intrusion. All of these systems would send logs to a SIAMaaS.

2. Answer: C

The action of remediation is often orchestrated with the intervention of security personnel. Remediation that is automated, requires no intervention. The creation of cases is automatic with a SOAR system. Alert generation is automatic with a SIEM.

3. Answer: D

The creation of a case is the first action that happens after a SOAR system receives an alert. The SOAR system then collects logs pertaining to the event. Then an alert is generated to security personnel, to allow them to either respond or review the case. The last action is response, which is when the SOAR system will remediate the security concern.

4. Answer: B

   Baseline detection is used to aid in the training of machine learning for user and entity behavior analytics (UEBA). Anomaly detection detects erratic behavior in events to produce alerts. Artificial Intelligence (AI) is a product of machine learning and other observed behavior analytics. Indicators of compromise (IoC) is a list of known URLs, IP addresses, and signatures to identify a threat actor.

5. Answer: A

   Indicators of compromise (IoC) is a method of detection that alerts on known malicious URLs and IP addresses, in addition to signatures, and other known indicators. Artificial Intelligence (AI) is used to analyze behavior patterns against machine learning and other observed behaviors. User and entity behavior analytics (UEBA) used machine language to identify abnormal user and host behavior. Endpoint detection and response (EDR) typically uses a mixture of signature-based and behavior-based detection methods to detect and respond to threats.

6. Answer: B

   Security orchestration, automation, and response (SOAR) systems are responsible for the response and remediation of security events. Security Information and Event Management (SIEM) are responsible for the creation of security alerts. An intrusion detection system (IDS) is used to detect intrusions, as its name state. Artificial Intelligence (AI) is a method of detection that uses advanced logic and machine learning to identify security alerts.

7. Answer: C

   If you process credit card payments, you must comply with Payment Card Industry Data Security Standard (PCI-DSS) regulations. The Federal Information Security Modernization Act (FISMA) is a law that requires government agencies and organization that work with the government to be compliant. The Family Educational Rights and Privacy Act (FERPA) is a federal law that protects the privacy of student education records. The General Data Protection Regulation (GDPR) is a European Union (EU) law governing how consumer data can be used and protected.

8. Answer: D

   Portability is not a main element of HIPPA compliance. Privacy, security, breach notification are all main elements of HIPPA compliance. Privacy requires your organization to keep patient information private. Security requires your organization to keep patient information secure. Breach notification requires you to notify patients, if their information is breached.

9. Answer: A

   The Federal Information Security Modernization Act (FISMA) is a law that requires government agencies and organization that work with the government to be compliant. The Family Educational Rights and Privacy Act (FERPA) is a federal law that protects the privacy of student education records. If you process credit card payments, you must comply with

Payment Card Industry Data Security Standard (PCI-DSS) regulations. The General Data Protection Regulation (GDPR) is a European Union (EU) law governing how consumer data can be used and protected.

10. Answer: A

If you work for a hospital and have a breach of patient information, you must notify the U.S. Department of Health and Human Services (HHS). The European Union (EU) is the unified government for most of Europe. A qualified security assessor (QSA) report is required for high volume PCI-DSS merchants. A data protection officer (DPO) is recommended for organizations that are required to comply with the GDPR regulations.

Chapter 12: Digital Forensics

1. Answer: D

The first step in this investigation is to contact the company's IT department and ask them to provide you with a list of employees who have access to the confidential data. This will help you to narrow down your list of suspects and focus your investigation. Obtaining a search warrant and seizing the employee's computer may be necessary, but it is not the first step in the investigation. Interviewing the employee or contacting the competitor is not recommended as it may compromise the investigation.

2. Answer: B

The first step in this investigation is to collect data from the affected server and preserve the evidence. This will allow you to conduct a forensic analysis of the data and determine the extent of the breach. Contacting the affected customers or compiling a report is not recommended as it may compromise the investigation.

3. Answer: D

Explanation: The final step in this investigation is to compile a report that explains what happened during the breach and identifies suspects or culprits if possible. The report should also contain recommendations for preventing future attacks. Contacting the affected customers or collecting data from the affected server is not recommended as it may compromise the investigation.

4. Answer: C

The Strategic attribution approach uses intelligence sources of information, such as human, signals, or geospatial intelligence, to attempt to corroborate and validate the findings of technical and operational attribution. This approach can often help confirm or disprove the identity of the attackers, and their relationship with other actors or entities.

5. Answer: E

The first stage of the Cyber Kill Chain model is Reconnaissance. This is the research stage of the operation where attackers scope out their target to identify any vulnerabilities and potential entry points. None of the options listed are correct.

6. Answer: C

The purpose of the Mitre ATT&CK knowledge base is to provide classification and documentation of adversarial actions across their lifecycle. This can help organizations to better understand the tactics, techniques, and procedures (TTPs) used by attackers and to develop more effective threat models. Options A and B are related to the Mitre ATT&CK knowledge base, they are not the primary purpose. Option D is a specific case for the knowledge base.

7. Answer: C

The purpose of the Diamond Model is to provide a taxonomy of adversarial actions across their lifecycle. This can help organizations to better understand the tactics, techniques, and procedures (TTPs) used by attackers and to develop more effective threat models. While options A and B are related to the Diamond Model, they are not the primary purpose. Option D is a specific use case for the Diamond Model, but it is not the primary purpose.

8. Answer: D

Explanation: TTPs can be used to support the development of an incident response methodology by describing the behavior and strategies of your adversaries. This can help organizations to better understand the tactics, techniques, and procedures (TTPs) used by attackers and to develop more effective incident response plans. While options A, B, and C are related to cybersecurity, they are not the primary use case for TTPs.

9. Answer: A

Artifacts, or sources of evidence, are digital traces left behind by activities on a system or network. This data can be used to understand the actions taken by an attacker during a cyber intrusion.

10. Answer: A

Explanation: The process of Chain of Custody in cybersecurity is the process of maintaining and documenting the handling of digital evidence from the moment it is collected until it is presented in a court of law. It ensures that the evidence remains in its original state and is admissible in court. While options B, C, and D are related to cybersecurity, they are not the primary purpose of Chain of Custody.

Chapter 13: Incident Response

1. Answer: A, B, E

DDoS (Distributed Denial of Service) attacks overwhelm a system with traffic, causing it to slow down or become unavailable. Supply chain attacks infiltrate an organization by targeting its suppliers or partners, introducing malware or gaining access to sensitive data. Phishing attacks send fraudulent messages to trick recipients into revealing sensitive information or installing malware. These incidents are considered security incidents because they threaten the confidentiality, integrity, and availability of information systems. Block Encryption is a method of encrypting data in fixed-size blocks using a cryptographic key. PKI

(Public Key Infrastructure) is a framework for managing digital certificates and public-key encryption. Both are security technologies used to protect data and secure communications, not incidents or attacks. Therefore, they are not considered security incidents.

2. Answer: D

   The Incident Response Plan details how to quickly identify an attack, the steps to take to minimize the impact, contain the blast radius, and remediate the cause to reduce exposure to future incidents. Network Benchmark, is used for performance measurement and not for incident handling. Eradication and Recovery Plan, focuses on removing threats and restoring systems but does not cover the entire incident response process. Containment Plan, only addresses the containment phase and not the full scope of incident response.

3. Answer: B

   The Incident Response Plan includes the business continuity plan, outlining procedures for restoring critical systems and data quickly in the event of an outage. Eradication and Recovery Plan, focuses on removing threats and restoring systems but does not cover the entire business continuity process. Incident Response Policy, provides guidelines and roles but does not detail specific continuity procedures. Incident Handling Plan, addresses the steps for managing incidents but not the broader continuity planning.

4. Answer: A

   Risk Assessments is the process used to identify vulnerabilities and the various types of security incidents that pose a risk to your organization and prioritize each type by its potential impact. Detection and Analysis, focuses on monitoring the network for suspicious activity and potential threats. Incident Handling, refers to the overall process of managing incidents but does not specifically prioritize risks. Identifying Attack Sources, involves tracing the origin of an attack but does not assess or prioritize vulnerabilities.

5. Answer: A, B, C

   The correct answers are CISA, NIST, and SANS, because most incident response plans follow frameworks developed by these organizations. Cisco, is a technology company that provides networking hardware and software but does not develop incident response frameworks. Homeland Security, is a government department responsible for public security but does not specifically develop incident response models.

6. Answer: B

   The Lessons Learned document reviews how effective your remediation methods and procedures were and identifies steps that can be improved. Chain of Custody, is used to document the handling of evidence. CSIRT, refers to the Computer Security Incident Response Team, which is responsible for managing incidents but does not specifically review remediation effectiveness. Eradication and Recovery, focuses on removing threats and restoring systems, but does not review the effectiveness of the procedures.

7. Answer: A

   The Containment Strategy process takes place at the beginning of the incident to prevent further damage and give you time to develop and implement a remediation. Evidence

Gathering, involves collecting data for analysis and legal purposes but does not prevent further damage. Identify Incident Precursors, involves recognizing early signs of potential incidents, but does not address immediate containment. Incident Preparation, involves planning and readiness activities before an incident occurs, not during the initial response.

8. Answer: A, C, D

Intrusion detection and protection products (IDPSs), Security Information and Event Management (SIEM) products, and Antivirus and antispam software are correct because these are sources of precursors that can help identify potential security incidents. GitHub, is a platform for version control and collaboration, not a source of precursors. Incident response team, is responsible for managing incidents but does not serve as a source of precursors.

9. Answer: B

The Lessons Learned is a document that details how well the staff performed in dealing with the incident, whether the documented procedures were followed and adequate, and what information was needed sooner. Eradication and Recovery, focuses on removing threats and restoring systems but does not review staff performance. Incident Handling, refers to the overall process of managing incidents but does not specifically evaluate performance. Precursors and Indicators, involves identifying early signs of potential incidents but does not assess staff performance.

10. Answer: C

Attack Vectors are attack executed from a website or web-based application, brute force, and impersonation are all methods used by attackers to gain unauthorized access to systems or data. Social Engineering, involves manipulating people to divulge confidential information. Ransomware, is a type of malware that encrypts data and demands a ransom. Insider Threats, involve malicious or negligent actions by authorized users. Phishing, involves tricking individuals into revealing sensitive information through deceptive messages.

Index

O

P

Online Test Bank

To help you study for your CCST Cisco Certified Support Technician Cybersecurity certification exam, register to gain one year of FREE access after activation to the online interactive test bank—included with your purchase of this book!

To access our learning environment, simply visit www.wiley.com/go/ sybextestprep, follow the instructions to register your book, and instantly gain one year of FREE access after activation to:

- Hundreds of practice test questions so you can practice in a timed and graded setting
- Flashcards
- A searchable glossary